Object-Oriented Programming
with C++

Second Edition

About the Author

E Balagurusamy is the Vice Chancellor, Anna University, Chennai. He is a teacher, trainer, and consultant in the fields of Information Technology and Management. He holds an ME (Hons) in Electrical Engineering and Ph.D in Systems Engineering from the Indian Institute of Technology, Roorkee. His areas of interest include Object-Oriented Software Engineering, Electronic Business, Technology Management, Business Process Re-engineering, and Total Quality Management.

A prolific writer, he has authored a large number of research papers and several books. His best selling books, among others include :

- Programming in BASIC, 3/e
- Programming in ANSI C, 2/e
- Programming with JAVA: A Primer, 2/e
- Programming in C#
- Numerical Methods, and
- Reliability Engineering

A recipient of numerous honours and awards, he has been listed in the Directory of Who's Who of Intellectuals and in the Directory of Distinguished Leaders in Education.

Object-Oriented Programming with C++

Second Edition

E Balagurusamy

Vice Chancellor
Anna University
Chennai.

Tata McGraw-Hill Publishing Company Limited

NEW DELHI

McGraw-Hill Offices

New Delhi New York St Louis San Francisco Auckland Bogotá
Caracas Kuala Lumpur Lisbon London Madrid Mexico City Milan
Montreal San Juan Santiago Singapore Sydney Tokyo Toronto

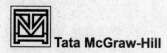
Tata McGraw-Hill

This edition can be exported from India only by the publishers,
Tata McGraw-Hill Publishing Company Limited

ISBN 0-07-040211-6

Published by Tata McGraw-Hill Publishing Company Limited,
7 West Patel Nagar, New Delhi 110 008, Typeset at
Krishtel eMaging Solutions, B1 Ansary, 39 Madley Rd, Chennai 17, and printed at
Gopsons Papers Ltd., A-14, Sector-60, Noida

Cover: Gopsons

The **McGraw-Hill** Companies

Preface
to the Second Edition

C++ is the most widely used object-oriented language today. It is faster and more powerful than Java, another popular object-oriented language, which lacks certain features such as pointers and multiple inheritance.

C++ has been undergoing changes during the last few years. They are basically meant to provide better control and conveniences to the C++ programmers. The ANSI/ISO C++ standards committee which reviewed all the changes, has standardized several new features. The Standard Template Library (STL) which was developed independently has now become a part of the C++ language. C++ is now called ANSI C++ or ANSI/ISO C++ or simply Standard C++. In this book, C++ generally refers to ANSI C++.

The changes in this edition are related to the new features of ANSI C++. Most of the programs in the book have been revised to make them compatible with ANSI C++. This mainly involves changes to the header files, the addition of namespace directive, and using the return type for the main function. Some programs containing C-style strings required more extensive changes due to the introduction of a new string class in ANSI C++. Major changes and additions include:

> ➤ Changes in the text to confirm to ANSI C++.
> ➤ Changes in the programs as per the ANSI C++ specifications.
> ➤ A more detailed discussion on templates and their applications.
> ➤ An independent chapter on managing exceptions in programs.
> ➤ A chapter on the manipulation of ANSI C++ strings.
> ➤ An introductory discussion on the Standard Template Library.
> ➤ A chapter to present briefly the new features of ANSI C++.

A thorough understanding of the standard language features and the standard library facilities would help the programmers gain better insights and design quality programs.

All the programs in this book have been tested on Microsoft Visual C++ Version 6.0. These programs would also run on the Borland C++ Builder 3.0 or any Turbo C++ Version that supports ANSI C++.

Finally, an Appendix named "C++ Proficiency Test" has been provided to test the level of mastery of the language features. All the readers are encouraged to take this test and review the concepts where necessary.

E BALAGURUSAMY

Preface
to the First Edition

C++ is an extension of C language which is widely used all over. It is a powerful modern language that combines the power, elegance and flexibility of C and the features of object-oriented programming. With its object-oriented capabilities such as data abstraction, inheritance and polymorphism, C++ offers significant software engineering benefits over C. Programming pandits expect that C++ will replace C as a general-purpose programming language. C++ is the language of the future.

This book is for programmers who wish to know all about C++ and object-oriented programming. It explains in a simple and easy-to-understand style the what, why and how of object-oriented programming using C++. The book assumes that the reader is already familiar with C language, although he need not be an expert C programmer. For those who have no C experience, this book should be used in conjunction with my book Programming in ANSI C also published by Tata McGraw-Hill or any other introductory book on ANSI C.

The book provides numerous examples and complete programs. The programs are meant to be both simple and educational. Wherever necessary, pictorial descriptions of concepts are included to facilitate better understanding. All the programs have been tested with Turbo C++ compiler on MS-DOS.

The book also presents the concept of object-oriented programming and discusses briefly the important elements of object-oriented analysis and design of systems. It is hoped that this book will help the reader to quickly move into the world of C++ and object-oriented programming.

There is no doubt that in spite of my strenuous efforts, errors might remain in the text. Programmers (who perhaps make many mistakes) are serious error-conscious people. I will be grateful if they could communicate to me any errors they discover.

E BALAGURUSAMY

Contents

1

Principles of Object-Oriented Programming

1.1 SOFTWARE CRISIS

Developments in software technology continue to be dynamic. New tools and techniques are announced in quick succession. This has forced the software engineers and industry to continuously look for new approaches to software design and development, and they are becoming more and more critical in view of the increasing complexity of software systems as well as the highly competitive nature of the industry. These rapid advances appear to have created a situation of crisis within the industry. The following issues need to be addressed to face this crisis:

- ● How to represent real-life entities of problems in system design?
- ● How to design systems with open interfaces?
- ● How to ensure reusability and extensibility of modules?
- ● How to develop modules that are tolerant to any changes in future?
- ● How to improve software productivity and decrease software cost?
- ● How to improve the quality of software?

- How to manage time schedules?
- How to industrialize the software development process?

Many software products are either not finished, or not used, or else are delivered with major errors. Figure 1.1 shows the fate of the US defence software projects undertaken in the 1970s. Around 50% of the software products were never delivered, and one-third of those which were delivered were never used. It is interesting to note that only 2% were used as delivered, without being subjected to any changes. This illustrates that the software industry has a remarkably bad record in delivering products.

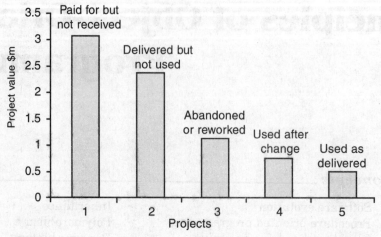

Fig. 1.1   *The state of US defence projects (according to the US government)*

Changes in user requirements have always been a major problem. Another study (Fig. 1.2) shows that more than 50% of the systems required modifications due to changes in user requirements and data formats. It only illustrates that, in a changing world with a dynamic business environment, requests for change are unavoidable and therefore systems must be adaptable and tolerant to changes.

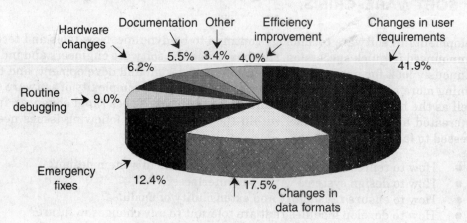

Fig. 1.2   *Breakdown of maintenance costs*

These studies and other reports on software implementation suggest that software products should be evaluated carefully for their quality before they are delivered and implemented. Some of the quality issues that must be considered for critical evaluation are:

1. Correctness
2. Maintainability
3. Reusability
4. Openness and interoperability
5. Portability
6. Security
7. Integrity
8. User friendliness

Selection and use of proper software tools would help resolving some of these issues.

1.2 SOFTWARE EVOLUTION

Ernest Tello, a well-known writer in the field of artificial intelligence, compared the evolution of software technology to the growth of a tree. Like a tree, the software evolution has had distinct phases or "layers" of growth. These layers were built up one by one over the last five decades as shown in Fig. 1.3, with each layer representing an improvement over the previous one. However, the analogy fails if we consider the life of these layers. In software systems, each of the layers continues to be functional, whereas in the case of trees, only the uppermost layer is functional.

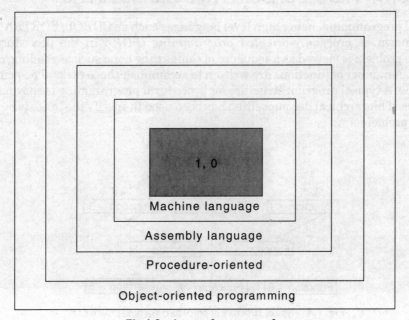

Fig 1.3 *Layers of computer software*

Alan Kay, one of the promoters of the object-oriented paradigm and the principal designer of Smalltalk, has said: "*As complexity increases, architecture dominates the basic material*". To build today's complex software it is just not enough to put together a sequence of programming statements and sets of procedures and modules; we need to incorporate sound construction techniques and program structures that are easy to comprehend, implement and modify.

Since the invention of the computer, many programming approaches have been tried. These include techniques such as *modular programming, top-down programming, bottom-up programming and structured programming*. The primary motivation in each has been the concern to handle the increasing complexity of programs that are reliable and maintainable. These techniques have become popular among programmers over the last two decades.

With the advent of languages such as C, structured programming became very popular and was the main technique of the 1980s. Structured programming was a powerful tool that enabled programmers to write moderately complex programs fairly easily. However, as the programs grew larger, even the structured approach failed to show the desired results in terms of bug-free, easy-to-maintain, and reusable programs.

Object-Oriented Programming (OOP) is an approach to program organization and development that attempts to eliminate some of the pitfalls of conventional programming methods by incorporating the best of structured programming features with several powerful new concepts. It is a new way of organizing and developing programs and has nothing to do with any particular language. However, not all languages are suitable to implement the OOP concepts easily.

1.3   A LOOK AT PROCEDURE-ORIENTED PROGRAMMING

Conventional programming, using high level languages such as COBOL, FORTRAN and C, is commonly known as *procedure-oriented programming (POP)*. In the procedure-oriented approach, the problem is viewed as a sequence of things to be done such as reading, calculating and printing. A number of functions are written to accomplish these tasks. The primary focus is on functions. A typical program structure for procedural programming is shown in Fig. 1.4. The technique of hierarchical decomposition has been used to specify the tasks to be completed for solving a problem.

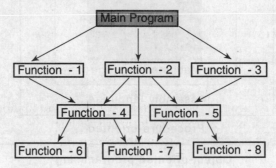

Fig. 1.4 *Typical structure of procedure-oriented programs*

Procedure-oriented programming basically consists of writing a list of instructions (or actions) for the computer to follow, and organizing these instructions into groups known as *functions*. We normally use a *flowchart* to organize these actions and represent the flow of control from one action to another. While we concentrate on the development of functions, very little attention is given to the data that are being used by various functions. What happens to the data? How are they affected by the functions that work on them?

In a multi-function program, many important data items are placed as *global* so that they may be accessed by all the functions. Each function may have its own *local data*. Figure 1.5 shows the relationship of data and functions in a procedure-oriented program.

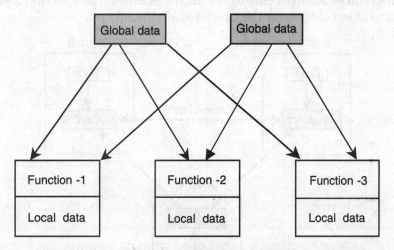

Fig. 1.5   *Relationship of data and functions in procedural programming*

Global data are more vulnerable to an inadvertent change by a function. In a large program it is very difficult to identify what data is used by which function. In case we need to revise an external data structure, we also need to revise all functions that access the data. This provides an opportunity for bugs to creep in.

Another serious drawback with the procedural approach is that it does not model real world problems very well. This is because functions are action-oriented and do not really correspond to the elements of the problem.

Some characteristics exhibited by procedure-oriented programming are:

- Emphasis is on doing things (algorithms).
- Large programs are divided into smaller programs known as functions.
- Most of the functions share global data.
- Data move openly around the system from function to function.
- Functions transform data from one form to another.
- Employs *top-down* approach in program design.

1.4 OBJECT-ORIENTED PROGRAMMING PARADIGM

The major motivating factor in the invention of object-oriented approach is to remove some of the flaws encountered in the procedural approach. OOP treats data as a critical element in the program development and does not allow it to flow freely around the system. It ties data more closely to the functions that operate on it, and protects it from accidental modification from outside functions. OOP allows decomposition of a problem into a number of entities called *objects* and then builds data and functions around these objects. The organization of data and functions in object-oriented programs is shown in Fig. 1.6. The data of an object can be accessed only by the functions associated with that object. However, functions of one object can access the functions of other objects.

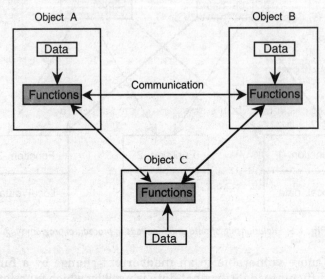

Fig 1.6 *Organization of data and functions in OOP*

Some of the striking features of object-oriented programming are:

- Emphasis is on data rather than procedure.
- Programs are divided into what are known as objects.
- Data structures are designed such that they characterize the objects.
- Functions that operate on the data of an object are tied together in the data structure.
- Data is hidden and cannot be accessed by external functions.
- Objects may communicate with each other through functions.
- New data and functions can be easily added whenever necessary.
- *Follows bottom-up* approach in program design.

Object-oriented programming is the most recent concept among programming paradigms and still means different things to different people. It is therefore important to have a working definition of object-oriented programming before we proceed further. We define "object-oriented programming as *an approach that provides a way of modularizing programs by creating partitioned memory area for both data and functions that can be used as templates for creating copies of such modules on demand.*" Thus, an object is considered to be a partitioned area of computer memory that stores data and set of operations that can access that data. Since the memory partitions are independent, the objects can be used in a variety of different programs without modifications.

1.5 BASIC CONCEPTS OF OBJECT-ORIENTED PROGRAMMING

It is necessary to understand some of the concepts used extensively in object-oriented programming. These include:

- Objects
- Classes
- Data abstraction and encapsulation
- Inheritance
- Polymorphism
- Dynamic binding
- Message passing

We shall discuss these concepts in some detail in this Section.

Objects

Objects are the basic run-time entities in an object-oriented system. They may represent a person, a place, a bank account, a table of data or any item that the program has to handle. They may also represent user-defined data such as vectors, time and lists. Programming problem is analyzed in terms of objects and the nature of communication between them. Program objects should be chosen such that they match closely with the real-world objects. Objects take up space in the memory and have an associated address like a record in Pascal, or a structure in C.

When a program is executed, the objects interact by sending messages to one another. For example, if "customer" and "account" are two objects in a program, then the customer object may send a message to the account object requesting for the bank balance. Each object contains data, and code to manipulate the data. Objects can interact without having to know details of each other's data or code. It is sufficient to know the type of message accepted, and the type of response returned by the objects. Although different authors represent them differently, Fig. 1.7 shows two notations that are popularly used in object-oriented analysis and design.

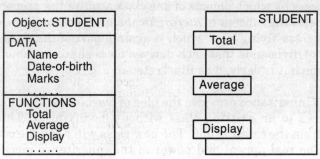

Fig. 1.7 *Two ways of representing an object*

Classes

We just mentioned that objects contain data, and code to manipulate that data. The entire set of data and code of an object can be made a user-defined data type with the help of a *class*. In fact, objects are variables of the type *class*. Once a class has been defined, we can create any number of objects belonging to that class. Each object is associated with the data of type class with which they are created. A class is thus a collection of objects of similar type. For example, mango, apple and orange are members of the class fruit. Classes are user-defined data types and behave like the built-in types of a programming language. The syntax used to create an object is no different than the syntax used to create an integer object in C. If fruit has been defined as a class, then the statement

```
fruit mango;
```

will create an object **mango** belonging to the class **fruit**.

Data Abstraction and Encapsulation

The wrapping up of data and functions into a single unit (called class) is known as *encapsulation*. Data encapsulation is the most striking feature of a class. The data is not accessible to the outside world, and only those functions which are wrapped in the class can access it. These functions provide the interface between the object's data and the program. This insulation of the data from direct access by the program is called *data hiding or information hiding*.

Abstraction refers to the act of representing essential features without including the background details or explanations. Classes use the concept of abstraction and are defined as a list of abstract *attributes* such as size, weight and cost, and *functions* to operate on these attributes. They encapsulate all the essential properties of the objects that are to be created. The attributes are sometimes called *data members* because they hold information. The functions that operate on these data are sometimes called *methods or member functions*.

Since the classes use the concept of data abstraction, they are known as *Abstract Data Types* (ADT).

Inheritance

Inheritance is the process by which objects of one class acquire the properties of objects of another class. It supports the concept of *hierarchical classification*. For example, the bird 'robin' is a part of the class 'flying bird' which is again a part of the class 'bird'. The principle behind this sort of division is that each derived class shares common characteristics with the class from which it is derived as illustrated in Fig. 1.8.

In OOP, the concept of inheritance provides the idea of *reusability*. This means that we can add additional features to an existing class without modifying it. This is possible by deriving a new class from the existing one. The new class will have the combined features of both the classes. The real appeal and power of the inheritance mechanism is that it

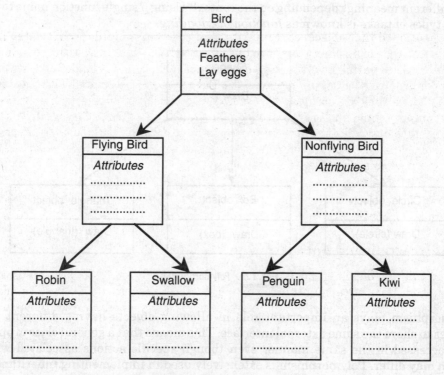

Fig. 1.8 *Property inheritance*

allows the programmer to reuse a class that is almost, but not exactly, what he wants, and to tailor the class in such a way that it does not introduce any undesirable side-effects into the rest of the classes.

Note that each sub-class defines only those features that are unique to it. Without the use of classification, each class would have to explicitly include all of its features.

Polymorphism

Polymorphism is another important OOP concept. Polymorphism, a Greek term, means the ability to take more than one form. An operation may exhibit different behaviours in different instances. The behaviour depends upon the types of data used in the operation. For example, consider the operation of addition. For two numbers, the operation will generate a sum. If the operands are strings, then the operation would produce a third string by concatenation. The process of making an operator to exhibit different behaviours in different instances is known as *operator overloading*.

Figure 1.9 illustrates that a single function name can be used to handle different number and different types of arguments. This is something similar to a particular word having several different meanings depending on the context. Using a single function name to perform different types of tasks is known as *function overloading*.

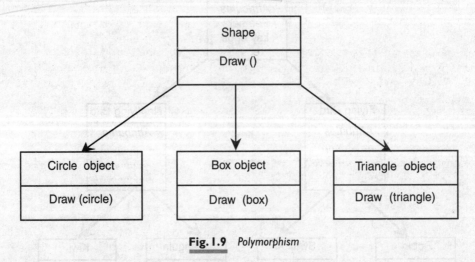

Fig. 1.9 *Polymorphism*

Polymorphism plays an important role in allowing objects having different internal structures to share the same external interface. This means that a general class of operations may be accessed in the same manner even though specific actions associated with each operation may differ. Polymorphism is extensively used in implementing inheritance.

Dynamic Binding

Binding refers to the linking of a procedure call to the code to be executed in response to the call. *Dynamic binding* (also known as late binding) means that the code associated with a given procedure call is not known until the time of the call at run-time. It is associated with polymorphism and inheritance. A function call associated with a polymorphic reference depends on the dynamic type of that reference.

Consider the procedure "draw" in Fig. 1.9. By inheritance, every object will have this procedure. Its algorithm is, however, unique to each object and so the draw procedure will be redefined in each class that defines the object. At run-time, the code matching the object under current reference will be called.

Message Passing

An object-oriented program consists of a set of objects that communicate with each other. The process of programming in an object-oriented language, therefore, involves the following basic steps:

1.   Creating classes that define objects and their behaviour,
2.   Creating objects from class definitions, and
3.   Establishing communication among objects.

Objects communicate with one another by sending and receiving information much the same way as people pass messages to one another. The concept of message passing makes it easier to talk about building systems that directly model or simulate their real-world counterparts.

A message for an object is a request for execution of a procedure, and therefore will invoke a function (procedure) in the receiving object that generates the desired result. *Message passing* involves specifying the name of the object, the name of the function (message) and the information to be sent. Example:

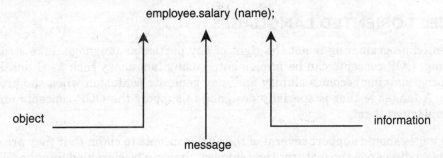

Objects have a life cycle. They can be created and destroyed. Communication with an object is feasible as long as it is alive.

1.6 BENEFITS OF OOP

OOP offers several benefits to both the program designer and the user. Object-orientation contributes to the solution of many problems associated with the development and quality of software products. The new technology promises greater programmer productivity, better quality of software and lesser maintenance cost. The principal advantages are:

- Through inheritance, we can eliminate redundant code and extend the use of existing
- classes.
- We can build programs from the standard working modules that communicate with one another, rather than having to start writing the code from scratch. This leads to saving of development time and higher productivity.
- The principle of data hiding helps the programmer to build secure programs that cannot be invaded by code in other parts of the program.
- It is possible to have multiple instances of an object to co-exist without any interference.
- It is possible to map objects in the problem domain to those in the program.
- It is easy to partition the work in a project based on objects.
- The data-centered design approach enables us to capture more details of a model in implementable form.
- Object-oriented systems can be easily upgraded from small to large systems.
- Message passing techniques for communication between objects makes the interface descriptions with external systems much simpler.
- Software complexity can be easily managed.

While it is possible to incorporate all these features in an object-oriented system, their importance depends on the type of the project and the preference of the programmer. There are a number of issues that need to be tackled to reap some of the benefits stated above. For instance, object libraries must be available for reuse. The technology is still developing and current products may be superseded quickly. Strict controls and protocols need to be developed if reuse is not to be compromised.

Developing a software that is easy to use makes it hard to build. It is hoped that the object-oriented programming tools would help manage this problem.

1.7   OBJECT-ORIENTED LANGUAGES

Object-oriented programming is not the right of any particular language. Like structured programming, OOP concepts can be implemented using languages such as C and Pascal. However, programming becomes clumsy and may generate confusion when the programs grow large. A language that is specially designed to support the OOP concepts makes it easier to implement them.

The languages should support several of the OOP concepts to claim that they are object-oriented. Depending upon the features they support, they can be classified into the following two categories:

1. Object-based programming languages, and
2. Object-oriented programming languages.

Object-based programming is the style of programming that primarily supports encapsulation and object identity. Major features that are required for object-based programming are:

- Data encapsulation
- Data hiding and access mechanisms
- Automatic initialization and clear-up of objects
- Operator overloading

Languages that support programming with objects are said to be object-based programming languages. They do not support inheritance and dynamic binding. Ada is a typical object-based programming language.

Object-oriented programming incorporates all of object-based programming features along with two additional features, namely, inheritance and dynamic binding. Object-oriented programming can therefore be characterized by the following statement:

```
Object-based features + inheritance + dynamic binding
```

Languages that support these features include C++, Smalltalk, Object Pascal and Java. There are a large number of object-based and object-oriented programming languages. Table 1.1 lists some popular general purpose OOP languages and their characteristics.

Table 1.1   Characteristics of Some OOP Languages

Characteristics	Simula *	Smalltalk *	Objective C	C++	Ada **	Object Pascal	Turbo Pascal	Eiffel *	Java *
Binding (early or late)	Both	Late	Both	Both	Early	Late	Early	Early	Both
Polymorphism	✓	✓	✓	✓	✓	✓	✓	✓	✓
Data hiding	✓	✓	✓	✓	✓	✓	✓	✓	✓
Concurrency	✓	Poor	Poor	Poor	Difficult	No	No	Promised	✓
Inheritance	✓	✓	✓	✓	No	✓	✓	✓	✓
Multiple Inheritance	No	✓	✓	✓	No	---	---	✓	No
Garbage Collection	✓	✓	✓	✓	No	✓	✓	✓	✓
Persistence	No	Promised	No	No	like 3GL	No	No	Some Support	✓
Genericity	No	No	No	✓	✓	N o	No	✓	No
Object Libraries	✓	✓	✓	✓	Not much	✓	✓	✓	✓

*   *Pure object-oriented languages*
**   *Object-based languages*
     Others are extended conventional languages

As seen from Table 1.1, all languages provide for polymorphism and data hiding. However, many of them do not provide facilities for concurrency, persistence and genericity. Eiffel, Ada and C++ provide generic facility which is an important construct for supporting reuse. However, persistence (a process of storing objects) is not fully supported by any of them. In Smalltalk, though the entire current execution state can be saved to disk, yet the individual objects cannot be saved to an external file.

Commercially, C++ is only 10 years old, Smalltalk and Objective C 13 years old, and Java only 5 years old. Although Simula has existed for more than two decades, it has spent most of its life in a research environment. The field is so new, however, that it should not be judged too harshly.

Use of a particular language depends on characteristics and requirements of an application, organizational impact of the choice, and reuse of the existing programs. C++ has now become the most successful, practical, general purpose OOP language, and is widely used in industry today.

1.8   APPLICATIONS OF OOP

OOP has become one of the programming buzzwords today. There appears to be a great deal of excitement and interest among software engineers in using OOP. Applications of OOP are beginning to gain importance in many areas. The most popular application of object-oriented programming, up to now, has been in the area of user interface design such as windows. Hundreds of windowing systems have been developed, using the OOP techniques.

Real-business systems are often much more complex and contain many more objects with complicated attributes and methods. OOP is useful in these types of applications because it can simplify a complex problem. The promising areas for application of OOP include:

- Real-time systems
- Simulation and modeling
- Object-oriented databases
- Hypertext, hypermedia and expertext
- AI and expert systems
- Neural networks and parallel programming
- Decision support and office automation systems
- CIM/CAM/CAD systems

The object-oriented paradigm sprang from the language, has matured into design, and has recently moved into analysis. It is believed that the richness of OOP environment will enable the software industry to improve not only the quality of software systems but also its productivity. Object-oriented technology is certainly going to change the way the software engineers think, analyze, design and implement future systems.

Summary

- Software technology has evolved through a series of phases during the last five decades.
- The most popular phase till recently was procedure-oriented programming (POP).
- POP employs *top-down* programming approach where a problem is viewed as a sequence of tasks to be performed. A number of functions are written to implement these tasks.
- POP has two major drawbacks, viz. (1) data move freely around the program and are therefore vulnerable to changes caused by any function in the program, and (2) it does not model very well the real-world problems.
- Object-oriented programming (OOP) was invented to overcome the drawbacks of the POP. It employs the *bottom-up* programming approach. It treats data as a critical element in the program development and does not allow it to flow freely around the system. It ties data more closely to the functions that operate on it in a data structure called **class**. This feature is called **data** *encapsulation*.
- In OOP, a problem is considered as a collection of a number of entities called **objects**. Objects are instances of classes.
- Insulation of data from direct access by the program is called *data hiding*.
- *Data abstraction* refers to putting together essential features without including background details.
- *Inheritance* is the process by which objects of one class acquire properties of objects of another class.

- *Polymorphism* means one name, multiple forms. It allows us to have more than one function with the same name in a program. It also allows overloading of operators so that an operation can exhibit different behaviours in different instances.
- *Dynamic binding* means that the code associated with a given procedure is not known until the time of the call at run-time.
- *Message passing* involves specifying the name of the object, the name of the function (message) and the information to be sent.
- Object-oriented technology offers several benefits over the conventional programming methods---the most important one being the reusability.
- Applications of OOP technology has gained importance in almost all areas of computing including real-time business systems.
- There are a number of languages that support object-oriented programming paradigm. Popular among them are C++, Smalltalk and Java. C++ has become an industry standard language today.

Key Terms

- Ada
- assembly language
- bottom-up programming
- C++
- classes
- concurrency
- data abstraction
- data encapsulation
- data hiding
- data members
- dynamic binding
- early binding
- Eiffel
- flowcharts
- function overloading
- functions
- garbage collection
- global data
- hierarchical classification
- inheritance
- Java
- late binding
- local data

- machine language
- member functions
- message passing
- methods
- modular programming
- multiple inheritance
- object libraries
- Object Pascal
- object-based programming
- Objective C
- object-oriented languages
- object-oriented programming
- objects
- operator overloading
- persistence
- polymorphism
- procedure-oriented programming
- reusability
- Simula
- Smalltalk
- structured programming
- top-down programming
- Turbo Pascal

Review Questions

1.1   *What do you think are the major issues facing the software industry today?*
1.2   *Briefly discuss the software evolution during the period 1950 – 1990.*

1.3   *What is procedure-oriented programming? What are its main characteristics?*

1.4   *Discuss an approach to the development of procedure-oriented programs.*

1.5   *Describe how data are shared by functions in a procedure-oriented program.*

1.6   *What is object-oriented programming? How is it different from the procedure-oriented programming?*

1.7   *How are data and functions organized in an object-oriented program?*

1.8   *What are the unique advantages of an object-oriented programming paradigm?*

1.9   *Distinguish between the following terms:*
    (a)   *Objects and classes*
    (b)   *Data abstraction and data encapsulation*
    (c)   *Inheritance and polymorphism*
    (d)   *Dynamic binding and message passing*

1.10 *What kinds of things can become objects in OOP?*

1.11 *Describe inheritance as applied to OOP.*

1.12 *What do you mean by dynamic binding? How is it useful in OOP?*

1.13 *How does object-oriented approach differ from object-based approach?*

1.14 *List a few areas of application of OOP technology.*

1.15 *State whether the following statements are TRUE or FALSE.*
    (a)   *In procedure-oriented programming, all data are shared by all functions.*
    (b)   *The main emphasis of procedure-oriented programming is on algorithms rather than on data.*
    (c)   *One of the striking features of object-oriented programming is the division of programs into objects that represent real-world entities.*
    (d)   *Wrapping up of data of different types into a single unit is known as encapsulation.*
    (e)   *One problem with OOP is that once a class is created it can never be changed.*
    (f)   *Inheritance means the ability to reuse the data values of one object by other objects.*
    (g)   *Polymorphism is extensively used in implementing inheritance.*
    (h)   *Object-oriented programs are executed much faster than conventional programs.*
    (i)   *Object-oriented systems can scale up better from small to large.*
    (j)   *Object-oriented approach cannot be used to create databases.*

2

Beginning with C++

Key Concepts

- ➤ C with classes
- ➤ C++ features
- ➤ Main function
- ➤ C++ comments
- ➤ Output operator
- ➤ Input operator
- ➤ Header file
- ➤ Return statement

- ➤ Namespace
- ➤ Variables
- ➤ Cascading of operators
- ➤ C++ program structure
- ➤ Client-server model
- ➤ Source file creation
- ➤ Compilation
- ➤ Linking

2.1 WHAT IS C++?

C++ is an object-oriented programming language. It was developed by Bjarne Stroustrup at AT&T Bell Laboratories in Murray Hill, New Jersey, USA, in the early 1980's. Stroustrup, an admirer of Simula67 and a strong supporter of C, wanted to combine the best of both the languages and create a more powerful language that could support object-oriented programming features and still retain the power and elegance of C. The result was C++. Therefore, C++ is an extension of C with a major addition of the class construct feature of Simula67. Since the class was a major addition to the original C language, Stroustrup initially called the new language 'C with classes'. However, later in 1983, the name was changed to C++. The idea of C++ comes from the C increment operator ++, thereby suggesting that C++ is an augmented (incremented) version of C.

During the early 1990's the language underwent a number of improvements and changes. In November 1997, the ANSI/ISO standards committee standardised these changes and added several new features to the language specifications.

C++ is a superset of C. Most of what we already know about C applies to C++ also. Therefore, almost all C programs are also C++ programs. However, there are a few minor differences that will prevent a C program to run under C++ compiler. We shall see these differences later as and when they are encountered. A comprehensive list of major differences between ANSI C and ANSI C++ is given in Appendix A.

The most important facilities that C++ adds on to C are classes, inheritance, function overloading, and operator overloading. These features enable creating of abstract data types, inherit properties from existing data types and support polymorphism, thereby making C++ a truly object-oriented language.

The object-oriented features in C++ allow programmers to build large programs with clarity, extensibility and ease of maintenance, incorporating the spirit and efficiency of C. The addition of new features has transformed C from a language that currently facilitates top-down, structured design, to one that provides bottom-up, object-oriented design.

2.2 APPLICATIONS OF C++

C++ is a versatile language for handling very large programs. It is suitable for virtually any programming task including development of editors, compilers, databases, communication systems and any complex real-life application systems.

- Since C++ allows us to create hierarchy-related objects, we can buildspecial object-oriented libraries which can be used later by many programmers.
- While C++ is able to map the real-world problem properly, the C part of C++ gives the language the ability to get close to the machine-level details.
- C++ programs are easily maintainable and expandable. When a new feature needs to be implemented, it is very easy to add to the existing structure of an object.
- It is expected that C++ will replace C as a general-purpose language in the near future.

2.3 A SIMPLE C++ PROGRAM

Let us begin with a simple example of a C++ program that prints a string on the screen.

```
                    PRINTING A STRING

#include <iostream> // include header file

using namespace std;

int main()
{
    cout << "C++ is better than C.\n"; // C++ statement
    return 0;
}                    // End of example
                         PROGRAM 2.1
```

This simple program demonstrates several C++ features.

Program Features

Like C, the C++ program is a collection of functions. The above example contains only one function, **main**(). As usual, execution begins at main(). Every C++ program must have a **main**(). C++ is a free-form language. With a few exceptions, the compiler ignores carriage returns and white spaces. Like C, the C++ statements terminate with semicolons.

Comments

C++ introduces a new comment symbol // (double slash). Comments start with a double slash symbol and terminate at the end of the line. A comment may start anywhere in the line, and whatever follows till the end of the line is ignored. Note that there is no closing symbol.

The double slash comment is basically a single line comment. Multiline comments can be written as follows:

```
// This is an example of
// C++ program to illustrate
// Some of its features
```

The C comment symbols /*, */ are still valid and are more suitable for multiline comments. The following comment is allowed:

```
/*  This is an example of
    C++ program to illustrate
    some of its features
*/
```

We can use either or both styles in our programs. Since this is a book on C++, we will use only the C++ style. However, remember that we can not insert a // style comment within the text of a program line. For example, the double slash comment cannot be used in the manner as shown below:

```
for(j=0; j<n; /* loops n times */ j++)
```

Output Operator

The only statement in Program 2.1 is an output statement. The statement

```
cout << "C++ is better than C.";
```

causes the string in quotation marks to be displayed on the screen. This statement introduces two new C++ features, cout and <<. The identifier cout (pronounced as 'C out') is a predefined object that represents the standard output stream in C++. Here, the standard output stream represents the screen. It is also possible to redirect the output to other output devices. We shall later discuss streams in detail.

The operator << is called the *insertion or put to* operator. It inserts (or sends) the contents of the variable on its right to the object on its left (Fig. 2.1).

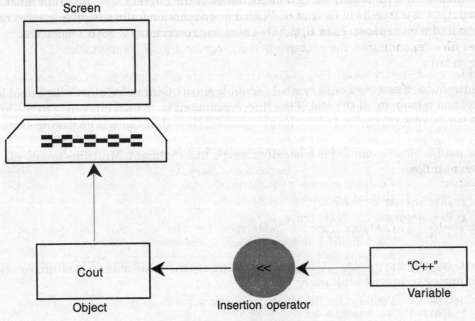

Fig. 2.1   *Output using insertion operator*

The object cout has a simple interface. If string represents a string variable, then the following statement will display its contents:

```
cout << string;
```

You may recall that the operator << is the bit-wise left-shift operator and it can still be used for this purpose. This is an example of how one operator can be used for different purposes, depending on the context. This concept is known as *operator overloading,* an important aspect of polymorphism. Operator overloading is discussed in detail in Chapter 7.

It is important to note that we can still use printf() for displaying an output. C++ accepts this notation. However, we will use cout << to maintain the spirit of C++.

The iostream File

We have used the following #include directive in the program:

```
#include <iostream>
```

This directive causes the preprocessor to add the contents of the iostream file to the program. It contains declarations for the identifier **cout** and the operator <<. Some old versions of C++ use a header file called iostream.h. This is one of the changes introduced by ANSI C++. (We should use iostream.h if the compiler does not support ANSI C++ features.)

The header file **iostream** should be included at the beginning of all programs that use input/output statements Note that the naming conventions for header files may vary. Some implementations use **iostream.hpp**; yet others **iostream.hxx**. We must include appropriate header files depending on the contents of the program and implementation.

Tables 2.1 and 2.2 provide lists of C++ standard library header files that may be needed in C++ programs. The header files with .h extension are "old style" files which should be used with old compilers. Table 2.1 also gives the version of these files that should be used with the ANSI standard compilers.

Table 2.1 Commonly used old-style header files

Header file	Contents and purpose	New version
<assert.h>	Contains macros and information for adding diagnostics that aid program debugging	<cassert>
<ctype.h>	Contains function prototypes for functions that test characters for certain properties, and function prototypes for functions that can be used to convert lowercase letters to uppercase letters and vice versa.	<cctype>
<float.h>	Contains the floating-point size limits of the system.	<cfloat>
<limits.h>	Contains the integral size limits of the system.	<climits>
<math.h>	Contains function prototypes for math library functions.	<cmath>
<stdio.h>	Contains function prototypes for the standard input/output library functions and information used by them.	<cstdio>
<stdlib.h>	Contains function prototypes for conversion of numbers to text, text to numbers, memory allocation, random numbers, and various other utility functions.	<cstdlib>
<string.h>	Contains function prototypes for C-style string processing functions.	<cstring>
<time.h>	Contains function prototypes and types for manipulating the time and date.	
<iostream.h>	Contains function prototypes for the standard input and standard output functions.	<iostream>
<iomanip.h>	Contains function prototypes for the stream manipulators that enable formatting of streams of data.	<iomanip>
<fstream.h>	Contains function prototypes for functions that perform input from files on disk and output to files on disk.	<fstream>

Table 2.2 New Header files included in ANSI C++

Header file	Contents and purpose
<utility>	Contains classes and functions that are used by many standard library header files.
<vector>, <list>, <deque> <queue>, <set>, <map>, <stack>, <bitset>	The header files contain classes that implement the standard library containers. Containers store data during a program's execution. We discuss these header files in Chapter14.
<functional>	Contains classes and functions used by algorithms of the standard library.
<memory>	Contains classes and functions used by the standard library to allocate memory to the standard library containers.
<iterator>	Contains classes for manipulating data in the standard library containers.
<algorithm>	Contains functions for manipulating data in the standard library containers.
<exception>, <stdexcept>	These header files contain classes that are used for exception handling.
<string>	Contains the definition of class string from the standard library. Discussed in Chapter 15
<sstream>	Contains function prototypes for functions that perform input from strings in memory and output to strings in memory.
<locale>	Contains classes and functions normally used by stream processing to process data in the natural form for different languages (e.g., monetary formats, sorting strings, character presentation, etc.)
<limits>	Contains a class for defining the numerical data type limits on each computer platform.
<typeinfo>	Contains classes for run-time type identification (determining data types at execution time).

Namespace

Namespace is a new concept introduced by the ANSI C++ standards committee. This defines a scope for the identifiers that are used in a program. For using the identifiers defined in the **namespace** scope we must include the using directive, like

```
using namespace std;
```

Here, **std** is the namespace where ANSI C++ standard class libraries are defined. All ANSI C++ programs must include this directive. This will bring all the identifiers defined in **std** to the current global scope. **using** and **namespace** are the new keywords of C++. Namespaces are discussed in detail in Chapter 16.

Return Type of main( )

In C++, main() returns an integer type value to the operating system. Therefore, every main() in C++ should end with a return(0) statement; otherwise a warning or an error might occur. Since **main()** returns an integer type value, return type for main() is explicitly specified as

int. Note that the default return type for all functions in C++ is **int**. The following **main** without type and return will run with a warning:

```
main()
{
    ......
    ......
}
```

2.4   MORE C++ STATEMENTS

Let us consider a slightly more complex C++ program. Assume that we would like to read two numbers from the keyboard and display their average on the screen. C++ statements to accomplish this is shown in Program 2.2.

```
                    AVERAGE OF TWO NUMBERS
    #include <iostream>

    using namespace std;

    int main()
    {
            float number1, number2,
                  sum, average;

            cout << "Enter two numbers: "; // prompt
            cin >> number1;          // Reads numbers
            cin >> number2;          // from keyboard

            sum = number1 + number2;
            average = sum/2;

            cout << "Sum = " << sum << "\n";
            cout << "Average = " << average << "\n";

            return 0;
    }
                         PROGRAM 2.2
```

The output of Program 2.2 is:

```
Enter two numbers: 6.5 7.5
Sum = 14
Average = 7
```

Variables

The program uses four variables number1, number2, sum, and average. They are declared as type float by the statement.

```
float number1, number2, sum, average;
```

All variables must be declared before they are used in the program.

Input Operator

The statement

```
cin >> number1;
```

is an input statement and causes the program to wait for the user to type in a number. The number keyed in is placed in the variable number1. The identifier cin (pronounced 'C in') is a predefined object in C++ that corresponds to the standard input stream. Here, this stream represents the keyboard.

The operator >> is known as *extraction or get from* operator. It extracts (or takes) the value from the keyboard and assigns it to the variable on its right (Fig. 2.2). This corresponds to the familiar scanf() operation. Like << , the operator >> can also be overloaded.

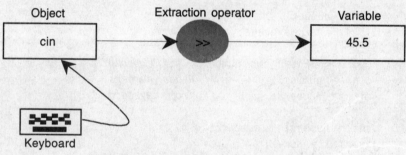

Fig. 2.2 *Input using extraction operator*

Cascading of I/O Operators

We have used the *insertion operator* << repeatedly in the last two statements for printing results.

The statement

```
cout << "Sum = " << sum << "\n";
```

first sends the string "Sum = " to cout and then sends the value of sum. Finally, it sends the newline character so that the next output will be in the new line. The multiple use of << in one statement is called cascading. When cascading an output operator, we should ensure necessary blank spaces between different items. Using the cascading technique, the last two statements can be combined as follows:

```
cout << "Sum = " << sum << "\n"
     << "Average = " << average << "\n";
```

This is one statement but provides two lines of output. If you want only one line of output, the statement will be:

```
cout << "Sum = " << sum << ","
     << "Average = " << average << "\n";
```

The output will be:

```
Sum = 14, Average = 7
```

We can also cascade input operator >> as shown below:

```
cin >> number1 >> number2;
```

The values are assigned from left to right. That is, if we key in two values, say, 10 and 20, then 10 will be assigned to number1 and 20 to number2.

2.5   AN EXAMPLE WITH CLASS

One of the major features of C++ is classes. They provide a method of binding together data and functions which operate on them. Like structures in C, classes are user-defined data types.

Program 2.3 shows the use of class in a C++ program.

USE OF CLASS

```
#include <iostream>
using namespace std;
class person
{
     char name[30];
     int age;

     public:
        void getdata(void);
        void display(void);
};
void person :: getdata(void)
{
     cout << "Enter name: ";
     cin >> name;
     cout << "Enter age: ";
     cin >> age;
}
```

```
void person :: display(void)
{
    cout << "\nName: " << name;
    cout << "\nAge: " << age;
}

int main()
{
    person p;

    p.getdata();
    p.display();

    return 0;
}
```

PROGRAM 2.3

The output of Program 2.3 is:

Enter Name: Ravinder
Enter Age: 30

Name: Ravinder
Age: 30

 cin can read only one word and therefore we cannot use names with blank spaces.

The program defines **person** as a new data of type class. The class person includes two basic data type items and two functions to operate on that data. These functions are called **member functions**. The main program uses **person** to declare variables of its type. As pointed out earlier, class variables are known as *objects*. Here, p is an object of type **person**. Class objects are used to invoke the functions defined in that class. More about classes and objects is discussed in Chapter 5.

2.6   STRUCTURE OF C++ PROGRAM

As it can be seen from the Program 2.3, a typical C++ program would contain four sections as shown in Fig. 2.3. These sections may be placed in separate code files and then compiled independently or jointly.

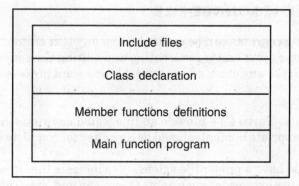

Fig. 2.3 *Structure of a C++ program*

It is a common practice to organize a program into three separate files. The class declarations are placed in a header file and the definitions of member functions go into another file. This approach enables the programmer to separate the abstract specification of the interface (class definition) from the implementation details (member functions definition). Finally, the main program that uses the class is placed in a third file which "includes" the previous two files as well as any other files required.

This approach is based on the concept of client-server model as shown in Fig. 2.4. The class definition including the member functions constitute the server that provides services to the main program known as client. The client uses the server through the public interface of the class.

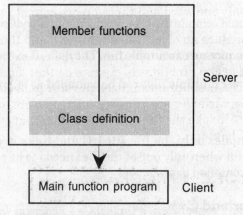

Fig. 2.4 *The client-server model*

2.7   CREATING THE SOURCE FILE

Like C programs, C++ programs can be created using any text editor. For example, on the UNIX, we can use vi or *ed* text editor for creating and editing the source code. On the DOS system, we can use *edlin* or any other editor available or a word processor system under non-document mode.

Some systems such as Turbo C++ provide an integrated environment for developing and editing programs. Appropriate manuals should be consulted for complete details.

The file name should have a proper file extension to indicate that it is a C++ program file. C++ implementations use extensions such as .c, .C, .cc, .cpp and .cxx. Turbo C++ and Borland C++ use .c for C programs and .cpp (C plus plus) for C++ programs. Zortech C++ system uses .cxx while UNIX AT&T version uses .C (capital C) and .cc. The operating system manuals should be consulted to determine the proper file name extensions to be used.

2.8   COMPILING AND LINKING

The process of compiling and linking again depends upon the operating system. A few popular systems are discussed in this section.

Unix AT&T C++

The process of implementation of a C++ program under UNIX is similar to that of a C program.We should use the "CC" (uppercase) command to compile the program. Remember, we use lowercase "cc" for compiling C programs. The command

```
CC example.C
```

at the UNIX prompt would compile the C++ program source code contained in the file **example.C**. The compiler would produce an object file **example.o** and then automatically link with the library functions to produce an executable file. The default executable filename is **a.out**.

A program spread over multiple files can be compiled as follows:

```
CC file1.C file2.o
```

The statement compiles only the file **file1.C** and links it with the previously compiled **file2.o** file.This is useful when only one of the files needs to be modified. The files that are not modified need not be compiled again.

Turbo C++ and Borland C++

Turbo C++ and Borland C++ provide an integrated program development environment under MS DOS. They provide a built-in editor and a menu bar which includes options such as File, Edit, Compile and Run.

We can create and save the source files under the **File option**, and edit them under the **Edit option**. We can then compile the program under the **Compile option** and execute it under the **Run option**. The **Run option** can be used without compiling the source code. In this case, the **RUN** command causes the system to compile, link and run the program in one step. Turbo C++ being the most popular compiler, creation and execution of programs under Turbo C++ system are discussed in detail in Appendix B.

Visual C++

It is a Microsoft application development system for C++ that runs under Windows. Visual C++ is a visual programming environment in which basic program components can be selected through menu choices, buttons, icons, and other predetermined methods. Development and execution of C++ programs under Windows are briefly explained in Appendix C.

Summary

- C++ is a superset of C language.
- C++ adds a number of object-oriented features such as objects, inheritance, function overloading and operator overloading to C. These features enable building of programs with clarity, extensibility and ease of maintenance.
- C++ can be used to build a variety of systems such as editors, compilers, databases, communication systems, and many more complex real-life application systems.
- C++ supports interactive input and output features and introduces a new comment symbol // that can be used for single line comments. It also supports C-style comments.
- Like C programs, execution of all C++ programs begins at **main( )** function and ends at **return( )** statement. The header file **iostream** should be included at the beginning of all programs that use input/output operations.
- All ANSI C++ programs must include **using namespace std** directive.
- A typical C++ program would contain four basic sections, namely, include files section, class declaration section, member function section and main function section.
- Like C programs, C++ programs can be created using any text editor.
- Most compiler systems provide an integrated environment for developing and executing programs. Popular systems are UNIX AT&T C++, Turbo C++ and Microsoft Visual C++.

Key Terms

- ➤ #include
- ➤ **a.out**
- ➤ Borland C++
- ➤ cascading
- ➤ **cin**
- ➤ class
- ➤ client
- ➤ comments

> ➤ **cout**
> ➤ edlin
> ➤ extraction operator
> ➤ **float**
> ➤ free-form
> ➤ get from operator
> ➤ input operator
> ➤ insertion operator
> ➤ **int**
> ➤ **iostream**
> ➤ **iostream.h**
> ➤ keyboard
> ➤ **main()**
> ➤ member functions
> ➤ MS-DOS
> ➤ **namespace**

> ➤ object
> ➤ operating systems
> ➤ operator overloading
> ➤ output operator
> ➤ put to operator
> ➤ return ()
> ➤ screen
> ➤ server
> ➤ Simula67
> ➤ text editor
> ➤ Turbo C++
> ➤ Unix AT&T C++
> ➤ **using**
> ➤ Visual C++
> ➤ Windows
> ➤ Zortech C++

Review Questions and Exercises

2.1 *State whether the following statements are TRUE or FALSE.*
   (a) *Since C is a subset of C++, all C programs will run under C++ compilers.*
   (b) *In C++, a function contained within a class is called a member function.*
   (c) *Looking at one or two lines of code, we can easily recognize whether a program is written in C or C++.*
   (d) *In C++, it is very easy to add new features to the existing structure of an object.*
   (e) *The concept of using one operator for different purposes is known as oerator overloading.*
   (f) *The output function printf() cannot be used in C++ programs.*

2.2 *Why do we need the preprocessor directive #include <iostream> ?*

2.3 *How does a main() function in C++ differ from main() in C?*

2.4 *What do you think is the main advantage of the comment / / in C++ as compared to the old C type comment?*

2.5 *Describe the major parts of a C++ program.*

2.6 *Find errors, if any, in the following C++ statements:*
   (a) *cout << "x=" x;*
   (b) *m = 5; / / n = 10; / / s = m + n;*
   (c) *cin >>x; >>y;*
   (d) *cout << \n "Name:" << name;*
   (e) *cout <<"Enter value:"; cin >> x;*
   (f) */ *Addition*/ z = x + y;*

2.7 *Write a program to display the following output using a single cout statement.*
   Maths = 90
   Physics = 77
   Chemistry = 69

2.8   Write a program to read two numbers from the keyboard and display the larger value on the screen.

2.9   Write a program to input an integer value from keyboard and display on screen "WELL DONE" that many times.

2.10 Write a program to read the values of a, b and c and display the value of x, where

$$x = a \ / \ b - c$$

Test your program for the following values:
(a)   a = 250, b = 85, c = 25
(b)   a = 300, b = 70, c = 70

2.11 Write a C++ program that will ask for a temperature in Fahrenheit and display it in Celsius.

2.12 Redo Exercise 2.11 using a class called **temp** and member functions.

3

Tokens, Expressions and Control Structures

Key Concepts

- ➢ Tokens
- ➢ Keywords
- ➢ Identifiers
- ➢ Data types
- ➢ User-defined types
- ➢ Derived types
- ➢ Symbolic constants
- ➢ Declaration of variables
- ➢ Initialization
- ➢ Reference variables
- ➢ Type compatibility

- ➢ Scope resolution
- ➢ Dereferencing
- ➢ Memory management
- ➢ Formatting the output
- ➢ Type casting
- ➢ Constructing expressions
- ➢ Special assignment expressions
- ➢ Implicit conversion
- ➢ Operator overloading
- ➢ Control structures

3.1 INTRODUCTION

As mentioned earlier, C++ is a superset of C and therefore most constructs of C are legal in C++ with their meaning unchanged. However, there are some exceptions and additions. In this chapter, we shall discuss these exceptions and additions with respect to tokens and control structures.

3.2 TOKENS

As we know, the smallest individual units in a program are known as tokens. C++ has the following tokens:

- Keywords
- Identifiers
- Constants
- Strings
- Operators

A C++ program is written using these tokens, white spaces, and the syntax of the language. Most of the C++ tokens are basically similar to the C tokens with the exception of some additions and minor modifications.

3.3   KEYWORDS

The keywords implement specific C++ language features. They are explicitly reserved identifiers and cannot be used as names for the program variables or other user-defined program elements.

Table 3.1 gives the complete set of C++ keywords. Many of them are common to both C and C++. The ANSI C keywords are shown in boldface. Additional keywords have been added to the ANSI C keywords in order to enhance its features and make it an object-oriented language. ANSI C++ standards committee has added some more keywords to make the language more versatile. These are shown separately. Meaning and purpose of all C++ keywords are given in Appendix D.

Table 3.1   C++ keywords

asm	**double**	new	**switch**
auto	**else**	operator	template
break	**enum**	private	this
case	**extern**	protected	throw
catch	**float**	public	try
char	**for**	**register**	**typedef**
class	friend	**return**	**union**
const	**goto**	**short**	**unsigned**
continue	**if**	**signed**	virtual
default	inline	**sizeof**	**void**
delete	**int**	**static**	**volatile**
do	**long**	**struct**	**while**
Added by ANSI C++			
bool	export	reinterpret_cast	typename
const_cast	false	static_cast	using
dynamic_cast	mutable	true	wchar_t
explicit	namespace	typeid	

Note: The ANSI C keywords are shown in bold face.

3.4   IDENTIFIERS AND CONSTANTS

Identifiers refer to the names of variables, functions, arrays, classes, etc. created by the programmer. They are the fundamental requirement of any language. Each language has its own rules for naming these identifiers. The following rules are common to both C and C++:

- Only alphabetic characters, digits and underscores are permitted.
- The name cannot start with a digit.
- Uppercase and lowercase letters are distinct.
- A declared keyword cannot be used as a variable name.

A major difference between C and C++ is the limit on the length of a name. While ANSI C recognizes only the first 32 characters in a name, ANSI C++ places no limit on its length and, therefore, all the characters in a name are significant.

Care should be exercised while naming a variable which is being shared by more than one file containing C and C++ programs. Some operating systems impose a restriction on the length of such a variable name.

Constants refer to fixed values that do not change during the execution of a program.

Like C, C++ supports several kinds of literal constants. They include integers, characters, floating point numbers and strings. Literal constant do not have memory locations. Examples:

```
123                // decimal integer
12.34              // floating point integer
037                // octal integer
0X2                // hexadecimal integer
"C++"              // string constant
'A'                // character constant
L'ab'              // wide-character constant
```

The **wchar_t** type is a wide-character literal introduced by ANSI C++ and is intended for character sets that cannot fit a character into a single byte. Wide-character literals begin with the letter L.

C++ also recognizes all the backslash character constants available in C.

C++ supports two types of string representation — the C-style character string and the string class type introduced with Standard C++. Although the use of the string class type is recommended, it is advisable to understand and use C-style strings in some situations. The string class type strings support many features and are discussed in detail in Chapter 15.

3.5   BASIC DATA TYPES

Data types in C++ can be classified under various categories as shown in Fig. 3.1.

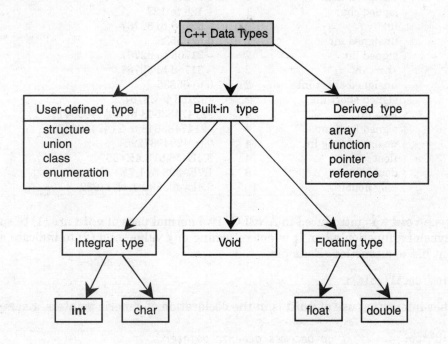

Fig.3.1   *Hierarchy of C++ data types*

Both C and C++ compilers support all the built-in (also known as *basic* or *fundamental*) data types. With the exception of **void**, the basic data types may have several *modifiers* preceding them to serve the needs of various situations. The modifiers **signed, unsigned, long**, and **short** may be applied to character and integer basic data types. However, the modifier **long** may also be applied to **double**. Data type representation is machine specific in C++. Table 3.2 lists all combinations of the basic data types and modifiers along with their size and range for a 16-bit word machine.

ANSI C++ committee has added two more data types, **bool** and **wchar_t**. They are discussed in Chapter 16.

Table 3.2   Size and Range of C++ Basic Data Types

Type	Bytes	Range
char	1	–128 to 127
unsigned char	1	0 to 255
signed char	1	– 128 to 127
int	2	– 32768 to 32767
unsigned int	2	0 to 65535
signed int	2	– 31768 to 32767
short int	2	– 31768 to 32767
unsigned short int	2	0 to 65535
signed short int	2	–32768 to 32767
long int	4	–2147483648 to 2147483647
signed long int	4	–2147483648 to 2147483647
unsigned long int	4	0 to 4294967295
float	4	3.4E–38 to 3.4E+38
double	8	1.7E–308 to 1.7E+308
long double	10	3.4E–4932 to 1.1E+4932

The type **void** was introduced in ANSI C. Two normal uses of **void** are (1) to specify the return type of a function when it is not returning any value, and (2) to indicate an empty argument list to a function. Example:

```
void funct1(void);
```

Another interesting use of **void** is in the declaration of generic pointers. Example:

```
void *gp;        // gp becomes generic pointer
```

A generic pointer can be assigned a pointer value of any basic data type, but it may not be dereferenced. For example,

```
int *ip;         // int pointer
gp = ip;         // assign int pointer to void pointer
```

are valid statements. But, the statement,

```
*ip = *gp;
```

is illegal. It would not make sense to dereference a pointer to a **void** value.

Assigning any pointer type to a **void** pointer without using a cast is allowed in both C++ and ANSI C. In ANSI C, we can also assign a **void** pointer to a non-**void** pointer without using a cast to non-void pointer type. This is not allowed in C++. For example,

```
void *ptr1;
char *ptr2;
ptr2 = ptr1;
```

are all valid statements in ANSI C but not in C++. A **void** pointer cannot be directly assigned to other type pointers in C++. We need to use a cast operator as shown below:

```
ptr2 = (char *)ptr1;
```

3.6 USER-DEFINED DATA TYPES

Structures and Classes

We have used user-defined data types such as **struct** and **union** in C. While these data types are legal in C++, some more features have been added to make them suitable for object-oriented programming. C++ also permits us to define another user-defined data type known as **class** which can be used, just like any other basic data type, to declare variables. The class variables are known as objects, which are the central focus of object-oriented programming. More about these data types is discussed later in Chapter 5.

Enumerated Data Type

An enumerated data type is another user-defined type which provides a way for attaching names to numbers, thereby increasing comprehensibility of the code. The **enum** keyword (from C) automatically enumerates a list of words by assigning them values 0,1,2, and so on. This facility provides an alternative means for creating symbolic constants. The syntax of an **enum** statement is similar to that of the **struct** statement. Examples:

```
enum shape{circle, square, triangle};
enum colour{red, blue, green, yellow};
enum position{off, on};
```

The enumerated data types differ slightly in C++ when compared with those in ANSI C. In C++, the tag names **shape, colour**, and **position** become new type names. By using these tag names, we can declare new variables. Examples:

```
shape ellipse;          // ellipse is of type shape
colour background;      // background is of type colour
```

ANSI C defines the types of **enums** to be **ints**. In C++, each enumerated data type retains its own separate type. This means that C++ does not permit an **int** value to be automatically converted to an **enum** value. Examples:

```
colour background = blue;        // allowed
colour background = 7;           // Error in C++
colour background = (colour) 7;  // OK
```

However, an enumerated value can be used in place of an **int** value.

```
int c = red;      // valid, colour type promoted to int
```

By default, the enumerators are assigned integer values starting with 0 for the first enumerator, 1 for the second, and so on. We can over-ride the default by explicitly assigning integer values to the enumerators. For example,

```
enum colour{red, blue=4, green=8};
enum colour{red=5, blue, green};
```

are valid definitions. In the first case, **red** is 0 by default. In the second case, **blue** is 6 and **green** is 7. Note that the subsequent initialized enumerators are larger by one than their predecessors.

C++ also permits the creation of anonymous **enums** (i.e., **enums** without tag names). Example:

```
enum{off, on};
```

Here, **off** is 0 and **on** is 1. These constants may be referenced in the same manner as regular constants. Examples:

```
int switch_1 = off;
int switch_2 = on;
```

In practice, enumeration is used to define symbolic constants for a **switch** statement. Example:

```
enum shape
{
   circle,
   rectangle,
   triangle
};

int main()
{
   cout << "Enter shape code:";
   int code;
   cin >> code;
   while(code >= circle && code <= triangle)
   {
           switch(code)
           {
                   case circle:
                   ......
                   ......
                   break;
                   case rectangle:
                   ......
```

```
                \
                ......
            break;
            case triangle:
                ......
                ......
            break;
        }
        cout << "Enter shape code:";
        cin >> code;
    }
    cout << "BYE \n";
    return 0;
}
```

ANSI C permits an **enum** to be defined within a structure or a class, but the **enum** is globally visible. In C++, an **enum** defined within a class (or structure) is local to that class (or structure) only.

3.7 DERIVED DATA TYPES

Arrays

The application of arrays in C++ is similar to that in C. The only exception is the way character arrays are initialized. When initializing a character array in ANSI C, the compiler will allow us to declare the array size as the exact length of the string constant. For instance,

```
    char string[3] = "xyz";
```

is valid in ANSI C. It assumes that the programmer intends to leave out the null character \0 in the definition. But in C++, the size should be one larger than the number of characters in the string.

```
    char string[4] = "xyz"; // O.K. for C++
```

Functions

Functions have undergone major changes in C++. While some of these changes are simple, others require a new way of thinking when organizing our programs. Many of these modifications and improvements were driven by the requirements of the object-oriented concept of C++. Some of these were introduced to make the C++ program more reliable and readable. All the features of C++ functions are discussed in Chapter 4.

Pointers

Pointers are declared and initialized as in C. Examples:

```
    int *ip;         // int pointer
    ip = &x;         // address of x assigned to ip
    *ip = 10;        // 10 assigned to x through indirection
```

C++ adds the concept of constant pointer and pointer to a constant.

```
char * const ptr1 = "GOOD";    // constant pointer
```

We cannot modify the address that **ptr1** is initialized to.

```
int const * ptr2 = &m;  // pointer to a constant
```

ptr2 is declared as pointer to a constant. It can point to any variable of correct type, but the contents of what it points to cannot be changed.

We can also declare both the pointer and the variable as constants in the following way:

```
const char * const cp = "xyz";
```

This statement declares cp as a constant pointer to the string which has been declared a constant. In this case, neither the address assigned to the pointer cp nor the contents it points to can be changed.

Pointers are extensively used in C++ for memory management and achieving polymorphism.

3.8 SYMBOLIC CONSTANTS

There are two ways of creating symbolic constants in C++:

- Using the qualifier **constant**, and
- Defining a set of integer constants using **enum** keyword.

In both C and C++, any value declared as **const** cannot be modified by the program in any way. However, there are some differences in implementation. In C++, we can use **const** in a constant expression, such as

```
const int size = 10;
char name[size];
```

This would be illegal in C. **const** allows us to create typed constants instead of having to use **#define** to create constants that have no type information.

As with **long** and **short**, if we use the **const** modifier alone, it defaults to **int**. For example,

```
const size = 10;
```

means

```
const int size = 10;
```

The *named constants* are just like variables except that their values cannot be changed.

C++ requires a **const** to be initialized. ANSI C does not require an initializer; if none is given, it initializes the **const** to 0.

The scoping of **const** values differs. A **const** in C++ defaults to the internal linkage and therefore it is local to the file where it is declared. In ANSI C, **const** values are global in nature. They are visible outside the file in which they are declared. However, they can be made local by declaring them as **static**. To give a **const** value an external linkage so that it can be referenced from another file, we must explicitly define it as an **extern** in C++. Example:

```
extern const total = 100;
```

Another method of naming integer constants is by enumeration as under;

```
enum {X,Y,Z};
```

This defines X, Y and Z as integer constants with values 0, 1, and 2 respectively. This is equivalent to:

```
const X = 0;
const Y = 1;
const Z = 2;
```

We can also assign values to X, Y, and Z explicitly. Example:

```
enum{X=100, Y=50, Z=200};
```

Such values can be any integer values. Enumerated data type has been discussed in detail in Section 3.6.

3.9 TYPE COMPATIBILITY

C++ is very strict with regard to type compatibility as compared to C. For instance, C++ defines **int, short int**, and **long int** as three different types. They must be cast when their values are assigned to one another. Similarly, **unsigned char, char**, and **signed char** are considered as different types, although each of these has a size of one byte. In C++, the types of values must be the same for complete compatibility, or else, a cast must be applied. These restrictions in C++ are necessary in order to support function overloading where two functions with the same name are distinguished using the type of function arguments.

Another notable difference is the way **char** constants are stored. In C, they are stored as **ints,** and therefore,

```
sizeof ('x')
```

is equivalent to

```
sizeof(int)
```

in C. In C++, however, **char** is not promoted to the size of **int** and therefore

```
sizeof('x')
```

equals

```
sizeof(char)
```

3.10 DECLARATION OF VARIABLES

We know that, in C, all variables must be declared before they are used in executable statements. This is true with C++ as well. However, there is a significant difference between C and C++ with regard to the place of their declaration in the program. C requires all the variables to be defined at the beginning of a scope. When we read a C program, we usually come across a group of variable declarations at the beginning of each scope level. Their actual use appears elsewhere in the scope, sometimes far away from the place of declaration. Before using a variable, we should go back to the beginning of the program to see whether it has been declared and, if so, of what type.

C++ allows the declaration of a variable anywhere in the scope. This means that a variable can be declared right at the place of its first use. This makes the program much easier to write and reduces the errors that may be caused by having to scan back and forth. It also makes the program easier to understand because the variables are declared in the context of their use.

The example below illustrates this point.

```
int main()
{
        float x;                        // declaration
        float sum = 0;

        for(int i=1; i<5; i++)          // declaration
        {
                cin >> x;
                sum = sum +x;
        }
        float average;                  // declaration
        average = sum/i;
        cout << average;

        return 0;
}
```

The only disadvantage of this style of declaration is that we cannot see all the variables used in a scope at a glance.

3.11   DYNAMIC INITIALIZATION OF VARIABLES

In C, a variable must be initialized using a constant expression, and the C compiler would fix the initialization code at the time of compilation. C++, however, permits initialization of the variables at run time. This is referred to as *dynamic initialization*. In C++, a variable can be initialized at run time using expressions at the place of declaration. For example, the following are valid initialization statements:

```
.....
.....
int n = strlen(string);
.....
float area = 3.14159 * rad * rad;
```

Thus, both the declaration and the initialization of a variable can be done simultaneously at the place where the variable is used for the first time. The following two statements in the example of the previous section

```
float average;  // declare where it is necessary
average = sum/i;
```

can be combined into a single statement:

```
float average = sum/i;  // initialize dynamically at run time
```

Dynamic initialization is extensively used in object-oriented programming. We can create exactly the type of object needed, using information that is known only at the run time.

3.12   REFERENCE VARIABLES

C++ introduces a new kind of variable known as the *reference* variable. A reference variable provides an *alias* (alternative name) for a previously defined variable. For example, if we make the variable **sum** a reference to the variable **total**, then **sum** and **total** can be used interchangeably to represent that variable. A reference variable is created as follows:

```
data-type & reference-name = variable-name
```

Example:

```
float total = 100;
float sum = total;
```

total is a **float** type variable that has already been declared; **sum** is the alternative name declared to represent the variable **total**. Both the variables refer to the same data object in the memory. Now, the statements

```
cout << total;
```

and

```
cout << sum;
```

both print the value 100. The statement

```
total = total + 10;
```

will change the value of both total and sum to 110. Likewise, the assignment

```
sum = 0;
```

will change the value of both the variables to zero.

A reference variable must be initialized at the time of declaration. This establishes the correspondence between the reference and the data object which it names. It is important to note that the initialization of a reference variable is completely different from assignment to it.

C++ assigns additional meaning to the symbol **&**. Here, **&** is not an address operator. The notation **float &** means reference to **float**. Other examples are:

```
int n[10];
int & x = n[10];          // x is alias for n[10]
char & a = '\n';          // initialize reference to a literal
```

The variable **x** is an alternative to the array element **n[10]**. The variable **a** is initialized to the newline constant. This creates a reference to the otherwise unknown location where the newline constant \n is stored.

The following references are also allowed:

```
i.   int x;
     int *p = &x;
     int & m = *p;

ii.  int & n = 50;
```

The first set of declarations causes **m** to refer to **x** which is pointed to by the pointer **p** and the statement in (ii) creates an **int** object with value 50 and name **n**.

A major application of reference variables is in passing arguments to functions. Consider the following:

```
void f(int & x)          // uses reference
{
   x = x+10;             // x is incremented; so also m
}
int main()
{
   int m = 10;
   f(m);                 // function call
   .....
   .....
}
```

When the function call **f(m)** is executed, the following initialization occurs:

```
int & x = m;
```

Thus x becomes an alias of m after executing the statement

```
f(m);
```

Such function calls are known as *call by reference*. This implementation is illustrated in Fig. 3.2. Since the variables **x** and **m** are aliases, when the function increments **x, m** is also incremented. The value of **m** becomes 20 after the function is executed. In traditional C, we accomplish this operation using pointers and dereferencing techniques.

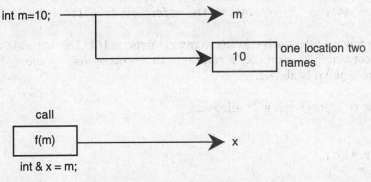

Fig. 3.2 *Call by reference mechanism*

The call by reference mechanism is useful in object-oriented programming because it permits the manipulation of objects by reference, and eliminates the copying of object parameters back and forth. It is also important to note that references can be created not only for built-in data types but also for user-defined data types such as structures and classes. References work wonderfully well with these user-defined data types.

3.13   OPERATORS IN C++

C++ has a rich set of operators. All C operators are valid in C++ also. In addition, C++ introduces some new operators. We have already seen two such operators, namely, the insertion operator <<, and the extraction operator >>. Other new operators are:

```
::       Scope resolution operator
::*      Pointer-to-member declarator
->*      Pointer-to-member operator
.*       Pointer-to-member operator
delete   Memory release operator
endl     Line feed operator
new      Memory allocation operator
setw     Field width operator
```

In addition, C++ also allows us to provide new definitions to some of the built-in operators. That is, we can give several meanings to an operator, depending upon the types of arguments used. This process is known as *operator overloading*.

3.14   SCOPE RESOLUTION OPERATOR

Like C, C++ is also a block-structured language. Blocks and scopes can be used in constructing programs. We know that the same variable name can be used to have different meanings in different blocks. The scope of the variable extends from the point of its declaration till the end of the block containing the declaration. A variable declared inside a block is said to be local to that block. Consider the following segment of a program:

```
.....
.....
{
   int x = 10;
   .....
   .....
}
.....
.....
{
   int x = 1;
   .....
   .....
}
```

The two declarations of x refer to two different memory locations containing different values. Statements in the second block cannot refer to the variable x declared in the first block, and vice versa. Blocks in C++ are often nested. For example, the following style is common:

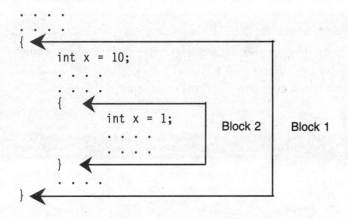

Block2 is contained in block1. Note that a declaration in an inner block *hides* a declaration of the same variable in an outer block and, therefore, each declaration of **x** causes it to refer to a different data object. Within the inner block, the variable **x** will refer to the data object declared therein.

In C, the global version of a variable cannot be accessed from within the inner block. C++ resolves this problem by introducing a new operator :: called the *scope resolution operator*. This can be used to uncover a hidden variable. It takes the following form:

```
:: variable-name
```

This operator allows access to the global version of a variable. For example, ::count means the global version of the variable count (and not the local variable count declared in that block). Program 3.1 illustrates this feature.

```
                        SCOPE RESOLUTION OPERATOR

    #include <iostream>
    using namespace std;
    int m = 10;          // global m

    int main()
    {
        int m = 20;      // m redeclared, local to main

        {
            int k = m;
            int m = 30;      // m declared again
                             // local to inner block

            cout <<   "we are in inner block \n";
            cout <<   "k = " << k << "\n";
            cout <<   "m = " << m << "\n";
            cout <<   "::m = " << ::m << "\n";
        }

                        PROGRAM 3.1
```

```
    cout << "\nWe are in outer block \n";
    cout << "m = " << m << "\n";
    cout << "::m = " << ::m << "\n";

    return 0;
}
```

PROGRAM 3.1

The output of Program 3.1 would be:

```
We are in inner block
k = 20
m = 30
::m = 10

We are in outer block
m = 20
::m = 10
```

In the above program, the variable **m** is declared at three places, namely, outside the **main()** function, inside the **main()**, and inside the inner block.

It is to be noted **::m** will always refer to the global **m**. In the inner block, ::m refers to the value 10 and not 20.

A major application of the scope resolution operator is in the classes to identify the class to which a member function belongs. This will be dealt in detail later when the classes are introduced.

3.15 MEMBER DEREFERENCING OPERATORS

As you know, C++ permits us to define a class containing various types of data and functions as members. C++ also permits us to access the class members through pointers. In order to achieve this, C++ provides a set of three pointer-to-member operators. Table 3.3 shows these operators and their functions.

Further details on these operators will be meaningful only after we discuss classes, and therefore we defer the use of member dereferencing operators until then.

Table 3.3   Member dereferencing operators

Operator	Function
::*	To declare a pointer to a member of a class
*	To access a member using object name and a pointer to that member
->*	To access a member using a pointer to the object and a pointer to that member

3.16 MEMORY MANAGEMENT OPERATORS

C uses **malloc()** and **calloc()** functions to allocate memory dynamically at run time. Similarly, it uses the function **free()** to free dynamically allocated memory. We use dynamic allocation techniques when it is not known in advance how much of memory space is needed. Although C++ supports these functions, it also defines two unary operators **new** and **delete** that perform the task of allocating and freeing the memory in a better and easier way. Since these operators manipulate memory on the free store, they are also known as *free store* operators.

An object can be created by using **new**, and destroyed by using **delete**, as and when required. A data object created inside a block with **new**, will remain in existence until it is explicitly destroyed by using **delete**. Thus, the lifetime of an object is directly under our control and is unrelated to the block structure of the program.

The **new** operator can be used to create objects of any type. It takes the following general form:

```
pointer-variable  =  new data-type;
```

Here, *pointer-variable* is a pointer of type *data-type*. The **new** operator allocates sufficient memory to hold a data object of type *data-type* and returns the address of the object. The *data-type* may be any valid data type. The *pointer-variable* holds the address of the memory space allocated. Examples:

```
p = new int;
q = new float;
```

where **p** is a pointer of type **int** and **q** is a pointer of type **float**. Here, **p** and **q** must have already been declared as pointers of appropriate types. Alternatively, we can combine the declaration of pointers and their assignments as follows:

```
int *p = new int;
float *q = new float;
```

Subsequently, the statements

```
*p = 25;
*q = 7.5;
```

assign 25 to the newly created **int** object and 7.5 to the **float** object.

We can also initialize the memory using the **new** operator. This is done as follows:

```
pointer-variable  =  new data-type(value);
```

Here, value specifies the initial value. Examples:

```
int *p = new int(25);
float *q = new float(7.5);
```

As mentioned earlier, **new** can be used to create a memory space for any data type including user-defined types such as arrays, structures and classes. The general form for a one-dimensional array is:

```
pointer-variable  =  new data-type[size];
```

Here, size specifies the number of elements in the array. For example, the statement

```
int *p = new int[10];
```

creates a memory space for an array of 10 integers. **p[0]** will refer to the first element, **p[1]** to the second element, and so on.

When creating multi-dimensional arrays with **new**, all the array sizes must be supplied.

```
array_ptr = new int[3][5][4];      // legal
array_ptr = new int[m][5][4];      // legal
array_ptr = new int[3][5][ ];      // illegal
array_ptr = new int[ ][5][4];      // illegal
```

The first dimension may be a variable whose value is supplied at runtime. All others must be constants.

The application of **new** to class objects will be discussed later in Chapter 6.

When a data object is no longer needed, it is destroyed to release the memory space for reuse. The general form of its use is:

```
delete pointer-variable;
```

The *pointer-variable* is the pointer that points to a data object created with **new**. Examples:

```
delete p;
delete q;
```

If we want to free a dynamically allocated array, we must use the following form of **delete**:

```
delete [size] pointer-variable;
```

The *size* specifies the number of elements in the array to be freed. The problem with this form is that the programmer should remember the size of the array. Recent versions of C++ do not require the size to be specified. For example,

```
delete [ ]p;
```

will delete the entire array pointed to by **p**.

What happens if sufficient memory is not available for allocation? In such cases, like **malloc()**, **new** returns a null pointer. Therefore, it may be a good idea to check for the pointer produced by **new** before using it. It is done as follows:

```
.....
.....
p = new int;
if(!p)
{
    cout << "allocation failed \n";
}
.....
.....
```

The **new** operator offers the following advantages over the function **malloc()**.

1. It automatically computes the size of the data object. We need not use the operator **sizeof**.
2. It automatically returns the correct pointer type, so that there is no need to use a type cast.
3. It is possible to initialize the object while creating the memory space.
4. Like any other operator, **new** and **delete** can be overloaded.

3.17 MANIPULATORS

Manipulators are operators that are used to format the data display. The most commonly used manipulators are **endl** and **setw**.

The **endl** manipulator, when used in an output statement, causes a linefeed to be inserted. It has the same effect as using the newline character "\n". For example, the statement

```
. . . . .
. . . . .
cout << "m = " << m << endl
     << "n = " << n << endl
     << "p = " << p << endl;
. . . . .
. . . . .
```

would cause three lines of output, one for each variable. If we assume the values of the variables as 2597, 14, and 175 respectively, the output will appear as shown below:

m = | 2 | 5 | 9 | 7 |

n = | 1 | 4 |

p = | 1 | 7 | 5 |

It is important to note that this form is not the ideal output. It should rather appear as under:

```
m = 2597
n =   14
p =  175
```

Here, the numbers are *right-justified*. This form of output is possible only if we can specify a common field width for all the numbers and force them to be printed right-justified. The **setw** manipulator does this job. It is used as follows:

```
cout << setw(5) << sum << endl;
```

The manipulator **setw(5)** specifies a field width 5 for printing the value of the variable sum. This value is right-justified within the field as shown below:

| | | 3 | 4 | 5 |

Program 3.2 illustrates the use of **endl** and **setw**.

USE OF MANIPULATORS

```
#include <iostream>
#include <iomanip>    // for setw

using namespace std;

int main()
{
    int Basic = 950, Allowance = 95, Total = 1045;
```

(Contd)

```
            cout << setw(10) << "Basic" << setw(10) << Basic << endl
                 << setw(10) << "Allowance" << setw(10) << Allowance << endl
                 << setw(10) << "Total" << setw(10) << Total << endl;

            return 0;
      }
```

PROGRAM 3.2

Output of this program is given below:

```
Basic        950
Allowance     95
Total       1045
```

 Character strings are also printed right-justified.

We can also write our own manipulators as follows:

```
#include <iostream>
ostream & symbol(ostream & output)
{
      return output << "\tRs";
}
```

The **symbol** is the new manipulator which represents **Rs**. The identifier **symbol** can be used whenever we need to display the string **Rs**.

3.18 TYPE CAST OPERATOR

C++ permits explicit type conversion of variables or expressions using the type cast operator.

Traditional C casts are augmented in C++ by a function-call notation as a syntactic alternative. The following two versions are equivalent:

```
(type-name) expression   // C notation
type-name (expression)   // C++ notation
```

Examples:

```
average = sum/(float)i;    // C notation
average = sum/float(i);    // C++ notation
```

A type-name behaves as if it is a function for converting values to a designated type. The function-call notation usually leads to simplest expressions. However, it can be used only if the type is an identifier. For example,

```
p = int * (q);
```

is illegal. In such cases, we must use C type notation.

```
p = (int *) q;
```

Alternatively, we can use **typedef** to create an identifier of the required type and use it in the functional notation.

```
typedef int * int_pt;
p = int_pt(q);
```

ANSI C++ adds the following new cast operators:

* const_cast
* static_cast
* dynamic_cast
* reinterpret_cast

Application of these operators is discussed in Chapter 16.

3.19 EXPRESSIONS AND THEIR TYPES

An expression is a combination of operators, constants and variables arranged as per the rules of the language. It may also include function calls which return values. An expression may consist of one or more operands, and zero or more operators to produce a value. Expressions may be of the following seven types:

* Constant expressions
* Integral expressions
* Float expressions
* Pointer expressions
* Relational expressions
* Logical expressions
* Bitwise expressions

An expression may also use combinations of the above expressions. Such expressions are known as *compound expressions*.

Constant Expressions

Constant Expressions consist of only constant values. Examples:

```
15
20 + 5 / 2.0
'x'
```

Integral Expressions

Integral Expressions are those which produce integer results after implementing all the automatic and explicit type conversions. Examples:

```
m
m * n - 5
m * 'x'
5 + int(2.0)
```

where **m** and **n** are integer variables.

Float Expressions

Float Expressions are those which, after all conversions, produce floating-point results. Examples:

```
x + y
x * y / 10
5 + float(10)
10.75
```

where **x** and **y** are floating-point variables.

Pointer Expressions

Pointer Expressions produce address values. Examples:

```
&m
ptr
ptr + 1
"xyz"
```

where **m** is a variable and **ptr** is a pointer.

Relational Expressions

Relational Expressions yield results of type **bool** which takes a value **true** or **false**. Examples:

```
x <= y
a+b == c+d
m+n > 100
```

When arithmetic expressions are used on either side of a relational operator, they will be evaluated first and then the results compared. Relational expressions are also known as *Boolean expressions*.

Logical Expressions

Logical Expressions combine two or more relational expressions and produces **bool** type results. Examples:

```
a>b  &&  x==10
x==10  ||  y==5
```

Bitwise Expressions

Bitwise Expressions are used to manipulate data at bit level. They are basically used for testing or shifting bits. Examples:

```
x << 3      // Shift three bit position to left
y >> 1      // Shift one bit position to right
```

Shift operators are often used for multiplication and division by powers of two.

ANSI C++ has introduced what are termed as *operator keywords* that can be used as alternative representation for operator symbols. Operator keywords are given in Chapter 16.

3.20 SPECIAL ASSIGNMENT EXPRESSIONS

Chained Assignment

```
x = (y = 10);
   or
x = y = 10;
```

First 10 is assigned to y and then to x.

A chained statement cannot be used to initialize variables at the time of declaration. For instance, the statement

```
float a = b = 12.34;        // wrong
```

is illegal. This may be written as

```
float a=12.34, b=12.34      // correct
```

Embedded Assignment

```
x = (y = 50) + 10;
```

(y = 50) is an assignment expression known as embedded assignment. Here, the value 50 is assigned to y and then the result 50+10 = 60 is assigned to x. This statement is identical to

```
y = 50;
x = y + 10;
```

Compound Assignment

Like C, C++ supports a *compound assignment operator* which is a combination of the assignment operator with a binary arithmetic operator. For example, the simple assignment statement

```
x = x + 10;
```

may be written as

```
x += 10;
```

The operator += is known as *compound assignment operator* or *short-hand assignment operator*. The general form of the compound assignment operator is:

```
variable1 op= variable2;
```

where *op* is a binary arithmetic operator. This means that

```
variable1 = variable1 op variable2;
```

3.21 IMPLICIT CONVERSIONS

We can mix data types in expressions. For example,

```
m = 5+2.75;
```

is a valid statement. Wherever data types are mixed in an expression, C++ performs the conversions automatically. This process is known as *implicit* or *automatic conversion*.

When the compiler encounters an expression, it divides the expressions into subexpressions consisting of one operator and one or two operands. For a binary operator, if the operands type differ, the compiler converts one of them to match with the other, using the rule that the "smaller" type is converted to the "wider" type. For example, if one of the operand is an **int** and the other is a **float**, the **int** is converted into a **float** because a **float** is wider than an **int**. The "water-fall" model shown in Fig. 3.3 illustrates this rule.

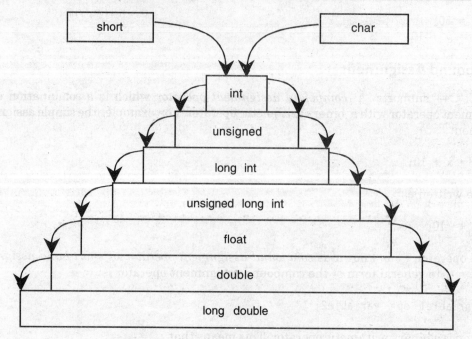

Fig. 3.3   *Water-fall model of type conversion*

Whenever a **char** or **short int** appears in an expression, it is converted to an **int**. This is called *integral widening conversion*. The implicit conversion is applied only after completing all integral widening conversions.

Type of results of mixed-mode arithmetic operations are summarised in Table 3.4.

Table 3.4   Results of Mixed-mode Operations

RHO \ LHO	char	short	int	long	float	double	long double
char	int	int	int	long	float	double	long double
short	int	int	int	long	float	double	long double
int	int	int	int	long	float	double	long double
long	long	long	long	long	float	double	long double
float	float	float	float	float	float	double	long double
double	double	double	double	double	double	double	long double
long double	long double	long double	long double	long double	long double	long double	long double

RHO – Right-hand operand
LHO – Left-hand operand

3.22 OPERATOR OVERLOADING

As stated earlier, overloading means assigning different meanings to an operation, depending on the context. C++ permits overloading of operators, thus allowing us to assign multiple meanings to operators. Actually, we have used the concept of overloading in C also. For example, the operator * when applied to a pointer variable, gives the value pointed to by the pointer. But it is also commonly used for multiplying two numbers. The number and type of operands decide the nature of operation to follow.

The input/output operators << and >> are good examples of operator overloading. Although the built-in definition of the << operator is for shifting of bits, it is also used for displaying the values of various data types. This has been made possible by the header file *iostream* where a number of overloading definitions for << are included. Thus, the statement

```
cout << 75.86;
```

invokes the definition for displaying a **double** type value, and

```
cout << "well done";
```

invokes the definition for displaying a **char** value. However, none of these definitions in *iostream* affect the built-in meaning of the operator.

Similarly, we can define additional meanings to other C++ operators. For example, we can define + operator to add two structures or objects. Almost all C++ operators can be overloaded with a few exceptions such as the member-access operators (**.** and **.***), conditional operator (?:), scope resolution operator (::) and the size operator (**sizeof**). Definitions for operator overloading are discussed in detail in Chapter 7.

3.23 OPERATOR PRECEDENCE

Although C++ enables us to add multiple meanings to the operators, yet their association and precedence remain the same. For example, the multiplication operator will continue having higher precedence than the add operator. Table 3.5 gives the precedence and associativity of all the C++ operators. The groups are listed in the order of decreasing precedence. The labels *prefix* and *postfix* distinguish the uses of ++ and --. Also, the symbols +, -, *, and & are used as both unary and binary operators.

A complete list of ANSI C++ operators and their meanings, precedence, associativity and use are given in Appendix E.

3.24 CONTROL STRUCTURES

In C++, a large number of functions are used that pass messages, and process the data contained in objects. A function is set up to perform a task. When the task is complex, many different

Table 3.5   Operator precedence and associativity

Operator	Associativity
::	left to right
-> . () [] postfix ++ postfix - -	left to right
prefix ++ prefix - - ~ ! unary + unary - unary * unary & (type) sizeof new delete	right to left
-> * *	left to right
* / %	left to right
+ -	left to right
<< >>	left to right
<< = >> =	left to right
= = !=	left to right
&	left to right
^	left to right
		left to right
&&	left to right
||	left to right
?:	left to right
= * = / = % = + = = << = >> = & = ^= |=	right to left
, (comma)	left to right

The unary operations assume higher precedence.

algorithms can be designed to achieve the same goal. Some are simple to comprehend, while others are not. Experience has also shown that the number of bugs that occur is related to the format of the program. The format should be such that it is easy to trace the flow of execution of statements. This would help not only in debugging but also in the review and maintenance of the program later. One method of achieving the objective of an accurate, error-resistant and maintainable code is to use one or any combination of the following three control structures:

1. Sequence structure (straight line)
2. Selection structure (branching)
3. Loop structure (iteration or repetition)

Figure 3.4 shows how these structures are implemented using *one-entry, one-exit* concept, a popular approach used in modular programming.

It is important to understand that all program processing can be coded by using only these three logic structures. The approach of using one or more of these basic control constructs in

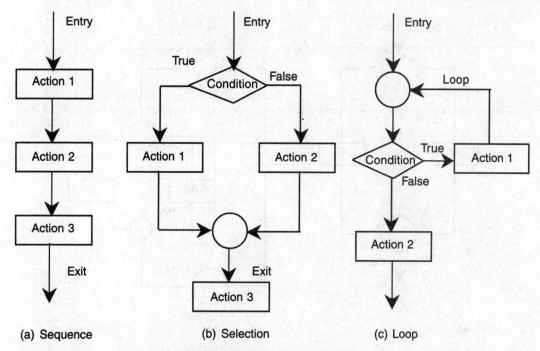

(a) Sequence   (b) Selection   (c) Loop

Fig. 3.4   *Basic control structures*

programming is known as *structured programming*, an important technique in software engineering.

Using these three basic constructs, we may represent a function structure either in detail or in summary form as shown in Figs 3.5 (a), (b) and (c).

Like C, C++ also supports all the three basic control structures, and implements them using various control statements as shown in Fig. 3.6. This shows that C++ combines the power of structured programming with the object-oriented paradigm.

The if statement

The **if** statement is implemented in two forms:

* Simple **if** statement
* **if...else** statement

Examples:

Form 1

```
if(expression is true)
{
        action1;
}
action2;
action3;
```

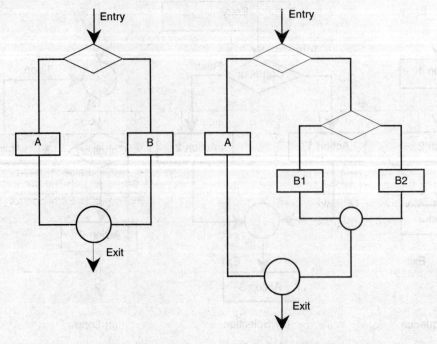

(a)   First level of abstraction   (b)   Second level of abstraction

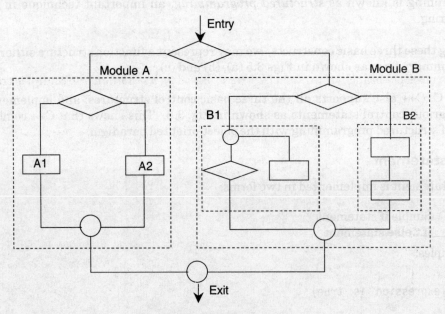

(c)   Detailed flow chart

Fig. 3.5   *Different levels of abstraction*

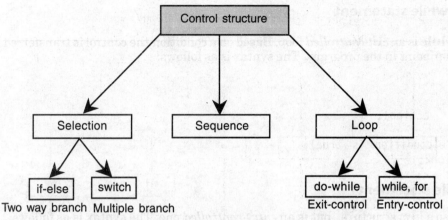

Fig. 3.6   *C++ statements to implement in two forms*

Form 2

```
if(expression is true)
{
      action1;
}
else
{
      action2;
}
action3;
```

The switch Statement

This is a multiple-branching statement where, based on a condition, the control is transferred to one of the many possible points. This is implemented as follows:

```
switch(expression)
{
      case1:
      {
      action1;
      }
      case2:
      {
      action2;
      }
      case3:
      {
      action3;
      default:
      {
      action4;
      }
}
action5;
```

The do-while statement

The **do-while** is an *exit-controlled* loop. Based on a condition, the control is transferred back to a particular point in the program. The syntax is as follows:

```
do
{
      action1;
}     .
while(condition is true);
action2;
```

The while statement

This is also a loop structure, but is an *entry-controlled* one. The syntax is as follows:

```
while(condition is true)
{
      action1;
}
action2;
```

The for statement

The **for** is an *entry-entrolled* loop and is used when an action is to be repeated for a predetermined number of times. The syntax is as follows:

```
for(initial value; test; increment)
{
      action1;
}
action2;
```

The syntax of the control statements in C++ is very much similar to that of C and therefore they are implemented as and when they are required.

Summary

- C++ provides various types of tokens that include keywords, identifiers, constants, strings, and operators.
- Identifiers refer to the names of variables, functions, arrays, classes, etc.
- C++ provides an additional use of **void**, for declaration of generic pointers.
- The enumerated data types differ slightly in C++. The tag names of the enumerated data types become new type names. That is, we can declare new variables using these tag names.
- In C++, the size of character array should be one larger than the number of characters in the string.

- C++ adds the concept of constant pointer and pointer to constant. In case of constant pointer we can not modify the address that the pointer is initialized to. In case of pointer to a constant, contents of what it points to cannot be changed.
- Pointers are widely used in C++ for memory management and to achieve polymorphism.
- C++ provides a qualifier called **const** to declare named constants which are just like variables except that their values can not be changed. A **const** modifier defaults to an **int**.
- C++ is very strict regarding type checking of variables. It does not allow to equate variables of two different data types. The only way to break this rule is type casting.
- C++ allows us to declare a variable anywhere in the program, as also its initialization at run time, using the expressions at the place of declaration.
- A reference variable provides an alternative name for a previously defined variable. Both the variables refer to the same data object in the memory. Hence, change in the value of one will also be reflected in the value of the other variable.
- A reference variable must be initialized at the time of declaration, which establishes the correspondence between the reference and the data object that it names.
- A major application of the scope resolution (::) operator is in the classes to identify the class to which a member function belongs.
- In addition to **malloc()**, **calloc()** and **free()** functions, C++ also provides two unary operators, **new** and **delete** to perform the task of allocating and freeing the memory in a better and easier way.
- C++ also provides manipulators to format the data display. The most commonly used manipulators are **endl** and **setw**.
- C++ supports seven types of expressions. When data types are mixed in an expression, C++ performs the conversion automatically using certain rules.
- C++ also permits explicit type conversion of variables and expressions using the type cast operators.
- Like C, C++ also supports the three basic control structures namely, sequence, selection and loop, and implements them using various control statements such as, **if, if...else, switch, do..while, while** and **for**.

Key Terms

➤ array	➤ compound assignment
➤ associativity	➤ compound expression
➤ automatic conversion	➤ **const**
➤ backslash character	➤ constant
➤ bitwise expression	➤ constant expression
➤ **bool**	➤ control structure
➤ boolean expression	➤ data types
➤ branching	➤ decimal integer
➤ call by reference	➤ declaration
➤ **calloc()**	➤ **delete**
➤ character constant	➤ dereferencing
➤ chained assignment	➤ derived-type
➤ **class**	➤ **do...while**

- ➤ embedded assignment
- ➤ **endl**
- ➤ entry control
- ➤ enumeration
- ➤ exit control
- ➤ explicit conversion
- ➤ expression
- ➤ float expression
- ➤ floating point integers
- ➤ **for**
- ➤ formatting
- ➤ free store
- ➤ **free()**
- ➤ function
- ➤ hexadecimal integer
- ➤ identifier
- ➤ **if**
- ➤ **if...else**
- ➤ implicit conversion
- ➤ initialization
- ➤ integer constant
- ➤ integral expression
- ➤ integral widening
- ➤ iteration
- ➤ keyword
- ➤ literal
- ➤ logical expression
- ➤ loop
- ➤ loop structure
- ➤ **malloc()**
- ➤ manipulator
- ➤ memory
- ➤ named constant
- ➤ **new**
- ➤ octal integer
- ➤ operator
- ➤ operator keywords

- ➤ operator overloading
- ➤ operator precedence
- ➤ pointer
- ➤ pointer expression
- ➤ pointer variable
- ➤ reference
- ➤ reference variable
- ➤ relational expression
- ➤ repetition
- ➤ scope resolution
- ➤ selection
- ➤ selection structure
- ➤ sequence
- ➤ sequence structure
- ➤ **setw**
- ➤ **sizeof()**
- ➤ straight line
- ➤ **string**
- ➤ string constant
- ➤ **struct**
- ➤ structure
- ➤ structured programming
- ➤ switch
- ➤ symbolic constant
- ➤ token
- ➤ type casting
- ➤ type compatibility
- ➤ **typedef**
- ➤ **union**
- ➤ user-defined type
- ➤ variable
- ➤ **void**
- ➤ water-fall model
- ➤ **wchar_t**
- ➤ **while**
- ➤ wide-character

Review Questions and Exercises

3.1   *Enumerate the rules of naming variables in C++. How do they differ from ANSI C rules?*

3.2   *An **unsigned int** can be twice as large as the **signed int**. Explain how?*

3.3   *Why does C++ have type modifiers?*

3.4   *What are the applications of **void** data type in C++?*

3.5   *Can we assign a **void** pointer to an **int** type pointer? If not, why? How can we achieve this?*

3.6   *Describe, with examples, the uses of enumeration data types.*

3.7   *Describe the differences in the implementation of **enum** data type in ANSI C and C++.*

3.8   *Why is an array called a derived data type?*

3.9   *The size of a **char** array that is declared to store a string should be one larger than the number of characters in the string. Why?*

3.10   *The **const** was taken from C++ and incorporated in ANSI C, although quite differently. Explain.*

3.11   *How does a constant defined by **const** differ from the constant defined by the preprocessor statement **#define**?*

3.12   *In C++, a variable can be declared anywhere in the scope. What is the significance of this feature?*

3.13   *What do you mean by dynamic initialization of a variable? Give an example.*

3.14   *What is a reference variable? What is its major use?*

3.15   *List at least four new operators added by C++ which aid OOP.*

3.16   *What is the application of the scope resolution operator :: in C++?*

3.17   *What are the advantages of using **new** operator as compared to the function **malloc()**?*

3.18   *Illustrate with an example, how the **setw** manipulator works.*

3.19   *How do the following statements differ?*
    (a)   *char * const p;*
    (b)   *char const *p;*

3.20   *Find errors, if any, in the following C++ statements.*
    (a)   *long float x;*
    (b)   *char *cp = vp;*   *// vp is a void pointer*
    (c)   *int code = three;*   *// three is an enumerator*
    (d)   *int *p = new;*   *// allocate memory with new*
    (e)   *enum (green, yellow, red);*
    (f)   *int const *p = total;*
    (g)   *const int array_size;*
    (h)   *for (i=1; int i<10; i++) cout << i << "\n";*
    (i)   *int & number = 100;*
    (j)   *float *p = new int [10];*
    (k)   *int public = 1000;*
    (l)   *char name[3] = "USA";*
    Note: In all the exercises that follow, use C++ features wherever possible.

3.21   *Write a function using reference variables as arguments to swap the values of a pair of integers.*

3.22   *Write a function that creates a vector of user-given size **M** using **new** operator.*

3.23   *Write a program to print the following output using **for** loops.*
    1
    22
    333
    4444
    55555
    . . . .

3.24   Write a program to evaluate the following investment equation
$$V = P(1 + r)^n$$
and print the tables which would give the value of V for various combination of the following values of P, r and n:
P: 1000, 2000, 3000, ..., 10,000
r: 0.10, 0.11, 0.12, ..., 0.20
n: 1, 2, 3, ..., 10
(Hint: P is the principal amount and V is the value of money at the end of n years. This equation can be recursively written as
$$V = P(1 + r)$$
$$P = V$$
In other words, the value of money at the end of the first year becomes the principal amount for the next year, and so on.

3.25   An election is contested by five candidates. The candidates are numbered 1 to 5 and the voting is done by marking the candidate number on the ballot paper. Write a program to read the ballots and **count** the votes cast for each candidate using an array variable count. In case, a number read is outside the range 1 to 5, the ballot should be considered as a 'spoilt ballot', and the program should also count the number of spoilt ballots.

3.26   A cricket team has the following table of batting figures for a series of test matches:

Player's name	Runs	Innings	Times not out
Sachin	8430	230	18
Saurav	4200	130	9
Rahul	3350	105	11
.	.	.	.
.	.	.	.

Write a program to read the figures set out in the above form, to calculate the batting averages and to print out the complete table including the averages.

3.27   Write programs to evaluate the following functions to 0.0001% accuracy.

(a) $\sin x = x - \dfrac{x^3}{3!} + \dfrac{x^5}{5!} - \dfrac{x^7}{7!} + \cdots\cdots$

(b) $SUM = 1 + (1/2)^2 + (1/3)^3 + (1/4)^4 + \cdots\cdots$

(c) $\cos x = 1 - \dfrac{x^2}{2!} + \dfrac{x^4}{4!} - \dfrac{x^6}{6!} + \cdots\cdots$

3.28.   Write a program to print a table of values of the function
$$y = e^{-x}$$
for x varying from 0 to 10 in steps of 0.1. The table should appear as follows.

TABLE FOR Y= EXP [–X]

X	0.1	0.2	0.3	0.4	0.5	0.6	0.7	0.8	0.9
0.0									
1.0									
.									
.									
9.0									

3.29   *Write a program to calculate the variance and standard deviation of N numbers.*

$$\text{Variance} = \frac{1}{N} \sum_{i=1}^{N} (x_1 - \bar{x})^2$$

$$\text{Standard Deviation} = \sqrt{\frac{1}{N} \sum_{i=1}^{N} (x_i - \bar{x})^2}$$

$$\text{where} \quad \bar{x} = \frac{1}{N} \sum_{i=1}^{N} x_1$$

3.30   *An electricity board charges the following rates to domestic users to discourage large consumption of energy:*
       For the first 100 units   -   60P per unit
       For next 200 units   -   80P per unit
       Beyond 300 units   -   90P per unit
       All users are charged a minimum of Rs. 50.00. If the total amount is more than Rs. 300.00 then an additional surcharge of 15% is added.
       Write a program to read the names of users and number of units consumed and print out the charges with names.

4

Functions in C++

4.1 INTRODUCTION

We know that functions play an important role in C program development. Dividing a program into functions is one of the major principles of top-down, structured programming. Another advantage of using functions is that it is possible to reduce the size of a program by calling and using them at different places in the program.

Recall that we have used a syntax similar to the following in developing C programs.

```
void show();    /* Function declaration */
main()
{
    .....
    show();         /* Function call */
    .....
}
void show()     /* Function definition */
{
    .....
    .....           /* Function body */
    .....
}
```

When the function is called, control is transferred to the first statement in the function body. The other statements in the function body are then executed and control returns to the main program when the closing brace is encountered. C++ is no exception. Functions continue to be the building blocks of C++ programs. In fact, C++ has added many new features to functions to make them more reliable and flexible. Like C++ operators, a C++ function can be overloaded to make it perform different tasks depending on the arguments passed to it. Most of these modifications are aimed at meeting the requirements of object-oriented facilities.

In this chapter, we shall briefly discuss the various new features that are added to C++ functions and their implementation.

4.2   THE MAIN FUNCTION

C does not specify any return type for the **main()** function which is the starting point for the execution of a program. The definition of **main()** would look like this:

```
main()
{
        // main program statements
}
```

This is perfectly valid because the **main()** in C does not return any value.

In C++, the **main()** returns a value of type **int** to the operating system. C++, therefore, explicitly defines **main()** as matching one of the following prototypes:

```
int main();
int main(int argc, char * argv[]);
```

The functions that have a return value should use the **return** statement for termination. The **main()** function in C++ is, therefore, defined as follows:

```
int main()
{
      ......
      ......
      return 0;
}
```

Since the return type of functions is **int** by default, the keyword **int** in the **main()** header is optional. Most C++ compilers will generate an error or warning if there is no **return** statement. Turbo C++ issues the warning

```
Function should return a value
```

and then proceeds to compile the program. It is good programming practice to actually return a value from **main()**.

Many operating systems test the return value (called *exit value*) to determine if there is any problem. The normal convention is that an exit value of zero means the program ran successfully, while a nonzero value means there was a problem. The explicit use of a **return(0)** statement will indicate that the program was successfully executed.

4.3   FUNCTION PROTOTYPING

Function *prototyping* is one of the major improvements added to C++ functions. The prototype describes the function interface to the compiler by giving details such as the number and type of arguments and the type of return values. With function prototyping, a *template* is always used when declaring and defining a function. When a function is called, the compiler uses the template to ensure that proper arguments are passed, and the return value is treated correctly. Any violation in matching the arguments or the return types will be caught by the compiler at the time of compilation itself. These checks and controls did not exist in the conventional C functions.

Remember, C also uses prototyping. But it was introduced first in C++ by Stroustrup and the success of this feature inspired the ANSI C committee to adopt it. However, there is a major difference in prototyping between C and C++. While C++ makes the prototyping essential, ANSI C makes it optional, perhaps, to preserve the compatibility with classic C.

Function prototype is a *declaration statement* in the calling program and is of the following form:

```
type function-name (argument-list);
```

The *argument-list* contains the types and names of arguments that must be passed to the function.

Example:

```
float volume(int x, float y, float z);
```

Note that each argument variable must be declared independently inside the parentheses. That is, a combined declaration like

```
float volume(int x, float y, z);
```

is illegal.

In a function declaration, the names of the arguments are *dummy* variables and therefore, they are optional. That is, the form

```
float volume(int, float, float);
```

is acceptable at the place of declaration. At this stage, the compiler only checks for the type of arguments when the function is called.

In general, we can either include or exclude the variable names in the argument list of prototypes. The variable names in the prototype just act as placeholders and, therefore, if names are used, they don't have to match the names used in the *function call or function definition*.

In the function definition, names are required because the arguments must be referenced inside the function. Example:

```
float volume(int a,float b,float c)
{
        float v = a*b*c;
        .....
        .....
}
```

The function **volume()** can be invoked in a program as follows:

```
float cube1 = volume(b1,w1,h1);   // Function call
```

The variable **b1, w1**, and **h1** are known as the actual parameters which specify the dimensions of **cube1**. Their types (which have been declared earlier) should match with the types declared in the prototype. Remember, the calling statement should not include type names in the argument list.

We can also declare a function with an *empty argument list*, as in the following example:

```
void display( );
```

In C++, this means that the function does not pass any parameters. It is identical to the statement

```
void display(void);
```

However, in C, an empty parentheses implies any number of arguments. That is, we have foregone prototyping. A C++ function can also have an 'open' parameter list by the use of ellipses in the prototype as shown below:

```
void do_something(...);
```

4.4 CALL BY REFERENCE

In traditional C, a function call passes arguments by value. The *called function* creates a new set of variables and copies the values of arguments into them. The function does not have access to the actual variables in the calling program and can only work on the copies of values. This mechanism is fine if the function does not need to alter the values of the original variables in the calling program. But, there may arise situations where we would like to change the values of variables in the *calling program*. For example, in bubble sort, we compare two adjacent elements in the list and interchange their values if the first element is greater than the second. If a function is used for *bubble sort*, then it should be able to alter the values of variables in the calling function, which is not possible if the call-by-value method is used.

Provision of the *reference variables* in C++ permits us to pass parameters to the functions by reference. When we pass arguments by reference, the 'formal' arguments in the called function become aliases to the 'actual' arguments in the calling function. This means that when the function is working with its own arguments, it is actually working on the original data. Consider the following function:

```
void swap(int a,int b)          // a and b are reference variables
{
    int t = a;                  // Dynamic initialization
    a = b;
    b = t;
}
```

Now, if **m** and **n** are two integer variables, then the function call

```
swap(m, n);
```

will exchange the values of **m** and **n** using their aliases (reference variables) **a** and **b**. Reference variables have been discussed in detail in Chapter 3. In traditional C, this is accomplished using *pointers* and *indirection* as follows:

```
void swap1(int *a, int *b)   /* Function definition */
{
     int t;
     t = *a;        /* assign the value at address a to t */
     *a = *b;       /* put the value at b into a   */
     *b = t;        /* put the value at t into b   */
}
```

This function can be called as follows:

```
swap1(x, y);      /* call by passing */
                  /* addresses of variables */
```

This approach is also acceptable in C++. Note that the call-by-reference method is neater in its approach.

4.5 RETURN BY REFERENCE

A function can also return a reference. Consider the following function:

```
int & max(int &x,int &y)
{
        if (x > y)
                return x;
        else
            return y;
}
```

Since the return type of **max()** is **int &,** the function returns reference to **x** or **y** (and not the values). Then a function call such as **max(a, b)** will yield a reference to either **a** or **b** depending on their values. This means that this function call can appear on the left-hand side of an assignment statement. That is, the statement

```
max(a,b) = -1;
```

is legal and assigns -1 to **a** if it is larger, otherwise -1 to **b**.

4.6 INLINE FUNCTIONS

One of the objectives of using functions in a program is to save some memory space, which becomes appreciable when a function is likely to be called many times. However, every time a function is called, it takes a lot of extra time in executing a series of instructions for tasks such as jumping to the function, saving registers, pushing arguments into the stack, and returning to the calling function. When a function is small, a substantial percentage of execution time may be spent in such overheads.

One solution to this problem is to use macro definitions, popularly known as *macros*. Preprocessor macros are popular in C. The major drawback with macros is that they are not really functions and therefore, the usual error checking does not occur during compilation.

C++ has a different solution to this problem. To eliminate the cost of calls to small functions, C++ proposes a new feature called *inline function*. An inline function is a function that is expanded in line when it is invoked. That is, the compiler replaces the function call with the corresponding function code (something similar to macros expansion). The inline functions are defined as follows:

```
inline function-header
{
    function body
}
```

Example:

```
inline double cube(double a)
{
    return(a*a*a);
}
```

The above inline function can be invoked by statements like

```
c = cube(3.0);
d = cube(2.5+1.5);
```

On the execution of these statements, the values of c and d will be 27 and 64 respectively. If the arguments are expressions such as 2.5 + 1.5, the function passes the value of the expression, 4 in this case. This makes the inline feature far superior to macros.

It is easy to make a function inline. All we need to do is to prefix the keyword **inline** to the function definition. All inline functions must be defined before they are called.

We should exercise care before making a function **inline**. The speed benefits of **inline** functions diminish as the function grows in size. At some point the overhead of the function call becomes small compared to the execution of the function, and the benefits of **inline** functions may be lost. In such cases, the use of normal functions will be more meaningful. Usually, the functions are made inline when they are small enough to be defined in one or two lines. Example:

```
inline double cube(double a) {return(a*a*a);}
```

Remember that the inline keyword merely sends a request, not a command, to the compiler. The compiler may ignore this request if the function definition is too long or too complicated and compile the function as a normal function.

Some of the situations where inline expansion may not work are:

1. For functions returning values, if a loop, a **switch**, or a **goto** exists.
2. For functions not returning values, if a return statement exists.
3. If functions contain **static** variables.
4. If **inline** functions are recursive.

Inline expansion makes a program run faster because the overhead of a function call and return is eliminated. However, it makes the program to take up more memory because the statements that define the inline function are reproduced at each point where the function is called. So, a trade-off becomes necessary.

Program 4.1 illustrates the use of inline functions.

```
                        INLINE FUNCTIONS
    #include <iostream>

    using namespace std;

            inline float mul(float x, float y)
```

```
        {
                return(x*y);
        }

        inline double div(double p, double q)
        {
                return(p/q);
        }

    int main()
    {
            float a = 12.345;
            float b = 9.82;

            cout << mul(a,b) << "\n";
            cout << div(a,b) << "\n";

            return 0;
    }
```

PROGRAM 4.1

The output of program 4.1 would be

```
121.228
1.25713
```

4.7 DEFAULT ARGUMENTS

C++ allows us to call a function without specifying all its arguments. In such cases, the function assigns a *default value* to the parameter which does not have a matching argument in the function call. Default values are specified when the function is declared. The compiler looks at the prototype to see how many arguments a function uses and alerts the program for possible default values. Here is an example of a prototype (i.e. function declaration) with default values:

```
float amount(float principal,int period,float rate=0.15);
```

The default value is specified in a manner syntactically similar to a variable initialization. The above prototype declares a default value of 0.15 to the argument **rate**. A subsequent function call like

```
value = amount(5000,7);         // one argument missing
```

passes the value of 5000 to **principal** and 7 to **period** and then lets the function use default value of 0.15 for rate. The call

```
value =  amount(5000,5,0.12);              // no missing argument
```

passes an explicit value of 0.12 to **rate**.

A default argument is checked for type at the time of declaration and evaluated at the time of call. One important point to note is that only the trailing arguments can have default values. It is important to note that we must add defaults from *right to left*. We cannot provide a default value to a particular argument in the middle of an argument list. Some examples of function declaration with default values are:

```
int mul(int i, int j=5, int k=10);        // legal
int mul(int i=5, int j);                  // illegal
int mul(int i=0, int j, int k=10);        // illegal
int mul(int i=2, int j=5, int k=10);      // legal
```

Default arguments are useful in situations where some arguments always have the same value. For instance, bank interest may remain the same for all customers for a particular period of deposit. It also provides a greater flexibility to the programmers. A function can be written with more parameters than are required for its most common application. Using default arguments, a programmer can use only those arguments that are meaningful to a particular situation. Program 4.2 illustrates the use of default arguments.

```
                        DEFAULT ARGUMENTS

    #include <iostream>

    using namespace std;

    int main()
    {
        float amount;

        float value(float p, int n, float r=0.15);   // prototype
        void printline(char ch='*', int len=40);      // prototype

        printline();                // uses default values for arguments

        amount = value(5000.00,5);       // default for 3rd argument

        cout << "\n         Final Value = " << amount << "\n\n";

        printline('=');   // use default value for 2nd argument

        return 0;
    }
    /*-----------------------------------------------------------*/
```

```
        float value(float p, int n, float r)
        {
                int year = 1;
                float sum = p;

                while(year <= n)
                {
                        sum = sum*(1+r);
                        year = year+1;
                }
                return(sum);
        }

        void printline(char ch, int len)
        {
                for(int i=1; i<=len; i++) printf("%c",ch);
                printf("\n");
        }
```

PROGRAM 4.2

The output of Program 4.2 would be:

```
************************************
        Final Value = 10056.8

========================================
```

Advantages of providing the default arguments are:

1.   We can use default arguments to add new parameters to the existing functions.
2.   Default arguments can be used to combine similar functions into one.

4.8   const ARGUMENTS

In C++, an argument to a function can be declared as const as shown below.

```
int strlen(const char *p);
int length(const string &s);
```

The qualifier **const** tells the compiler that the function should not modify the argument. The compiler will generate an error when this condition is violated. This type of declaration is significant only when we pass arguments by reference or pointers.

4.9   FUNCTION OVERLOADING

As stated earlier, *overloading* refers to the use of the same thing for different purposes. C++ also permits overloading of functions. This means that we can use the same function name to create functions that perform a variety of different tasks. This is known as *function polymorphism* in OOP.

Using the concept of function overloading; we can design a family of functions with one function name but with different argument lists. The function would perform different operations depending on the argument list in the function call. The correct function to be invoked is determined by checking the number and type of the arguments but not on the function type. For example, an overloaded **add()** function handles different types of data as shown below:

```
// Declarations
int add(int a, int b);                  // prototype 1
int add(int a, int b, int c);           // prototype 2
double add(double x, double y);         // prototype 3
double add(int p, double q);            // prototype 4
double add(double p, int q);            // prototype 5

// Function calls
cout << add(5, 10);         // uses prototype 1
cout << add(15, 10.0);      // uses prototype 4
cout << add(12.5, 7.5);     // uses prototype 3
cout << add(5, 10, 15);     // uses prototype 2
cout << add(0.75, 5);       // uses prototype 5
```

A function call first matches the prototype having the same number and type of arguments and then calls the appropriate function for execution. A best match must be unique. The function selection involves the following steps:

1. The compiler first tries to find an exact match in which the types of actual arguments are the same, and use that function.
2. If an exact match is not found, the compiler uses the integral promotions to the actual arguments, such as,

    char to **int**
    float to **double**

    to find a match.
3. When either of them fails, the compiler tries to use the built-in conversions (the implicit assignment conversions) to the actual arguments and then uses the function whose match is unique. If the conversion is possible to have multiple matches, then the compiler will generate an error message. Suppose we use the following two functions:

    ```
    long square(long n)
    double square(double x)
    ```

A function call such as

```
square(10)
```

will cause an error because **int** argument can be converted to either **long** or **double**, thereby creating an ambiguous situation as to which version of **square()** should be used.

4. If all of the steps fail, then the compiler will try the user-defined conversions in combination with integral promotions and built-in conversions to find a unique match. User-defined conversions are often used in handling class objects.

Program 4.3 illustrates function overloading.

FUNCTION OVERLOADING

```
// Function volume() is overloaded three times

#include <iostream>

using namespace std;

// Declarations (prototypes)
int volume(int);
double volume(double, int);
long volume(long, int, int);

int main()
{
        cout << volume(10) << "\n";
        cout << volume(2.5,8) << "\n";
        cout << volume(100L,75,15) << "\n";

        return 0;
}

// Function definitions

int volume(int s)   // cube
{
        return(s*s*s);
}

double volume(double r, int h)    // cylinder
{
        return(3.14519*r*r*h);
}

long volume(long l, int b, int h) // rectangular box
{
        return(l*b*h);
}
```

PROGRAM 4.3

The output of Program 4.3 would be:

```
1000
157.26
112500
```

Overloading of the functions should be done with caution. We should not overload unrelated functions and should reserve function overloading for functions that perform closely related tasks. Sometimes, the default arguments may be used instead of overloading. This may reduce the number of functions to be defined.

Overloaded functions are extensively used for handling class objects. They will be illustrated later when the classes are discussed in the next chapter.

4.10   FRIEND AND VIRTUAL FUNCTIONS

C++ introduces two new types of functions, namely, friend function and virtual function. They are basically introduced to handle some specific tasks related to class objects. Therefore, discussions on these functions have been reserved until after the class objects are discussed. The friend functions are discussed in Sec. 5.15 of the next chapter and virtual functions in Sec. 9.5 of Chapter 9.

4.11   MATH LIBRARY FUNCTIONS

The standard C++ supports many math functions that can be used for performing certain commonly used calculations. Most frequently used math library functions are summarized in Table 4.1.

Table 4.1   Commonly used math library functions

Function	Purposes
ceil(x)	Rounds x to the smallest integer not less than x ceil(8.1) = 9.0 and ceil(-8.8) = -8.0
cos(x)	Trigonometric cosine of x (x in radians)
exp(x)	Exponential function e^x.
fabs(x)	Absolute value of x. If x>0 then abs(x) is x If x=0 then abs(x) is 0.0 If x<0 then abs(x) is $-x$
floor(x)	Rounds x to the largest integer not greater than x floor(8.2) = 8.0 and floor(-8.8 = -9.0
log(x)	Natural logarithm of x(base e)
log10(x)	Logarithm of x(base 10)
pow(x,y)	x raised to power y(x^y)
sin(x)	Trigonometric sine of x (x in radians)
sqrt(x)	Square root of x
tan(x)	Trigonometric tangent of x (x in radians)

The argument variables **x** and **y** are of type **double** and all the functions return the data type **double**.

To use the math library functions, we must include the header file **math.h** in conventional C++ and **cmath** in ANSI C++.

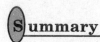

Summary

- It is possible to reduce the size of program by calling and using functions at different places in the program.
- In C++ the main() returns a value of type **int** to the operating system. Since the return type of functions is **int** by default, the keyword **int** in the main() header is optional. Most C++ compilers issue a warning, if there is no return statement.
- Function prototyping gives the compiler the details about the functions such as the number and types of arguments and the type of return values.
- Reference variables in C++ permit us to pass parameters to the functions by reference. A function can also return a reference to a variable.
- When a function is declared inline the compiler replaces the function call with the respective function code. Normally, a small size function is made as **inline**.
- The compiler may ignore the inline declaration if the function declaration is too long or too complicated and hence compile the function as a normal function.
- C++ allows us to assign default values to the function parameters when the function is declared. In such a case we can call a function without specifying all its arguments. The defaults are always added from right to left.
- In C++, an argument to a function can be declared as **const**, indicating that the function should not modify the argument.
- C++ allows function overloading. That is, we can have more than one function with the same name in our program. The compiler matches the function call with the exact function code by checking the number and type of the arguments.
- C++ supports two new types of functions, namely **friend** functions and **virtual** functions.
- Many mathematical computations can be carried out using the library functions supported by the C++ standard library.

Key Terms

- ➤ actual arguments
- ➤ argument list
- ➤ bubble sort
- ➤ call by reference
- ➤ call by value
- ➤ called function

- ➤ calling program
- ➤ calling statement
- ➤ **cmath**
- ➤ **const** arguments
- ➤ declaration statement
- ➤ default arguments

➤ default values	➤ macros
➤ dummy variables	➤ **main()**
➤ ellipses	➤ math library
➤ empty argument list	➤ **math.h**
➤ exit value	➤ overloading
➤ formal arguments	➤ pointers
➤ **friend** functions	➤ polymorphism
➤ function call	➤ prototyping
➤ function definition	➤ reference variable
➤ function overloading	➤ return by reference
➤ function polymorphism	➤ **return** statement
➤ function prototype	➤ return type
➤ indirection	➤ **return()**
➤ **inline**	➤ template
➤ inline functions	➤ virtual functions

Review Questions and Exercises

4.1   State whether the following statements are TRUE or FALSE.

(a) A function argument is a value returned by the function to the calling program.

(b) When arguments are passed by value, the function works with the original arguments in the calling program.

(c) When a function returns a value, the entire function call can be assigned to a variable.

(d) A function can return a value by reference.

(e) When an argument is passed by reference, a temporary variable is created in the calling program to hold the argument value.

(f) It is not necessary to specify the variable name in the function prototype.

4.2   What are the advantages of function prototypes in C++?

4.3   Describe the different styles of writing prototypes.

4.4   Find errors, if any, in the following function prototypes.

(a) float average(x,y);

(b) int mul(int a,b);

(c) int display(...);

(d) void Vect(int? &V, int & size);

(e) void print(float data [], size = 20);

4.5   What is the main advantage of passing arguments by reference?

4.6   When will you make a function **inline**? Why?

4.7   How does an **inline** function differ from a preprocessor macro?

4.8   When do we need to use default arguments in a function?

4.9   What is the significance of an empty parenthesis in a function declaration?

4.10   What do you meant by overloading of a function? When do we use this concept?

4.11 *Comment on the following function definitions:*

```
(a) int *f( )
    {
        int m = 1;
        ....
        ....
        return(&m);
    }
(b) double f( )
    {
        ....
        ....
        return(1);
    }
(c) int & f()
    {
        int n = 10;
        ....
        ....
        return(n);
    }
```

4.12 *Find errors, if any, in the following function definition for displaying a matrix:*

```
void display(int A[ ] [ ], int m, int n)
{
    for(i=0; i<m; i++)
        for(j=0; j<n; j++)
            cout << " " << A[i][j];
    cout << "\n";
}
```

4.13 *Write a function to read a matrix of size m x n from the keyboard.*

4.14 *Write a program to read a matrix of size m x n from the keyboard and display the same on the screen. Use the functions discussed in Exercises 4.12 and 4.13.*

4.15 *Rewrite the program of Exercise 4.14 to make the row parameter of the matrix as a default argument.*

4.16 *The effect of a default argument can be alternatively achieved by overloading. Discuss with an example.*

4.17 *Write a macro that obtains the largest of three numbers.*

4.18 *Redo Exercise 4.17 using inline function. Test the function using a **main** program.*

4.19 *Write a function **power()** to raise a number **m** to a power **n**. The function takes a **double** value for **m** and **int** value for **n**, and returns the result correctly. Use a default value of 2 for n to make the function to calculate squares when this argument is omitted. Write a **main** that gets the values of **m** and **n** from the user to test the function.*

4.20 *Write a function that performs the same operation as that of Exercise 4.19 but takes an **int** value for **m**. Both the functions should have the same name. Write a **main** that calls both the functions. Use the concept of function overloading.*

5
Classes and Objects

5.1 INTRODUCTION

The most important feature of C++ is the "class". Its significance is highlighted by the fact that Stroustrup initially gave the name "C with classes" to his new language. A class is an extension of the idea of structure used in C. It is a new way of creating and implementing a user-defined data type. We shall discuss, in this chapter, the concept of class by first reviewing the traditional structures found in C and then the ways in which classes can be designed, implemented and applied.

5.2 C STRUCTURES REVISITED

We know that one of the unique features of the C language is structures. They provide a method for packing together data of different types. A structure is a convenient tool for handling a group of logically related data items. It is a user-defined data type with a *template* that serves to define its data properties. Once the structure type has been defined, we can create variables of that type using declarations that are similar to the built-in type declarations. For example, consider the following declaration:

```
struct student
{
        char    name[20];
        int     roll_number;
        float total_marks;
};
```

The keyword **struct** declares **student** as a new data type that can hold three fields of different data types. These fields are known as *structure members* or *elements*. The identifier student, which is referred to as *structure name* or *structure tag*, can be used to create variables of type student. Example:

```
struct student A;    // C declaration
```

A is a variable of type student and has three member variables as defined by the template. Member variables can be accessed using the *dot* or *period operator* as follows:

```
strcpy(A.name, "John");
A.roll_number = 999;
A.total_marks = 595.5;
Final_total = A.total_marks + 5;
```

Structures can have arrays, pointers or structures as members.

Limitations of C Structures

The standard C does not allow the struct data type to be treated like built-in types. For example, consider the following structure:

```
struct complex
{
        float x;
        float y;
};
        struct complex c1, c2, c3;
```

The complex numbers c1, c2, and c3 can easily be assigned values using the dot operator, but we cannot add two complex numbers or subtract one from the other. For example,

```
c3 = c1 + c2;
```

is illegal in C.

Another important limitation of C structures is that they do not permit *data hiding*. Structure members can be directly accessed by the structure variables by any function anywhere in their scope. In other words, the structure members are public members.

Extensions to Structures

C++ supports all the features of structures as defined in C. But C++ has expanded its capabilities further to suit its OOP philosophy. It attempts to bring the user-defined types as close as possible to the built-in data types, and also provides a facility to hide the data which is one of the main precepts of OOP. *Inheritance*, a mechanism by which one type can inherit characteristics from other types, is also supported by C++.

In C++, a structure can have both variables and functions as members. It can also declare some of its members as 'private' so that they cannot be accessed directly by the external functions.

In C++, the structure names are stand-alone and can be used like any other type names. In other words, the keyword struct can be omitted in the declaration of structure variables. For example, we can declare the student variable A as

```
student A;    // C++ declaration
```

Remember, this is an error in C.

C++ incorporates all these extensions in another user-defined type known as **class**. There is very little syntactical difference between structures and classes in C++ and, therefore, they can be used interchangeably with minor modifications. Since class is a specially introduced data type in C++, most of the C++ programmers tend to use the structures for holding only data, and classes to hold both the data and functions. Therefore, we will not discuss structures any further.

The only difference between a structure and a class in C++ is that, by default, the members of a class are *private*, while, by default, the members of a structure are *public*.

5.3   SPECIFYING A CLASS

A class is a way to bind the data and its associated functions together. It allows the data (and functions) to be hidden, if necessary, from external use. When defining a class, we are creating a new *abstract data type* that can be treated like any other built-in data type. Generally, a class specification has two parts:

1.   Class declaration
2.   Class function definitions

The class declaration describes the type and scope of its members. The class function definitions describe how the class functions are implemented.

The general form of a class declaration is:

```
class class_name
{
        private:
                variable declarations;
                function declarations;
        public;
                variable declarations;
                function declaration;
};
```

The **class** declaration is similar to a **struct** declaration. The keyword **class** specifies, that what follows is an abstract data of type *class_name*. The body of a class is enclosed within braces and terminated by a semicolon. The class body contains the declaration of variables and functions. These functions and variables are collectively called *class members*. They are usually grouped under two sections, namely, *private* and *public* to denote which of the members are *private* and which of them are *public*. The keywords **private** and **public** are known as visibility labels. Note that these keywords are followed by a colon.

The class members that have been declared as private can be accessed only from within the class. On the other hand, public members can be accessed from outside the class also. The data hiding (using private declaration) is the key feature of object-oriented programming. The use of the keyword private is optional. By default, the members of a class are **private**. If both the labels are missing, then, by default, all the members are **private**. Such a class is completely hidden from the outside world and does not serve any purpose.

The variables declared inside the class are known as *data members* and the functions are known as *member functions*. Only the member functions can have access to the private data members and private functions. However, the public members (both functions and data) can be accessed from outside the class. This is illustrated in Fig. 5.1. The binding of data and functions together into a single class-type variable is referred to as *encapsulation*.

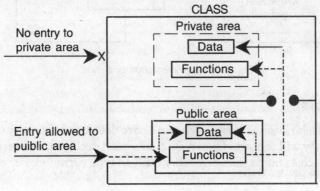

Fig. 5.1   *Data hiding in classes*

A Simple Class Example

A typical class declaration would look like:

```
class item
{
        int number;                   // variables declaration
        float cost;                   // private by default
    public:
        void getdata(int a, float b); // functions declaration
        void putdata(void);           // using prototype
};
```

We usually give a class some meaningful name, such as **item**. This name now becomes a new type identifier that can be used to declare *instances* of that class type. The class item contains two data members and two function members. The data members are private by default while both the functions are public by declaration. The function **getdata()** can be used to assign values to the member variables number and cost, and **putdata()** for displaying their values. These functions provide the only access to the data members from outside the class. This means that the data cannot be accessed by any function that is not a member of the class **item**. Note that the functions are declared, not defined. Actual function definitions will appear later in the program. The data members are usually declared as **private** and the member functions as **public**. Figure 5.2 shows two different notations used by the OOP analysts to represent a class.

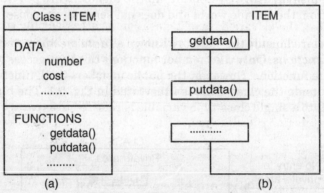

Fig. 5.2 *Representation of a class*

Creating Objects

Remember that the declaration of **item** as shown above does not define any objects of **item** but only specifies *what* they will contain. Once a class has been declared, we can create variables of that type by using the class name (like any other built-in type variable). For example,

```
item x;      // memory for x is created
```

creates a variable **x** of type **item**. In C++, the class variables are known as *objects*. Therefore, **x** is called an object of type **item**. We may also declare more than one object in one statement. Example:

```
item x, y, z;
```

The declaration of an object is similar to that of a variable of any basic type. The necessary memory space is allocated to an object at this stage. Note that class specification, like a structure, provides only a *template* and does not create any memory space for the objects.

Objects can also be created when a class is defined by placing their names immediately after the closing brace, as we do in the case of structures. That is to say, the definition

```
class item
{
    .....
    .....
    .....

}x,y,z;
```

would create the objects **x, y** and **z** of type **item**. This practice is seldom followed because we would like to declare the objects close to the place where they are used and not at the time of class definition.

Accessing Class Members

As pointed out earlier, the private data of a class can be accessed only through the member functions of that class. The **main()** cannot contain statements that access **number** and **cost** directly. The following is the format for calling a member function:

```
object-name.function-name (actual-arguments);
```

For example, the function call statement

```
x.getdata(100,75.5);
```

is valid and assigns the value 100 to **number** and 75.5 to **cost** of the object **x** by implementing the **getdata()** function. The assignments occur in the actual function. Please refer Sec. 5.4 for further details.

Similarly, the statement

```
x.putdata();
```

would display the values of data members. Remember, a member function can be invoked only by using an object (of the same class). The statement like

```
    getdata(100,75.5);
```

has no meaning. Similarly, the statement

```
    x.number = 100;
```

is also illegal. Although **x** is an object of the type **item** to which **number** belongs, the number (declared private) can be accessed only through a member function and not by the object directly.

It may be recalled that objects communicate by sending and receiving messages. This is achieved through the member functions. For example,

```
    x.putdata();
```

sends a message to the object **x** requesting it to display its contents.

A variable declared as public can be accessed by the objects directly. Example:

```
class xyz
{
        int x;
        int y;
    public:
        int z;
};
    .....
    .....
xyz p;
p.x = 0;        // error, x is private
p.z = 10        // OK, z is public
    .....
    .....
```

The use of data in this manner defeats the very idea of data hiding and therefore should be avoided.

5.4   DEFINING MEMBER FUNCTIONS

Member functions can be defined in two places:

*   Outside the class definition.
*   Inside the class definition.

It is obvious that, irrespective of the place of definition, the function should perform the same task. Therefore, the code for the function body would be identical in both the cases. However, there is a subtle difference in the way the function header is defined. Both these approaches are discussed in detail in this section.

Outside the Class Definition

Member functions that are declared inside a class have to be defined separately outside the class. Their definitions are very much like the normal functions. They should have a function header and a function body. Since C++ does not support the old version of function definition, the *ANSI prototype* form must be used for defining the function header.

An important difference between a member function and a normal function is that a member function incorporates a membership 'identity label' in the header. This 'label' tells the compiler which **class** the function belongs to. The general form of a member function definition is:

```
return-type class-name :: function-name (argument declaration)
{
        Function body
}
```

The membership label class-name :: tells the compiler that the function *function-name* belongs to the class *class-name*. That is, the scope of the function is restricted to the *class-name* specified in the header line. The symbol :: is called the *scope resolution* operator.

For instance, consider the member functions **getdata()** and **putdata()** as discussed above. They may be coded as follows:

```
void item :: getdata(int a, float b)
{
        number = a;
        cost = b;
}
void item :: putdata(void)
{
        cout << "Number :" << number << "\n";
        cout << "Cost   :" << cost   << "\n";
}
```

Since these functions do not return any value, their return-type is void. Function arguments are declared using the ANSI prototype.

The member functions have some special characteristics that are often used in the program development. These characteristics are :

* Several different classes can use the same function name. The 'membership label' will resolve their scope.
* Member functions can access the private data of the class. A non-member function cannot do so. (However, an exception to this rule is a *friend* function discussed later.)
* A member function can call another member function directly, without using the dot operator.

Inside the Class Definition

Another method of defining a member function is to replace the function declaration by the actual function definition inside the class. For example, we could define the item class as follows:

```
class item
{
    int number;
    float cost;
  public:
    void getdata(int a, float b);     // declaration

    // inline function

    void putdata(void);   // definition inside the class
    {
        cout << number  <<  "\n";
        cout << cost    <<  "\n";
    }
};
```

When a function is defined inside a class, it is treated as an inline function. Therefore, all the restrictions and limitations that apply to an **inline** function are also applicable here. Normally, only small functions are defined inside the class definition.

5.5   A C++ PROGRAM WITH CLASS

All the details discussed so far are implemented in Program 5.1.

```
                        CLASS IMPLEMENTATION
    #include <iostream>

    using namespace std;

    class item
    {
        int number;   // private by default
        float cost;   // private by default
      public:
        void getdata(int a, float b);       // prototype declaration,
                                            // to be defined
        // Function defined inside class
        void putdata(void)
        {
            cout << "number :" << number << "\n";
```

```
            cout << "cost   :" << cost   << "\n";
        }
};
//........... Member Function Definition ...............

void item :: getdata(int a, float b)      // use membership label
{
        number = a;   // private variables
        cost = b;     // directly used
}
//.................... Main Program ....................

int main()
{
        item x;        // create object x

        cout <<  "\nobject x "  <<  "\n";

        x.getdata(100, 299.95);            // call member function
        x.putdata();                       // call member function

        item y;                            // create another object

        cout <<  "\nobject y"  << "\n";

        y.getdata(200, 175.50);
        y.putdata();

        return 0;
}
```

PROGRAM 5.1

This program features the class **item**. This class contains two private variables and two public functions. The member function **getdata()** which has been defined outside the class supplies values to both the variables. Note the use of statements such as

```
number = a;
```

in the function definition of **getdata()**. This shows that the member functions can have direct access to private data items.

The member function **putdata()** has been defined inside the class and therefore behaves like an **inline** function. This function displays the values of the private variables **number** and **cost**.

The program creates two objects, x and y in two different statements. This can be combined in one statement.

```
item x, y;        // creates a list of objects
```

Here is the output of Program 5.1:

```
object x
number  :100
cost    :299.95
```

```
object y
number  :200
cost    :175.5
```

For the sake of illustration we have shown one member function as **inline** and the other as an 'external' member function. Both can be defined as **inline** or external functions.

5.6   MAKING AN OUTSIDE FUNCTION INLINE

One of the objectives of OOP is to separate the details of implementation from the class definition. It is therefore good practice to define the member functions outside the class.

We can define a member function outside the class definition and still make it inline by just using the qualifier **inline** in the header line of function definition. Example:

```
class item
{
     .....
     .....
  public:
       void getdata(int a, float b);        // declaration
};

inline void item :: getdata(int a, float b) // definition
{
       number = a;
       cost = b;
}
```

5.7   NESTING OF MEMBER FUNCTIONS

We just discussed that a member function of a class can be called only by an object of that class using a dot operator. However, there is an exception to this. A member function can be called by using its name inside another member function of the same class. This is known as *nesting of member functions*. Program 5.2 illustrates this feature.

NESTING OF MEMBER FUNCTIONS

```cpp
#include <iostream>

using namespace std;

class set
{
        int m, n;
   public:
        void input(void);
        void display(void);
        int largest(void);
};

int set :: largest(void)
{
        if(m >= n)
                return(m);
        else
                return(n);
}

void set :: input(void)
{
        cout << "Input values of m and n" << "\n";
        cin >> m >> n;
}

void set :: display(void)
{
        cout << "Largest value = "
                << largest() << "\n";          // calling member function
}

int main()
{
        set A;
        A.input();
        A.display();

        return 0;
}
```

The output of Program 5.2 would be:

```
Input values of m and n
25  18
Largest value = 25
```

5.8 PRIVATE MEMBER FUNCTIONS

Although it is normal practice to place all the data items in a private section and all the functions in public, some situations may require certain functions to be hidden (like private data) from the outside calls. Tasks such as deleting an account in a customer file, or providing increment to an employee are events of serious consequences and therefore the functions handling such tasks should have restricted access. We can place these functions in the private section.

A private member function can only be called by another function that is a member of its class. Even an object cannot invoke a private function using the dot operator. Consider a class as defined below:

```
class sample
{
    int m;
    void read(void);           // private member function
  public:
    void update(void);
    void write(void);
};
```

If **s1** is an object of **sample**, then

```
s1.read();      // won't work; objects cannot access
                // private members
```

is illegal. However, the function **read()** can be called by the function **update()** to update the value of **m**.

```
void sample :: update(void)
{
    read();      // simple call; no object used
}
```

5.9 ARRAYS WITHIN A CLASS

The arrays can be used as member variables in a class. The following class definition is valid.

```
const int size=10;        // provides value for array size

class array
{
      int a[size];        // 'a' is int type array
   public:
      void setval(void);
      void display(void);
};
```

The array variable **a[ ]** declared as a private member of the class **array** can be used in the member functions, like any other array variable. We can perform any operations on it. For instance, in the above class definition, the member function **setval()** sets the values of elements of the array **a[ ]**, and **display()** function displays the values. Similarly, we may use other member functions to perform any other operations on the array values.

Let us consider a shopping list of items for which we place an order with a dealer every month. The list includes details such as the code number and price of each item. We would like to perform operations such as adding an item to the list, deleting an item from the list and printing the total value of the order. Program 5.3 shows how these operations are implemented using a class with arrays as data members.

```
                      PROCESSING SHOPPING LIST

   #include <iostream>

   using namespace std;

   const m=50;

   class ITEMS
   {
          int itemCode[m];
          float itemPrice[m];
          int count;
       public:
          void CNT(void){count = 0;}         // initializes count to 0
          void getitem(void);
          void displaySum(void);
          void remove(void);
          void displayItems(void);
   };
   //=========================================================
   void ITEMS :: getitem(void)               // assign values to data
                                              // members of item
```

(Contd)

```cpp
{
        cout << "Enter item code :";
        cin >> itemCode[count];

        cout << "Enter item cost :";
        cin >> itemPrice[count];
        count++;
}
void ITEMS :: displaySum(void)              // display total value of
                                            // all items
{
        float sum = 0;
for(int i=0;  i<count;  i++)
                sum = sum + itemPrice[i];

        cout << "\nTotal value :" << sum << "\n";
}
void ITEMS :: remove(void)                  // delete a specified item
{
        int a;
        cout << "Enter item code :";
        cin >> a;

        for(int i=0;  i<count;  i++)
                if(itemCode[i]  == a)
                        itemPrice[i]  = 0;
}

void ITEMS :: displayItems(void)            // displaying items
{
        cout << "\nCode   Price\n";

        for(int i=0;  i<count;  i++)
        {
                cout <<"\n" << itemCode[i];
                cout <<"    " << itemPrice[i];
        }
        cout << "\n";
}
//========================================================

int main()
{
        ITEMS  order;
        order.CNT();
        int x;
```

(Contd)

```
        do              // do....while loop
        {
                cout << "\nYou can do the following;"
                     << "Enter appropriate number \n";
                cout << "\n1 : Add an item ";
                cout << "\n2 : Display total value";
                cout << "\n3 : Delete an item";
                cout << "\n4 : Display all items";
                cout << "\n5 : Quit";
                cout << "\n\nWhat is your option?";

                cin >> x;

                switch(x)
                {
                        case 1 : order.getitem(); break;
                        case 2 : order.displaySum(); break;
                        case 3 : order.remove(); break;
                        case 4 : order.displayItems(); break;
                        case 5 : break;
                        default : cout << "Error in input; try again\n";
                }

        } while(x != 5);                    // do...while ends

        return 0;
}
```

PROGRAM 5.3

The output of Program 5.3 would be:

```
You can do the following; Enter appropriate number
1 : Add an item
2 : Display total value
3 : Delete an item
4 : Display all items
5 : Quit

What is your option?1
Enter item code :111
Enter item cost :100

You can do the following; Enter appropriate number
1 : Add an item
```

(Contd)

```
2 : Display total value
3 : Delete an item
4 : Display all items
5 : Quit

What is your option?1
Enter item code :222
Enter item cost :200

You can do the following; Enter appropriate number
1 : Add an item
2 : Display total value
3 : Delete an item
4 : Display all items
5 : Quit

What is your option?1
Enter item code :333
Enter item cost :300

You can do the following; Enter appropriate number
1 : Add an item
2 : Display total value
3 : Delete an item
4 : Display all items
5 : Quit

What is your option?2
Total value :600

You can do the following; Enter appropriate number
1 : Add an item
2 : Display total value
3 : Delete an item
4 : Display all items
5 : Quit

What is your option?3
Enter item code :222

You can do the following; Enter appropriate number
1 : Add an item
2 : Display total value
3 : Delete an item
4 : Display all items
5 : Quit
```

```
What is your option?4

Code        Price
111         100
222         0
333         300

You can do the following; Enter appropriate number
1 : Add an item
2 : Display total value
3 : Delete an item
4 : Display all items
5 : Quit

What is your option?5
```

The program uses two arrays, namely **itemCode**[ ] to hold the code number of items and **itemPrice**[ ] to hold the prices. A third data member **count** is used to keep a record of items in the list. The program uses a total of four functions to implement the operations to be performed on the list. The statement

```
const int m = 50;
```

defines the size of the array members.

The first function **CNT**( ) simply sets the variable **count** to zero. The second function **getitem**() gets the item code and the item price interactively and assigns them to the array members **itemCode[count]** and **itemPrice[count]**. Note that inside this function **count** is incremented after the assignment operation is over. The function **displaySum**( ) first evaluates the total value of the order and then prints the value. The fourth function **remove**() deletes a given item from the list. It uses the item code to locate it in the list and sets the price to zero indicating that the item is not 'active' in the list. Lastly, the function **displayItems**( ) displays all the items in the list.

The program implements all the tasks using a menu-based user interface.

5.10 MEMORY ALLOCATION FOR OBJECTS

We have stated that the memory space for objects is allocated when they are declared and not when the class is specified. This statement is only partly true. Actually, the member functions are created and placed in the memory space only once when they are defined as a part of a class specification. Since all the objects belonging to that class use the same member functions, no separate space is allocated for member functions when the objects are created. Only space for member variables is allocated separately for each object. Separate memory locations for the objects are essential, because the member variables will hold different data values for different objects. This is shown in Fig. 5.3.

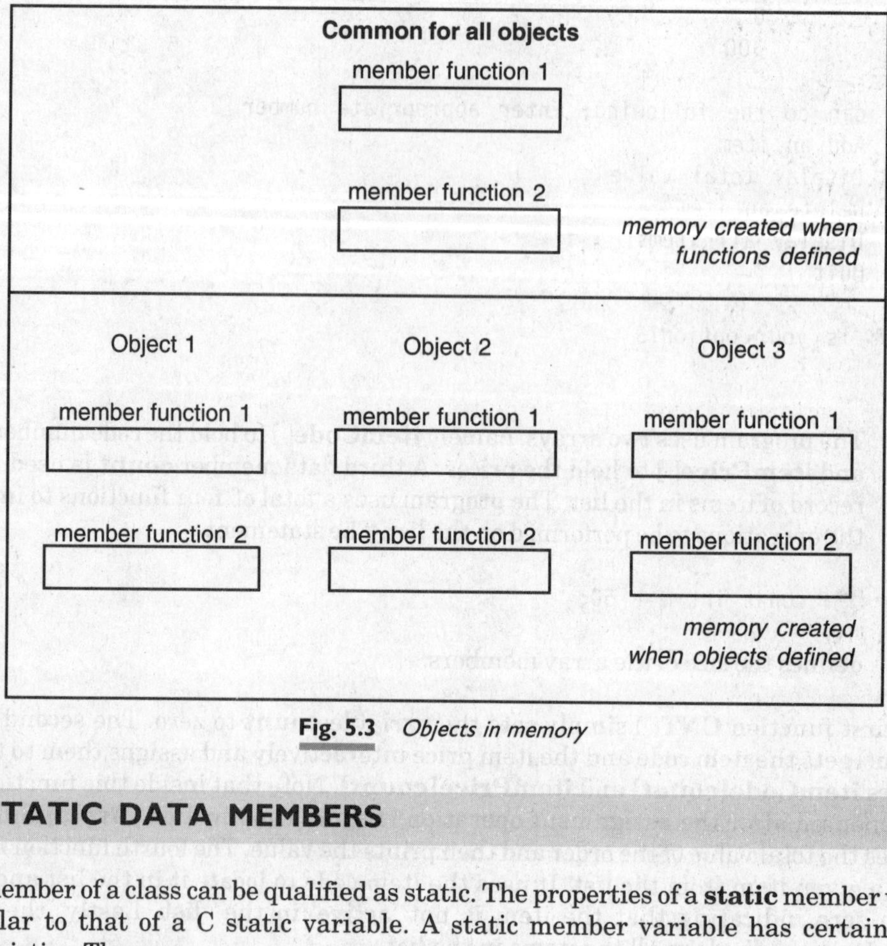

Common for all objects

member function 1

member function 2

memory created when functions defined

Object 1   Object 2   Object 3

member function 1   member function 1   member function 1

member function 2   member function 2   member function 2

memory created when objects defined

Fig. 5.3   *Objects in memory*

5.11 STATIC DATA MEMBERS

A data member of a class can be qualified as static. The properties of a **static** member variable are similar to that of a C static variable. A static member variable has certain special characteristics. These are :

* It is initialized to zero when the first object of its class is created. No other initialization is permitted.
* Only one copy of that member is created for the entire class and is shared by all the objects of that class, no matter how many objects are created.
* It is visible only within the class, but its lifetime is the entire program.

Static variables are normally used to maintain values common to the entire class. For example, a static data member can be used as a counter that records the occurrences of all the objects. Program 5.4 illustrates the use of a static data member.

STATIC CLASS MEMBER

```cpp
#include <iostream>

using namespace std;

class item
{
        static int count;
        int number;
    public:
        void getdata(int a)
        {
                number = a;
                count ++;
        }
        void getcount(void)
        {
                cout << "count: ";
                cout << count  << "\n";
        }
};

int item :: count;

int main()
{
        item a, b, c;           // count is initialized to zero
        a.getcount();           // display count
        b.getcount();
        c.getcount();

        a.getdata(100);         // getting data into object a
        b.getdata(200);         // getting data into object b
        c.getdata(300);         // getting data into object c

        cout << "After reading data" << "\n";

        a.getcount();           // display count
        b.getcount();
        c.getcount();

        return 0;
}
```

PROGRAM 5.4

The output of the Program 5.4 would be:

```
count: 0
count: 0
count: 0
After reading data
count: 3
count: 3
count: 3
```

 Notice the following statement in the program:

```
int item :: count;    // definition of static data member
```

Note that the type and scope of each **static** member variable must be defined outside the class definition. This is necessary because the static data members are stored separately rather than as a part of an object. Since they are associated with the class itself rather than with any class object, they are also known as *class variables*.

The **static** variable **count** is initialized to zero when the objects are created. The count is incremented whenever the data is read into an object. Since the data is read into objects three times, the variable count is incremented three times. Because there is only one copy of count shared by all the three objects, all the three output statements cause the value 3 to be displayed. Figure 5.4 shows how a static variable is used by the objects.

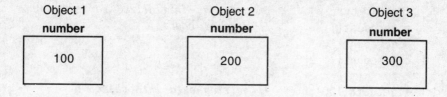

Fig. 5.4   *Sharing of a static data member*

Static variables are like non-inline member functions as they are declared in a class declaration and defined in the source file. While defining a static variable, some initial value can also be assigned to the variable. For instance, the following definition gives count the initial value 10.

```
int item :: count = 10;
```

5.12 STATIC MEMBER FUNCTIONS

Like **static** member variable, we can also have **static** member functions. A member function that is declared **static** has the following properties:

* A **static** function can have access to only other static members (functions or variables) declared in the same class.
* A **static** member function can be called using the class name (instead of its objects) as follows:

class-name :: function-name;

Program 5.5 illustrates the implementation of these characteristics. The **static** function **showcount()** displays the number of objects created till that moment. A count of number of objects created is maintained by the **static** variable count.

The function **showcode()** displays the code number of each object.

```
                    STATIC MEMBER FUNCTION

    #include <iostream>

    using namespace std;

    class test
    {
        int code;
        static int count;          // static member variable
      public:
        void setcode(void)
        {
        code = ++count;
        }
        void showcode(void)
        {
        cout << "object number: " << code << "\n";
        }
        static void showcount(void)      // static member function
        {
```

(Contd)

```
                    cout << "count: " << count << "\n";
                    }
            };

            int test :: count;
            int main()
            {
                    test t1, t2;

                    t1.setcode();
                    t2.setcode();

                    test :: showcount();      // accessing static function

                    test t3;
                    t3.setcode();

                    test :: showcount();

                    t1.showcode();
                    t2.showcode();
                    t3.showcode();

                    return 0;
            }
```

PROGRAM 5.5

Output of Program 5.5:

```
    count: 2
    count: 3
    object number: 1
    object number: 2
    object number: 3
```

 Note that the statement

```
    code = ++count;
```

is executed whenever **setcode( )** function is invoked and the current value of **count** is assigned to **code**. Since each object has its own copy of **code**, the value contained in **code** represents a unique number of its object.

Remember, the following function definition will not work:

```
static void showcount()
{
    cout << code;     // code is not static
}
```

5.13 ARRAYS OF OBJECTS

We know that an array can be of any data type including **struct**. Similarly, we can also have arrays of variables that are of the type **class**. Such variables are called *arrays of objects*. Consider the following class definition:

```
class employee
{
        char name[30];
        float age;
    public:
        void getdata(void);
        void putdata(void);
};
```

The identifier **employee** is a user-defined data type and can be used to create objects that relate to different categories of the employees. Example:

```
employee  manager[3];       // array of manager
employee  foreman[15];      // array of foreman
employee  worker[75];       // array of worker
```

The array **manager** contains three objects(managers), namely, **manager[0], manager[1]** and **manager[2]**, of type **employee** class. Similarly, the **foreman** array contains 15 objects (foremen) and the **worker** array contains 75 objects(workers).

Since an array of objects behaves like any other array, we can use the usual array-accessing methods to access individual elements, and then the dot member operator to access the member functions. For example, the statement

```
manager[i].putdata();
```

will display the data of the ith element of the array **manager**. That is, this statement requests the object **manager[i]** to invoke the member function **putdata()**.

An array of objects is stored inside the memory in the same way as a multi-dimensional array. The array manager is represented in Fig. 5.5. Note that only the space for data items of the objects is created. Member functions are stored separately and will be used by all the objects.

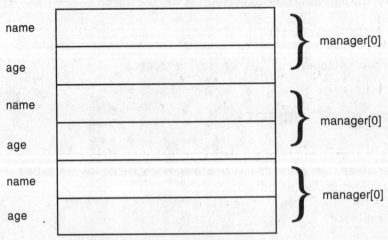

Fig. 5.5   *Storage of data items of an object array*

Program 5.6 illustrates the use of object arrays.

```
                            ARRAYS OF OBJECTS

#include <iostream>

using namespace std;

class employee
{
        char   name[30];       // string as class member
        float  age;
   public:
        void getdata(void);
        void putdata(void);
};
void employee :: getdata(void)
{
        cout << "Enter name: ";
        cin  >> name;
        cout << "Enter age:   ";
        cin  >> age;
}
void employee :: putdata(void)
{
        cout << "Name: " << name << "\n";
        cout << "Age:   " << age  << "\n";
}
```

(*Contd*)

```
      const int size=3;
      int main()
      {
            employee manager[size];
            for(int i=0; i<size; i++)
            {
                  cout << "\nDetails of manager" << i+1 << "\n";
                  manager[i].getdata();
            }
            cout <<   "\n";
            for(i=0; i<size; i++)
            {
                  cout << "\nManager" << i+1 << "\n";
                  manager[i].putdata();
            }

            return 0;
      }
```

PROGRAM 5.6

This being an interactive program, the input data and the program output are shown below:

```
Interactive input
      Details of manager1
      Enter name: xxx
      Enter age:  45

      Details of manager2
      Enter name: yyy
      Enter age:  37

      Details of manager3
      Enter name: zzz
      Enter age:  50

Program output
      Manager1
      Name: xxx
      Age:  45

      Manager2
      Name: yyy
      Age:  37

      Manager3
      Name: zzz
      Age:  50
```

5.14   OBJECTS AS FUNCTION ARGUMENTS

Like any other data type, an object may be used as a function argument. This can be done in two ways:

- A copy of the entire object is passed to the function.
- Only the address of the object is transferred to the function.

The first method is called *pass-by-value*. Since a copy of the object is passed to the function, any changes made to the object inside the function do not affect the object used to call the function. The second method is called *pass-by-reference*. When an address of the object is passed, the called function works directly on the actual object used in the call. This means that any changes made to the object inside the function will reflect in the actual object. The pass-by reference method is more efficient since it requires to pass only the address of the object and not the entire object.

Program 5.7 illustrates the use of objects as function arguments. It performs the addition of time in the hour and minutes format.

```
                         OBJECTS AS ARGUMENTS
    #include <iostream>

    using namespace std;

    class time
    {
          int  hours;
          int  minutes;
      public:
          void gettime(int h, int m)
          { hours = h; minutes = m; }
          void puttime(void)
          {
                  cout << hours << " hours and ";
                  cout << minutes << " minutes " << "\n";
          }
          void sum(time, time);  // declaration with objects as arguments
    };
    void time :: sum(time t1, time t2)      // t1, t2 are objects
    {
          minutes = t1.minutes + t2.minutes;
          hours = minutes/60;
          minutes = minutes%60;
          hours = hours + t1.hours + t2.hours;
    }
```

(Contd)

```
int main()
{
    time T1, T2, T3;

    T1.gettime(2,45);      // get T1
    T2.gettime(3,30);      // get T2

    T3.sum(T1,T2);         // T3=T1+T2

    cout << "T1 = "; T1.puttime();      // display T1
    cout << "T2 = "; T2.puttime();      // display T2
    cout << "T3 = "; T3.puttime();      // display T3

    return 0;
}
```

PROGRAM 5.7

The output of Program 5.7 would be:

```
T1 = 2 hours and 45 minutes
T2 = 3 hours and 30 minutes
T3 = 6 hours and 15 minutes
```

Since the member function **sum( )** is invoked by the object **T3**, with the objects **T1** and **T2** as arguments, it can directly access the hours and minutes variables of **T3**. But, the members of **T1** and **T2** can be accessed only by using the dot operator (like **T1.hours** and **T1.minutes**). Therefore, inside the function sum(), the variables **hours** and **minutes** refer to **T3**, **T1.hours** and **T1.minutes** refer to **T1**, and **T2.hours** and **T2.minutes** refer to **T2**.

Figure 5.6 illustrates how the members are accessed inside the function **sum()**.

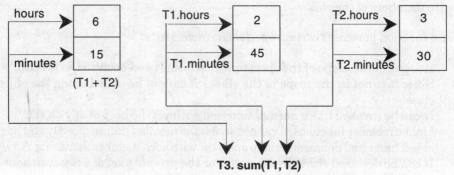

Fig. 5.6   *Accessing members of objects within a called function*

An object can also be passed as an argument to a non-member function. However, such functions can have access to the **public member** functions only through the objects passed as arguments to it. These functions cannot have access to the private data members.

5.15   FRIENDLY FUNCTIONS

We have been emphasizing throughout this chapter that the private members cannot be accessed from outside the class. That is, a non-member function cannot have an access to the private data of a class. However, there could be a situation where we would like two classes to share a particular function. For example, consider a case where two classes, **manager** and **scientist**, have been defined. We would like to use a function **income_tax()** to operate on the objects of both these classes. In such situations, C++ allows the common function to be made friendly with both the classes, thereby allowing the function to have access to the private data of these classes. Such a function need not be a member of any of these classes.

To make an outside function "friendly" to a class, we have to simply declare this function as a **friend** of the class as shown below:

```
class ABC
{
        .....
        .....
    public:
        .....
        .....
        friend void xyz(void); // declaration
};
```

The function declaration should be preceded by the keyword **friend**. The function is defined elsewhere in the program like a normal C++ function. The function definition does not use either the keyword **friend** or the scope operator ::. The functions that are declared with the keyword friend are known as friend functions. A function can be declared as a **friend** in any number of classes. A friend function, although not a member function, has full access rights to the private members of the class.

A friend function possesses certain special characteristics:

- It is not in the scope of the class to which it has been declared as **friend**.
- Since it is not in the scope of the class, it cannot be called using the object of that class.
- It can be invoked like a normal function without the help of any object.
- Unlike member functions, it cannot access the member names directly and has to use an object name and dot membership operator with each member name.(e.g. A.x).
- It can be declared either in the public or the private part of a class without affecting its meaning.
- Usually, it has the objects as arguments.

The friend functions are often used in operator overloading which will be discussed later.

Program 5.8 illustrates the use of a friend function.

```
                         FRIEND FUNCTION
    #include <iostream>

    using namespace std;

    class sample
    {
          int a;
          int b;
       public:
          void setvalue() {a=25; b=40; }
          friend float mean(sample s);
    };
    float mean(sample s)
    {
          return float(s.a + s.b)/2.0;
    }

    int main()
    {
          sample X;      // object X
          X.setvalue();
          cout << "Mean value = " << mean(X) << "\n";

          return 0;
    }
                          PROGRAM 5.8
```

The output of Program 5.8 would be:

```
Mean value = 32.5
```

The friend function accesses the class variables **a** and **b** by using the dot operator and the object passed to it. The function call **mean(X)** passes the object **X** by value to the friend function.

Member functions of one class can be **friend** functions of another class. In such cases, they are defined using the scope resolution operator which is shown as follows:

```
class X
{
    .....
    .....
    int fun1();         // member function of X
    .....
};

class Y
{
    .....
    .....
    friend int X :: fun1();      // fun1() of X
                                 // is friend of Y
    .....
};
```

The function **fun1()** is a member of **class X** and a **friend** of class **Y**.

We can also declare all the member functions of one class as the friend functions of another class. In such cases, the class is called a **friend class**. This can be specified as follows:

```
class Z
{
    .....
    friend class X;   // all member functions of X are
                      // friends to Z
};
```

Program 5.9 demonstrates how friend functions work as a bridge between the classes.

```
                 A FUNCTION FRIENDLY TO TWO CLASSES
    #include <iostream>

    using namespace std;

    class ABC;   // Forward declaration
    //------------------------------------------------------------//
    class XYZ
    {
          int x;
       public:
          void setvalue(int i) {x = i;}
          friend void max(XYZ, ABC);
    };
    //------------------------------------------------------------//
```

(Contd)

```
class ABC
{
        int a;
   public:
        void setvalue(int i) {a = i;}
        friend void max(XYZ, ABC);
};
//-------------------------------------------------------//
void max(XYZ m, ABC n)        // Definition of friend
{
        if(m.x >= n.a)
                cout << m.x;
        else
                cout << n.a;
}
//-------------------------------------------------------//
int main()
{
        ABC abc;
        abc.setvalue(10);
        XYZ xyz;
        xyz.setvalue(20);
        max(xyz, abc);

        return 0;
}
```

PROGRAM 5.9

The output of Program 5.9 would be:

20

The function max() has arguments from both **XYZ** and **ABC**. When the function max() is declared as a friend in **XYZ** for the first time, the compiler will not acknowledge the presence of ABC unless its name is declared in the beginning as

```
class ABC;
```

This is known as 'forward' declaration.

As pointed out earlier, a friend function can be called by reference. In this case, local copies of the objects are not made. Instead, a pointer to the address of the object is passed and the called function directly works on the actual object used in the call.

This method can be used to alter the values of the private members of a class. Remember, altering the values of private members is against the basic principles of data hiding. It should be used only when absolutely necessary.

Program 5.10 shows how to use a common friend function to exchange the private values of two classes. The function is called by reference.

```
                    SWAPPING PRIVATE DATA OF CLASSES

    #include <iostream>

    using namespace std;

    class class_2;

    class class_1
    {
        int value1;
      public:
        void indata(int a) {value1 = a;}
        void display(void) {cout << value1 << "\n";}
        friend void exchange(class_1 &, class_2 &);
    };

    class class_2
    {
        int value2;
      public:
        void indata(int a) {value2 = a;}
        void display(void) {cout << value2 << "\n";}
        friend void exchange(class_1 &, class_2 &);
    };

    void exchange(class_1 & x, class_2 & y)
    {
        int temp = x.value1;
        x.value1 = y.value2;
        y.value2 = temp;
    }

    int main()
    {
        class_1 C1;
        class_2 C2;

        C1.indata(100);
```

(Contd)

```
            C2.indata(200);

            cout << "Values before exchange" << "\n";
            C1.display();
            C2.display();

            exchange(C1, C2);    // swapping

            cout << "Values after exchange " << "\n";
            C1.display();
            C2.display();

            return 0;
    }
```

PROGRAM 5.10

The objects x and y are aliases of **C1** and **C2** respectively. The statements

```
int temp = x.value1
x.value1 = y.value2;
y.value2 = temp;
```

directly modify the values of **value1** and **value2** declared in **class_1** and **class_2**.

Here is the output of Program 5.10:

```
Values before exchange
100
200
Values after exchange
200
100
```

5.16 RETURNING OBJECTS

A function can not only receive objects as arguments but also can return them. The example in Program 5.11 illustrates how an object can be created (within a function) and returned to another function.

RETURNING OBJECTS

```
#include <iostream>

using namespace std;
```

(Contd)

```
class complex            // x + iy form
{
      float x;                // real part
      float y;                // imaginary part
  public:
      void input(float real, float imag)
      { x = real; y = imag; }

      friend complex sum(complex, complex);

      void show(complex);
};

complex sum(complex c1, complex c2)
{
      complex c3;            // objects c3 is created
      c3.x = c1.x + c2.x;
      c3.y = c1.y + c2.y;
      return(c3);            // returns object c3
}

void complex :: show(complex c)
{
      cout << c.x << " + j" << c.y << "\n";
}

int main()
{
      complex A, B, C;

      A.input(3.1, 5.65);
      B.input(2.75, 1.2);

      C = sum(A, B);        // C = A + B

      cout << "A = "; A.show(A);
      cout << "B = "; B.show(B);
      cout << "C = "; C.show(C);

      return 0;
}
```

PROGRAM 5.11

Upon execution, Program 5.11 would generate the following output:

```
A = 3.1 + j5.65
B = 2.75 + j1.2
C = 5.85 + j6.85
```

The program adds two complex numbers **A** and **B** to produce a third complex number **C** and displays all the three numbers.

5.17 const MEMBER FUNCTIONS

If a member function does not alter any data in the class, then we may declare it as a **const** member function as follows:

```
void mul(int, int) const;
double get_balance() const;
```

The qualifier **const** is appended to the function prototypes (in both declaration and definition). The compiler will generate an error message if such functions try to alter the data values.

5.18 POINTERS TO MEMBERS

It is possible to take the address of a member of a class and assign it to a pointer. The address of a member can be obtained by applying the operator & to a "fully qualified" class member name. A class member pointer can be declared using the operator ::* with the class name. For example, given the class

```
class A
{
   private:
       int m;
   public:
       void show();
};
```

We can define a pointer to the member m as follows:

```
int A::* ip = &A :: m;
```

The **ip** pointer created thus acts like a class member in that it must be invoked with a class object. In the statement above, the phrase **A::*** means "pointer-to-member of **A** class". The phrase **&A::m** means the "address of the m member of A class".

Remember, the following statement is not valid:

```
int *ip = &m;   // won't work
```

This is because **m** is not simply an **int** type data. It has meaning only when it is associated with the class to which it belongs. The scope operator must be applied to both the pointer and the member.

The pointer **ip** can now be used to access the member **m** inside member functions (or friend functions). Let us assume that **a** is an object of **A** declared in a member function. We can access **m** using the pointer **ip** as follows:

```
cout << a.*ip;   // display
cout << a.m;     // same as above
```

Now, look at the following code:

```
ap = &a;              // ap is pointer to object a
cout << ap -> *ip;    // display m
cout << ap -> m; // same as above
```

The *dereferencing operator* ->* is used to access a member when we use pointers to both the object and the member. The *dereferencing* operator.* is used when the object itself is used with the member pointer. Note that ***ip** is used like a member name.

We can also design pointers to member functions which, then, can be invoked using the dereferencing operators in the **main** as shown below :

```
(object-name .* pointer-to-member function) (10);
(pointer-to-object ->* pointer-to-member function) (10)
```

The precedence of ( ) is higher than that of .* and ->*, so the parentheses are necessary.

Program 5.12 illustrates the use of dereferencing operators to access the class members.

```
                    DEREFERENCING OPERATORS
    #include <iostream>

    using namespace std;

    class M
    {
        int x;
        int y;
      public:
        void set_xy(int a, int b)
        {
            x = a;
            y = b;
        }
```

(Contd)

```
              friend int sum(M m);
      };
      int sum(M m)
      {
              int M ::* px = &M :: x;
              int M ::* py = &M :: y;
              M *pm = &m;
              int S = m.*px + pm->*py;
              return S;
      }


      int main()
      {
              M n;
              void (M :: *pf)(int,int) = &M :: set_xy;
              (n.*pf)(10,20);
              cout << "SUM = " << sum(n) << "\n";

              M *op = &n;
              (op->*pf)(30,40);
              cout << "SUM = " << sum(n) << "\n";

              return 0;
      }
```

PROGRAM 5.12

The output of Program 5.12 would be:

```
sum = 30
sum = 70
```

5.19 LOCAL CLASSES

Classes can be defined and used inside a function or a block. Such classes are called local classes. Examples:

```
void test(int a)        // function
{
      .....
      .....
      class student      // local class
      {
            .....
            .....         // class definition
```

```
        .....
    };
    .....
    .....
    student s1(a);      // create student object
    .....               // use student object
}
```

Local classes can use global variables (declared above the function) and static variables declared inside the function but cannot use automatic local variables. The global variables should be used with the scope operator (::).

There are some restrictions in constructing local classes. They cannot have static data members and member functions must be defined inside the local classes. Enclosing function cannot access the private members of a local class. However, we can achieve this by declaring the enclosing function as a friend.

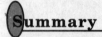

Summary

- A class is an extension to the structure data type. A class can have both variables and functions as members.
- By default, members of the class are private whereas that of structure are public.
- Only the member functions can have access to the private data members and private functions. However the public members can be accessed from outside the class.
- In C++, the class variables are called objects. With objects we can access the public members of a class using a dot operator.
- We can define the member functions inside or outside the class. The difference between a member function and a normal function is that a member function uses a membership 'identity' label in the header to indicate the class to which it belongs.
- The memory space for the objects is allocated when they are declared. Space for member variables is allocated separately for each object, but no separate space is allocated for member functions.
- A data member of a class can be declared as a **static** and is normally used to maintain values common to the entire class.
- The static member variables must be defined outside the class.
- A static member function can have access to the static members declared in the same class and can be called using the class name.
- C++ allows us to have arrays of objects.
- We may use objects as function arguments.
- A function declared as a **friend** is not in the scope of the class to which it has been declared as friend. It has full access to the private members of the class.
- A function can also return an object.
- If a member function does not alter any data in the class, then we may declare it as a **const** member function. The keyword **const** is appended to the function prototype.
- It is also possible to define and use a class inside a function. Such a class is called a local class.

Key Terms

- ➤ abstract data type
- ➤ arrays of objects
- ➤ **class**
- ➤ class declaration
- ➤ class members
- ➤ class variables
- ➤ **const** member functions
- ➤ data hiding
- ➤ data members
- ➤ dereferencing operator
- ➤ dot operator
- ➤ elements
- ➤ encapsulation
- ➤ **friend** functions
- ➤ inheritance
- ➤ **inline** functions
- ➤ local class
- ➤ member functions
- ➤ nesting of member functions

- ➤ objects
- ➤ pass-by-reference
- ➤ pass-by-value
- ➤ period operator
- ➤ **private**
- ➤ prototype
- ➤ **public**
- ➤ scope operator
- ➤ scope resolution
- ➤ static data members
- ➤ static member functions
- ➤ static variables
- ➤ **struct**
- ➤ structure
- ➤ structure members
- ➤ structure name
- ➤ structure tag
- ➤ template

Review Questions and Exercises

5.1 *How do structures in C and C++ differ?*

5.2 *What is a class? How does it accomplish data hiding?*

5.3 *How does a C++ structure differ from a C++ class?*

5.4 *What are objects? How are they created?*

5.5 *How is a member function of a class defined?*

5.6 *Can we use the same function name for a member function of a class and an outside function in the same program file? If yes, how are they distinguished? If no, give reasons.*

5.7 *Describe the mechanism of accessing data members and member functions in the following cases:*
   (a) *Inside the **main** program.*
   (b) *Inside a member function of the same class.*
   (c) *Inside a member function of another class.*

5.8 *When do we declare a member of a class **static**?*

5.9 *What is a friend function? What are the merits and demerits of using friend functions?*

5.10 *State whether the following statements are TRUE or FALSE.*
   (a) *Data items in a class must always be private.*
   (b) *A function designed as private is accessible only to member functions of that class.*

(c)   *A function designed as public can be accessed like any other ordinary functions.*
(d)   *Member functions defined inside a class specifier become inline functions by default.*
(e)   *Classes can bring together all aspects of an entity in one place.*
(f)   *Class members are public by default.*
(g)   *Friend functions have access to only public members of a class.*
(h)   *An entire class can be made a friend of another class.*
(i)   *Functions cannot return class objects.*
(j)   *Data members can be initialized inside class specifier.*

5.11   *Define a class to represent a bank account. Include the following members:*
Data members
1.   *Name of the depositor*
2.   *Account number*
3.   *Type of account*
4.   *Balance amount in the account*
Member functions
1.   *To assign initial values*
2.   *To deposit an amount*
3.   *To withdraw an amount after checking the balance*
4.   *To display name and balance*
Write a main program to test the program.

5.12   *Write a class to represent a vector (a series of float values). Include member functions to perform the following tasks:*
(a)   *To create the vector*
(b)   *To modify the value of a given element*
(c)   *To multiply by a scalar value*
(d)   *To display the vector in the form (10, 20, 30, ...)*
Write a program to test your class.

5.13   *Modify the class and the program of Exercise 5.11 for handling 10 customers.*

5.14   *Modify the class and program of Exercise 5.12 such that the program would be able to add two vectors and display the resultant vector. (Note that we can pass objects as function arguments.)*

5.15   *Create two classes DM and DB which store the value of distances. DM stores distances in metres and centimetres and DB in feet and inches. Write a program that can read values for the class objects and add one object of DM with another object of DB.*
Use a friend function to carry out the addition operation. The object that stores the results may be a DM object or DB object, depending on the units in which the results are required.
The display should be in the format of feet and inches or metres and cenitmetres depending on the object on display.

6

Constructors and Destructors

Key Concepts

- ➤ Constructing objects
- ➤ Constructors
- ➤ Constructor overloading
- ➤ Default argument constructor
- ➤ Copy constructor
- ➤ Constructing matrix objects

- ➤ Automatic initialization
- ➤ Parameterized constructors
- ➤ Default constructor
- ➤ Dynamic initialization
- ➤ Dynamic constuctor
- ➤ Destructors

6.1 INTRODUCTION

We have seen, so far, a few examples of classes being implemented. In all the cases, we have used member functions such as **putdata()** and **setvalue()** to provide initial values to the private member variables. For example, the following statement

```
A.input();
```

invokes the member function **input()**, which assigns the initial values to the data items of object **A**. Similarly, the statement

```
x.getdata(100,299.95);
```

passes the initial values as arguments to the function **getdata()**, where these values are assigned to the private variables of object **x**. All these 'function call' statements are used with the appropriate objects that have already been created. These functions cannot be used to initialize the member variables at the time of creation of their objects.

Providing the initial values as described above does not conform with the philosophy of C++ language. We stated earlier that one of the aims of C++ is to create user-defined data types such as **class**, that behave very similar to the built-in types. This means that we should be able to initialize a **class** type variable (object) when it is declared, much the same way as initialization of an ordinary variable. For example,

```
int m = 20;
float x = 5.75;
```

are valid initialization statements for basic data types.

Similarly, when a variable of built-in type goes out of scope, the compiler automatically destroys the variable. But it has not happened with the objects we have so far studied. It is therefore clear that some more features of classes need to be explored that would enable us to initialize the objects when they are created and destroy them when their presence is no longer necessary.

C++ provides a special member function called the constructor which enables an object to initialize itself when it is created. This is known as *automatic initialization* of objects. It also provides another member function called the *destructor* that destroys the objects when they are no longer required.

6.2   CONSTRUCTORS

A constructor is a 'special' member function whose task is to initialize the objects of its class. It is special because its name is the same as the class name. The constructor is invoked whenever an object of its associated class is created. It is called constructor because it constructs the values of data members of the class.

A constructor is declared and defined as follows:

```
// class with a constructor

class integer
{
    int m, n;
    public:
        integer(void);         // constructor declared
        .....
        .....
};
integer :: integer(void)       // constructor defined
{
    m = 0; n = 0;
}
```

When a class contains a constructor like the one defined above, it is guaranteed that an object created by the class will be initialized automatically. For example, the declaration

```
integer int1;          // object int1 created
```

not only creates the object **int1** of type **integer** but also initializes its data members **m** and **n** to zero. There is no need to write any statement to invoke the constructor function (as we do with the normal member functions). If a 'normal' member function is defined for zero initialization, we would need to invoke this function for each of the objects separately. This would be very inconvenient, if there are a large number of objects.

A constructor that accepts no parameters is called the *default constructor*. The default constructor for **class A is A::A()**. If no such constructor is defined, then the compiler supplies a default constructor. Therefore a statement such as

```
A a;
```

invokes the default constructor of the compiler to create the object **a**.

The constructor functions have some special characteristics. These are :

* They should be declared in the public section.
* They are invoked automatically when the objects are created.
* They do not have return types, not even void and therefore, and they cannot return values.
* They cannot be inherited, though a derived class can call the base class constructor.
* Like other C++ functions, they can have default arguments.
* Constructors cannot be **virtual**. (Meaning of virtual will be discussed later in Chapter 9.)
* We cannot refer to their addresses.
* An object with a constructor (or destructor) cannot be used as a member of a union.
* They make 'implicit calls' to the operators **new** and **delete** when memory allocation is required.

Remember, when a constructor is declared for a class, initialization of the class objects becomes mandatory.

6.3 PARAMETERIZED CONSTRUCTORS

The constructor **integer()**, defined above, initializes the data members of all the objects to zero. However, in practice it may be necessary to initialize the various data elements of different objects with different values when they are created. C++ permits us to achieve this objective by passing arguments to the constructor function when the objects are created. The constructors that can take arguments are called *parameterized constructors*.

The constructor **integer()** may be modified to take arguments as shown below:

```
class integer
{
        int m, n;
    public:
        integer(int x, int y);          // parameterized constructor
        .....
        .....
};
integer :: integer(int x, int y)
{
        m = x; n = y;
}
```

When a constructor has been parameterized, the object declaration statement such as

```
integer int1;
```

may not work. We must pass the initial values as arguments to the constructor function when an object is declared. This can be done in two ways:

* By calling the constructor explicitly.
* By calling the constructor implicitly.

The following declaration illustrates the first method:

```
integer int1 = integer(0,100);    // explicit call
```

This statement creates an integer object int1 and passes the values 0 and 100 to it. The second is implemented as follows:

```
integer int1(0,100);              // implicit call
```

This method, sometimes called the shorthand method, is used very often as it is shorter, looks better and is easy to implement.

Remember, when the constructor is parameterized, we must provide appropriate arguments for the constructor. Program 6.1 demonstrates the passing of arguments to the constructor functions.

CLASS WITH CONSTRUCTORS

```cpp
#include <iostream>

using namespace std;

class integer
{
    int m, n;
  public:
    integer(int, int);                      // constructor declared

    void display(void)
    {
       cout << " m = " << m  << "\n";
       cout << " n = " << n  << "\n";
    }
};

integer :: integer(int x, int y)            // constructor defined
{
    m = x;  n = y;
}

int main()
{
   integer int1(0,100);                     // constructor called implicitly

   integer int2 = integer(25, 75);          // constructor called explicitly

   cout << "\nOBJECT1" << "\n";
   int1.display();

   cout << "\nOBJECT2" << "\n";
   int2.display();

   return 0;
}
```

PROGRAM 6.1

Program 6.1 displays the following output:

```
OBJECT1
m = 0
n = 100
```

```
OBJECT2
m = 25
n = 75
```

The constructor functions can also be defined as **inline** functions. Example:

```
class integer
{
    int m, n;
  public:
    integer(int x, int y)    // Inline constructor
    {
        m = x; y = n;
    }
    .....
    .....
};
```

The parameters of a constructor can be of any type except that of the class to which it belongs. For example,

```
class A
{
    .....
    .....
    public:
        A(A);
};
```

is illegal.

However, a constructor can accept a *reference* to its own class as a parameter. Thus, the statement

```
class A
{
    .....
    .....
    public:
        A(A&);
};
```

is valid. In such cases, the constructor is called the *copy constructor*.

6.4   MULTIPLE CONSTRUCTORS IN A CLASS

So far we have used two kinds of constructors. They are:

```
integer();          // No arguments
integer(int, int);  // Two arguments
```

In the first case, the constructor itself supplies the data values and no values are passed by the calling program. In the second case, the function call passes the appropriate values from **main()**. C++ permits us to use both these constructors in the same class. For example, we could define a class as follows:

```
class integer
{
     int m, n;
  public:
     integer(){m=0; n=0;}         // constructor 1
     integer(int a, int b)
     {m = a; n = b;}              // constructor 2
     integer(integer & i)
     {m = i.m;  n = i.n;}         // constructor 3
};
```

This declares three constructors for an **integer** object. The first constructor receives no arguments, the second receives two **integer** arguments and the third receives one integer object as an argument. For example, the declaration

```
integer I1;
```

would automatically invoke the first constructor and set both **m** and **n** of **I1** to zero. The statement

```
integer I2(20,40);
```

would call the second constructor which will initialize the data members **m** and **n** of **I2** to 20 and 40 respectively. Finally, the statement

```
integer I3(I2);
```

would invoke the third constructor which copies the values of **I2** into **I3**. In other words, it sets the value of every data element of **I3** to the value of the corresponding data element of **I2**. As mentioned earlier, such a constructor is called the *copy constructor*. We learned in Chapter 4 that the process of sharing the same name by two or more functions is referred to as function overloading. Similarly, when more than one constructor function is defined in a class, we say that the constructor is overloaded.

Program 6.2 shows the use of overloaded constructors.

```
                    OVERLOADED CONSTRUCTORS

#include <iostream>

using namespace std;

class complex
{
      float x, y;
  public:
      complex(){ }                         // constructor no arg
      complex(float a) {x = y = a;}        // constructor-one arg
      complex(float real, float imag)      // constructor-two args
      {x = real; y = imag;}

      friend complex sum(complex, complex);
      friend void show(complex);
};
complex sum(complex c1, complex c2)        // friend
{
      complex c3;
      c3.x = c1.x + c2.x;
      c3.y = c1.y + c2.y;
      return(c3);
}
void show(complex c)          // friend
{
      cout << c.x << " + j" << c.y << "\n";
}

int main()
{
      complex A(2.7, 3.5);          // define & initialize
      complex B(1.6);               // define & initialize
      complex C;                    // define

      C = sum(A, B);                // sum() is a friend
      cout << "A = "; show(A);      // show() is also friend
      cout << "B = "; show(B);
      cout << "C = "; show(C);

// Another way to give initial values (second method)

      complex P,Q,R;                // define P, Q and R
```

(Contd)

```
        P = complex(2.5,3.9);      // initialize P
        Q = complex(1.6,2.5);      // initialize Q
        R = sum(P,Q);

        cout << "\n";
        cout << "P = "; show(P);
        cout << "Q = "; show(Q);
        cout << "R = "; show(R);

        return 0;
}
```

PROGRAM 6.2

The output of Program 6.2 would be:

```
A = 2.7 + j3.5
B = 1.6 + j1.6
C = 4.3 + j5.1

P = 2.5 + j3.9
Q = 1.6 + j2.5
R = 4.1 + j6.4
```

There are three constructors in the class **complex**. The first constructor, which takes no arguments, is used to create objects which are not initialized; the second, which takes one argument, is used to create objects and initialize them; and the third, which takes two arguments, is also used to create objects and initialize them to specific values. Note that the second method of initializing values looks better.

Let us look at the first constructor again.

```
complex(){ }
```

It contains the empty body and does not do anything. We just stated that this is used to create objects without any initial values. Remember, we have defined objects in the earlier examples without using such a constructor. Why do we need this constructor now?. As pointed out earlier, C++ compiler has an *implicit constructor* which creates objects, even though it was not defined in the class.

This works fine as long as we do not use any other constructors in the class. However, once we define a constructor, we must also define the "do-nothing" implicit constructor. This constructor will not do anything and is defined just to satisfy the compiler.

6.5   CONSTRUCTORS WITH DEFAULT ARGUMENTS

It is possible to define constructors with default arguments. For example, the constructor complex() can be declared as follows:

```
complex(float real, float imag=0);
```

The default value of the argument **imag** is zero. Then, the statement

```
complex C(5.0);
```

assigns the value 5.0 to the **real** variable and 0.0 to **imag** (by default). However, the statement

```
complex C(2.0,3.0);
```

assigns 2.0 to **real** and 3.0 to **imag**. The actual parameter, when specified, overrides the default value. As pointed out earlier, the missing arguments must be the trailing ones.

It is important to distinguish between the default constructor **A::A()** and the default argument constructor **A::A(int = 0)**. The default argument constructor can be called with either one argument or no arguments. When called with no arguments, it becomes a default constructor. When both these forms are used in a class, it causes ambiguity for a statement such as

```
A a;
```

The ambiguity is whether to 'call' **A::A() or A::A(int = 0)**.

6.6   DYNAMIC INITIALIZATION OF OBJECTS

Class objects can be initialized dynamically too. That is to say, the initial value of an object may be provided during run time. One advantage of dynamic initialization is that we can provide various initialization formats, using overloaded constructors. This provides the flexibility of using different format of data at run time depending upon the situation.

Consider the long term deposit schemes working in the commercial banks. The banks provide different interest rates for different schemes as well as for different periods of investment. Program 6.3 illustrates how to use the class variables for holding account details and how to construct these variables at run time using dynamic initialization.

DYNAMIC INITIALIZATION OF CONSTRUCTORS

```
// Long-term fixed deposit system
#include <iostream>
using namespace std;
```

(Contd)

```
class Fixed_deposit
{
        long int P_amount;          // Principal amount
        int      Years;             // Period of investment
        float    Rate;              // Interest rate
        float    R_value;           // Return value of amount
  public:
        Fixed_deposit(){ }
        Fixed_deposit(long int p, int y, float r=0.12);
        Fixed_deposit(long int p, int y, int r);
        void display(void);
};
Fixed_deposit :: Fixed_deposit(long int p, int y, float r)
{
        P_amount = p;
        Years = y;
        Rate = r;
        R_value = P_amount;
        for(int i = 1; i <= y; i++)
             R_value = R_value * (1.0 + r);

}


Fixed_deposit :: Fixed_deposit(long int p, int y, int r)
{
        P_amount = p;
        Years = y;
        Rate = r;
        R_value = P_amount;

        for(int i=1; i<=y; i++)
            R_value = R_value*(1.0+float(r)/100);

}


void Fixed_deposit :: display(void)
{
        cout << "\n"
            << "Principal Amount = " << P_amount << "\n"
            << "Return Value     = " << R_value  << "\n";

}

int main()
{
        Fixed_deposit FD1, FD2, FD3;   // deposits created

        long int p;                     // principal amount
```

(Contd)

```
    int      y;                    // investment period, years
    float    r;                    // interest rate, decimal form
    int      R;                    // interest rate, percent form

    cout << "Enter amount,period,interest rate(in percent)"<<"\n";
    cin >> p >> y >> R;
    FD1 = Fixed_deposit(p,y,R);

    cout << "Enter amount,period,interest rate(decimal form)" << "\n";
    cin >> p >> y >> r;
    FD2 = Fixed_deposit(p,y,r);

    cout << "Enter amount and period" << "\n";
    cin >> p >> y;
    FD3 = Fixed_deposit(p,y);

    cout << "\nDeposit 1";
    FD1.display();

    cout << "\nDeposit 2";
    FD2.display();

    cout << "\nDeposit 3";
    FD3.display();

    return 0;
}
```

PROGRAM 6.3

The output of Program 6.3 would be:

```
Enter amount,period,interest rate(in percent)
10000 3 18
Enter amount,period,interest rate(in decimal form)
10000 3 0.18
Enter amount and period
10000 3

Deposit 1
Principal Amount = 10000
Return Value     = 16430.3

Deposit 2
Principal Amount = 10000
Return Value     = 16430.3
```

```
Deposit 3
Principal Amount = 10000
Return Value     = 14049.3
```

The program uses three overloaded constructors. The parameter values to these constructors are provided at run time. The user can provide input in one of the following forms:

1. Amount, period and interest in decimal form.
2. Amount, period and interest in percent form.
3. Amount and period.

Since the constructors are overloaded with the appropriate parameters, the one that matches the input values is invoked. For example, the second constructor is invoked for the forms (1) and (3), and the third is invoked for the form (2). Note that, for form (3), the constructor with default argument is used. Since input to the third parameter is missing, it uses the default value for **r**.

6.7 COPY CONSTRUCTOR

We briefly mentioned about the copy constructor in Sec. 6.3. We used the copy constructor

```
integer(integer &i);
```

in Sec. 6.4 as one of the overloaded constructors.

As stated earlier, a copy constructor is used to declare and initialize an object from another object. For example, the statement

```
integer I2(I1);
```

would define the object I2 and at the same time initialize it to the values of I1. Another form of this statement is

```
integer I2 = I1;
```

The process of initializing through a copy constructor is known as *copy initialization*. Remember, the statement

```
I2 = I1;
```

will not invoke the copy constructor. However, if **I1** and **I2** are objects, this statement is legal and simply assigns the values of **I1** to **I2**, member-by-member. This is the task of the overloaded assignment operator(=). We shall see more about this later.

A copy constructor takes a reference to an object of the same class as itself as an argument. Let us consider a simple example of constructing and using a copy constructor as shown in Program 6.4.

```
                        COPY CONSTRUCTOR

    #include <iostream>

    using namespace std;

    class code
    {
        int id;
      public:
        code(){ }                   // constructor
        code(int a) { id = a;}      // constructor again
        code(code & x)              // copy constructor

        {
                id = x.id;          // copy in the value
        }
        void display(void)
        {
                cout << id;
        }
    };

    int main()
    {
        code A(100);   // object A is created and initialized
        code B(A);     // copy constructor called
        code C = A;    // copy constructor called again

        code D;// D is created, not initialized
        D = A;         // copy constructor not called

        cout << "\n id of A: "; A.display();
        cout << "\n id of B: "; B.display();
        cout << "\n id of C: "; C.display();
        cout << "\n id of D: "; D.display();

        return 0;
    }
```

PROGRAM 6.4

The output of Program 6.4 is shown below

```
id of A: 100
id of B: 100
id of C: 100
id of D: 100
```

A reference variable has been used as an argument to the copy constructor. We cannot pass the argument by value to a copy constructor.

When no copy constructor is defined, the compiler supplies its own copy constructor.

6.8 DYNAMIC CONSTRUCTORS

The constructors can also be used to allocate memory while creating objects. This will enable the system to allocate the right amount of memory for each object when the objects are not of the same size, thus resulting in the saving of memory. Allocation of memory to objects at the time of their construction is known as dynamic construction of objects. The memory is allocated with the help of the new operator. Program 6.5 shows the use of new, in constructors that are used to construct strings in objects.

```
                        CONSTRUCTORS WITH new

#include <iostream>
#include <string>

using namespace std;

class String
{
      char *name;
      int  length;
   public:
      String()          // constructor-1
      {
          length = 0;
          name = new char[length + 1];
      }

      String(char *s)   // constructor-2
      {
          length = strlen(s);
          name = new char[length + 1];      // one additional
                                            // character for \0
          strcpy(name, s);
      }

      void display(void)
      {cout << name << "\n";}
```

(Contd)

```
        void join(String &a, String &b);
};

void String :: join(String &a, String &b)
{
        length = a.length + b.length;
        delete name;
        name = new char[length+1];          // dynamic allocation

        strcpy(name, a.name);
        strcat(name, b.name);
};

int main()
{
        char *first = "Joseph ";
        String name1(first), name2("Louis "),name3("Lagrange"),s1,s2;

        s1.join(name1, name2);
        s2.join(s1, name3);
        name1.display();
        name2.display();
        name3.display();
        s1.display();
        s2.display();

        return 0;
}
```

PROGRAM 6.5

The output of Program 6.5 would be:

```
Joseph
Louis
Lagrange
Joseph Louis
Joseph Louis Lagrange
```

This Program uses two constructors. The first is an empty constructor that allows us to declare an array of strings. The second constructor initializes the **length** of the string, allocates necessary space for the string to be stored and creates the string itself. Note that one additional character space is allocated to hold the end-of-string character '\0'.

The member function **join( )** concatenates two strings. It estimates the combined length of the strings to be joined, allocates memory for the combined string and then creates the same using the string functions **strcpy( )** and **strcat( )**. Note that in the function **join( )**, **length** and **name** are members of the object that calls the function, while **a.length** and **a.name** are members of the argument object **a**. The **main( )** function program concatenates three strings into one string. The output is as shown below:

```
Joseph Louis Lagrange
```

6.9 CONSTRUCTING TWO-DIMENSIONAL ARRAYS

We can construct matrix variables using the class type objects. The example in Program 6.6 illustrates how to construct a matrix of size m x n.

CONSTRUCTING MATRIX OBJECTS

```cpp
#include <iostream>

using namespace std;

class matrix
{
        int **p;        // pointer to matrix
        int d1,d2;      // dimensions
    public:
        matrix(int x, int y);
        void get_element(int i, int j, int value)
        {p[i][j]=value;}
        int & put_element(int i, int j)
        {return p[i][j];}
};
matrix :: matrix(int x, int y)
{
        d1 = x;
        d2 = y;
        p = new int *[d1];               // creates an array pointer
        for(int i = 0; i < d1; i++)
            p[i] = new int[d2];          // creates space for each row
}

int main()
{
        int m, n;

        cout << "Enter size of matrix: ";
        cin  >> m >> n;
```

(Contd)

```
    matrix A(m,n);              // matrix object A constructed

    cout << "Enter matrix elements row by row \n";
    int i, j, value;

    for(i = 0; i < m; i++)
         for(j = 0; j < n; j++)
         {
                cin >> value;
                A.get_element(i,j,value);
         }
    cout << "\n";
    cout << A.put_element(1,2);

    return 0;
};
```

PROGRAM 6.6

The output of a sample run of Program 6.6 is as follows.

```
Enter size of matrix: 3 4
Enter matrix elements row by row
11 12 13 14
15 16 17 18
19 20 21 22

17
```

17 is the value of the element (1,2).

The constructor first creates a vector pointer to an **int** of size **d1**. Then, it allocates, iteratively an **int** type vector of size **d2** pointed at by each element **p[i]**. Thus, space for the elements of a d1 X d2 matrix is allocated from free store as shown below:

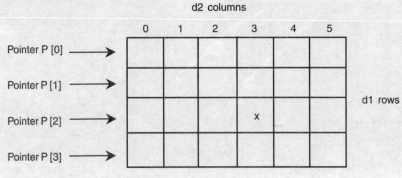

x represents the element P[2] [3]

6.10   const OBJECTS

We may create and use constant objects using **const** keyword before object declaration. For example, we may create X as a constant object of the class **matrix** as follows:

```
const matrix X(m,n); // object X is constant
```

Any attempt to modify the values of **m** and **n** will generate compile-time error. Further, a constant object can call only **const** member functions. As we know, a **const** member is a function prototype or function definition where the keyword const appears after the function's signature.

Whenever **const** objects try to invoke non-**const** member functions, the compiler generates errors.

6.11   DESTRUCTORS

A *destructor*, as the name implies, is used to destroy the objects that have been created by a constructor. Like a constructor, the destructor is a member function whose name is the same as the class name but is preceded by a tilde. For example, the destructor for the class integer can be defined as shown below:

```
~integer(){ }
```

A destructor never takes any argument nor does it return any value. It will be invoked implicitly by the compiler upon exit from the program (or block or function as the case may be) to clean up storage that is no longer accessible. It is a good practice to declare destructors in a program since it releases memory space for future use.

Whenever **new** is used to allocate memory in the constructors, we should use **delete** to free that memory. For example, the destructor for the **matrix** class discussed above may be defined as follows:

```
matrix :: ~matrix()
{
      for(int i=0; i<d1; i++)
      delete p[i];
      delete p;
}
```

This is required because when the pointers to objects go out of scope, a destructor is not called implicitly.

The example below illustrates that the destructor has been invoked implicitly by the compiler.

IMPLEMENTATION OF DESTRUCTORS

```cpp
#include <iostream>

using namespace std;

int count = 0;

class alpha
{
  public:
    alpha()
    {
        count++;
        cout << "\nNo.of object created " << count;
    }

    ~alpha()
    {
        cout << "\nNo.of object destroyed " << count;
        count--;
    }
};

int main()
{
    cout << "\n\nENTER MAIN\n";

    alpha A1, A2, A3, A4;
    {
        cout << "\n\nENTER BLOCK1\n";
        alpha A5;
    }

    {
        cout << "\n\nENTER BLOCK2\n";
        alpha  A6;
    }
    cout << "\n\nRE-ENTER MAIN\n";

    return 0;
}
```

PROGRAM 6.7

The output of a sample run of Program 6.7 is shown below:

```
ENTER MAIN

No.of object created 1
No.of object created 2
No.of object created 3
No.of object created 4

ENTER BLOCK1

No.of object created 5
No.of object destroyed 5

ENTER BLOCK2

No.of object created 5
No.of object destroyed 5

RE-ENTER MAIN

No.of object destroyed 4
No.of object destroyed 3
No.of object destroyed 2
No.of object destroyed 1
```

As the objects are created and destroyed, they increase and decrease the count. Notice that after the first group of objects is created, **A5** is created, and then destroyed, **A6** is created, and then destroyed. Finally, the rest of the objects are also destroyed. When the closing brace of a scope is encountered, the destructors for each object in the scope are called. Note that the objects are destroyed in the reverse order of creation.

Summary

- C++ provides a special member function called the constructor which enables an object to initialize itself when it is created. This is known as *automatic initialization* of objects.
- A constructor has the same name as that of a class.
- Constructors are normally used to initialize variables and to allocate memory.
- Similar to normal functions, constructors may be overloaded.
- When an object is created and initialized at the same time, a copy constructor gets called.

- We may make an object **const** if it does not modify any of its data values.
- C++ also provides another member function called the destructor that destroys the objects when they are no longer required.

Key Terms

➤ automatic initialization	➤ explicit call
➤ **Const**	➤ implicit call
➤ Constructor	➤ implicit constructor
➤ constructor overloading	➤ initialization
➤ copy constructor	➤ **new**
➤ copy initialization	➤ parameterized constructor
➤ default argument	➤ reference
➤ default constructor	➤ shorthand method
➤ **Delete**	➤ **strcat()**
➤ Destructor	➤ **strcpy()**
➤ dynamic construction	➤ **strlen()**
➤ dynamic initialization	➤ **virtual**

Review Questions and Exercises

6.1   *What is a constructor? Is it mandatory to use constructors in a class?*

6.2   *How do we invoke a constructor function?*

6.3   *List some of the special properties of the constructor functions.*

6.4   *What is a parameterized constructor?*

6.5   *Can we have more than one constructors in a class? If yes, explain the need for such a situation.*

6.6   *What do you mean by dynamic initialization of objects? Why do we need to do this?*

6.7   *How is dynamic initialization of objects achieved?*

6.8   *Distinguish between the following two statements:*

```
time  T2(T1);
time  T2 = T1;
```

T1 and T2 are objects of **time** class.

6.9   *Describe the importance of destructors.*

6.10 *State whether the following statements are TRUE or FALSE.*

(a) *Constructors, like other member functions, can be declared anywhere in the class.*

(b) *Constructors do not return any values.*

(c) *A constructor that accepts no parameter is known as the default constructor.*

(d) *A class should have at least one constructor.*

(e) *Destructors never take any argument.*

6.11 *Design constructors for the classes designed in Exercises 5.11 through 5.15 of Chapter 5.*

6.12 *Define a class* **String** *that could work as a user-defined string type. Include constructors that will enable us to create an uninitialized string*

```
String s1; // string with length 0
```

and also to initialize an object with a string constant at the time of creation like

```
String s2("Well done!");
```

Include a function that adds two strings to make a third string. Note that the statement

```
s2 = s1;
```

will be perfectly reasonable expression to copy one string to another.

Write a complete program to test your class to see that it does the following tasks:

(a) *Creates uninitialized string objects.*

(b) *Creates objects with string constants.*

(c) *Concatenates two strings properly.*

(d) *Displays a desired string object.*

6.13 *A book shop maintains the inventory of books that are being sold at the shop. The list includes details such as author, title, price, publisher and stock position. Whenever a customer wants a book, the sales person inputs the title and author and the system searches the list and displays whether it is available or not. If it is not, an appropriate message is displayed. If it is, then the system displays the book details and requests for the number of copies required. If the requested copies are available, the total cost of the requested copies is displayed; otherwise the message "Required copies not in stock" is displayed.*

Design a system using a class called **books** *with suitable member functions and constructors. Use* **new** *operator in constructors to allocate memory space required.*

6.14 *Improve the system design in Exercise 6.13 to incorporate the following features:*

(a) *The price of the books should be updated as and when required. Use a private member function to implement this.*

(b) *The stock value of each book should be automatically updated as soon as a transaction is completed.*

(c) *The number of successful and unsuccessful transactions should be recorded for the purpose of statistical analysis. Use* **static** *data members to keep count of transactions.*

6.15 *Modify the program of Exercise 6.14 to demonstrate the use of pointers to access the members.*

Operator Overloading and Type Conversions

Key Concepts

➤ Overloading
➤ Operator functions
➤ Overloading unary operators
➤ String manipulations
➤ Basic to class type
➤ Class to class type

➤ Operator overloading
➤ Overloading binary operators
➤ Using friends for overloading
➤ Type conversions
➤ Class to basic type
➤ Overloading rules

7.1 INTRODUCTION

Operator overloading is one of the many exciting features of C++ language. It is an important technique that has enhanced the power of extensibility of C++. We have stated more than once that C++ tries to make the user-defined data types behave in much the same way as the built-in types. For instance, C++ permits us to add two variables of user-defined types with the same syntax that is applied to the basic types. This means that C++ has the ability to provide the operators with a special meaning for a data type. The mechanism of giving such special meanings to an operator is known as *operator overloading*.

Operator overloading provides a flexible option for the creation of new definitions for most of the C++ operators. We can almost create a new language of our own by the creative use of the function and operator overloading techniques. We can overload (give additional meaning to) all the C++ operators except the following:

- Class member access operators (., .*).
- Scope resolution operator (::).
- Size operator (**sizeof**).
- Conditional operator (?:).

The excluded operators are very few when compared to the large number of operators which qualify for the operator overloading definition.

Although the *semantics* of an operator can be extended, we cannot change its *syntax*, the grammatical rules that govern its use such as the number of operands, precedence and associativity. For example, the multiplication operator will enjoy higher precedence than the addition operator. Remember, when an operator is overloaded, its original meaning is not lost. For instance, the operator +, which has been overloaded to add two vectors, can still be used to add two integers.

7.2   DEFINING OPERATOR OVERLOADING

To define an additional task to an operator, we must specify what it means in relation to the class to which the operator is applied. This is done with the help of a special function, called *operator function*, which describes the task. The general form of an operator function is:

```
return type classname :: operator (op-arglist)
{
        Function body        // task defined
}
```

where *return type* is the type of value returned by the specified operation and *op* is the operator being overloaded. The *op* is preceded by the keyword **operator**. **operator** *op* is the function name.

Operator functions must be either member functions (non-static) or friend functions. A basic difference between them is that a friend function will have only one argument for unary operators and two for binary operators, while a member function has no arguments for unary operators and only one for binary operators. This is because the object used to invoke the member function is passed implicitly and therefore is available for the member function. This is not the case with **friend** functions. Arguments may be passed either by value or by reference. Operator functions are declared in the class using prototypes as follows:

```
vector operator+(vector);              // vector addition
vector operator-();                    // unary minus
friend vector operator+(vector,vector); // vector addition
friend vector operator-(vector);       // unary minus
vector operator-(vector &a);           // subtraction
int operator==(vector);                // comparison
friend int operator==(vector,vector)   // comparison
```

vector is a data type of **class** and may represent both magnitude and direction (as in physics and engineering) or a series of points called elements (as in mathematics).

The process of overloading involves the following steps:

1.   Create a class that defines the data type that is to be used in the overloading operation.
2.   Declare the operator function **operator** *op*() in the public part of the class.
     It may be either a member function or a **friend** function.
3.   Define the operator function to implement the required operations.

Overloaded operator functions can be invoked by expressions such as

    op x or x op

for unary operators and

    x op y

for binary operators. *op* x (or x *op*) would be interpreted as

    operator op (x)

for **friend** functions. Similarly, the expression x op y would be interpreted as either

    x.operator op (y)

in case of member functions, or

    operator op (x,y)

in case of **friend** functions. When both the forms are declared, standard argument matching is applied to resolve any ambiguity.

7.3   OVERLOADING UNARY OPERATORS

Let us consider the unary minus operator. A minus operator when used as a unary, takes just one operand. We know that this operator changes the sign of an operand when applied to a basic data item. We will see here how to overload this operator so that it can be applied to an object in much the same way as is applied to an **int** or **float** variable. The unary minus when applied to an object should change the sign of each of its data items.

Program 7.1 shows how the unary minus operator is overloaded.

```
                    [ OVERLOADING UNARY MINUS ]

    #include <iostream>

    using namespace std;

    class space
```

(Contd)

```
{
    int x;
    int y;
    int z;
  public:
    void getdata(int a, int b, int c);
    void display(void);
    void operator-();              // overload unary minus
};
void space :: getdata(int a, int b, int c)
{
    x = a;
    y = b;
    z = c;
}
void space :: display(void)
{
    cout << x << " ";
    cout << y << " " ;
    cout << z << "\n";
}
void space :: operator-()
{
    x = -x;
    y = -y;
    z = -z;
}

int main()
{
    space S;
    S.getdata(10, -20, 30);

    cout << "S : ";
    S.display();

    -S;                       // activates operator-() function

    cout << "S : ";
    S.display();

    return 0;
}
```

PROGRAM 7.1

The Program 7.1 produces the following output:

```
S : 10 -20  30
S : -10  20 -30
```

The function **operator** – ( ) takes no argument. Then, what does this operator function do?. It changes the sign of data members of the object **S**. Since this function is a member function of the same class, it can directly access the members of the object which activated it.

Remember, a statement like

```
S2 = -S1;
```

will not work because, the function **operator**–() does not return any value. It can work if the function is modified to return an object.

It is possible to overload a unary minus operator using a friend function as follows:

```
friend void operator-(space &s);        // declaration
        void operator-(space &s)         // definition
{
        s.x = -s.x;
        s.y = -s.y;
        s.z = -s.z;
}
```

Note that the argument is passed by reference. It will not work if we pass argument by value because only a copy of the object that activated the call is passed to operator-(). Therefore, the changes made inside the operator function will not reflect in the called object.

7.4 OVERLOADING BINARY OPERATORS

We have just seen how to overload a unary operator. The same mechanism can be used to overload a binary operator. In Chapter 6, we illustrated, how to add two complex numbers using a friend function. A statement like

```
C = sum(A, B);        // functional notation.
```

was used. The functional notation can be replaced by a natural looking expression

```
C = A + B;        // arithmetic notation
```

by overloading the + operator using an operator+() function. The Program7.2 illustrates how this is accomplished.

```
                     [ OVERLOADING + OPERATOR ]

#include <iostream>

using namespace std;

class complex
{
      float x;                         // real part
      float y;                         // imaginary part
    public:
      complex(){ }                     // constructor 1
      complex(float real, float imag)  // constructor 2
      { x = real; y = imag; }
      complex operator+(complex);
      void display(void);
};

complex complex :: operator+(complex c)
{
      complex temp;            // temporary
      temp.x = x + c.x;        // these are
      temp.y = y + c.y;        // float additions
      return(temp);
}

void complex :: display(void)
{
      cout << x << " + j" << y << "\n";
}

int main()
{
      complex C1, C2, C3;      // invokes constructor 1
      C1 = complex(2.5, 3.5);  // invokes constructor 2
      C2 = complex(1.6, 2.7);
      C3 = C1 + C2;

      cout << "C1 = "; C1.display();
      cout << "C2 = "; C2.display();
      cout << "C3 = "; C3.display();

      return 0;
}
```

PROGRAM 7.2

The output of Program 7.2 would be:

```
C1 = 2.5 + j3.5
C2 = 1.6 + j2.7
C3 = 4.1 + j6.2
```

Let us have a close look at the function **operator+( )** and see how the operator overloading is implemented.

```
complex complex :: operator+(complex c)
{
    complex temp;
    temp.x = x + c.x;
    temp.y = y + c.y;
    return(temp);
}
```

We should note the following features of this function:

1. It receives only one **complex** type argument explicitly.
2. It returns a **complex** type value.
3. It is a member function of **complex**.

The function is expected to add two complex values and return a complex value as the result but receives only one value as argument. Where does the other value come from? Now let us look at the statement that invokes this function:

```
C3 = C1 + C2;              // invokes operator+() function
```

We know that a member function can be invoked only by an object of the same class. Here, the object **C1** takes the responsibility of invoking the function and **C2** plays the role of an argument that is passed to the function. The above **invocation** statement is equivalent to

```
C3 = C1.operator+(C2);          // usual function call syntax
```

Therefore, in the **operator+()** function, the data members of **C1** are accessed directly and the data members of **C2** (that is passed as an argument) are accessed using the dot operator. Thus, both the objects are available for the function. For example, in the statement

```
temp.x = x + c.x;
```

c.x refers to the object **C2** and x refers to the object **C1**. **temp.x** is the real part of **temp** that has been created specially to hold the results of addition of **C1** and **C2**. The function returns the complex temp to be assigned to **C3**. Figure 7.1 shows how this is implemented.

As a rule, in overloading of binary operators, the *left-hand* operand is used to invoke the operator function and the *right- hand* operand is passed as an argument.

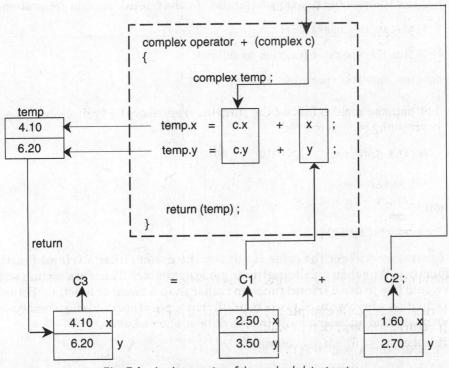

Fig. 7.1 *Implementation of the overloaded + operator*

We can avoid the creation of the **temp** object by replacing the entire function body by the following statement:

```
return complex((x+c.x),(y+c.y));    // invokes constructor 2
```

What does it mean when we use a class name with an argument list? When the compiler comes across a statement like this, it invokes an appropriate constructor, initializes an object with no name and returns the contents for copying into an object. Such an object is called a temporary object and goes out of space as soon as the contents are assigned to another object. Using *temporary objects* can make the code shorter, more efficient and better to read.

7.5 OVERLOADING BINARY OPERATORS USING FRIENDS

As stated earlier, **friend** functions may be used in the place of member functions for overloading a binary operator, the only difference being that a **friend** function requires two arguments to be explicitly passed to it, while a member function requires only one.

The complex number program discussed in the previous section can be modified using a **friend** operator function as follows:

1. Replace the member function declaration by the **friend** function declaration.

```
friend complex operator+(complex, complex);
```

2. Redefine the operator function as follows:

```
complex operator+(complex a, complex b)
{
    return complex((a.x+b.x),(a.y+b.y));
}
```

In this case, the statement

```
C3 = C1 + C2;
```

is equivalent to

```
C3 = operator+(C1, C2);
```

In most cases, we will get the same results by the use of either a **friend** function or a member function. Why then an alternative is made available? There are certain situations where we would like to use a **friend** function rather than a member function. For instance, consider a situation where we need to use two different types of operands for a binary operator, say, one an object and another a built-in type data as shown below,

```
A = B + 2; (or A = B * 2;)
```

where **A** and **B** are objects of the same class. This will work for a member function but the statement

```
A = 2 + B; (or A = 2 * B)
```

will not work. This is because the left-hand operand which is responsible for invoking the member function should be an object of the same class. However **friend** function allows both approaches. How?

It may be recalled that an object need not be used to invoke a **friend** function but can be passed as an argument. Thus, we can use a friend function with a built-in type data as the *left-hand* operand and an object as the *right-hand* operand. Program 7.3 illustrates this, using scalar *multiplication* of a vector. It also shows how to overload the input and output operators >> and <<.

```
[ OVERLOADING OPERATORS USING FRIENDS ]
#include <iostream.h>

const size = 3;

class vector
{
    int v[size];
```

(Contd)

```
    public:
        vector();                      // constructs null vector
        vector(int *x);                // constructs vector from array
        friend vector operator *(int a, vector b);          // friend 1
        friend vector operator *(vector b, int a);          // friend 2
        friend istream & operator >> (istream &, vector &);
        friend ostream & operator << (ostream &, vector &);
};

vector :: vector()
{
        for(int i=0; i<size; i++)
            v[i] = 0;
}

vector :: vector(int *x)
{
        for(int i=0; i<size; i++)
            v[i] = x[i];
}

vector operator *(int a, vector b)
{
        vector c;

        for(int i=0; i < size; i++)
            c.v[i] = a * b.v[i];
        return c;
}

        vector operator *(vector b, int a)
{
        vector c;

        for(int i=0; i<size; i++)
            c.v[i] = b.v[i] * a;
        return c;
}

istream & operator >> (istream &din, vector &b)

{
        for(int i=0; i<size; i++)
            din >> b.v[i];
        return(din);
}
```

(Contd)

```
    ostream & operator <<   (ostream &dout, vector &b)
    {
            dout << "(" << b.v[0];

            for(int i=1; i<size; i++)
                    dout << ", " << b.v[i];
            dout << ")";
            return(dout);
    }

    int x[size] = {2,4,6};

    int main()
    {
            vector m;               // invokes constructor 1
            vector n = x;           // invokes constructor 2

            cout << "Enter elements of vector m " << "\n";
            cin >> m;               // invokes operator>>() function

            cout << "\n";
            cout << "m = " << m << "\n";        // invokes operator <<()

            vector p, q;

            p = 2 * m;              // invokes friend 1
            q = n * 2;              // invokes friend 2

            cout << "\n";
            cout << "p = " << p << "\n";        // invokes operator<<()
            cout << "q = " << q << "\n";

            return 0;
    }
```

PROGRAM 7.3

Shown below is the output of Program 7.3:

```
Enter elements of vector m
5 10 15

m = (5, 10, 15)
p = (10, 20, 30)
q = (4, 8, 12)
```

The program overloads the operator * two times, thus overloading the operator function operator*() itself. In both the cases, the functions are explicitly passed two arguments and they are invoked like any other overloaded function, based on the types of its arguments. This enables us to use both the forms of scalar multiplication such as

```
p = 2 * m;        // equivalent to p = operator*(2,m);
q = n * 2;        // equivalent to q = operator*(n,2);
```

The program and its output are largely self-explanatory.   The first constructor

```
vector();
```

constructs a vector whose elements are all zero. Thus

```
vector m;
```

creates a vector m and initializes all its elements to 0. The second constructor

```
vector(int ?x);
```

creates a vector and copies the elements pointed to by the pointer argument x into it. Therefore, the statements

```
int x[3] = {2, 4, 6};
vector n = x;
```

create n as a vector with components 2, 4, and 6.

 We have used vector variables like **m** and **n** in input and output statements just like simple variables. This has been made possible by overloading the operators >> and << using the functions:

```
friend istream & operator>>(istream &, vector &);
friend ostream & operator<<(ostream &, vector &);
```

istream and **ostream** are classes defined in the **iostream.h** file which has been included in the program.

7.6 MANIPULATION OF STRINGS USING OPERATORS

ANSI C implements strings using character arrays, pointers and string functions. There are no operators for manipulating the strings. One of the main drawbacks of string manipulations in C is that whenever a string is to be copied, the programmer must first determine its length and allocate the required amount of memory.

Although these limitations exist in C++ as well, it permits us to create our own definitions of operators that can be used to manipulate the strings very much similar to the decimal numbers. (Recently, ANSI C++ committee has added a new class called **string** to the C++ class library that supports all kinds of string manipulations. String manipulations using the **string** class are discussed in Chapter 15.

For example, we shall be able to use statements like

```
string3 = string1 + string2;
if(string1 >= string2) string = string1;
```

Strings can be defined as class objects which can be then manipulated like the built-in types. Since the strings vary greatly in size, we use *new* to allocate memory for each string and a pointer variable to point to the string array. Thus we must create string objects that can hold these two pieces of information, namely, length and location which are necessary for string manipulations. A typical string class will look as follows:

```
class string
{
      char  *p;        // pointer to string
      int  len;        // length of string
   public:
      .....            // member functions
      .....            // to initialize and
      .....            // manipulate strings
};
```

We shall consider an example to illustrate the application of overloaded operators to strings. The example shown in Program 7.4 overloads two operators, + and <= just to show how they are implemented. This can be extended to cover other operators as well.

```
                     MATHEMATICAL OPERATIONS ON STRINGS

    #include <string.h>
    #include <iostream.h>

    class string
    {
            char *p;
            int len;
       public:
            string() {len = 0; p = 0;}        // create null string
            string(const char * s);           // create string from arrays
            string(const string & s);         // copy constructor
            string(){delete p;}               // destructor

            // + operator
            friend string operator+(const string &s, const string &t);

            // <= operator
            friend int operator<=(const string &s, const string &t);
            friend void show(const string s);
    };
```

(Contd)

```
string :: string(const char *s)
{
    len = strlen(s);
    p   = new char[len+1];
    strcpy(p,s);
}

string :: string(const string & s)
{
    len = s.len;
    p   = new char[len+1];

    strcpy(p,s.p);
}


// overloading + operator
string operator+(const string &s, const string &t)
{
    string temp;
    temp.len = s.len + t.len;
    temp.p = new char[temp.len+1];
    strcpy(temp.p,s.p);
    strcat(temp.p,t.p);
    return(temp);
}
// overloading <= operator
int operator<=(const string &s, const string &t)
{
    int m = strlen(s.p);
    int n = strlen(t.p);

    if(m <= n)   return(1);

    else return(0);
}
void show(const string s)
{
    cout << s.p;
}

int main()
{
    string s1 = "New ";
    string s2 = "York";
    string s3 = "Delhi";
    string t1,t2,t3;
```

(Contd)

```
          t1 = s1;
          t2 = s2;
          t3 = s1+s3;

          cout << "\nt1 = ";  show(t1);
          cout << "\nt2 = ";  show(t2);
          cout << "\n";
          cout << "\nt3 = ";  show(t3);
          cout << "\n\n";

          if(t1 <= t3)
          {
                  show(t1);
                  cout << " smaller than ";
                  show(t3);
                  cout << "\n";
          }
          else
          {
                  show(t3);
                  cout << " smaller than ";
                  show(t1);
                  cout << "\n";
          }

          return 0;
    }
```

PROGRAM 7.4

The following is the output of Program 7.4.

```
t1 = New
t2 = York

t3 = New Delhi

New   smaller than New Delhi
```

7.7 RULES FOR OVERLOADING OPERATORS

Although it looks simple to redefine the operators, there are certain restrictions and limitations in overloading them. Some of them are listed below:

1. Only existing operators can be overloaded. New operators cannot be created.
2. The overloaded operator must have at least one operand that is of user-defined type.

3. We cannot change the basic meaning of an operator. That is to say, we cannot redefine the plus(+) operator to subtract one value from the other.
4. Overloaded operators follow the syntax rules of the original operators. They cannot be overridden.
5. There are some operators that cannot be overloaded. (See Table 7.1.)
6. We cannot use **friend** functions to overload certain operators. (See Table 7.2.) However, member functions can be used to overload them.
7. Unary operators, overloaded by means of a member function, take no explicit arguments and return no explicit values, but, those overloaded by means of a friend function, take one reference argument (the object of the relevant class).
8. Binary operators overloaded through a member function take one explicit argument and those which are overloaded through a friend function take two explicit arguments.
9. When using binary operators overloaded through a member function, the left hand operand must be an object of the relevant class.
10. Binary arithmetic operators such as +, -, *, and / must explicitly return a value. They must not attempt to change their own arguments.

Table 7.1   Operators that cannot be overloaded

Sizeof	Size of operator
.	Membership operator
.*	Pointer-to-member operator
::	Scope resolution operator
?:	Conditional operator

Table 7.2   Where a friend cannot be used

=	Assignment operator
( )	Function call operator
[ ]	Subscripting operator
->	Class member access operator

7.8   TYPE CONVERSIONS

We know that when constants and variables of different types are mixed in an expression, C applies automatic type conversion to the operands as per certain rules. Similarly, an assignment operation also causes the automatic type conversion. The type of data to the right of an assignment operator is automatically converted to the type of the variable on the left. For example, the statements

```
int m;
float x = 3.14159;
m = x;
```

convert **x** to an integer before its value is assigned to **m**. Thus, the fractional part is truncated. The type conversions are automatic as long as the data types involved are built-in types.

What happens when they are user-defined data types?

Consider the following statement that adds two objects and then assigns the result to a third object.

```
v3 = v1 + v2;        // v1, v2 and v3 are class type objects
```

When the objects are of the same class type, the operations of addition and assignment are carried out smoothly and the compiler does not make any complaints. We have seen, in the case of class objects, that the values of all the data members of the right-hand object are simply copied into the corresponding members of the object on the left-hand. What if one of the operands is an object and the other is a built-in type variable? Or, what if they belong to two different classes?

Since the user-defined data types are designed by us to suit our requirements, the compiler does not support automatic type conversions for such data types. We must, therefore, design the conversion routines by ourselves, if such operations are required.

Three types of situations might arise in the data conversion between uncompatible types:

1. Conversion from basic type to class type.
2. Conversion from class type to basic type.
3. Conversion from one class type to another class type.

We shall discuss all the three cases in detail.

Basic to Class Type

The conversion from basic type to class type is easy to accomplish. It may be recalled that the use of constructors was illustrated in a number of examples to initialize objects. For example, a constructor was used to build a vector object from an **int** type array. Similarly, we used another constructor to build a string type object from a **char*** type variable. These are all examples where constructors perform a *defacto* type conversion from the argument's type to the constructor's class type.

Consider the following constructor:

```
string :: string(char *a)
{
        length = strlen(a);
        P = new char[length+1];
        strcpy(P,a);
}
```

This constructor builds a **string** type object from a **char*** type variable **a**. The variables **length** and **p** are data members of the class **string**. Once this constructor has been defined in the string class, it can be used for conversion from **char*** type to string type. Example:

```
string s1, s2;
char? name1 = "IBM PC";
char? name2 = "Apple Computers";
s1 = string(name1);
s2 = name2;
```

The statement

```
s1 = string(name1);
```

first converts **name1** from **char*** type to **string** type and then assigns the string type values to the object **s1**. The statement

```
s2 = name2;
```

also does the same job by invoking the constructor implicitly.

Let us consider another example of converting an **int** type to a **class** type.

```
class time
{
    int  hrs;
    int mins;
  public:
    ....
    ....
    time(int t)                    // constructor
    {
        hours = t/60;              // t in minutes
        mins  = t%60;
    }
};
```

The following conversion statements can be used in a function:

```
time = T1;                 // object T1 created
int duration = 85;
T1 = duration;             // int to class type
```

After this conversion, the **hrs** member of **T1** will contain a value of 1 and **mins** member a value of 25, denoting 1 hours and 25 minutes.

The constructors used for the type conversion take a single argument whose type is to be converted.

In both the examples, the left-hand operand of = operator is always a **class** object. Therefore, we can also accomplish this conversion using an overloaded = operator.

Class to Basic Type

The constructors did a fine job in type conversion from a basic to class type. What about the conversion from a class to basic type? The constructor functions do not support this operation. Luckily, C++ allows us to define an overloaded *casting operator* that could be used to convert a class type data to a basic type. The general form of an overloaded casting operator function, usually referred to as a *conversion function*, is:

```
operator typename()
{
    .....
    ..... (Function statements)
    .....
}
```

This function converts a class type data to *typename*. For example, the **operator double()** converts a class object to type **double**, the **operator int()** converts a class type object to type int, and so on.

Consider the following conversion function:

```
vector :: operator double()
{
    double sum = 0;
    for(int i=0; i<size; i++)
        sum = sum + v[i] * u[i];
    return sqrt(sum);
}
```

This function converts a vector to the corresponding scalar magnitude. Recall that the magnitude of a vector is given by the square root of the sum of the squares of its components. The operator **double()** can be used as follows:

```
double length = double(V1);
    or
double length = V1;
```

where **V1** is an object of type **vector**. Both the statements have exactly the same effect. When the compiler encounters a statement that requires the conversion of a class type to a basic type, it quietly calls the casting operator function to do the job.

The casting operator function should satisfy the following conditions:

- It must be a class member.
- It must not specify a return type.
- It must not have any arguments.

Since it is a member function, it is invoked by the object and, therefore, the values used for conversion inside the function belong to the object that invoked the function. This means that the function does not need an argument.

In the string example described in the previous section, we can do the conversion from string to **char*** as follows:

```
string :: operator char*()
{
        return(p);
}
```

One Class to Another Class Type

We have just seen data conversion techniques from a basic to class type and a class to basic type. But there are situations where we would like to convert one class type data to another class type.

Example:

```
objX = objY;    // objects of different types
```

objX is an object of class **X** and **objY** is an object of class **Y**. The **class Y** type data is converted to the **class X** type data and the converted value is assigned to the **objX**. Since the conversion takes place from **class Y** to **class X, Y** is known as the *source* class and **X** is known as the *destination* class.

Such conversions between objects of different classes can be carried out by either a constructor or a conversion function. The compiler treats them the same way. Then, how do we decide which form to use? It depends upon where we want the type-conversion function to be located in the source class or in the destination class.

We know that the casting operator function

```
operator  typename()
```

converts the class object *of which it is a member* to *typename*. The *typename* may be a built-in type or a user-defined one (another class type). In the case of conversions between objects, *typename* refers to the destination class. Therefore, when a class needs to be converted, a casting operator function can be used (i.e. source class). The conversion takes place in the source class and the result is given to the destination class object.

Now consider a single-argument constructor function which serves as an instruction for converting the *argument's type* to the class type of *which it is a member*. This implies that the argument belongs to the *source* class and is passed to the *destination* class for conversion. This makes it necessary that the conversion constructor be placed in the destination class. Figure 7.2 illustrates these two approaches.

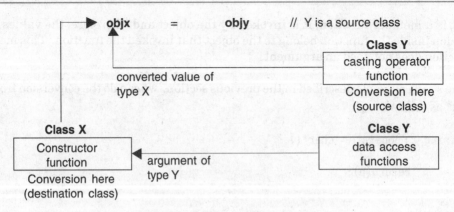

Fig. 7.2 *Conversion between objects*

Table 7.3 provides a summary of all the three conversions. It shows that the conversion from a class to any other type (or any other class) should make use of a casting operator in the source class. On the other hand, to perform the conversion from any other type/class to a class type, a constructor should be used in the destination class.

Table 7.3   Type conversions

Conversion required	Conversion takes place in	
	Source class	Destination class
Basic → class	Not applicable	Constructor
Class → basic	Casting operator	Not applicable
Class → class	Casting operator	Constructor

When a conversion using a constructor is performed in the destination class, we must be able to access the data members of the object sent (by the source class) as an argument. Since data members of the source class are private, we must use special access functions in the source class to facilitate its data flow to the destination class.

A Data Conversion Example

Let us consider an example of an inventory of products in store. One way of recording the details of the products is to record their code number, total items in the stock and the cost of each item. Another approach is to just specify the item code and the value of the item in the stock. The example shown in Program 7.5 uses two classes and shows how to convert data of one type to another.

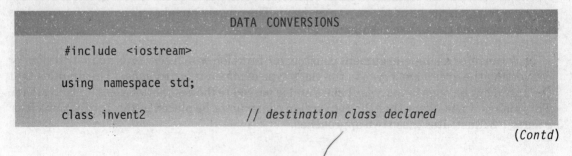

```
                          DATA CONVERSIONS

    #include <iostream>

    using namespace std;

    class invent2              // destination class declared
```

(Contd)

```
        class invent1          // source class
        {
              int code;         // item code
              int items;        // no. of items
              float price;      // cost of each item
      public:
          invent1(int a, int b, float c)
          {
              code = a;
              items = b;
              price = c;
          }
          void putdata()
          {
              cout << "Code:  " << code  << "\n";
              cout << "Items: " << items << "\n";
              cout << "Value: " << price << "\n";
          }
          int getcode() {return code;}
          int getitems() {return items;}
          int getprice() {return price;}
          operator float() {return(items * price);}

          /* operator invent2()      // invent1 to invent2
          {
              invent2 temp;
              temp.code = code;
              temp.value = price * items;
              return temp;
          } */
        };       // End of source class

class invent2          // destination class
{
        int code;
        float value;
      public:
          invent2()
          {
              code = 0; value = 0;
          }
          invent2(int x, float y)     // constructor for
                                      // initialization
          {
              code = x;
              value = y;
          }
```

```
        void putdata()
        {
            cout << "Code:   " << code  << "\n";
            cout << "Value: " << value << "\n\n";
        }
        invent2(invent1 p)          // constructor for conversion
        {
            code = p.getcode();
            value =    p.getitems() * p.getprice();
        }
};    // End of destination class

    int main()
    {
        invent1 s1(100,5,140.0);
        invent2 d1;
        float total_value;

        /* invent1 To float  */
        total_value = s1;

        /* invent1 To invent2 */
        d1 = s1;

        cout << "Product details - invent1 type" << "\n";
        s1.putdata();

        cout << "\nStock value" << "\n";
        cout << "Value = " << total_value << "\n\n";

        cout << "Product details-invent2 type" << "\n";
        d1.putdata();

        return 0;
    }
```

PROGRAM 7.5

Following is the output of Program 7.5:

```
Product details-invent1 type
Code:  100
Items: 5
Value: 140
```

```
Stock value
Value = 700
Product details-invent2 type
Code:  100
Value: 700
```

We have used the conversion function

```
operator float( )
```

in the class **invent1** to convert the **invent1** type data to a **float**. The constructor

```
invent2 (invent1)
```

is used in the class **invent2** to convert the **invent1** type data to the **invent2** type data.

Remember that we can also use the casting operator function

```
operator invent2()
```

in the class invent1 to convert **invent1** type to **invent2** type. However, it is important that we do not use both the constructor and the casting operator for the same type conversion, since this introduces an ambiguity as to how the conversion should be performed.

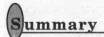ummary

- Operator overloading is one of the important features of C++ language. It is called compile time polymorphism.
- Using overloading feature we can add two user defined data types such as objects, with the same syntax, just as basic data types.
- We can overload almost all the C++ operators except the following:
  - class member access operators(., .*)
  - scope resolution operator (::)
  - size operator(sizeof)
  - conditional operator(?:)
- Operator overloading is done with the help of a special function, called operator function, which describes the special task to an operator.
- There are certain restrictions and limitations in overloading operators. Operator functions must either be member functions (non-static) or friend functions. The overloading operator must have at least one operand that is of user-defined type.
- The compiler does not support automatic type conversions for the user defined data types. We can use casting operator functions to achieve this.
- The casting operator function should satisfy the following conditions:
  - It must be a class member.
  - It must not specify a return type.
  - It must not have any arguments.

Key Terms

- arithmetic notation
- binary operators
- casting
- casting operator
- constructor
- conversion function
- destination class
- **friend**
- **friend** function
- functional notation
- manipulating strings

- operator
- operator function
- operator overloading
- scalar multiplication
- semantics
- **sizeof**
- source class
- syntax
- temporary object
- type conversion
- unary operators

Review Questions and Exercises

7.1 *What is operator overloading?*

7.2 *Why is it necessary to overload an operator?*

7.3 *What is an operator function? Describe the syntax of an operator function*

7.4 *How many arguments are required in the definition of an overloaded unary operator?*

7.5 *A class alpha has a constructor as follows:*
    alpha(int a, double b);
Can we use this constructor to convert types?

7.6 *What is a conversion function? How is it created? Explain its syntax.*

7.7 *A friend function cannot be used to overload the assignment operator =. Explain why?*

7.8 *When is a friend function compulsory? Give an example.*

7.9 *We have two classes X and Y. If **a** is an object of X and b is an object of **Y** and we want to say **a** = **b**; What type of conversion routine should be used and where?*

7.10 *State whether the following statements are TRUE or FALSE.*

(a) *Using the operator overloading concept, we can change the meaning of an operator.*

(b) *Operator overloading works when applied to class objects only.*

(c) *Friend functions cannot be used to overload operators.*

(d) *When using an overloaded binary operator, the left operand is implicitly passed to the member function.*

(e) *The overloaded operator must have at least one operand that is user-defined type.*

(f) *Operator functions never return a value.*

(g) *Through operator overloading, a class type data can be converted to a basic type data.*

(h) *A constructor can be used to convert a basic type to a class type data.*

Note

For all the exercises that follow, build a demonstration program to test your code.

7.11   *Create a class* ***FLOAT*** *that contains one float data member. Overload all the four arithmetic operators so that they operate on the objects of* ***FLOAT***.

7.12   *Design a class* ***Polar*** *which describes a point in the plane using polar coordinates* ***radius*** *and* ***angle***. *A point in polar coordinates is shown below (Fig. 7.3).*

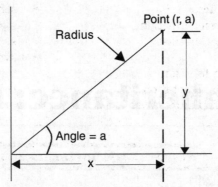

Fig. 7.3   *Polar coordinates of a point*

Use the overloaded + operator to add two objects of Polar.

Note that we cannot add polar values of two points directly. This requires first the conversion of points into rectangular co-ordinates, then adding the corresponding rectangular co-ordinates and finally converting the result back into polar co-ordinates. You need to use the following trigonometric formulae:

```
x  =  r * cos(a);
y  =  r * sin(a);
a  =  atan(x/y);      // arc tangent
r  =  sqrt(x*x + y*y);
```

7.13   *Create a class* ***MAT*** *of size* ***m x n***. *Define all possible matrix operations for* ***MAT*** *type objects.*

7.14   *Define a class String. Use overloaded == operator to compare two strings.*

7.15   *Define two classes* ***Polar*** *and* ***Rectangle*** *to represent points in the polar and rectangle systems. Use conversion routines to convert from one system to the other.*

8

Inheritance: Extending Classes

Key Concepts

- ➤ Reusability
- ➤ Inheritance
- ➤ Single inheritance
- ➤ Multiple inheritance
- ➤ Multilevel inheritance
- ➤ Hybrid inheritance
- ➤ Hierarchical inheritance
- ➤ Defining a derived class

- ➤ Inheritiing private members
- ➤ Virtual base class
- ➤ Direct base class
- ➤ Indirect base class
- ➤ Abstract class
- ➤ Defining derived class constructors
- ➤ Nesting of classes

8.1 INTRODUCTION

Reusability is yet another important feature of OOP. It is always nice if we could reuse something that already exists rather than trying to create the same all over again. It would not only save time and money but also reduce frustration and increase reliability. For instance, the reuse of a class that has already been tested, debugged and used many times can save us the effort of developing and testing the same again.

Fortunately, C++ strongly supports the concept of *reusability*. The C++ classes can be reused in several ways. Once a class has been written and tested, it can be adapted by other programmers to suit their requirements. This is basically done by creating new classes, reusing the properties of the existing ones. The mechanism of deriving a new class from an old one is called *inheritance (or derivation)*. The old class is referred to as the *base class* and the new one is called the *derived class or subclass*.

The derived class inherits some or all of the traits from the base class. A class can also inherit properties from more than one class or from more than one level. A derived class with only one base class, is called *single inheritance* and one with several base classes is called *multiple inheritance*. On the other hand, the traits of one class may be inherited by more than one class. This process is known as *hierarchical inheritance*. The mechanism of deriving a class from another 'derived class' is known as *multilevel inheritance*. Figure 8.1 shows various forms of inheritance that could be used for writing extensible programs. The direction of arrow indicates the direction of inheritance. (Some authors show the arrow in opposite direction meaning "inherited from".)

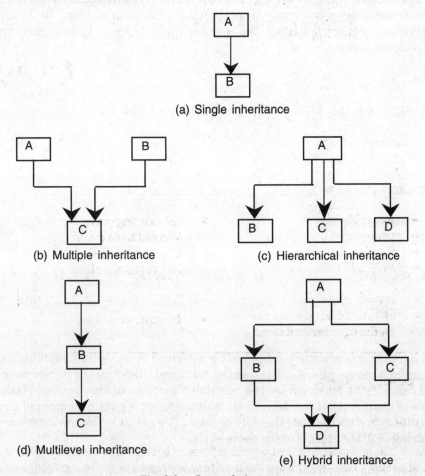

Fig. 8.1   *Forms of inheritance*

8.2 DEFINING DERIVED CLASSES

A derived class can be defined by specifying its relationship with the base class in addition to its own details. The general form of defining a derived class is:

```
class derived-class-name  : visibility-mode base-class-name
{
       .....//
       .....//   members of derived class
       .....//
};
```

The colon indicates that the *derived-class-name* is derived from the *base-class-name*. The *visibility-mode* is optional and, if present, may be either **private** or **public**. The default visibility-mode is **private**. Visibility mode specifies whether the features of the base class are *privately derived or publicly derived*.

Examples:

```
class ABC: private XYZ      // private derivation
{
       members of ABC
};

class ABC: public XYZ       // public derivation
{
       members of ABC
};

class ABC: XYZ              // private derivation by default
{
       members of ABC
};
```

When a base class is *privately inherited* by a derived class, 'public members' of the base class become 'private members' of the derived class and therefore the public members of the base class can only be accessed by the member functions of the derived class. They are inaccessible to the objects of the derived class. Remember, a public member of a class can be accessed by its own objects using the *dot operator*. The result is that no member of the base class is accessible to the objects of the derived class.

On the other hand, when the base class is *publicly inherited*, 'public members' of the base class become 'public members' of the derived class and therefore they are accessible to the objects of the derived class. In *both the cases, the private members are not inherited* and therefore, the private members of a base class will never become the members of its derived class.

In inheritance, some of the base class data elements and member functions are 'inherited' into the derived class. We can add our own data and member functions and thus extend the functionality of the base class. Inheritance, when used to modify and extend the capabilities of the existing classes, becomes a very powerful tool for incremental program development.

8.3 SINGLE INHERITANCE

Let us consider a simple example to illustrate inheritance. Program 8.1 shows a base class B and a derived class D. The class B contains one private data member, one public data member, and three public member functions. The class D contains one private data member and two public member functions.

```
                SINGLE INHERITANCE : PUBLIC

    #include <iostream>

    using namespace std;

    class B
    {
        int a;                  // private; not inheritable
      public:
        int b;                  // public; ready for inheritance
        void get_ab();
        int  get_a(void);
        void show_a(void);
    };

    class D : public B          // public derivation
    {
        int c;
      public:
        void mul(void);
        void display(void);
    };
    //------------------------------------------------------------
    void B :: get_ab(void)
    {
        a = 5; b = 10;
    }
    int B :: get_a()
    {
        return a;
    }
    void B :: show_a()
    {
        cout << "a = " << a << "\n";
    }
```

(Contd)

```
        void D :: mul()
        {
                c = b * get_a();
        }
        void D :: display()
        {
                cout << "a = " << get_a() << "\n";
                cout << "b = " << b << "\n";
                cout << "c = " << c << "\n\n";
        }
        //-----------------------------------------------------------
        int main()
        {
                D d;

                d.get_ab();
                d.mul();
                d.show_a();
                d.display();

                d.b = 20;
                d.mul();
                d.display();

                return 0;
        }
```

PROGRAM 8.1

Given below is the output of Program 8.1:

```
a = 5
a = 5
b = 10
c = 50

a = 5
b = 20
c = 100
```

The class **D** is a public derivation of the base class **B**. Therefore, **D** inherits all the **public** members of **B** and retains their visibility. Thus a **public** member of the base class **B** is also a public member of the derived class **D**. The **private** members of **B** cannot be inherited by **D**. The class **D**, in effect, will have more members than what it contains at the time of declaration as shown in Fig. 8.2.

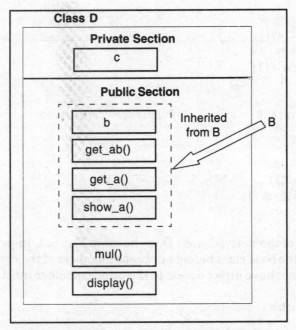

Fig. 8.2   *Adding more members to a class (by public derivation)*

The program illustrates that the objects of class **D** have access to all the public members of **B**. Let us have a look at the functions **show_a()** and **mul()**:

```
void show_a()
{
      cout << "a = " << a << "\n";
}

void mul()
{
      c = b * get_a();          // c = b * a
}
```

Although the data member **a** is private in **B** and cannot be inherited, objects of **D** are able to access it through an inherited member function of **B**.

Let us now consider the case of private derivation.

```
class B
{
      int a;
   public:
```

```
        int b;
        void get_ab();
 void get_a();
        void show_a();
};

class D : private B          // private derivation
{
        int c;
    public:
        void mul();
        void display();
};
```

The membership of the derived class **D** is shown in Fig. 8.3. In **private** derivation, the **public** members of the base class become **private** members of the derived class. Therefore, the objects of **D** can not have direct access to the public member functions of **B**.

The statements such as

```
d.get_ab();      // get_ab() is private
d.get_a();       // so also get_a()
d.show_a();      // and show_a()
```

will not work. However, these functions can be used inside **mul()** and **display()** like the normal functions as shown below:

```
void mul()
{
     get_ab();
     c = b * get_a();
}

void display()
{
     show_a();          // outputs value of 'a'
     cout << "b = " << b << "\n"
          << "c = " << c << "\n\n";
}
```

Program 8.2 incorporates these modifications for private derivation. Please compare this with Program 8.1.

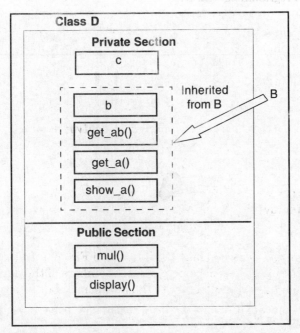

Fig. 8.3 *Adding more members to a class (by private derivation)*

```
                    SINGLE INHERITANCE : PRIVATE

#include <iostream>

using namespace std;

class B
{
    int a;            // private; not inheritable
  public:
    int b;            // public; ready for inheritance
    void get_ab();
    int  get_a(void);
    void show_a(void);
};

class D : private B        // private derivation
{
    int c;
  public:
    void mul(void);
    void display(void);
};

//-------------------------------------------------------------
```

(Contd)

```
void B :: get_ab(void)
{
    cout << "Enter values for a and b:";
    cin >> a >> b;
}

int B :: get_a()
{
    return a;
}

void B :: show_a()
{
    cout << "a = " << a << "\n";
}

void D :: mul()
{
    get_ab();
    c = b * get_a();          // 'a' cannot be used directly
}

void D :: display()
{
    show_a();                  // outputs value of 'a'
    cout << "b = " << b << "\n"
         << "c = " << c << "\n\n";
}

//-----------------------------------------------------------

int main()
{
    D d;

    // d.get_ab();  WON'T WORK
    d.mul();
    // d.show_a();  WON'T WORK
    d.display();

    // d.b = 20;      WON'T WORK; b has become private
    d.mul();
    d.display();

    return 0;
}
```

PROGRAM 8.2

The output of Program 8.2 would be:

```
Enter values for a and b:5 10
a = 5
b = 10
c = 50
Enter values for a and b:12 20
a = 12
b = 20
c = 240
```

Suppose a base class and a derived class define a function of the same name. What will happen when a derived class object invokes the function?. In such cases, the derived class function supersedes the base class definition. The base class function. will be called only if the derived class does not redefine the function.

8.4   MAKING A PRIVATE MEMBER INHERITABLE

We have just seen how to increase the capabilities of an existing class without modifying it. We have also seen that a private member of a base class cannot be inherited and therefore it is not available for the derived class directly. What do we do if the **private** data needs to be inherited by a derived class? This can be accomplished by modifying the visibility limit of the **private** member by making it **public**. This would make it accessible to all the other functions of the program, thus taking away the advantage of data hiding.

C++ provides a third *visibility modifier*, **protected**, which serve a limited purpose in inheritance. A member declared as **protected** is accessible by the member functions within its class and any class *immediately* derived from it. It *cannot* be accessed by the functions outside these two classes. A class can now use all the three visibility modes as illustrated below:

```
class alpha
{
  private:             // optional
    .....              // visible to member functions
    .....              // within its class
  protected:
    .....              // visible to member functions
    .....              // of its own and derived class
  public:
    .....              // visible to all functions
    .....              // in the program
```

When a **protected** member is inherited in **public** mode, it becomes **protected** in the derived class too and therefore is accessible by the member functions of the derived class. It is also ready for further inheritance. A **protected** member, inherited in the **private** mode derivation, becomes **private** in the derived class. Although it is available to the member functions of the derived class, it is not available for further inheritance (since **private** members cannot be inherited). Figure 8.4 is the pictorial representation for the two levels of derivation.

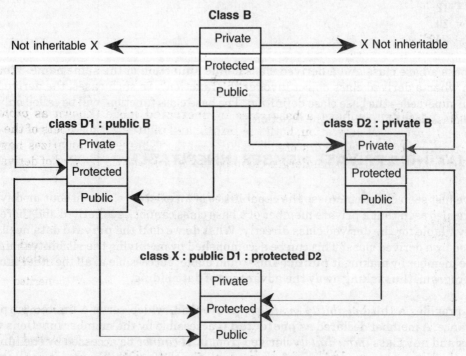

Fig. 8.4   *Effect of inheritance on the visibility of members*

The keywords **private**, **protected**, and **public** may appear in any order and any number of times in the declaration of a class. For example,

```
class beta
{
    protected:
        .....
    public:
        .....
    private:
        .....
    public:
        .....
};
```

is a valid class definition.

However, the normal practice is to use them as follows:

```
class beta
{
    .....
    .....                    // private by default

    protected:

        .....

    public:

        .....

}
```

It is also possible to inherit a base class in **protected** mode (known as *protected derivation*). In protected derivation, both the **public** and **protected** members of the base class become **protected** members of the derived class. Table 8.1 summarizes how the visibility of base class members undergoes modifications in all the three types of derivation.

Table 8.1   Visibility of inherited members

Base class visibility	Derived class visibility		
	Public derivation	**Private derivation**	**Protected derivation**
Private ⟶	Not inherited	Not inherited	Not inherited
Protected ⟶	Protected	Private	Protected
Public ⟶	Public	Private	Protected

Now let us review the access control to the **private** and **protected** members of a class. What are the various functions that can have access to these members? They could be:

1. A function that is a friend of the class.
2. A member function of a class that is a friend of the class.
3. A member function of a derived class.

While the friend functions and the member functions of a friend class can have direct access to both the **private** and **protected** data, the member functions of a derived class can directly access only the **protected** data. However, they can access the **private** data through the member functions of the base class. Figure 8.5 illustrates how the access control mechanism works in various situations. A simplified view of access control to the members of a class is shown in Fig. 8.6.

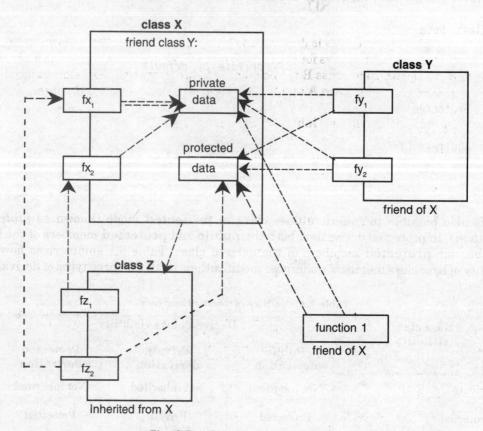

Fig. 8.5   *Access mechanism in classes*

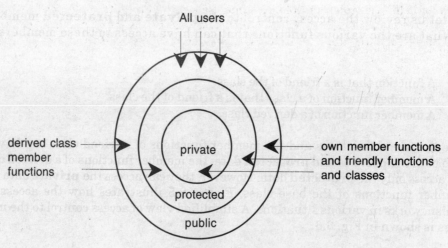

Fig. 8.6   *A simple view of access control to the members of a class*

8.5 MULTILEVEL INHERITANCE

It is not uncommon that a class is derived from another derived class as shown in Fig. 8.7. The class **A** serves as a base class for the derived class **B**, which in turn serves as a base class for the derived class **C**. The class **B** is known as *intermediate* base class since it provides a link for the inheritance between **A** and **C**. The chain **ABC** is known as *inheritance path*.

A derived class with multilevel inheritance is declared as follows:

```
class A{.....};            // Base class
class B: public A {.....}; // B derived from A
class C: public B {.....}; // C derived from B
```

This process can be extended to any number of levels.

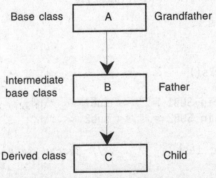

Fig. 8.7 *Multilevel inheritance*

Let us consider a simple example. Assume that the test results of a batch of students are stored in three different classes. Class **student** stores the roll-number, class **test** stores the marks obtained in two subjects and class **result** contains the **total** marks obtained in the test. The class **result** can inherit the details of the marks obtained in the test and the roll-number of students through multilevel inheritance. Example:

```
class student
{
      protected:
      int roll_number;
   public:
      void get_number(int);
      void put_number(void);
};
void student :: get_number(int a)
{
      roll_number = a;
```

```
}
void student :: put_number()
{
        cout << "Roll Number: " << roll_number << "\n";
}

class test : public student        // First level derivation
{
    protected:
        float sub1;
        float sub2;
    public:
        void get_marks(float, float);
        void put_marks(void);
};
void test :: get_marks(float x, float y)
{
        sub1 = x;
        sub2 = y;
}
void test :: put_marks()
{
        cout << "Marks in SUB1 = " << sub1 << "\n";
        cout << "Marks in SUB2 = " << sub2 << "\n";
}
class result : public test             // Second level derivation
{
        float total;              // private by default
    public:
        void display(void);
};
```

The class **result**, after inheritance from 'grandfather' through 'father', would contain the following members:

```
    private:
        float total;               // own member
    protected:
        int roll_number;           // inherited from  student via test
        float sub1;                // inherited from test
        float sub2;                // inherited from test
    public:
      void get_number(int);        // from student via test
      void put_number(void);       // from student via test
      void get_marks(float, float); // from test
      void put_marks(void);        // from test
      void display(void);          // own member
```

The inherited functions **put_number()** and **put_marks()** can be used in the definition of **display()** function:

```
void result :: display(void)
{
      total = sub1 + sub2;
      put_number();
      put_marks();
      cout << "Total = " << total << "\n";
}
```

Here is a simple **main()** program:

```
int main()
{
      result student1;                    // student1 created
      student1.get_number(111);
      student1.get_marks(75.0, 59.5);
      student1.display();

      return 0;
}
```

This will display the result of **student1**. The complete program is shown in Program 8.3.

```
                    MULTILEVEL INHERITANCE

      #include <iostream>

      using namespace std;

      class student
      {
         protected:
             int roll_number;
         public:
             void get_number(int);
             void put_number(void);
      };
      void student :: get_number(int a)
      {
             roll_number = a;
      }

      void student :: put_number()
      {
             cout << "Roll Number: " << roll_number << "\n";
```

(Contd)

```
    }
    class test : public student        // First level derivation
    {
      protected:
        float sub1;
        float sub2;
      public:
        void get_marks(float, float);
        void put_marks(void);
    };

    void test :: get_marks(float x, float y)
    {
        sub1 = x;
        sub2 = y;
    }

    void test :: put_marks()
    {
        cout << "Marks in SUB1 = " << sub1 << "\n";
        cout << "Marks in SUB2 = " << sub2 << "\n";
    }

    class result : public test          // Second level derivation
    {
        float total;                    // private by default
      public:
        void display(void);
    };

    void result :: display(void)
    {
        total = sub1 + sub2;
        put_number();
        put_marks();
        cout << "Total = " << total << "\n";
    }

    int main()
    {
        result student1;           // student1 created

        student1.get_number(111);
        student1.get_marks(75.0, 59.5);

        student1.display();

        return 0;
    }
```

PROGRAM 8.3

Program 8.3 displays the following output:

```
Roll Number: 111
Marks in SUB1 = 75
Marks in SUB2 = 59.5
Total = 134.5
```

8.6 MULTIPLE INHERITANCE

A class can inherit the attributes of two or more classes as shown in Fig. 8.8. This is known as *multiple inheritance*. Multiple inheritance allows us to combine the features of several existing classes as a starting point for defining new classes. It is like a child inheriting the physical features of one parent and the intelligence of another.

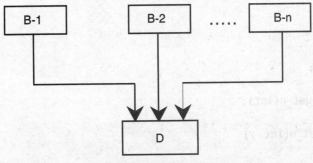

Fig. 8.8   *Multiple inheritance*

The syntax of a derived class with multiple base classes is as follows:

```
class D: visibility B-1, visibility B-2 ...
{
    .....
    .....(Body of D)
    .....
};
```

where, *visibility* may be either **public** or **private**. The base classes are separated by commas.

Example:

```
class P : public M, public N
{
    public:
        void display(void);
};
```

Classes M and N have been specified as follows:

```
class M
{
   protected:
       int m;
   public:
       void get_m(int);
};
void M :: get_m(int x)
{
       m = x;
}
class N
{
   protected:
       int n;
   public:
       void get_n(int);
};
void N :: get_n(int y)
{
       n = y;
}
```

The derived class **P**, as declared above, would, in effect, contain all the members of **M** and **N** in addition to its own members as shown below:

```
class P
{
   protected:

       int m;                          // from M
       int n;                          // from N

   public:

           void get_m(int);            // from M
           void get_n(int);            // from N
           void display(void)          // own member

};
```

The member function display() can be defined as follows:

```
void P :: display(void)
{
    cout << "m = " << m << "\n";
    cout << "n = " << n << "\n";
    cout << "m*n =" << m*n << "\n";
};
```

The main() function which provides the user-interface may be written as follows:

```
main()
{
    P p;
    p.get_m(10);
    p.get_n(20);
    p.display();
}
```

Program 8.4 shows the entire code illustrating how all the three classes are implemented in multiple inheritance mode.

```
                    MULTIPLE  INHERITANCE

    #include <iostream>

    using namespace std;

    class M
    {
      protected:
          int m;
      public:
          void get_m(int);
    };

    class N
    {
      protected:
          int n;
      public:
          void get_n(int);
    };

    class P : public M, public N
    {
      public:
```

(Contd)

```
            void display(void);
    };

    void M :: get_m(int x)
    {
        m = x;
    }

    void N :: get_n(int y)
    {
        n = y;
    }

    void P :: display(void)
    {
        cout << "m = " << m << "\n";
        cout << "n = " << n << "\n";
        cout << "m*n = " << m*n << "\n";
    }

    int main()
    {
        P p;

        p.get_m(10);
        p.get_n(20);
        p.display();

        return 0;
    }
```

PROGRAM 8.4

The output of Program 8.4 would be:

```
m = 10
n = 20
m*n = 200
```

Ambiguity Resolution in Inheritance

Occasionally, we may face a problem in using the multiple inheritance, when a function with the same inheritance appears in more than one base class. Consider the following two classes.

```
class M
{
  public:
    void display(void)
```

```
        {
          cout << "Class M\n";
        }
    };

    class N
    {
      public:
        void display(void)
        {
            cout << "Class N\n";
        }
    };
```

Which **display()** function is used by the derived class when we inherit these two classes? We can solve this problem by defining a named instance within the derived class, using the class resolution operator with the function as shown below:

```
    class P : public M, public N
    {
      public:
        void display(void)        // overrides display() of M and N
        {
            M :: display();
        }
    };
```

We can now use the derived class as follows:

```
    int main()
    {
        P p;
        p.display();
    }
```

Ambiguity may also arise in single inheritance applications. For instance, consider the following situation:

```
    class A
    {
      public:
        void display()
        {
            cout << "A\n";
        }
    };
```

```
class B : public A
{
  public:
   void display()
   {
        cout << "B\n";
   }
};
```

In this case, the function in the derived class overrides the inherited function and, therefore, a simple call to **display()** by **B** type object will invoke function defined in **B** only. However, we may invoke the function defined in **A** by using the scope resolution operator to specify the class.

Example:

```
int main()
{
    B b;                    // derived class object
    b.display();            // invokes display() in B
    b.A::display();         // invokes display() in A
    b.B::display();         // invokes display() in B

    return 0;
}
```

This will produce the following output:

```
B
A
B
```

8.7 HIERARCHICAL INHERITANCE

We have discussed so far how inheritance can be used to modify a class when it did not satisfy the requirements of a particular problem on hand. Additional members are added through inheritance to extend the capabilities of a class. Another interesting application of inheritance is to use it as a support to the hierarchical design of a program. Many programming problems can be cast into a hierarchy where certain features of one level are shared by many others below that level.

As an example, Fig. 8.9 shows a hierarchical classification of students in a university. Another example could be the classification of accounts in a commercial bank as shown in Fig. 8.10. All the students have certain things in common and, similarly, all the accounts possess certain common features.

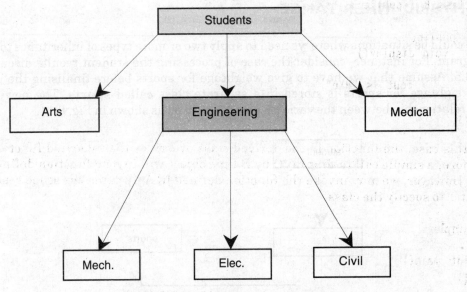

Fig. 8.9 *Hierarchical classification of students*

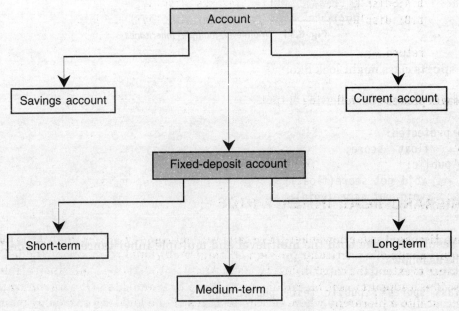

Fig. 8.10 *Classification of bank accounts*

In C++, such problems can be easily converted into class hierarchies. The base class will include all the features that are common to the subclasses. A *subclass* can be constructed by inheriting the properties of the base class. A subclass can serve as a base class for the lower level classes and so on.

8.8 HYBRID INHERITANCE

There could be situations where we need to apply two or more types of inheritance to design a program. For instance, consider the case of processing the student results discussed in Sec. 8.5. Assume that we have to give weightage for sports before finalising the results. The weightage for sports is stored in a separate class called **sports**. The new inheritance relationship between the various classes would be as shown in Fig. 8.11.

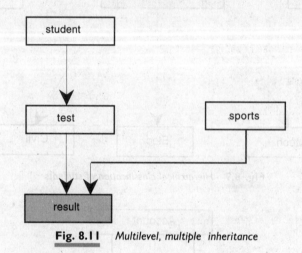

Fig. 8.11 *Multilevel, multiple inheritance*

The **sports** class might look like:

```
class sports
{
    protected:
        float  score;
    public:
        void get_score(float);
        void put_score(void);
};
```

The result will have both the multilevel and multiple inheritances and its declaration would be as follows:

```
class sports : public test, public sports
{
    .....
    .....
};
```

Where test itself is a derived class from student. That is

```
class test : public student
{
    .....
    .....
};
```

Program 8.5 illustrates the implementation of both multilevel and multiple inheritance.

```
                      HYBRID  INHERITANCE

#include <iostream>

using namespace std;

class student
{
  protected:
    int   roll_number;
  public:
    void get_number(int a)
    {
       roll_number = a;
    }
    void put_number(void)
    {
      cout << "Roll No: " << roll_number << "\n";
    }
};

class test : public student
{
  protected:
    float part1, part2;
  public:
    void get_marks(float x, float y)
    {
      part1 = x;  part2 = y;
    }
    void put_marks(void)
    {
      cout << "Marks obtained: " << "\n"
           << "Part1 = " << part1 << "\n"
           << "Part2 = " << part2 << "\n";
    }
};
```

(Contd)

```cpp
class sports
{
    protected:
        float score;
    public:
        void get_score(float s)
        {
            score = s;
        }
        void put_score(void)
        {
            cout << "Sports wt: " << score << "\n\n";
        }
};

class result : public test, public sports
{
        float total;
    public:
        void display(void);
};

void result :: display(void)
{
        total = part1 + part2 + score;

        put_number();
        put_marks();
        put_score();

        cout << "Total Score: " << total << "\n";
}

int main()
{
        result student_1;
        student_1.get_number(1234);
        student_1.get_marks(27.5, 33.0);
        student_1.get_score(6.0);
        student_1.display();

        return 0;
}
```

PROGRAM 8.5

Here is the output of Program 8.5:

```
Roll No: 1234
Marks obtained:
Part1 = 27.5
Part2 = 33
Sports wt: 6

Total Score: 66.5
```

8.9 VIRTUAL BASE CLASSES

We have just discussed a situation which would require the use of both the multiple and multilevel inheritance. Consider a situation where all the three kinds of inheritance, namely, multilevel, multiple and hierarchical inheritance, are involved. This is illustrated in Fig. 8.12. The 'child' has two *direct base classes* 'parent1' and 'parent2' which themselves have a common base class 'grandparent'. The 'child' inherits the traits of 'grandparent' via two separate paths. It can also inherit directly as shown by the broken line. The 'grandparent' is sometimes referred to as *indirect base class*.

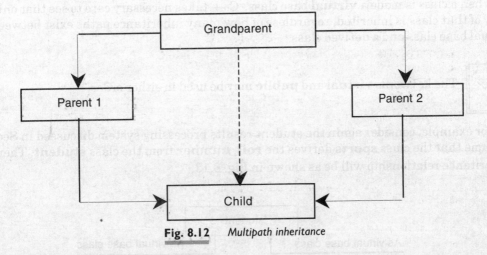

Fig. 8.12 *Multipath inheritance*

Inheritance by the 'child' as shown in Fig. 8.12 might pose some problems. All the public and protected members of 'grandparent' are inherited into 'child' twice, first via 'parent1' and again via 'parent2'. This means, 'child' would have *duplicate* sets of the members inherited from 'grandparent'. This introduces ambiguity and should be avoided.

The duplication of inherited members due to these multiple paths can be avoided by making the common base class (ancestor class) as *virtual base class* while declaring the direct or intermediate base classes which is shown as follow:

```
class A                          // grandparent
{
    .....
    .....
};
class B1 : virtual public A     // parent1
{
    .....
    .....
};
class B2 : public virtual A     // parent2
{
    .....
    .....
};
class C : public B1, public B2  // child
{
    .....                       // only one copy of A
    .....                       // will be inherited
};
```

When a class is made a **virtual** base class, C++ takes necessary care to see that only one copy of that class is inherited, regardless of how many inheritance paths exist between the virtual base class and a derived class.

The keywords **virtual** and **public** may be used in either order.

For example, consider again the student results processing system discussed in Sec. 8.8. Assume that the class **sports** derives the **roll_number** from the class **student**. Then, the inheritance relationship will be as shown in Fig. 8.13.

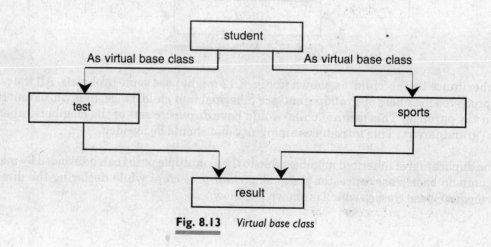

Fig. 8.13   *Virtual base class*

A program to implement the concept of virtual base class is illustrated in Program 8.6.

```
                      VIRTUAL BASE CLASS

#include <iostream>

using namespace std;

class student
{
  protected:
     int roll_number;
  public:
     void get_number(int a)
     {
         roll_number = a;
     }
     void put_number(void)
     {
         cout << "Roll No: " << roll_number << "\n";
     }
};

class test : virtual public student
{
  protected:
     float part1, part2;
  public:
     void get_marks(float x, float y)
     {
         part1 = x;   part2 = y;
     }
     void put_marks(void)
     {
         cout << "Marks obtained: " << "\n"
              << "Part1 = " << part1 << "\n"
              << "Part2 = " << part2 << "\n";
     }
};

class sports : public virtual student
{
  protected:
     float score;
  public:
     void get_score(float s)
```

(Contd)

```
            {
                score = s;
            }
        void put_score(void)
            {
                cout << "Sports wt: " << score << "\n\n";
            }
};

class result : public test, public sports
{
        float total;
    public:
        void display(void);
};

void result :: display(void)
{
        total = part1 + part2 + score;

        put_number();
        put_marks();
        put_score();

        cout << "Total Score: " << total << "\n";
}

int main()
{
        result student_1;
        student_1.get_number(678);
        student_1.get_marks(30.5, 25.5);
        student_1.get_score(7.0);
        student_1.display();

        return 0;
}
```

PROGRAM 8.6

The output of Program 8.6 would be:

```
Roll No: 678
Marks obtained:
Part1 = 30.5
Part2 = 25.5
Sport wt: 7

Total Score: 63
```

8.10 ABSTRACT CLASSES

An *abstract class* is one that is not used to create objects. An abstract class is designed only to act as a base class (to be inherited by other classes). It is a design concept in program development and provides a base upon which other classes may be built. In the previous example, the **student** class is an abstract class since it was not used to create any objects.

8.11 CONSTRUCTORS IN DERIVED CLASSES

As we know, the constructors play an important role in initializing objects. We did not use them earlier in the derived classes for the sake of simplicity. One important thing to note here is that, as long as no base class constructor takes any arguments, the derived class need not have a constructor function. However, if any base class contains a constructor with one or more arguments, then it is *mandatory* for the derived class to have a constructor and pass the arguments to the base class constructors. Remember, while applying inheritance we usually create objects using the derived class. Thus, it makes sense for the derived class to pass arguments to the base class constructor. When both the derived and base classes contain constructors, the base constructor is executed first and then the constructor in the derived class is executed.

In case of multiple inheritance, the base classes are constructed *in the order in which they appear in the declaration of the derived class*. Similarly, in a multilevel inheritance, the constructors will be executed *in the order of inheritance*.

Since the derived class takes the responsibility of supplying initial values to its base classes, we supply the initial values that are required by all the classes together, when a derived class object is declared. How are they passed to the base class constructors so that they can do their job? C++ supports a special argument passing mechanism for such situations.

The constructor of the derived class receives the entire list of values as its arguments and passes them on to the base constructors in the order in which they are declared in the derived class. The base constructors are called and executed before executing the statements in the body of the derived constructor.

The general form of defining a derived constructor is:

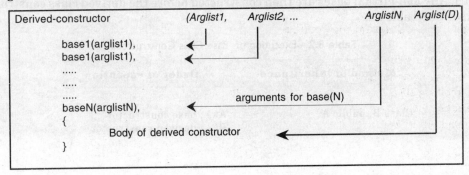

The header line of *derived-constructor* function contains two parts separated by a colon(:). The first part provides the declaration of the arguments that are passed to the *derived-constructor* and the second part lists the function calls to the base constructors.

base1(arglist1), base2(arglist2) ... are function calls to base constructors **base1()**, **base2()**, ... and therefore *arglist1, arglist2, ...* etc. represent the actual parameters that are passed to the base constructors. *Arglist1* through *ArglistN* are the argument declarations for base constructors *base1* through *baseN*. *ArglistD* provides the parameters that are necessary to initialize the members of the derived class.

Example:

```
D(int a1, int a2, float b1, float b2, int d1):
A(a1, a2),        /* call to constructor A */
B(b1, b2)         /* call to constructor B */
{
    d = d1;        // executes its own body
}
```

A(a1, a2) invokes the base constructor **A()** and B(b1, b2) invokes another base constructor **B()**. The constructor **D()** supplies the values for these four arguments. In addition, it has one argument of its own. The constructor **D()** has a total of five arguments. **D()** may be invoked as follows:

```
. . . . .
D objD(5, 12, 2.5, 7.54, 30);
. . . . .
```

These values are assigned to various parameters by the constructor **D()** as follows:

```
5    ──────→   a1
12   ──────→   a2
2.5  ──────→   b1
7.54 ──────→   b2
30   ──────→   d1
```

The constructors for virtual base classes are invoked before any non-virtual base classes. If there are multiple virtual base classes, they are invoked in the order in which they are declared. Any non-virtual bases are then constructed before the derived class constructor is executed. See Table 8.2.

Table 8.2 Execution of Base Class Constructors

Method of inheritance	Order of execution

Class B: public A
{
};
	A( ) ; base constructor
	B( ) ; derived constructor

class A : public B, public C
{
};
	B( ) ; base(first)
	C( ) ; base(second)
	A( ) ; derived

class A : public B, virtual public C
{
};
	C( ) ; virtual base
	B( ) ; ordinary base
	A( ) ; derived

Program 8.7 illustrates how constructors are implemented when the classes are inherited.

CONSTRUCTORS IN DERIVED CLASS

```cpp
#include <iostream>

using namespace std;

class alpha
{
    int x;
  public:
    alpha(int i)
    {
        x = i;
        cout << "alpha initialized \n";
    }
    void show_x(void)
    { cout << "x = " << x << "\n"; }
};

class beta
{
    float y;
  public:
    beta(float j)
    {
        y = j;
        cout << "beta initialized \n";
    }
    void show_y(void)
    { cout << "y = " << y << "\n"; }
};

class gamma: public beta, public alpha
{
    int m, n;
```

(Contd)

```
    public:
        gamma(int a, float b, int c, int d):
            alpha(a), beta(b)
        {
            m = c;
            n = d;
            cout << "gamma initialized \n";
        }
        void show_mn(void)
        {
            cout << "m = " << m << "\n"
                 << "n = " << n << "\n";
        }
};

int main()
{
        gamma g(5, 10.75, 20, 30);
        cout << "\n";
        g.show_x();
        g.show_y();
        g.show_mn();

        return 0;
}
```

PROGRAM 8.7

The output of Program 8.7 would be:

```
beta initialized
alpha initialized
gamma initialized

x = 5
y = 10.75
m = 20
n = 30
```

beta is initialized first, although it appears second in the derived constructor. This is because it has been declared first in the derived class header line. Also, note that **alpha(a)** and **beta(b)** are function calls. Therefore, the parameters should not include types.

C++ supports another method of initializing the class objects. This method uses what is known as initialization list in the constructor function. This takes the following form:

```
constructor  (arglist)  :  intialization-section
{
     assignment-section
}
```

The *assignment-section* is nothing but the body of the constructor function and is used to assign initial values to its data members. The part immediately following the colon is known as the *initialization section*. We can use this section to provide initial values to the base constructors and also to initialize its own class members. This means that we can use either of the sections to initialize the data members of the constructors class. The initialization section basically contains a list of initializations separated by commas. This list is known as *initialization list*. Consider a simple example:

```
class XYZ
{
     int a;
     int b;
  public:
     XYZ(int i, int j) : a(i), b(2 * j) { }
};

main()
{
     XYZ x(2, 3);
}
```

This program will initialize **a** to 2 and **b** to 6. Note how the data members are initialized, just by using the variable name followed by the initialization value enclosed in the parenthesis (like a function call). Any of the parameters of the argument list may be used as the initialization value and the items in the list may be in any order. For example, the constructor **XYZ** may also be written as:

```
XYZ(int i, int j) : b(i), a(i + j) { }
```

In this case, **a** will be initialized to 5 and **b** to 2. Remember, the data members are initialized in the order of declaration, independent of the order in the initialization list. This enables us to have statements such as

```
XYZ(int i, int j) : a(i), b(a * j) { }
```

Here **a** is initialized to 2 and **b** to 6. Remember, **a** which has been declared first is initialized first and then its value is used to initialize **b**. However, the following will not work:

```
XYZ(int i, int j) : b(i), a(b * j) { }
```

because the value of **b** is not available to **a** which is to be initialized first.

The following statements are also valid:

```
XYZ(int i, int j) : a(i) {b = j;}
XYZ(int i, int j) { a = i; b = j;}
```

We can omit either section, if it is not needed. Program 8.8 illustrates the use of initialization lists in the base and derived constructors.

INITIALIZATION LIST IN CONSTRUCTORS

```
#include <iostream>

using namespace std;

class alpha
{
    int x;
  public:
    alpha(int i)
    {
        x = i;
        cout << "\n alpha constructed";
    }

    void show_alpha(void)
    {
        cout << " x = " << x << "\n";
    }
};

class beta
{
    float p, q;
  public:
    beta(float a, float b): p(a), q(b+p)
    {
        cout << "\n beta constructed";
    }
    void show_beta(void)
    {
        cout << " p = " << p << "\n";
        cout << " q = " << q << "\n";
    };
};
class gamma : public beta, public alpha
```

(Contd)

```
{
        int u,v;
    public:
        gamma(int a, int b, float c):
                alpha(a*2), beta(c,c), u(a)
        { v = b; cout << "\n gamma constructed"; }

        void show_gamma(void)
        {
                cout << " u = " << u << "\n";
                cout << " v = " << v << "\n";
        }
};

int main()
{
        gamma g(2, 4, 2.5);

        cout << "\n\n Display member values " << "\n\n";

        g.show_alpha();
        g.show_beta();
        g.show_gamma();

        return 0;
};
```

PROGRAM 8.8

The output of Program 8.8 would be:

```
beta constructed
alpha constructed
gamma constructed

Display member values

x = 4
p = 2.5
q = 5
u = 2
v = 4
```

The argument list of the derived constructor **gamma** contains only three parameters **a**, **b** and **c** which are used to initialize the five data members contained in all the three classes.

8.12 MEMBER CLASSES: NESTING OF CLASSES

Inheritance is the mechanism of deriving certain properties of one class into another. We have seen in detail how this is implemented using the concept of derived classes. C++ supports yet another way of inheriting properties of one class into another. This approach takes a view that an object can be a collection of many other objects. That is, a class can contain objects of other classes as its members as shown below:

```
class alpha {....};
class beta {....};
class gamma
{
        alpha a;            // a is an object of alpha class
        beta b;             // b is an object of beta class
        .....
};
```

All objects of **gamma** class will contain the objects **a** and **b**. This kind of relationship is called *containership* or *nesting*. Creation of an object that contains another object is very different than the creation of an independent object. An independent object is created by its constructor when it is declared with arguments. On the other hand, a nested object is created in two stages. First, the member objects are created using their respective constructors and then the other 'ordinary' members are created. This means, constructors of all the member objects should be called before its own constructor body is executed. This is accomplished using an initialization list in the constructor of the nested class.

Example:

```
class gamma
{
        .....
        alpha a;         // a is object of alpha
        beta b;          // b is object of beta
    public:
        gamma(arglist): a(arglist1), b(arglist2)
        {
                // constructor body
        }
};
```

arglist is the list of arguments that is to be supplied when a **gamma** object is defined. These parameters are used for initializing the members of **gamma**. *arglist1* is the argument list for the constructor of **a** and *arglist2* is the argument list for the constructor of **b**. *arglist1* and *arglist2* may or may not use the arguments from *arglist*. Remember, **a**(*arglist1*) and **b**(*arglist2*) are function calls and therefore the arguments do not contain the data types. They are simply variables or constants.

Example:

```
gamma(int x, int y, float z) : a(x), b(x,z)
{
      Assignment section(for ordinary other members)
}
```

We can use as many member objects as are required in a class. For each member object we add a constructor call in the initializer list. The constructors of the member objects are called in the order in which they are declared in the nested class.

Summary

- The mechanism of deriving a new class from an old class is called inheritance. Inheritance provides the concept of reusability. The C++ classes can be reused using inheritance.
- The derived class inherits some or all of the properties of the base class.
- A derived class with only one base class is called single inheritance.
- A class can inherit properties from more than one class which is known as multiple inheritance.
- A class can be derived from another derived class which is known as multilevel inheritance.
- When the properties of one class are inherited by more than one class, it is called hierarchical inheritance.
- A private member of a class cannot be inherited either in public mode or in private mode.
- A protected member inherited in public mode becomes protected, whereas inherited in private mode becomes private in the derived class.
- A public member inherited in public mode becomes public, whereas inherited in private mode becomes private in the derived class.
- The friend functions and the member functions of a friend class can directly access the private and protected data.
- The member functions of a derived class can directly access only the protected and public data. However, they can access the private data through the member functions of the base class.
- Multipath inheritance may lead to duplication of inherited members from a 'grandparent' base class. This may be avoided by making the common base class a virtual base class.
- In multiple inheritance, the base classes are constructed in the order in which they appear in the declaration of the derived class.
- In multilevel inheritance, the constructors are executed in the order of inheritance.
- A class can contain objects of other classes. This is known as containership or nesting.

Key Terms

➤ abstract class	➤ inheritance path
➤ access control	➤ initialization list
➤ access mechanism	➤ initialization section
➤ ancestor class	➤ intermediate base
➤ assignment section	➤ member classes
➤ base class	➤ multilevel inheritance
➤ base constructor	➤ multiple inheritance
➤ child class	➤ nesting
➤ common base class	➤ **private**
➤ containership	➤ private derivation
➤ derivation	➤ private members
➤ derived class	➤ privately derived
➤ derived constructor	➤ **protected**
➤ direct base class	➤ protected members
➤ dot operator	➤ **public**
➤ duplicate members	➤ public derivation
➤ father class	➤ public members
➤ **friend**	➤ publicly derived
➤ grandfather class	➤ reusability
➤ grandparent class	➤ single inheritance
➤ hierarchical inheritance	➤ subclass
➤ hybrid inheritance	➤ virtual base class
➤ indirect base class	➤ visibility mode
➤ inheritance	➤ visibility modifier

Review Questions and Exercises

8.1   *What does inheritance mean in C++?*

8.2   *What are the different forms of inheritance? Give an example for each.*

8.3   *Describe the syntax of the single inheritance in C++.*

8.4   *We know that a private member of a base class is not inheritable. Is it anyway possible for the objects of a derived class to access the private members of the base class? If yes, how? Remember, the base class cannot be modified.*

8.5   *How do the properties of the following two derived classes differ?*
   a)   `class D1: private B{//...};`
   b)   `class D2: public B{//...};`

8.6   *When do we use the protected visibility specifier to a class member?*

8.7   *Describe the syntax of multiple inheritance. When do we use such an inheritance?*

8.8   *What are the implications of the following two definitions?*
   a)   `class A: public B, public C{//....};`
   b)   `class A: public C, public B{//....};`

8.9   *What is a virtual base class?*

8.10 *When do we make a class virtual?*

8.11 *What is an abstract class?*

8.12 *In what order are the class constructors called when a derived class object is created?*

8.13 *Class D is derived from class B. The class D does not contain any data members of its own. Does the class D require constructors? If yes, why?*

8.14 *What is containership? How does it differ from inheritance?*

8.15 *Describe how an object of a class that contains objects of other classes created?*

8.16 *State whether the following statements are TRUE or FALSE:*

   (a) *Inheritance helps in making a general class into a more specific class.*

   (b) *Inheritance aids data hiding.*

   (c) *One of the advantages of inheritance is that it provides a conceptual framework.*

   (d) *Inheritance facilitates the creation of class libraries.*

   (e) *Defining a derived class requires some changes in the base class.*

   (f) *A base class is never used to create objects.*

   (g) *It is legal to have an object of one class as a member of another class.*

   (h) *We can prevent the inheritance of all members of the base class by making base class virtual in the definition of the derived class.*

8.17 *Find errors in the following program. State reasons.*

```
// Program test
#include <iostream.h>

class X
{
        private:
            int x1;
        protected:
            int x2;
        public:
            int x3;
};

class Y: public X
{
    public:
        void f()
        {
            int y1,y2,y3;
            y1 = x1;
            y2 = x2;
            y3 = x3;
        }
};

class Z: X
{
    public:
```

```
            void f()
            {
                    int z1,z2,z3;
                    z1 = x1;
                    z2 = x2;
                    z3 = x3;
            }
};
main()
{
            int m,n,p;
            Y y;
            m = y.x1;
            n = y.x2;
            p = y.x3;
            Z z;
            m = z.x1;
            n = z.x2;
            p = z.x3;
}
```

8.18 *Debug the following program.*

```
// Test program
#include <iostream.h>

class B1
{
        int b1;
    public:
        void display();
        {
                cout << b1 <<"\n";
        }
};

class B2
{
        int b2;
    public:
        void display();
        {
                cout << b2 <<"\n";
        }
```

```
class D: public B1, public B2
{
        // nothing here
};
main()
{
        D d;
        d.display()
        d.B1::display();
        d.B2::display();
}
```

8.19 *Assume that a bank maintains two kinds of accounts for customers, one called as savings account and the other as current account. The savings account provides compound interest and withdrawal facilities but no cheque book facility. The current account provides cheque book facility but no interest. Current account holders should also maintain a minimum balance and if the balance falls below this level, a service charge is imposed.*

Create a class **account** *that stores customer name, account number and type of account. From this derive the classes* **cur_acct** *and* **sav_acct** *to make them more specific to their requirements. Include necessary member functions in order to achieve the following tasks:*

(a) *Accept deposit from a customer and update the balance.*

(b) *Display the balance.*

(c) *Compute and deposit interest.*

(d) *Permit withdrawal and update the balance.*

(e) *Check for the minimum balance, impose penalty, necessary, and update the balance.*

Do not use any constructors. Use member functions to initialize the class members.

8.20 *Modify the program of Exercise 8.19 to include constructors for all the three classes.*

8.21 *An educational institution wishes to maintain a database of its employees. The database is divided into a number of classes whose hierarchical relationships are shown in Fig. 8.13. The figure also shows the minimum information required for each class. Specify all the classes and define functions to create the database and retrieve individual information as and when required.*

8.22 *The database created in Exercise 8.21 does not include educational information of the staff. It has been decided to add this information to teachers and officers (and not for typists) which will help the management in decision making with regard to training, promotion, etc. Add another data class called* **education** *that holds two pieces of educational information, namely, highest qualification in general education and highest professional qualification. This class should be inherited by the* **class teacher** *and* **officer**. *Modify the program of Exercise 8.21 to incorporate these additions.*

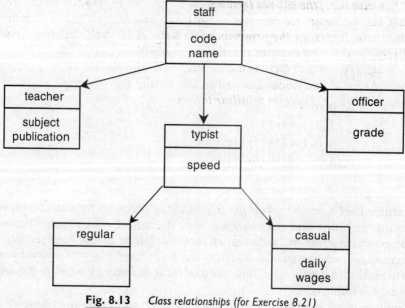

Fig. 8.13   *Class relationships (for Exercise 8.21)*

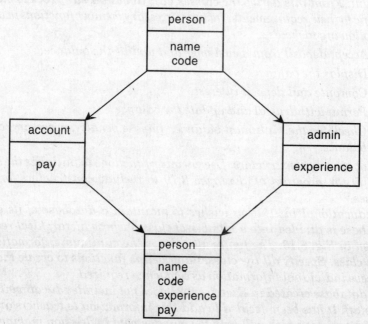

Fig. 8.14   *Multipath inheritance (for Exercise 8.23)*

8.23   *Consider a class network of Fig. 8.14. The class **master** derives information from both account and admin classes which in turn derive information from the class **person**. Define all the four classes and write a program to create, update and display the information contained in **master** objects.*

8.24 *In Exercise 8.21, the classes* **teacher**, **officer**, *and* **typist** *are derived from the class* **staff**. *As we know, we can use container classes in place of inheritance in some situations. Redesign the program of Exercise 8.21 such that the classes* **teacher**, **officer**, *and* **typist** *contain the objects of* **staff**.

8.25 *We have learned that OOP is well suited for designing simulation programs. Using the techniques and tricks learned so far, design a program that would simulate a simple real-world system familiar to you.*

9

Pointers, Virtual Functions and Polymorphism

Key Concepts _____

- ➤ Polymorphism
- ➤ Pointers to objects
- ➤ this pointer

- ➤ Pointers to derived classes
- ➤ Virtual functions
- ➤ Pure virtual function

9.1 INTRODUCTION

Polymorphism is one of the crucial features of OOP. It simply means 'one name, multiple forms'. We have already seen how the concept of *polymorphism* is implemented using the overloaded functions and operators. The overloaded member functions are 'selected' for invoking by matching arguments, both type and number. This information is known to the compiler at the compile time and, therefore, compiler is able to select the appropriate function for a particular call at the compile time itself. This is called *early binding or static binding or static linking*. Also known as *compile time polymorphism*, early binding simply means that an object is bound to its function call at compile time.

Now let us consider a situation where the function name and prototype is the same in both the base and derived classes. For example, consider the following class definitions:

```
class A
{
    int x;
  public:
    void show() {....}        // show() in base class
};
```

```
class B: public A
{
    int y;
  public:
    void show() {....}      // show() in derived class
};
```

How do we use the member function **show()** to print the values of objects of both the classes **A** and **B**?. Since the prototype of **show()** is the same in both the places, the function is not overloaded and therefore static binding does not apply. We have seen earlier that, in such situations, we may use the class resolution operator to specify the class while invoking the functions with the derived class objects.

It would be nice if the appropriate member function could be selected while the program is running. This is known as *run time polymorphism*. How could it happen? C++ supports a mechanism known as *virtual function* to achieve run time polymorphism. Please refer Fig. 9.1.

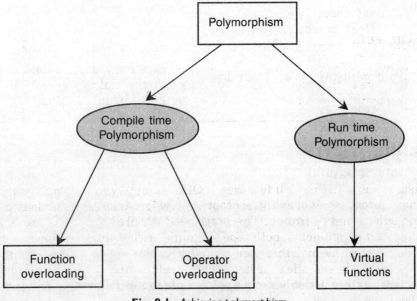

Fig. 9.1 *Achieving polymorphism*

At run time, when it is known what class objects are under consideration, the appropriate version of the function is invoked. Since the function is linked with a particular class much later after the compilation, this process is termed as *late binding*. It is also known as *dynamic binding* because the selection of the appropriate function is done dynamically at run time.

Dynamic binding is one of the powerful features of C++. This requires the use of pointers to objects. We shall discuss in detail how the object pointers and virtual functions are used to implement dynamic binding.

9.2 POINTERS TO OBJECTS

We have already seen how to use pointers to access the class members. As stated earlier, a pointer can point to an object created by a class. Consider the following statement:

```
item x;
```

where **item** is a class and x is an object defined to be of type item. Similarly we can define a pointer **it_ptr** of type **item** as follows:

```
item *it_ptr;
```

Object pointers are useful in creating objects at run time. We can also use an object pointer to access the public members of an object. Consider a class **item** defined as follows:

```
class item
{
        int code;
        float price;
    public:
        void getdata(int a, float b)
        {
            code = a;
            price = b;
        }

        void show(void)
        {
            cout << "Code : " << code << "\n";
                 << "Price: " << price << "\n\n";
        }
};
```

Let us declare an **item** variable x and a pointer **ptr** to x as follows:

```
item x;
item *ptr = &x;
```

The pointer **ptr** is initialized with the address of x.

We can refer to the member functions of **item** in two ways, one by using the *dot operator* and *the object*, and another by using the *arrow operator* and the *object pointer*. The statements

```
x.getdata(100,75.50);
x.show();
```

are equivalent to

```
ptr->getdata(100, 75.50);
ptr->show();
```

Since ***ptr** is an alias of **x**, we can also use the following method:

```
(*ptr).show();
```

The parentheses are necessary because the dot operator has higher precedence than the *indirection operator* *.

We can also create the objects using pointers and **new** operator as follows:

```
item *ptr = new item;
```

This statement allocates enough memory for the data members in the object structure and assigns the address of the memory space to **ptr**. Then **ptr** can be used to refer to the members as shown below:

```
ptr -> show();
```

If a class has a constructor with arguments and does not include an empty constructor, then we must supply the arguments when the object is created.

We can also create an array of objects using pointers. For example, the statement

```
item *ptr = new item[10];    // array of 10 objects
```

creates memory space for an array of 10 objects of **item**. Remember, in such cases, if the class contains constructors, it must also contain an empty constructor.

Program 9.1, illustrates the use of pointers to objects.

```
                       POINTERS TO OBJECTS

    #include <iostream>

    using namespace std;

    class item
    {
        int code;
        float price;
    public:
```

(Contd)

```
        void getdata(int a, float b)
        {
                code = a;
                price = b;
        }

        void show(void)
        {
                cout << "Code : " << code << "\n";
                cout << "Price: " << price << "\n";
        }
};

const int size = 2;

int main()
{
    item *p = new item [size];
    item *d = p;
    int x, i;
    float y;

    for(i=0; i<size; i++)
    {
            cout << "Input code and price for item" << i+1;
            cin >> x >> y;
            p->getdata(x,y);
            p++;
    }

    for(i=0; i<size; i++)
    {
            cout << "Item:" << i+1 << "\n";
            d->show();
            d++;
    }

    return 0;
}
```

PROGRAM 9.1

The output of Program 9.1 will be:

```
Input code and price for item1 40 500
Input code and price for item2 50 600
```

```
Item:1
Code : 40
Price: 500
Item:2
Code : 50
Price: 600
```

In Program 9.1 we created space dynamically for two objects of equal size. But this may not be the case always. For example, the objects of a class that contain character strings would not be of the same size. In such cases, we can define an array of pointers to objects that can be used to access the individual objects. This is illustrated in Program 9.2.

```
                 ARRAY OF POINTERS TO OBJECTS

    #include <iostream>
    #include <cstring>

    using namespace std;

    class city
    {
       protected:
         char *name;
         int len;
       public:
         city()

         {
             len = 0;
             name = new char[len+1];
         }
         void getname(void)
         {
             char *s;
             s = new char[30];

             cout << "Enter city name:";
             cin >> s;
             len = strlen(s);
             name = new char[len + 1];
             strcpy(name, s);
         }
         void printname(void)
         {
             cout << name << "\n";
         }
```

(Contd)

```
    };

    int main()
    {
        city *cptr[10];              // array of 10 pointers to cities

        int n = 1;
        int option;

        do
        {
            cptr[n] = new city; // create new city
            cptr[n]->getname();
            n++;
            cout << "Do you want to enter one more name?\n";
            cout << "(Enter 1 for yes 0 for no):";
            cin >> option;
        }
        while(option);

        cout << "\n\n";
        for(int i=1; i<=n; i++)
        {
            cptr[i]->printname();
        }

        return 0;
    }
```

PROGRAM 9.2

The output of Program 9.2 would be:

```
Enter city name:Hyderabad
Do you want to enter one more name?
(Enter 1 for yes 0 for no);1
Enter city name:Secunderabad
Do you want to enter one more name?
(Enter 1 for yes 0 for no);1
Enter city name:Malkajgiri
Do you want to enter one more name?
(Enter 1 for yes 0 for no);0

Hyderabad
Secunderabad
Malkajgiri
```

9.3   this POINTER

C++ uses a unique keyword called **this** to represent an object that invokes a member function. **this** is a pointer that points to the object for which *this* function was called. For example, the function call **A.max()** will set the pointer **this** to the address of the object **A**. The starting address is the same as the address of the first variable in the class structure.

This unique pointer is automatically passed to a member function when it is called. The pointer **this** acts as an *implicit* argument to all the member functions. Consider the following simple example:

```
class ABC
{
        int a;
        .....
        .....
};
```

The private variable 'a' can be used directly inside a member function, like

```
a = 123;
```

We can also use the following statement to do the same job:

```
this->a = 123;
```

Since C++ permits the use of shorthand form **a = 123**, we have not been using the pointer **this** explicitly so far. However, we have been implicitly using the pointer **this** when overloading the operators using member function.

Recall that, when a binary operator is overloaded using a member function, we pass only one argument to the function. The other argument is implicitly passed using the pointer **this**. One important application of the pointer **this** is to return the object it points to. For example, the statement

```
return *this;
```

inside a member function will return the object that invoked the function. This statement assumes importance when we want to compare two or more objects inside a member function and return the *invoking object* as a result. Example:

```
person & person :: greater(person & x)
{
        if x.age > age
            return x;                    // argument object
        else
```

```
        return *this;              // invoking object
}
```

Suppose we invoke this function by the call

```
max = A.greater(B);
```

The function will return the object **B** (argument object) if the age of the person **B** is greater than that of **A**, otherwise, it will return the object **A** (invoking object) using the pointer **this**. Remember, the dereference operator * produces the contents at the address contained in the pointer. A complete program to illustrate the use of **this** is given in Program 9.3.

```
                        this POINTER

    #include <iostream>
    #include <cstring>

    using namespace std;

    class person
    {
        char name[20];
        float age;
      public:
        person(char *s, float a)
        {
            strcpy(name, s);
            age = a;
        }
        person & person :: greater(person & x)

        {
            if(x.age >= age)
                return x;
            else
                return *this;
        }

        void display(void)
        {
            cout << "Name: " << name << "\n"
                 << "Age:  " << age << "\n";
        }
    };

    int main()
```

(Contd)

```
{
         person P1("John", 37.50),
                P2("Ahmed", 29.0),
                P3("Hebber", 40.25);

         person P = P1.greater(P3);        // P3.greater(P1)
         cout << "Elder person is: \n";
         P.display();

         P = P1.greater(P2);               // P2.greater(P1)
         cout << "Elder person is: \n";
         P.display();

         return 0;
}
```

PROGRAM 9.3

The output of Program 9.3 would be:

```
Elder person is:
Name: Hebber
Age:  40.25
Elder person is:
Name: John
Age:  37.5
```

9.4 POINTERS TO DERIVED CLASSES

We can use pointers not only to the base objects but also to the objects of derived classes. Pointers to objects of a base class are type-compatible with pointers to objects of a derived class. Therefore, a single pointer variable can be made to point to objects belonging to different classes. For example, if **B** is a base class and **D** is a derived class from **B**, then a pointer declared as a pointer to **B** can also be a pointer to **D**. Consider the following declarations:

```
B *cptr;        // pointer to class B type variable
B  b;           // base object
D  d;           // derived object
cptr = &b;      // cptr points to object b
```

We can make **cptr** to point to the object **d** as follows:

```
cptr = &d;      // cptr points to object d
```

This is perfectly valid with C++ because **d** is an object derived from the class **B**.

However, there is a problem in using **cptr** to access the public members of the derived class **D**. Using **cptr**, we can access only those members which are inherited from **B** and not the members that originally belong to **D**. In case a member of **D** has the same name as one of the members of **B**, then any reference to that member by **cptr** will always access the base class member.

Although C++ permits a base pointer to point to any object derived from that base, the pointer cannot be directly used to access all the members of the derived class. We may have to use another pointer *declared* as pointer to the derived type.

Program 9.4 illustrates how pointers to a derived object are used.

```
                    POINTERS TO DERIVED OBJECTS

    #include <iostream>

    using namespace std;

    class BC
    {
      public:
        int b;
        void show()
        { cout << "b = " << b << "\n";}
    };

        class DC : public BC

    {
      public:
        int d;
        void show()
        { cout << "b = " << b << "\n"
               << "d = " << d << "\n";
        }
    };

    int main()
    {
        BC *bptr;                   // base pointer
        BC base;
        bptr = &base;               // base address

        bptr->b = 100;              // access BC via base pointer
        cout << "bptr points to base object \n";
        bptr -> show();
```

(Contd)

```
      // derived class
      DC derived;
      bptr = &derived;          // address of derived object
      bptr -> b = 200;          // access DC via base pointer

      /* bptr -> d = 300;*/     // won't work
      cout << "bptr now points to derived object \n";
      bptr -> show();           // bptr now points to derived object

      /* accessing d using a pointer of type derived class DC */

      DC *dptr;                 // derived type pointer
      dptr = &derived;
      dptr->d = 300;

      cout << "dptr is derived type pointer\n";
      dptr -> show();

      cout << "using ((DC *)bptr)\n";
      ((DC *)bptr) -> d = 400;
      ((DC *)bptr) -> show();

      return 0;
}
```

PROGRAM 9.4

Program 9.4 produces the following output:

```
bptr points base object
b = 100
bptr now points to derived object
b = 200
dptr is derived type pointer
b = 200
d = 300
using ((DC ?)bptr)
b = 200
d = 400
```

We have used the statement

```
bptr -> show();
```

two times. First, when **bptr** points to the base object, and second when **bptr** is made to point to the derived object. But, both the times, it executed **BC::show()** function and displayed the content of the base object. However, the statements

```
dptr -> show();
((DC *) bptr) -> show(); // cast bptr to DC type
```

display the contents of the **derived** object. This shows that, although a base pointer can be made to point to any number of derived objects, it cannot directly access the members defined by a derived class.

9.5   VIRTUAL FUNCTIONS

As mentioned earlier, polymorphism refers to the property by which objects belonging to different classes are able to respond to the same message, but in different forms. An essential requirement of polymorphism is therefore the ability to refer to objects without any regard to their classes. This necessitates the use of a single pointer variable to refer to the objects of different classes. Here, we use the pointer to base class to refer to all the derived objects. But, we just discovered that a base pointer, even when it is made to contain the address of a derived class, always executes the function in the base class. The compiler simply ignores the contents of the pointer and chooses the member function that matches the type of the pointer. How do we then achieve polymorphism?. It is achieved using what is known as 'virtual' functions.

When we use the same function name in both the base and derived classes, the function in base class is declared as *virtual* using the keyword **virtual** preceding its normal declaration. When a function is made **virtual, C++** determines which function to use at run time based on the type of object pointed to by the base pointer, rather than the type of the pointer. Thus, by making the base pointer to point to different objects, we can execute different versions of the **virtual** function. Program 9.5 illustrates this point.

```
                        VIRTUAL FUNCTIONS

    #include <iostream>

    using namespace std;

    class Base
    {
      public:
        void display() {cout << "\n Display base ";}
        virtual void show() {cout << "\n show base";}
    };
    class Derived : public Base
    {
      public:
        void display() {cout << "\n Display derived";}
```

(Contd)

```
            void show() {cout << "\n show derived";}
};

int main()
{
    Base B;
    Derived D;
    Base *bptr;

    cout << "\n bptr points to Base \n";
    bptr = &B;
    bptr -> display();    // calls Base version
    bptr -> show();       // calls Base version

    cout << "\n\n bptr points to Derived\n";
    bptr = &D;
    bptr -> display();    // calls Base version
    bptr -> show();       // calls Derived version

    return 0;
}
```

PROGRAM 9.5

The output of Program 9.5 would be:

```
bptr points to Base

Display base
Show base

bptr points to Derived

Display base
Show derived
```

When **bptr** is made to point to the object **D**, the statement

        bptr -> display();

calls only the function associated with the **Base** (i.e. **Base :: display**( )), whereas the statement

        bptr -> show();

calls the **Derived** version of **show()**. This is because the function **display()** has not been made **virtual** in the **Base** class.

One important point to remember is that, we must access **virtual** functions through the use of a pointer declared as a pointer to the base class. Why can't we use the object name (with the dot operator) the same way as any other member function to call the virtual functions?. We can, but remember, run time polymorphism is achieved only when a virtual function is accessed through a pointer to the base class.

Let us take an example where **virtual** functions are implemented in practice. Consider a book shop which sells both books and video-tapes. We can create a class known as **media** that stores the title and price of a publication. We can then create two derived classes, one for storing the number of pages in a book and another for storing the playing time of a tape. Figure 9.2 shows the class hierarchy for the book shop.

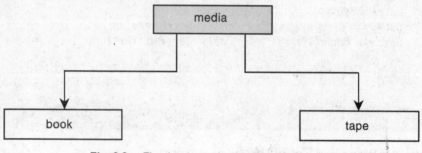

Fig. 9.2 *The class hierarchy for the book shop*

The classes are implemented in Program 9.6. A function **display()** is used in all the classes to display the class contents. Notice that the function **display()** has been declared virtual in media, the base class.

In the **main** program we create a heterogeneous list of pointers of type **media** as shown below:

```
media *list[2]; = { &book1; [1], &tape1};
```

The base pointers **list[0]** and **list[1]** are initialized with the addresses of objects **book1** and **tape1** respectively.

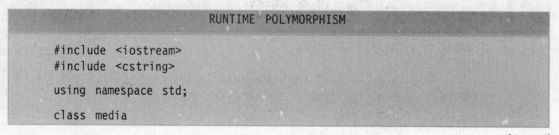

```
                    RUNTIME POLYMORPHISM

    #include <iostream>
    #include <cstring>

    using namespace std;

    class media
```

(Contd)

```
{
  protected:
      char  title[50];
      float price;
  public:
      media(char *s, float a)
      {
          strcpy(title, s);
          price = a;
      }
      virtual void display() { }      // empty virtual function
};

class book: public media
{
      int pages;
  public:
      book(char *s, float a, int p):media(s,a)
      {
          pages = p;
      }
      void display();
};

class tape :public media
{
      float time;
  public:
      tape(char * s, float a, float t):media(s, a)
      {
          time = t;
      }
      void display();
};

void book :: display()
{
      cout << "\n Title: " << title;
      cout << "\n Pages: " << pages;
      cout << "\n Price: " << price;
}
void tape :: display()
{
      cout << "\n Title: " << title;
      cout << "\n play time: " << time << "mins";
      cout << "\n price: " << price;
```

(Contd)

```
        }

    int main()
    {
            char * title = new char[30];
            float price, time;
            int pages;

            // Book details
            cout << "\n ENTER BOOK DETAILS\n";
            cout << " Title:"; cin >> title;
            cout << " Price: "; cin >> price;
            cout << " Pages: "; cin >> pages;

            book book1(title, price, pages);

            // Tape details
            cout << "\n ENTER TAPE DETAILS\n";
            cout << " Title: "; cin >> title;
            cout << " Price: "; cin >> price;
            cout << " Play time (mins): "; cin >> time;

            tape tape1(title, price, time);

            media* list[2];
            list[0] = &book1;
            list[1] = &tape1;

            cout << "\n MEDIA DETAILS";

            cout << "\n ......BOOK......";
            list[0] -> display();        // display book details

            cout << "\n ......TAPE......";
            list[1] -> display();        // display tape details

            result 0;
    }
```

PROGRAM 9.6

The output of Program 9.6 would be:

```
ENTER BOOK DETAILS
Title:Programming_in_ANSI_C
Price: 88
```

```
Pages: 400

ENTER TAPE DETAILS
Title: Computing_Concepts
Price: 90
Play time (mins): 55

MEDIA DETAILS
......BOOK......
Title:Programming_in_ANSI_C
Pages: 400
Price: 88

.....TAPE......
Title: Computing_Concepts
Play time: 55mins
Price: 90
```

Rules for Virtual Functions

When virtual functions are created for implementing late binding, we should observe some basic rules that satisfy the compiler requirements:

1. The virtual functions must be members of some class.
2. They cannot be static members.
3. They are accessed by using object pointers.
4. A virtual function can be a friend of another class.
5. A virtual function in a base class must be defined, even though it may not be used.
6. The prototypes of the base class version of a virtual function and all the derived class versions must be identical. If two functions with the same name have different prototypes, C++ considers them as overloaded functions, and the virtual function mechanism is ignored.
7. We cannot have virtual constructors, but we can have virtual destructors.
8. While a base pointer can point to any type of the derived object, the reverse is not true. That is to say, we cannot use a pointer to a derived class to access an object of the base type.
9. When a base pointer points to a derived class, incrementing or decrementing it will not make it to point to the next object of the derived class. It is incremented or decremented only relative to its base type. Therefore, we should not use this method to move the pointer to the next object.
10. If a virtual function is defined in the base class, it need not be necessarily redefined in the derived class. In such cases, calls will invoke the base function.

9.6   PURE VIRTUAL FUNCTIONS

It is normal practice to declare a function virtual inside the base class and redefine it in the derived classes. The function inside the base class is seldom used for performing any task. It only serves as a *placeholder*. For example, we have not defined any object of class media and therefore the function display() in the base class has been defined 'empty'. Such functions are called "do-nothing" functions.

A "do-nothing" function may be defined as follows:

```
virtual void display() = 0;
```

Such functions are called *pure virtual* functions. A pure virtual function is a function declared in a base class that has no definition relative to the base class. In such cases, the compiler requires each derived class to either define the function or redeclare it as a pure virtual function. Remember that a class containing pure virtual functions cannot be used to declare any objects of its own. As stated earlier, such classes are called *abstract base classes*. The main objective of an abstract base class is to provide some traits to the derived classes and to create a base pointer required for achieving run time polymorphism.

Summary

- Polymorphism simply means one name having multiple forms.
- There are two types of polymorphism, namely, compile time polymorphism and run time polymorphism.
- Functions and operators overloading are examples of compile time polymorphism. The overloaded member functions are selected for invoking by matching arguments, both type and number. The compiler knows this information at the compile time and, therefore, compiler is able to select the appropriate function for a particular call at the compile time itself. This is called early or static binding or static linking. It means that an object is bound to its function call at compile time.
- In run time polymorphism, an appropriate member function is selected while the program is running. C++ supports run time polymorphism with the help of virtual functions. It is called late or dynamic binding because the appropriate function is selected dynamically at run time. Dynamic binding requires use of pointers to objects and is one of the powerful features of C++.
- Object pointers are useful in creating objects at run time. It can be used to access the public members of an object, along with an arrow operator.
- A **this** pointer refers to an object that currently invokes a member function. For example, the function call **a.show()** will set the pointer 'this' to the address of the object 'a'.
- Pointers to objects of a base class type are compatible with pointers to objects of a derived class. Therefore, we can use a single pointer variable to point to objects of base class as well as derived classes.
- When a function is made virtual, C++ determines which function to use at run time based on the type of object pointed to by the base pointer, rather than the type of the pointer. By making the base pointer to point to different objects, we can execute different versions of the virtual function.
- Run time polymorphism is achieved only when a virtual function is accessed

through a pointer to the base class. It cannot be achieved using object name along with the dot operator to access virtual function.

- We can have virtual destructors but not virtual constructors.
- If a virtual function is defined in the base class, it need not be necessarily redefined in the derived class. In such cases, the respective calls will invoke the base class function.
- A virtual function, equated to zero is called a pure virtual function. It is a function declared in a base class that has no definition relative to the base class. A class containing such pure function is called an abstract class.

Key Terms

➤ Abstract base classes	➤ invoking object
➤ argument object	➤ late binding
➤ arrow operator	➤ **new** operator
➤ base address	➤ object pointer
➤ base object	➤ operator overloading
➤ base pointer	➤ placeholder
➤ class hierarchy	➤ pointers
➤ compile time	➤ polymorphism
➤ compile time polymorphism	➤ pure virtual function
➤ Derived object	➤ run time
➤ do-nothing function	➤ run time polymorphism
➤ dot operator	➤ static binding
➤ dynamic binding	➤ static linking
➤ early binding	➤ **this** pointer
➤ function overloading	➤ virtual constructors
➤ Implicit argument	➤ virtual destructors
➤ indirection operator	➤ virtual function

Review Questions and Exercises

9.1 *What does polymorphism mean in C++ language?*

9.2 *How is polymorphism achieved at (a) compile time, and (b) run time?*

9.3 *Discuss the different ways by which we can access public member functions of an object.*

9.4 *Explain, with an example, how you would create space for an array of objects using pointers.*

9.5 *What does **this** pointer point to?*

9.6 *What are the applications of **this** pointer?*

9.7 *What is a virtual function?*

9.8 *Why do we need virtual functions?*

9.9 *When do we make a virtual function "pure"? What are the implications of making a function a pure virtual function?*

9.10   *State which of the following statements are TRUE or FALSE.*
   (a) Virtual functions are used to create pointers to base classes.
   (b) Virtual functions allow us to use the same function call to invoke member functions of objects of different classes.
   (c) A pointer to a base class cannot be made to point to objects of derived class.
   *(d) **this** pointer points to the object that is currently used to invoke a function.*
   *(e) **this** pointer can be used like any other pointer to access the members of the object it points to.*
   *(f) **this** pointer can be made to point to any object by assigning the address of the object.*
   (g) Pure virtual functions force the programmer to redefine the virtual function inside the derived classes.

9.11   *Correct the errors in the following program.*

```
class test
{
    private:
        int m;
    public:
        void getdata()
        {
            cout <<"Enter number:";
            cin >> m;
        }
        void display()
        {
            cout << m;
        }
};

main()
{
        test T;
        T->getdata();
        T->display();

        test *p;
        p = new test;
        p.getdata();
        (*p).display();
}
```

9.12   *Debug and run the following program. What will be the output?*

```
#include <iostream.h>
class A
{
```

```
        protected:
            int a,b;
        public:
            A(int x = 0, int y)
            {
                a = x;
                b = y;
            }
            virtual void print();
    };
    class B: public A
    {
        private:
            float p,q;
        public:
            B(int m, int n, float u, float v)
            {
                p = u;
                q = v;
            }
            B() {p = q = 0;}
            void input(float u, float v);
            virtual void print(float);
    };
    void A::print(void)
    {
        cout << A values: << a <<""<< b <<"\n";
    }
    void B::print(float)
    {
        cout <<B values:<< u <<""<< v <<"\n";
    }
    void B::input(float x, float y)
    {
        p = x;
        q = y;
    }
    main()
    {
        A a1(10,20), *ptr;
        B b1;
        b1.input(7.5,3.142);

        ptr = &a1;
        ptr->print();

        ptr = &b1;
        ptr->print();
```

9.13 *Create a base class called **shape**. Use this class to store two **double** type values that could be used to compute the area of figures. Derive two specific classes called **triangle** and **rectangle** from the base **shape**. Add to the base class, a member function **get_data()** to initialize base class data members and another member function **display_area()** to compute and display the area of figures. Make **display_area()** as a virtual function and redefine this function in the derived classes to suit their requirements.*

Using these three classes, design a program that will accept dimensions of a triangle or a rectangle interactively, and display the area.

Remember the two values given as input will be treated as lengths of two sides in the case of rectangles, and as base and height in the case of triangles, and used as follows:

```
Area of rectangle = x * y
Area of triangle = 1/2 * x * y
```

9.14 *Extend the above program to display the area of circles. This requires addition of a new derived class 'circle' that computes the area of a circle. Remember, for a circle we need only one value, its radius, but the get_data() function in the base class requires two values to be passed. (Hint: Make the second argument of get_data() function as a default one with zero value.)*

9.15 *Run the above program with the following modifications:*

(a) *Remove the definition of **display_area()** from one of the derived classes.*

(b) *In addition to the above change, declare the **display_area()** as **virtual** in the base class **shape**.*

Comment on the output in each case.

10

Managing Console I/O Operations

10.1 INTRODUCTION

Every program takes some data as input and generates processed data as output following the familiar input-process-output cycle. It is, therefore, essential to know how to provide the input data and how to present the results in a desired form. We have, in the earlier chapters, used **cin** and **cout** with the operators >> and << for the input and output operations. But we have not so far discussed as to how to control the way the output is printed. C++ supports a rich set of I/O functions and operations to do this. Since these functions use the advanced features of C++ (such as classes, derived classes and virtual functions), we need to know a lot about them before really implementing the C++ I/O operations.

Remember, C++ supports all of C's rich set of I/O functions. We can use any of them in the C++ programs. But we restrained from using them due to two reasons. First, I/O methods in C++ support the concepts of OOP and secondly, I/O methods in C cannot handle the user-defined data types such as class objects.

C++ uses the concept of *stream* and *stream classes* to implement its I/O operations with the console and disk files. We will discuss in this chapter, how stream classes support the console- oriented input-output operations. File-oriented I/O operations will be discussed in the next chapter.

10.2   C++ STREAMS

The I/O system in C++ is designed to work with a wide variety of devices including terminals, disks, and tape drives. Although each device is very different, the I/O system supplies an interface to the programmer that is independent of the actual device being accessed. This interface is known as *stream*.

A stream is a sequence of bytes. It acts either as a *source* from which the input data can be obtained or as a *destination* to which the output data can be sent. The source stream that provides data to the program is called the *input stream* and the destination stream that receives output from the program is called the *output stream*. In other words, a program *extracts* the bytes from an input stream and *inserts* bytes into an output stream as illustrated in Fig. 10.1.

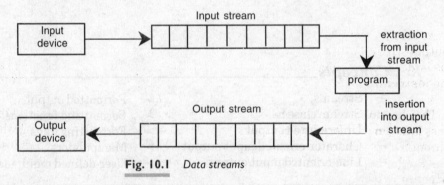

Fig. 10.1   *Data streams*

The data in the input stream can come from the keyboard or any other storage device. Similarly, the data in the output stream can go to the screen or any other storage device. As mentioned earlier, a stream acts as an interface between the program and the input/output device. Therefore, a C++ program handles data (input or output) independent of the devices used.

C++ contains several pre-defined streams that are automatically opened when a program begins its execution. These include cin and cout which have been used very often in our earlier programs. We know that cin represents the input stream connected to the standard input device (usually the keyboard) and cout represents the output stream connected to the standard output device (usually the screen). Note that the keyboard and the screen are default options. We can redirect streams to other devices or files, if necessary.

10.3   C++ STREAM CLASSES

The C++ I/O system contains a hierarchy of classes that are used to define various streams to deal with both the console and disk files. These classes are called *stream classes*. Figure 10.2 shows the hierarchy of the stream classes used for input and output operations with the console unit.

These classes are declared in the header file *iostream*. This file should be included in all the programs that communicate with the console unit.

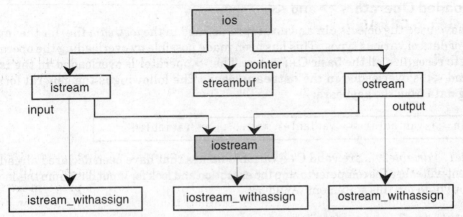

Fig. 10.2   *Stream classes for console I/O operations*

As seen in the Fig. 10.2, **ios** is the base class for **istream** (input stream) and **ostream** (output stream) which are, in turn, base classes for **iostream** (input/output stream). The class **ios** is declared as the virtual base class so that only one copy of its members are inherited by the **iostream**.

The class **ios** provides the basic support for formatted and unformatted I/O operations. The class **istream** provides the facilities for formatted and unformatted input while the class **ostream** (through inheritance) provides the facilities for formatted output. The class **iostream** provides the facilities for handling both input and output streams. Three classes, namely, **istream_withassign, ostream_withassign**, and **iostream_withassign** add assignment operators to these classes. Table 10.1 gives the details of these classes.

Table 10.1   Stream classes for console operations

Class name	Contents
ios (General input/output stream class)	• Contains basic facilities that are used by all other input and output classes • Also contains a pointer to a buffer object (**streambuf** object) • Declares constants and functions that are necessary for handling formatted input and output operations
istream (input stream)	• Inherits the properties of **ios** • Declares input functions such as **get()**, **getline()** and **read()** • Contains overloaded extraction operator >>
ostream (output stream)	• Inherits the properties of ios • Declares output functions **put()** and **write()** • Contains overloaded insertion operator <<
iostream (input/output stream)	• Inherits the properties of **ios istream** and **ostream** through multiple inheritance and thus contains all the input and output functions
streambuf	• Provides an interface to physical devices through buffers • Acts as a base for **filebuf** class used ios files

10.4 UNFORMATTED I/O OPERATIONS

Overloaded Operators >> and <<

We have used the objects **cin** and **cout** (pre-defined in the *iostream* file) for the input and output of data of various types. This has been made possible by overloading the operators >> and << to recognize all the basic C++ types. The >> operator is overloaded in the **istream** class and << is overloaded in the **ostream** class. The following is the general format for reading data from the keyboard:

```
cin >> variable1 >> variable2 >> .... >> variableN
```

variable1, variable2, ... are valid C++ variable names that have been declared already. This statement will cause the computer to stop the execution and look for input data from the keyboard. The input data for this statement would be:

```
data1 data2 ...... dataN
```

The input data are separated by white spaces and should match the type of variable in the **cin** list. Spaces, newlines and tabs will be skipped.

The operator >> reads the data character by character and assigns it to the indicated location. The reading for a variable will be terminated at the encounter of a white space or a character that does not match the destination type. For example, consider the following code:

```
int code;
cin >> code;
```

Suppose the following data is given as input:

```
4258D
```

The operator will read the characters upto 8 and the value 4258 is assigned to **code.** The character D remains in the input stream and will be input to the next **cin** statement. The general form for displaying data on the screen is:

```
cout << item1 << item2 << .... << itemN
```

The items *item1* through *itemN* may be variables or constants of any basic type. We have used such statements in a number of examples illustrated in previous chapters.

put() and get() Functions

The classes **istream** and **ostream** define two member functions **get()** and **put()** respectively to handle the single character input/output operations. There are two types of **get()** functions. We can use both **get(char *)** and **get(void)** prototypes to fetch a character including the blank space, tab and the newline character. The **get(char *)** version assigns the input character to its argument and the **get(void)** version returns the input character.

Since these functions are members of the input/output stream classes, we must invoke them using an appropriate object.

Example:

```
char c;
cin.get(c);              // get a character from keyboard
                         // and assign it to c

while(c != '\n')
{
        cout << c;       // display the character on screen
        cin.get(c);      // get another character
}
```

This code reads and displays a line of text (terminated by a newline character). Remember, the operator >> can also be used to read a character but it will skip the white spaces and newline character. The above **while** loop will not work properly if the statement

```
cin >> c;
```

is used in place of

```
cin.get(c);
```

  Try using both of them and compare the results.

The **get(void)** version is used as follows:

```
.....
char c;
c = cin.get(); // cin.get(c); replaced
.....
.....
```

The value returned by the function **get**() is assigned to the variable **c**.

The function **put**(), a member of **ostream** class, can be used to output a line of text, character by character. For example,

```
cout.put('x');
```

displays the character **x** and

```
cout.put(ch);
```

displays the value of variable **ch.**

The variable **ch** must contain a character value. We can also use a number as an argument to the function **put**(). For example,

```
cout.put(68);
```

displays the character D. This statement will convert the **int** value 68 to a **char** value and display the character whose ASCII value is 68.

The following segment of a program reads a line of text from the keyboard and displays it on the screen.

```
char c;
cin.get(c);              // read a character

while(c != '\n')
{
        cout.put(c);     // display the character on screen
        cin.get(c);
}
```

Program 10.1 illustrates the use of these two character handling functions.

```
               CHARACTER I/O   WITH get() AND put()

#include <iostream>

using namespace std;

int main()
{
   int count = 0;
   char c;

   cout << "INPUT TEXT\n";

   cin.get(c);

   while(c != '\n')
   {
        cout.put(c);
        count++;
        cin.get(c);
   }
   cout << "\nNumber of characters = " << count << "\n";

   return 0;
}

                        PROGRAM 10.1
```

```
Input
      Object Oriented Programming
Output
      Object Oriented Programming
      Number of characters = 27
```

When we type a line of input, the text is sent to the program as soon as we press the RETURN key. The program then reads one character at a time using the statement **cin.get(c);** and displays it using the statement **cout.put(c);.** The process is terminated when the newline character is encountered.

getline() and write() Functions

We can read and display a line of text more efficiently using the line-oriented input/output functions **getline**() and **write**(). The **getline**() function reads a whole line of text that ends with a newline character (transmitted by the RETURN key). This function can be invoked by using the object **cin** as follows:

```
cin.getline (line, size);
```

This function call invokes the function **getline**() which reads character input into the variable line. The reading is terminated as soon as either the newline character '\n' is encountered or size-1 characters are read (whichever occurs first). The newline character is read but not saved. Instead, it is replaced by the null character. For example, consider the following code:

```
char   name[20];
cin.getline(name, 20);
```

Assume that we have given the following input through the keyboard:

```
Bjarne Stroustrup <press RETURN>
```

This input will be read correctly and assigned to the character array **name**. Let us suppose the input is as follows:

```
Object Oriented Programming   <press RETURN>
```

In this case, the input will be terminated after reading the following 19 characters:

```
Object Oriented Pro
```

Remember, the two blank spaces contained in the string are also taken into account.

We can also read strings using the operator >> as follows:

```
cin >> name;
```

But remember **cin** can read strings that do not contain white spaces. This means that **cin** can read just one word and not a series of words such as "Bjarne Stroustrup". But it can read the following string correctly:

    Bjarne_Stroustrup

After reading the string, **cin** automatically adds the terminating null character to the character array.

Program 10.2 demonstrates the use of >> and **getline**() for reading the strings.

```
                    READING STRINGS WITH getline()

#include <iostream>

using namespace std;

int main()
{
    int size = 20;
    char city[20];

    cout << "Enter city name: \n";
    cin  >> city;
    cout << "City name:" << city << "\n\n";

    cout << "Enter city name again: \n";
    cin.getline(city, size);
    cout << "City name now: " << city << "\n\n";

    cout << "Enter another city name: \n";
    cin.getline(city, size);
    cout << "New city name: " << city << "\n\n";

    return 0;
}
                          PROGRAM 10.2
```

The output of Program 10.2 would be:

    First run
            Enter city name:
            Delhi
            City name: Delhi

            Enter city name again:
            City name now:

```
        Enter another city name:
        Chennai
        New city name: Chennai
```

Second run
```
        Enter city name:
        New Delhi
        City name: New

        Enter city name again:
        City name now: Delhi

        Enter another city name:
        Greater Bombay
        New city name: Greater Bombay
```

During first run, the newline character '\n' at the end of "Delhi" which is waiting in the input queue is read by the **getline()** that follows immediately and therefore it does not wait for any response to the prompt 'Enter city name again:'. The character '\n' is read as an empty line. During the second run, the word "Delhi" (that was not read by cin) is read by the function **getline()** and, therefore, here again it does not wait for any input to the prompt 'Enter city name again:'. Note that the line of text "Greater Bombay" is correctly read by the second **cin.getline(city,size);** statement.

The **write()** function displays an entire line and has the following form:

```
cout.write (line, size)
```

The first argument line represents the name of the string to be displayed and the second argument size indicates the number of characters to display. Note that it does not stop displaying the characters automatically when the null character is encountered. If the size is greater than the length of line, then it displays beyond the bounds of line. Program 10.3 illustrates how **write**() method displays a string.

```
                DISPLAYING STRINGS WITH write()

#include <iostream>
#include <string>

using namespace std;

int main()
{
    char * string1 = "C++ ";
    char * string2 = "Programming";
    int m = strlen(string1);
    int n = strlen(string2);
```

```
        for(int i=1; i<n; i++)
        {
            cout.write(string2,i);
            cout << "\n";
        }

        for(i=n; i>0; i-)
        {
            cout.write(string2,i);
            cout << "\n";
        }

        // concatenating strings
        cout.write(string1,m).write(string2,n);

        cout << "\n";

        // crossing the boundary
        cout.write(string1,10);

        return 0;
}
```

PROGRAM 10.3

Look at the output of Program 10.3:

```
P
Pr
Pro
Prog
Progr
Progra
Program
Programm
Programmi
Programmin
Programming
Programmin
Programmi
Programm
Program
Progra
Progr
Prog
Pro
Pr
P
C++ Programming
C++ Progr
```

The last line of the output indicates that the statement

```
cout.write(string1, 10);
```

displays more characters than what is contained in **string1.**

It is possible to concatenate two strings using the **write**() function. The statement

```
cout.write(string1, m).write(string2, n);
```

is equivalent to the following two statements:

```
cout.write(string1, m);
cout.write(string2, n);
```

10.5   FORMATTED CONSOLE I/O OPERATIONS

C++ supports a number of features that could be used for formatting the output. These features include:

- **ios** class functions and flags.
- Manipulators.
- User-defined output functions.

The **ios** class contains a large number of member functions that would help us to format the output in a number of ways. The most important ones among them are listed in Table 10.2.

Table 10.2   ios format functions

Function	Task
Width ()	To specify the required field size for displaying an output value
precision ()	To specify the number of digits to be displayed after the decimal point of a float value
fill()	To specify a character that is used to fill the unused portion of a field
setf()	To specify format flags that can control the form of output display (such as left-justification and right-justification)
unsetf()	To clear the flags specified

Manipulators are special functions that can be included in the I/O statements to alter the format parameters of a stream. Table 10.3 shows some important manipulator functions that are frequently used. To access these manipulators, the file iomanip should be included in the program.

Table 10.3   Manipulators

Manipulators	Equivalent ios function
setw()	width()
setprecision()	precision()
setfill()	fill()
setiosflags()	setf()
resetiosflags()	unsetf()

In addition to these functions supported by the C++ library, we can create our own manipulator functions to provide any special output formats. The following sections will provide details of how to use the pre-defined formatting functions and how to create new ones.

Defining Field Width: width()

We can use the **width()** function to define the width of a field necessary for the output of an item. Since, it is a member function, we have to use an object to invoke it, as shown below:

```
cout.width(w);
```

where w is the field width (number of columns). The output will be printed in a field of w characters wide at the right end of the field. The **width()** function can specify the field width for only one item (the item that follows immediately). After printing one item (as per the specifications) it will revert back to the default. For example, the statements

```
cout.width(5);
cout << 543  << 12 << "\n";
```

will produce the following output:

		5	4	3	1	2

The value 543 is printed right-justified in the first five columns. The specification width(5) does not retain the setting for printing the number 12. This can be improved as follows:

```
cout.width(5);
cout << 543;
cout.width(5);
cout << 12  << "\n";
```

This produces the following output:

		5	4	3				1	2

Remember that the field width should be specified for each item separately. C++ never truncates the values and therefore, if the specified field width is smaller than the size of the value to be printed, C++ expands the field to fit the value. Program 10.4 demonstrates how the function **width()** works.

```
                SPECIFYING FIELD SIZE WITH width()

#include <iostream>

using namespace std;

int main()
{
    int items[4] = {10,8,12,15};
    int cost[4] = {75,100,60,99};

    cout.width(5);
    cout <<  "ITEMS";
    cout.width(8);
    cout << "COST";

    cout.width(15);
    cout << "TOTAL VALUE"  << "\n";

    int sum = 0;

    for(int i=0; i<4; i++)
    {
        cout.width(5);
        cout << items[i];

        cout.width(8);
        cout << cost[i];

        int value = items[i] * cost[i];
        cout.width(15);
        cout << value << "\n";
        sum = sum + value;
    }
    cout << "\n Grand Total = ";

    cout.width(2);
    cout << sum << "\n";

    return 0;
}
                            PROGRAM 10.4
```

The output of Program 10.4 would be:

```
ITEMS        COST TOTAL VALUE

   10          75     750
    8         100     800
```

```
    12            60         720
    15            99         1485


Grand Total = 3755
```

A field of width two has been used for printing the value of sum and the result is not truncated. A good gesture of C++ !

Setting Precision: precision()

By default, the floating numbers are printed with six digits after the decimal point. However, we can specify the number of digits to be displayed after the decimal point while printing the floating-point numbers. This can be done by using the **precision()** member function as follows:

```
cout.precision(d);
```

where d is the number of digits to the right of the decimal point. For example, the statements

```
cout.precision(3);
cout << sqrt(2) << "\n";
cout << 3.14159 << "\n";
cout << 2.50032 << "\n";
```

will produce the following output:

```
1.141    (truncated)
3.142    (rounded to the nearest cent)
2.5      (no trailing zeros)
```

Not that, unlike the function **width()**, **precision()** retains the setting in effect until it is reset. That is why we have declared only one statement for the precision setting which is used by all the three outputs.

We can set different values to different precision as follows:

```
cout.precision(3);
cout << sqrt(2)   << "\n";
cout.precision(5);              // Reset the precision
cout << 3.14159   << "\n";
```

We can also combine the field specification with the precision setting. Example:

```
cout.precision(2);
cout.width(5);
cout << 1.2345;
```

The first two statements instruct: "print two digits after the decimal point in a field of five character width". Thus, the output will be:

	1		2	3

Program 10.5 shows how the functions **width()** and **precision()** are jointly used to control the output format.

```
              PRECISION SETTING WITH precision()

#include <iostream>
#include <cmath>

using namespace std;

int main()
{
        cout << "Precision set to 3 digits \n\n";
        cout.precision(3);

        cout.width(10);
        cout << "VALUE";
        cout.width(15);
        cout << "SQRT_OF_VALUE" << "\n";

        for(int n=1; n<=5; n++)
        {
                cout.width(8);
                cout << n;
                cout.width(13);
                cout << sqrt(n)   << "\n";
        }

        cout << "\n Precision set to 5 digits \n\n";
        cout.precision(5);              // precision parameter changed
        cout << " sqrt(10) = " << sqrt(10) << "\n\n";

        cout.precision(0);              // precision set to default
        cout << " sqrt(10) = " << sqrt(10) << " (default setting)\n";

        return 0;
}
```

PROGRAM 10.5

Here is the output of Program 10.5

```
Precision set to 3 digits
        VALUE    SQRT_OF_VALUE
          1            1
          2          1.41
          3          1.73
          4            2
          5          2.24

Precision set to 5 digits

sqrt(10) = 3.1623

sqrt(10) = 3.162278 (default setting)
```

Observe the following from the output:
1. The output is rounded to the nearest cent (i.e., 1.6666 will be 1.67 for two digit precision but 3333 will be 1.33).
2. Trailing zeros are truncated.
3. Precision setting stays in effect until it is reset.
4. Default precision is 6 digits.

Filling and Padding: fill()

We have been printing the values using much larger field widths than required by the values. The unused positions of the field are filled with white spaces, by default. However, we can use the fill() function to fill the unused positions by any desired character. It is used in the following form:

```
cout.fill (ch);
```

Where *ch* represents the character which is used for filling the unused positions. Example:

```
cout.fill('*');
cout.width(10);
cout << 5250  << "\n";
```

The output would be:

*	*	*	*	*	*	5	2	5	0

Financial institutions and banks use this kind of padding while printing cheques so that no one can change the amount easily. Like **precision()**, **fill()** stays in effect till we change it. See Program 10.6 and its output.

```
                    PADDING WITH fill()

#include <iostream>

using namespace std;

int main( )
{     cout.fill('<');

      cout.precision(3);
      for(int n=1; n<=6; n++)
      {
           cout.width(5);
           cout << n;
           cout.width(10);
           cout << 1.0 / float(n) << "\n";
           if (n == 3)
               cout.fill ('>');
      }
      cout << "\nPadding changed \n\n";
      cout.fill ('#');      // fill( ) reset
      cout.width (15);
      cout << 12.345678    << "\n";

      return 0;
}
```

                    PROGRAM 10.6

The output of Program 10.6 would be:

```
<<<<1<<<<<<<<<1
<<<<2<<<<<<<0.5
<<<<3<<<<<0.333
>>>>4>>>>>>0.25
>>>>5>>>>>>>0.2
>>>>6>>>>>0.167

Padding changed

###########12.3
```

Formatting Flags, Bit-fields and setf()

We have seen that when the function **width()** is used, the value (whether text or number) is printed right-justified in the field width created. But, it is a usual practice to print the text left-justified. How do we get a value printed left-justified? Or, how do we get a floating-point number printed in the scientific notation?

The **setf()**, a member function of the **ios** class, can provide answers to these and many other formatting questions. The **setf()** (*setf* stands for set flags) function can be used as follows:

```
cout.setf(arg1,arg2)
```

The *arg1* is one of the formatting *flags* defined in the class **ios**. The formatting flag specifies the format action required for the output. Another **ios** constant, *arg2*, known as bit *field* specifies the group to which the formatting flag belongs.

Table 10.4 shows the bit fields, flags and their format actions. There are three bit fields and each has a group of format flags which are mutually exclusive Examples:

```
cout.setf(ios::left, ios::adjustfied);
cout.setf(ios::scientific, ios::floatfield);
```

Note that the first argument should be one of the group members of the second argument.

Table 10.4   Flags and bit fields for setf() function

Format required	Flag (arg1)	Bit-field (arg2)
Left-justified output	ios :: left	ios :: adjustfield
Right-justified output	ios :: right	ios :: adjustfield
Padding after sign or base Indicator (like +##20)	ios :: internal	ios :: adjustfield
Scientific notation	ios :: scientific	ios :: floatfield
Fixed point notation	ios :: fixed	ios :: floatfield
Decimal base	ios :: doc	ios :: basefield
Octal base	ios :: oct	ios :: basefield
Hexadecimal base	ios :: hex	ios :: basefield

Consider the following segment of code:

```
cout.fill('*');
cout.setf(ios::left, ios::adjustfield);
cout.width(15);
cout << "TABLE 1" <<  "\n";
```

This will produce the following output:

T	A	B	L	E		1	*	*	*	*	*	*	*	*

The statements

```
cout.fill ('*');
cout.precision(3);
cout.setf(ios::internal, ios::adjustfield);
cout.setf(ios::scientific, ios::floatfield);
cout.width(15);

cout << -12.34567  << "\n";
```

will produce the following output:

-	*	*	*	*	*	1	.	2	3	5	e	+	0	1

The sign is left-justified and the value is right left- justified. The space between them is padded with stars. The value is printed accurate to three decimal places in the scientific notation.

Displaying Trailing Zeros and Plus Sign

If we print the numbers 10.75, 25.00 and 15.50 using a field width of, say, eight positions, with two digits precision, then the output will be as follows:

				1	0	.	7	5
							2	5
				1	5	.	5

Note that the trailing zeros in the second and third items have been truncated.

Certain situations, such as a list of prices of items or the salary statement of employees, require trailing zeros to be shown. The above output would look better if they are printed as follows:

```
10.75
25.00
15.50
```

The **setf()** can be used with the flag **ios::showpoint** as a single argument to achieve this form of output. For example,

```
cout.setf(ios::showpoint);      // display trailing zeros
```

would cause cout to display trailing zeros and trailing decimal point. Under default precision, the value 3.25 will be displayed as 3.250000. Remember, the default precision assumes a precision of six digits.

Similarly, a plus sign can be printed before a positive number using the following statement:

```
cout.setf(ios::showpos);        // show +sign
```

For example, the statements

```
cout.setf(ios::showpoint);
cout.setf(ios::showpos);
cout.precision(3);
cout.setf(ios::fixed, ios::floatfield);
cout.setf(ios::internal, ios::adjustfield);
cout.width(10);
cout << 275.5 << "\n";
```

will produce the following output:

+			2	7	5	.	5	0	0

The flags such as **showpoint** and **showpos** do not have any bit fields and therefore are used as single arguments in **setf()**. This is possible because the **setf()** has been declared as an overloaded function in the class **ios**. Table 10.5 lists the flags that do not possess a named bit field. These flags are not mutually exclusive and therefore can be set or cleared independently.

Table 10.5 Flags that do not have bit fields

Flag	Meaning
ios :: showbase	Use base indicator on output
ios :: showpos	Print + before positive numbers
ios :: showpoint	Show trailing decimal point and zeroes
ios :: uppercase	Use uppercase letters for hex output
ios :: skipus	Skip white space on input
ios :: unitbuf	Flush all streams after insertion
ios :: stdio	Flush **stdout** and **stderr** after insertion

Program 10.7 demonstrates the setting of various formatting flags using the overloaded **setf()** function.

```
                    FORMATTING WITH FLAGS IN setf()
#include <iostream>
#include <cmath>

using namespace std;

int main()
{
        cout.fill('*');
        cout.setf(ios::left, ios::adjustfield);
        cout.width(10);
        cout << "VALUE";

        cout.setf(ios::right, ios::adjustfield);
        cout.width(15);
        cout << "SQRT OF VALUE" << "\n";

        cout.fill('.');
        cout.precision(4);
        cout.setf(ios::showpoint);
        cout.setf(ios::showpos);
        cout.setf(ios::fixed, ios::floatfield);

        for(int n=1; n<=10; n++)
        {
                cout.setf(ios::internal, ios::adjustfield);
                cout.width(5);
                cout << n;

                cout.setf(ios::right, ios::adjustfield);
                cout.width(20);
                cout << sqrt(n)  << "\n";
        }

        // floatfield changed
        cout.setf(ios::scientific, ios::floatfield);
        cout << "\nSQRT(100) = " << sqrt(100) << "\n";

        return 0;
}
```

PROGRAM 10.7

The output of Program 10.7 would be:

```
VALUE*********SQRT OF VALUE
+...1...............+1.0000
+...2...............+1.4142
+...3...............+1.7321
```

```
+...4...............+2.0000
+...5...............+2.2361
+...6...............+2.4495
+...7...............+2.6458
+...8...............+2.8284
+...9...............+3.0000
+..10...............+3.1623

SQRT(100) = +1.0000e+001
```

1. The flags set by **setf()** remain effective until they are reset or unset.
2. A format flag can be reset any number of times in a program.
3. We can apply more than one format controls jointly on an output value.
4. The setf() sets the specified flags and leaves others unchanged.

10.6 MANAGING OUTPUT WITH MANIPULATORS

The header file *iomanip* provides a set of functions called *manipulators* which can be used to manipulate the output formats. They provide the same features as that of the **ios** member functions and flags. Some manipulators are more convenient to use than their counterparts in the class **ios**. For example, two or more manipulators can be used as a chain in one statement as shown below:

```
cout << manip1 << manip2 << manip3 << item;
cout << manip1 << item1  << manip2 << item2;
```

This kind of concatenation is useful when we want to display several columns of output.

The most commonly used manipulators are shown in Table 10.6. The table also gives their meaning and equivalents. To access these manipulators, we must include the file *iomanip* in the program.

Table 10.6   Manipulators and their meanings

Manipulator	Meaning	Equivalent
setw (int w)		
setprecision(int d)	Set the field width to w.	width( )
	Set the floating point precision to d.	precision( )
setfill(int c)	Set the fill character to c.	fill( )
setiosflags(long f)	Set he format flag f.	setf( )
resetiosflags(long f)	Clear the flag specified by f.	unsetf( )
Endif	Insert new line and flush stream.	"\n"

Some examples of manipulators are given below:

```
cout << setw(10) << 12345;
```

This statement prints the value 12345 right-justified in a field width of 10 characters. The output can be made left-justified by modifying the statement as follows:

```
cout << setw(10) << setiosflags(ios::left) << 12345;
```

One statement can be used to format output for two or more values.   For example, the statement

```
cout    << setw(5)  << setprecision(2) << 1.2345
        << setw(10) << setprecision(4) << sqrt(2)
        << setw(15) << setiosflags(ios::scientific) << sqrt(3);
        << endl;
```

will print all the three values in one line with the field sizes of 5, 10, and 15 respectively. Note that each output is controlled by different sets of format specifications.

We can jointly use the manipulators and the **ios** functions in a program. The following segment of code is valid:

```
cout.setf(ios::showpoint);
cout.setf(ios::showpos);
cout << setprecision(4);
cout << setiosflags(ios::scientific);
cout << setw(10) << 123.45678;
```

There is a major difference in the way the manipulators are implemented as compared to the **ios** member functions. The **ios** member function return the previous format state which can be used later, if necessary. But the manipulator does not return the previous format state. In case, we need to save the old format states, we must use the **ios** member functions rather than the manipulators. Example:

```
cout.precision(2);          // previous state
int p = cout.precision(4);      // current state;
```

When these statements are executed, **p** will hold the value of 2 (previous state) and the new format state will be 4. We can restore the previous format state as follows:

```
cout.precision(p);      // p = 2
```

Program 10.8 illustrates the formatting of the output values using both manipulators and **ios** functions.

```
                     FORMATTING WITH MANIPULATORS
#include <iostream>
#include <iomanip>

using namespace std;

int main()
{
      cout.setf(ios::showpoint);

      cout << setw(5)   <<  "n"
           << setw(15) << "Inverse_of_n"
           << setw(15) << "Sum_of_terms\n\n";

      double term, sum = 0;

      for(int n=1; n<=10; n++)
      {
           term = 1.0 / float(n);
           sum  = sum + term;

           cout << setw(5) << n
                << setw(14) << setprecision(4)
                << setiosflags(ios::scientific) << term
                << setw(13) << resetiosflags(ios::scientific)
                << sum << endl;
      }
      return 0;
}
```

PROGRAM 10.8

The output of Program 10.8 would be:

n	Inverse_of_n	Sum_of_terms
1	1.0000e+000	1.0000
2	5.0000e-001	1.5000
3	3.3333e-001	1.8333
4	2.5000e-001	2.0833
5	2.0000e-001	2.2833
6	1.6667e-001	2.4500
7	1.4286e-001	2.5929
8	1.2500e-001	2.7179
9	1.1111e-001	2.8290
10	1.0000e-001	2.9290

Designing Our Own Manipulators

We can design our own manipulators for certain special purposes. The general form for creating a manipulator without any arguments is:

```
ostream & manipulator (ostream & output)
{
    .....
    ..... (code)
    .....
    return output;
}
```

Here, the *manipulator* is the name of the manipulator under creation. The following function defines a manipulator called **unit** that displays "inches":

```
ostream & unit(ostream & output)
{
        output << " inches";
        return output;
}
```

The statement

```
cout << 36 << unit;
```

will produce the following output

```
36 inches
```

We can also create manipulators that could represent a sequence of operations. Example:

```
ostream & show(ostream & output)
{
        output.setf(ios::showpoint);
        output.setf(ios::showpos);
        output << setw(10);
        return output;
}
```

This function defines a manipulator called **show** that turns on the flags **showpoint** and **showpos** declared in the class **ios** and sets the field width to 10.

Program 10.9 illustrates the creation and use of the user-defined manipulators. The program creates two manipulators called **currency** and **form** which are used in the **main** program.

```
                        USER-DEFINED MANIPULATORS

#include <iostream>
#include <iomanip>

using namespace std;

// user-defined manipulators

ostream & currency(ostream & output)
{
     output << "Rs";
     return output;
}

ostream & form(ostream & output)
{
     output.setf(ios::showpos);
     output.setf(ios::showpoint);
     output.fill('*');
     output.precision(2);
     output << setiosflags(ios::fixed)
             << setw(10);
     return output;
}

int main()
{
     cout << currency << form << 7864.5;

     return 0;
}
```

PROGRAM 10.9

The output of Program 10.9 would be:

Rs**+7864.50

Note that **form** represents a complex set of format functions and manipulators.

Summary

- In C++, the I/O system is designed to work with different I/O devices. This I/O system supplies an interface called 'stream' to the programmer, which is independent of the actual device being used.

- A stream is a sequence of bytes and serves as a source or destination for an I/O data.
- The source stream that provides data to the program is called the *input stream* and the destination stream that receives output from the program is called the *output stream*.
- The C++ I/O system contains a hierarchy of stream classes used for input and output operations. These classes are declared in the header file **'iostream'**.
- **cin** represents the input stream connected to the standard input device and **cout** represents the output stream connected to the standard output device.
- The **istream** and **ostream** classes define two member functions **get()** and **put()** to handle the single character I/O operations.
- The >> operator is overloaded in the **istream** class as an extraction operator and the << operator is overloaded in the **ostream** class as an insertion operator.
- We can read and write a line of text more efficiently using the line oriented I/O functions **getline()** and **write()** respectively.
- The **ios** class contains the member functions such as **width()**, **precision()**, **fill()**, **setf()**, **unsetf()** to format the output.
- The header file **'iomanip'** provides a set of manipulator functions to manipulate output formats. They provide the same features as that of **ios** class functions.
- We can also design our own manipulators for certain special purposes.

Key Terms

- adjustfield
- basefield
- bit-fields
- console I/O operations
- decimal base
- destination stream
- field width
- **fill()**
- filling
- fixed point notation
- flags
- floatfield
- formatted console I/O
- formatting flags
- formatting functions
- **get()**
- **getline()**
- hexadecimal base
- input stream
- internal
- **ios**
- iomanip
- iostream
- istream
- left-justified
- manipulator
- octal base
- ostream
- output stream
- padding
- **precision()**
- **put()**
- **resetiosflags()**
- right-justified
- scientific notation
- **setf()**
- **setfill()**
- **setiosflags()**
- **setprecision()**
- setting precision
- **setw()**
- showbase
- showpoint
- showpos
- skipus
- source stream
- standard input device
- standard output device

> stream classes   ➤ unsetf()
> streambuf   ➤ width()
> streams   ➤ write()
> unitbuf

Review Questions and Exercises

10.1   *What is a stream?*
10.2   *Describe briefly the features of I/O system supported by C++.*
10.3   *How do the I/O facilities in C++ differ from that in C?*
10.4   *Why are the words such as **cin** and **cout** not considered as keywords?*
10.5   *How is **cout** able to display various types of data without any special instructions?*
10.6   *Why is it necessary to include the file iostream in all our programs?*
10.7   *Discuss the various forms of **get()** function supported by the input stream. How are they used?*
10.8   *How do the following two statements differ in operation?*

```
cin >> c;
cin.get(c);
```

10.9   *Both **cin** and **getline()** function can be used for reading a string. Comment.*
10.10 *Discuss the implications of size parameter in the following statement:*

```
cout.write(line, size);
```

10.11 *What does the following statement do?*

```
cout.write(s1,m).write(s2,n);
```

10.12 *What role does the **iomanip** file play?*
10.13 *What is the role of **file()** function? When do we use this function?*
10.14 *Discuss the syntax of **set()** function.*
10.15 *What is the basic difference between manipulators and **ios** member functions in implementation? Give examples.*
10.16 *State whether the following statements are TRUE or FALSE.*

(a)   *A C++ stream is a file.*
(b)   *C++ never truncates data.*
(c)   *The main advantage of **width()** function is that we can use one width specification for more than one items.*
(d)   *The **get(void)** function provides a single-character input that does not skip over the white spaces.*
(e)   *The header file **iomanip** can be used in place of iostream.*
(f)   *We cannot use both the C I/O functions and C++ I/O functions in the same program.*

(g)   *A programmer can define a manipulator that could represent a set of format functions.*

10.17 *State errors, if any, in the following statements.*

(a)   `cout << (void*) amount;`

(b)   `cout << put("John");`

(c)   `cout << width();`

(d)   `int p = cout.width(10);`

(e)   `cout.width(10).precision(3);`

(f)   `cout.setf(ios::scientific,ios::left);`

(g)   `ch = cin.get();`

(h)   `cin.get().get();`

(i)   `cin.get(c).get();`

(j)   `cout << setw(5) << setprecision(2);`

(k)   `cout << resetiosflags(ios::left |ios::showpos);`

10.18 *What will be the result of the following program segment?*

```
for(i=0.25;  i<=1.0;  i=i+0.25)
{
        cout.precision(5);
        cout.width(7);
        cout << i;
        cout.width(10);
        cout <<i*i<< "\n";
}
cout  << setw(10)  << "TOTAL ="
      << setw(20)  << setprecision(2)  << 1234.567
      << endl;
```

10.19 *Discuss the syntax for creating user-defined manipulators. Design a single manipulator to provide the following output specifications for printing float values:*

(a)   *10 columns width*

(b)   *Right-justified*

(c)   *Two digits precision*

(d)   *Filling of unused places with **

(e)   *Trailing zeros shown*

10.20 *Write a program to read a list containing item name, item code, and cost interactively and produce a three column output as shown below.*

NAME	CODE	COST
Turbo C++	1001	250.95
C Primer	905	95.70
.....	...	.....
.....	...	.....
.....	...	.....

Note that the name and code are left-justified and the cost is right-justified with a precision of two digits. Trailing zeros are shown.

10.21 *Modify the above program to fill the unused spaces with hyphens.*

10.22 *Write a program which reads a text from the keyboard and displays the following information on the screen in two columns:*

(a)   *Number of lines*

(b)   *Number of words*

(c)   *Number of characters*

Strings should be left-justified and numbers should be right-justified in a suitable field width.

11

Working with Files

11.1 INTRODUCTION

Many real-life problems handle large volumes of data and, in such situations, we need to use some devices such as floppy disk or hard disk to store the data. The data is stored in these devices using the concept of *files*. A file is a collection of related data stored in a particular area on the disk. Programs can be designed to perform the read and write operations on these files.

A program typically involves either or both of the following kinds of data communication:

1. Data transfer between the console unit and the program.
2. Data transfer between the program and a disk file.

This is illustrated in Fig. 11.1.

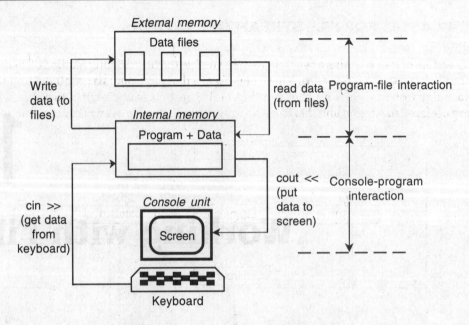

Fig. 11.1   *Console-program-file interaction*

We have already discussed the technique of handling data communication between the console unit and the program. In this chapter, we will discuss various methods available for storing and retrieving the data from files.

The I/O system of C++ handles file operations which are very much similar to the console input and output operations. It uses file streams as an interface between the programs and the files. The stream that supplies data to the program is known as *input stream* and the one that receives data from the program is known as *output stream*. In other words, the input stream extracts (or reads) data from the file and the output stream inserts (or writes) data to the file. This is illustrated in Fig. 11.2.

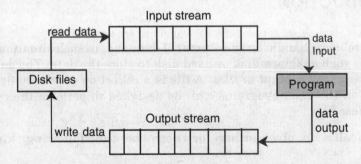

Fig. 11.2   *File input and output streams*

The input operation involves the creation of an input stream and linking it with the program and the input file. Similarly, the output operation involves establishing an output stream with the necessary links with the program and the output file.

11.2   CLASSES FOR FILE STREAM OPERATIONS

The I/O system of C++ contains a set of classes that define the file handling methods. These include **ifstream, ofstream** and **fstream**. These classes are derived from **fstreambase** and from the corresponding *iostream* class as shown in Fig.11.3. These classes, designed to manage the disk files, are declared in *fstream* and therefore we must include this file in any program that uses files.

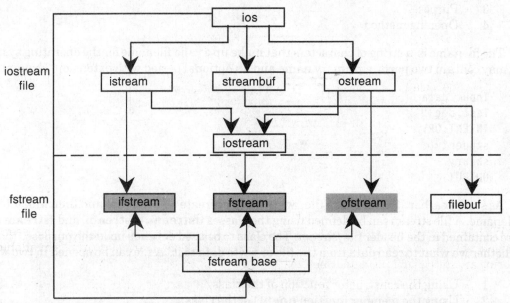

Fig. 11.3   *Stream classes for file operations (contained in fstream file)*

Table 11.1 shows the details of file stream classes. Note that these classes contain many more features. For more details, refer to the manual.

Table 11.1   Details of file stream classes

Class	Contents
filebuf	Its purpose is to set the file buffers to read and write. Contains **Openprot** constant used in the **open()** of file stream classes. Also contain **close()** and **open()** as members.
fstreambase	Provides operations common to the file streams. Serves as a base for **fstream, ifstream** and **ofstream** class. Contains **open()** and **close()** functions.
ifstream	Provides input operations. Contains **open()** with default input mode. Inherits the functions **get()**, **getline()**, **read()**, **seekg()** and **tellg()** functions from **istream**.
Ofstream	Provides output operations. Contains **open()** with default output mode. Inherits **put()**, **seekp()**, **tellp()**, and **write()**, functions from **ostream**.
fstream	Provides support for simultaneous input and output operations. Contains **open()** with default input mode. Inherits all the functions from **istream** and **ostream** classes through **iostream**.

11.3 OPENING AND CLOSING A FILE

If we want to use a disk file, we need to decide the following things about the file and its intended use:

1. Suitable name for the file.
2. Data type and structure.
3. Purpose.
4. Opening method.

The filename is a string of characters that make up a valid filename for the operating system. It may contain two parts, a primary name and an optional period with extension. Examples:

```
Input.data
Test.doc
INVENT.ORY
student
salary
OUTPUT
```

As stated earlier, for opening a file, we must first create a file stream and then link it to the filename. A file stream can be defined using the classes **ifstream, ofstream,** and **fstream** that are contained in the header file *fstream*. The class to be used depends upon the purpose, that is, whether we want to read data from the file or write data to it. A file can be opened in two ways:

1. Using the constructor function of the class.
2. Using the member function **open()** of the class.

The first method is useful when we use only one file in the stream. The second method is used when we want to manage multiple files using one stream.

Opening Files Using Constructor

We know that a constructor is used to initialize an object while it is being created. Here, a filename is used to initialize the file stream object. This involves the following steps:

1. Create a file stream object to manage the stream using the appropriate class. That is to say, the class **ofstream** is used to create the output stream and the class **ifstream** to create the input stream.
2. Initialize the file object with the desired filename.

For example, the following statement opens a file named "results" for output:

```
ofstream outfile("results");    // output only
```

This creates **outfile** as an **ofstream** object that manages the output stream. This object can be any valid C++ name such as **o_file, myfile** or **fout**. This statement also opens the file **results** and attaches it to the output stream **outfile**. This is illustrated in Fig. 11.4.

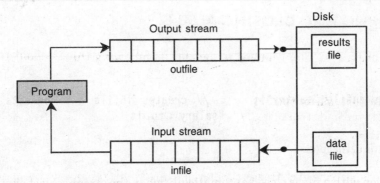

Fig. 11.4   *Two file streams working on separate files*

Similarly, the following statement declares **infile** as an **ifstream** object and attaches it to the file **data** for reading (input).

```
ifstream   infile("data");   // input only
```

The program may contain statements like:

```
outfile << "TOTAL";
outfile << sum;
infile  >> number;
infile  >> string;
```

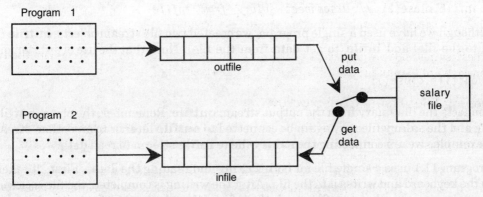

Fig. 11.5   *Two file streams working on one file*

We can also use the same file for both reading and writing data as shown in Fig. 11.5. The programs would contain the following statements:

```
Program1
.....
.....
ofstream outfile("salary");          // creates outfile and connects
                                     // "salary" to it
```

```
    . . . . .
    . . . . .
Program2
    . . . . .
    . . . . .
    ifstream infile("salary");       // creates infile and connects
                              // "salary" to it
    . . . . .
    . . . . .
```

The connection with a file is closed automatically when the stream object expires (when the program terminates). In the above statement, when the *program1* is terminated, the **salary** file is disconnected from the **outfile** stream. Similar action takes place when the *program 2* terminates.

Instead of using two programs, one for writing data (output) and another for reading data (input), we can use a single program to do both the operations on a file. Example.

```
    . . . . .
    . . . . .
      outfile.close();                  // Disconnect salary from outfile
      ifstream infile("salary");      // and connect to infile
    . . . . .
    . . . . .
    infile.close(); // Disconnect salary from infile
```

Although we have used a single program, we created two file stream objects, **outfile** (to put data to the file) and **infile** (to get data from the file). Note that the use of a statement like

```
    outfile.close();
```

disconnects the file salary from the output stream **outfile**. Remember, the object **outfile** still exists and the **salary** file may again be connected to **outfile** later or to any other stream. In this example, we are connecting the **salary** file to **infile** stream to read data.

Program 11.1 uses a single file for both writing and reading the data. First, it takes data from the keyboard and writes it to the file. After the writing is completed, the file is closed. The program again opens the same file, reads the information already written to it and displays the same on the screen.

```
                        WORKING WITH SINGLE FILE

    // Creating files with constructor function

    #include <iostream.h>
    #include <fstream.h>

    int main()
```

(Contd)

```
{
        ofstream outf("ITEM");          // connect ITEM file to outf

        cout << "Enter item name:";
        char name[30];
        cin >> name;                    // get name from key board and

        outf << name << "\n";           // write to file ITEM

        cout << "Enter item cost:";
        float cost;
        cin >> cost;                    // get cost from key board and

         outf << cost << "\n";          // write to file ITEM

        outf.close();                   // Disconnect ITEM file from outf

        ifstream inf("ITEM");           // connect ITEM file to inf

        inf >>  name;                   // read name from file ITEM
        inf >> cost;                    // read cost from file ITEM
        cout << "\n";
        cout << "Item name:" << name << "\n";
        cout << "Item cost:" << cost << "\n";

        inf.close();                    // Disconnect ITEM from inf

        return 0;
}
```

PROGRAM 11.1

The output of Program 11.1 would be:

```
Enter item name:CD-ROM
Enter item cost:250

Item name:CD-ROM
Item cost:250
```

C aution !

When a file is opened for *writing only*, a new file is created if there is no file of that name. If a file by that name exists already, then its contents are deleted and the file is presented as a clean file. We shall discuss later how to open an existing file for updating it without losing its original contents.

Opening Files Using open()

As stated earlier, the function **open()** can be used to open multiple files that use the same stream object. For example, we may want to process a set of files sequentially. In such cases, we may create a single stream object and use it to open each file in turn. This is done as follows:

```
file-stream-class stream-object;
stream-object.open ("filename");
```

Example:

```
ofstream outfile;              // Create stream (for output)
outfile.open("DATA1");         // Connect stream to DATA1
.....
.....
outfile.close();               // Disconnect stream from DATA1
outfile.open("DATA2");         // Connect stream to DATA2
.....
.....
outfile.close();               // Disconnect stream from DATA2
.....
.....
```

The above program segment opens two files in sequence for writing the data. Note that the first file is closed before opening the second one. This is necessary because a stream can be connected to only one file at a time. See Program 11.2 and Fig. 11.6.

```
                    WORKING WITH MULTIPLE FILES

    // Creating files with open() function

    #include <iostream.h>
    #include <fstream.h>

    int main()
    {
        ofstream fout;                    // create output stream
        fout.open("country");             // connect "country" to it

        fout << "United States of America\n";
        fout << "United Kingdom\n";
        fout << "South Korea\n";

        fout.close();                     // disconnect "country" and

        fout.open("capital");             // connect "capital"

        fout    << "Washington\n";
```

(Contd)

```
        fout    << "London\n";
        fout    << "Seoul\n";

        fout.close();                        // disconnect "capital"

        // Reading the files
        const int N = 80;                    // size of line
        char line[N];

        ifstream fin;                        // create input stream
        fin.open("country");                 // connect "country" to it

        cout <<"contents of country file\n";

        while(fin)                           // check end-of-file
        {
                fin.getline(line, N);        // read a line
                cout << line ;               // display it
        }

        fin.close();                         // disconnect "country" and

        fin.open("capital");                 // connect "capital"

        cout << "\nContents of capital file \n";

        while(fin)
        {
                fin.getline(line, N);
                cout << line ;
        }
        fin.close();

        return 0;
}
```

PROGRAM 11.2

The output of Program 11.2 would be:

```
Contents of country file
United States of America
United  Kingdom
South  Korea

Contents of capital file
Washington
London
Seoul
```

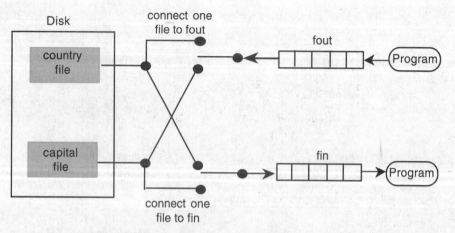

Fig. 11.6 *Streams working on multiple files*

At times we may require to use two or more files simultaneously. For example, we may require to merge two sorted files into a third sorted file. This means, both the sorted files have to be kept open for reading and the third one kept open for writing. In such cases, we need to create two separate input streams for handling the two input files and one output stream for handling the output file. See Program 11.3.

```
                   READING FROM TWO FILES SIMULTANEOUSLY

    // Reads the files created in Program 11.2

    #include <iostream.h>
    #include <fstream.h>
    #include <stdlib.h>              // for exit() function

    int main()
    {
      const  int SIZE = 80;
      char line[SIZE];

      ifstream fin1, fin2;      // create two input streams
      fin1.open("country");
      fin2.open("capital");

      for(int i=1; i<=10; i++)
      {
            if(fin1.eof() != 0)
            {
                  cout << "Exit from country \n";
                  exit(1);
```

(Contd)

```
            }
        fin1.getline(line, SIZE);
        cout << "Capital of "<< line ;

        if(fin2.eof() != 0)
        {
            cout << "Exit from capital\n";
            exit(1);
        }

        fin2.getline(line,SIZE);
        cout << line << "\n";
    }
    return 0;
}
```

PROGRAM 11.3

The output of Program 11.3 would be:

```
Capital of United States of America
Washington

Capital of United Kingdom
London
Capital of South Korea
Seoul
```

11.4 DETECTING END-OF FILE

Detection of the end-of-file condition is necessary for preventing any further attempt to read data from the file. This was illustrated in Program 11.2 by using the statement

```
while(fin)
```

An **ifstream** object, such as **fin**, returns a value of 0 if any error occurs in the file operation including the end-of-file condition. Thus, the **while** loop terminates when **fin** returns a value of zero on reaching the end-of-file condition. Remember, this loop may terminate due to other failures as well. (We will discuss other error conditions later.)

There is another approach to detect the end-of-file condition. Note that we have used the following statement in Program 11.3:

```
if(fin1.eof() != 0) {exit(1);}
```

eof() is a member function of **ios** class. It returns a non-zero value if the end-of-file(EOF) condition is encountered, and a zero, otherwise. Therefore, the above statement terminates the program on reaching the end of the file.

11.5 MORE ABOUT OPEN(): FILE MODES

We have used **ifstream** and **ofstream** constructors and the function **open()** to create new files as well as to open the existing files. Remember, in both these methods, we used only one argument that was the filename. However, these functions can take two arguments, the second one for *specifying the file mode*. The general form of the function **open()** with two arguments is:

```
stream-object.open("filename", mode);
```

The second *argument mode* (called file mode parameter) specifies the purpose for which the file is opened. How did we then open the files without providing the second argument in the previous examples?

The prototype of these class member functions contain default values for the second argument and therefore they use the default values in the absence of the actual values. The default values are as follows:

```
ios::in  for ifstream functions meaning open for reading only.
ios::out for ofstream functions meaning open for writing only.
```

The *file mode* parameter can take one (or more) of such constants defined in the class **ios**. Table 11.2 lists the file mode parameters and their meanings.

Table 11.2   File mode parameters

Parameter	Meaning
ios :: app	Append to end-of-life
ios :: ate	Go to end-of-life on opening
ios :: binary	Binary file
ios :: in	Open file for reading only
ios :: nocreate	Open fails if the file does not exist
ios :: noreplace	Open files if the file already exists
ios :: out	Open file for writing only
ios :: trunc	Delete the contents of the file if it exists

1. Opening a file in **ios::out** mode also opens it in the **ios::trunc** mode by default.
2. Both **ios:app** and **ios::ate** take us to the end of the file when it is opened. The difference between the two parameters is that the **ios::app** allows us to add data to the end of the file only, while **ios::ate** mode permits us to add data or to modify the existing data anywhere in the file. In both the cases, a file is created by the specified name, if it does not exist.
3. The parameter **ios::app** can be used only with the files capable of output.
4. Creating a stream using **ifstream** implies input and creating a stream using **ofstream** implies output. So in these cases it is not necessary to provide the mode parameters.
5. The **fstream** class does not provide a mode by default and therefore, we must provide the mode explicitly when using an object of **fstream** class.
6. The *mode* can combine two or more parameters using the bitwise OR operator (symbol |) shown as follows:

```
fout.open("data", ios::app | ios:: nocreate)
```

This opens the file in the append mode but fails to open the file if it does not exist.

11.6   FILE POINTERS AND THEIR MANIPULATIONS

Each file has two associated pointers known as the *file pointers*. One of them is called the input pointer (*or get pointer*) and the other is called the output pointer (*or put pointer*). We can use these pointers to move through the files while reading or writing. The input pointer is used for reading the contents of a given file location and the output pointer is used for writing to a given file location. Each time an input or output operation takes place, the appropriate pointer is automatically advanced.

Default Actions

When we open a file in read-only mode, the input pointer is automatically set at the beginning so that we can read the file from the start. Similarly, when we open a file in write-only mode, the existing contents are deleted and the output pointer is set at the beginning. This enables us to write to the file from the start. In case, we want to open an existing file to add more data, the file is opened in 'append' mode. This moves the output pointer to the end of the file (i.e. the end of the existing contents). See Fig. 11.7.

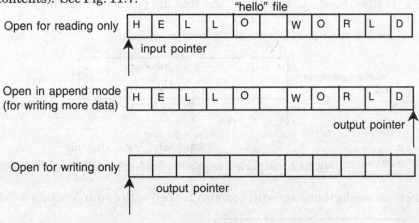

Fig. 11.7   *Action on file pointers while opening a file*

Functions for Manipulation of File Pointers

All the actions on the file pointers as shown in Fig.11.7 take place automatically by default. How do we then move a file pointer to any other desired position inside the file? This is possible only if we can take control of the movement of the file pointers ourselves. The file stream classes support the following functions to manage such situations:

- **seekg()**   Moves get pointer (input) to a specified location.
- **seekp()**   Moves put pointer(output) to a specified location.
- **tellg()**   Gives the current position of the get pointer.

- **tellp()**   Gives the current position of the put pointer.

For example, the statement

```
infile.seekg(10);
```

moves the file pointer to the byte number 10. Remember, the bytes in a file are numbered beginning from zero. Therefore, the pointer will be pointing to the 11th byte in the file.

Consider the following statements:

```
ofstream   fileout;
fileout.open("hello", ios::app);
int p = fileout.tellp();
```

On execution of these statements, the output pointer is moved to the end of the file "hello" and the value of **p** will represent the number of bytes in the file.

Specifying the offset

We have just now seen how to move a file pointer to a desired location using the 'seek' functions. The argument to these functions represents the absolute position in the file. This is shown in Fig. 11.8.

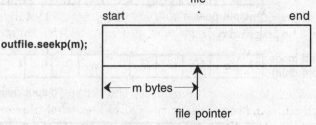

Fig. 11.8   *Action of a single argument seek function*

'Seek' functions **seekg()** and **seekp()** can also be used with two arguments as follows:

```
seekg (offset, refposition);
seekp (offset, refposition);
```

The parameter *offset* represents the number of bytes the file pointer is to be moved from the location specified by the parameter *refposition*. The *refposition* takes one of the following three constants defined in the **ios** class:

- **ios::beg**   start of the file
- **ios::cur**   current position of the pointer
- **ios::end**   End of the file

The **seekg()** function moves the associated file's 'get' pointer while the **seekp()** function moves the associated file's 'put' pointer. Table 11.3 lists some sample pointer offset calls and their actions. **fout** is an **ofstream** object.

Table 11.3   Pointer offset calls

Seek call	Action
fout.seekg(o, ios::beg);	Go to start
fout.seekg(o, ios::cur);	Stay at the current position
fout.seekg(o, ios::end);	Go to the end of file
Fout.seekg(m,ios::beg);	Move to (m + 1)th byte in the file
fout.seekg(m,ios::cur);	Go forward by m byte form the current position
fout.seekg(-m,ios::cur);	Go backward by m bytes from the current position
fout.seekg(-m,ios::end);	Go backward by m bytes form the end

11.7   SEQUENTIAL INPUT AND OUTPUT OPERATIONS

The file stream classes support a number of member functions for performing the input and output operations on files. One pair of functions, **put()** and **get()**, are designed for handling a single character at a time. Another pair of functions, **write()** and **read()**, are designed to write and read blocks of *binary* data.

put() and get() Functions

The function **put()** writes a single character to the associated stream. Similarly, the function **get()** reads a single character from the associated stream. Program 11.4 illustrates how these functions work on a file. The program requests for a string. On reeiving the string, the program writes it, character by character, to the file using the **put()** function in a **for** loop. Note that the length of the string is used to terminate the **for** loop.

The program then displays the contents of the file on the screen. It uses the function **get()** to fetch a character from the file and continues to do so until the end-of-file condition is reached. The character read from the file is displayed on the screen using the operator <<.

```
                   I/O OPERATIONS ON CHARACTERS
      #include <iostream.h>
      #include <fstream.h>
      #include <string.h>

      int main()
      {
            char string[80];

            cout << "Enter a string \n";
            cin >> string;

            int len = strlen(string);
```

```
        fstream file;                 // input and output stream
        file.open("TEXT", ios::in | ios:: out);

        for(int i=0; i<len; i++)
        file.put(string[i]);          // put a character to file

        file.seekg(0);                // go to the start

    char  ch;
    while(file)
    {
        file.get(ch);                 // get a character from file
        cout << ch;                   // display it on screen
    }
    return 0;
}
```

PROGRAM 11.4

The output of Program 11.4 would be:

```
Enter a string
Cobol_Programming      input
Cobol_Programming      output
```

We have used an **fstream** object to open the file. Since an **fstream** object can handle both the input and output simultaneously, we have opened the file in **ios::in | ios::out** mode. After writing the file, we want to read the entire file and display its contents. Since the file pointer has already moved to the end of the file, we must bring it back to the start of the file. This is done by the statement

```
file.seekg(0);
```

write() and read() Functions

The functions **write()** and **read()**, unlike the functions **put()** and **get()**, handle the data in binary form. This means that the values are stored in the disk file in the same format in which they are stored in the internal memory. Figure 11.9 shows how an **int** value 2594 is stored in the *binary* and *character* formats. An **int** takes two bytes to store its value in the binary form, irrespective of its size. But a 4 digit int will take four bytes to store it in the character form.

The binary format is more accurate for storing the numbers as they are stored in the exact internal representation. There are no conversions while saving the data and therefore saving is much faster.

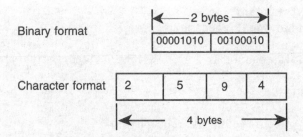

Fig. 11.9   *Binary and character formats of an integer value*

The binary input and output functions takes the following form:

```
infile. read ((char *) & V, sizeof (V));
outfile.write ((char *) & V, sizeof (V));
```

These functions take two arguments. The first is the address of the variable **V**, and the second is the length of that variable in bytes. The address of the variable must be cast to type **char *** (i.e. pointer to character type). Program 11.5 illustrates how these two functions are used to save an array of **float** numbers and then recover them for display on the screen.

```
                    I/O OPERATIONS ON BINARY FILES

    #include <iostream.h>
    #include <fstream.h>
    #include <iomanip.h>

    const char * filename = "BINARY";

    int main()
    {
        float height[4] = {175.5,153.0,167.25,160.70};

        ofstream outfile;
        outfile.open(filename);

        outfile.write((char *) & height, sizeof(height));

        outfile.close();            // close the file for reading

        for(int i=0; i<4; i++)      // clear array from memory
            height[i] = 0;
```

(*Contd*)

```
            ifstream infile;
            infile.open(filename);

            infile.read((char *) & height, sizeof(height));

            for(i=0; i<4; i++)
            {
                cout.setf(ios::showpoint);
                cout << setw(10) << setprecision(2)
                    << height[i];
            }
            infile.close();

            return 0;
        }
```

PROGRAM 11.5

The output of Program 11.5 would be:

175.50   153.00   167.25

Reading and Writing a Class Object

We mentioned earlier that one of the shortcomings of the I/O system of C is that it cannot handle user-defined data types such as class objects. Since the class objects are the central elements of C++ programming, it is quite natural that the language supports features for writing to and reading from the disk files objects directly. The binary input and output functions **read()** and **write()** are designed to do exactly this job. These functions handle the entire structure of an object as a single unit, using the computer's internal representation of data. For instance, the function **write()** copies a class object from memory byte by byte with no conversion. One important point to remember is that only data members are written to the disk file and the member functions are not.

Program 11.6 illustrates how class objects can be written to and read from the disk files. The length of the object is obtained using the **sizeof** operator. This length represents the sum total of lengths of all data members of the object.

READING AND WRITING CLASS OBJECTS

```
    #include <iostream.h>
    #include <fstream.h>
    #include <iomanip.h>

    class INVENTORY
    {
        char    name[10];      // item name
        int     code;          // item code
```

(Contd)

READING AND WRITING CLASS OBJECTS

```cpp
    float cost;                    // cost of each item
  public:
    void readdata(void);
    void writedata(void);
};
void INVENTORY :: readdata(void)      // read from keyboard
{
    cout << "Enter name: "; cin >> name;
    cout << "Enter code: "; cin >> code;
    cout << "Enter cost: "; cin >> cost;
}
void INVENTORY :: writedata(void) // formatted display on
{                                 // screen
    cout << setiosflags(ios::left)
         << setw(10) << name
         << setiosflags(ios::right)
         << setw(10) << code
         << setprecision(2)
         << setw(10) << cost
         << endl;
}
int main()
{
    INVENTORY item[3];             // Declare array of 3 objects
    fstream file;                  // Input and output file
    file.open("STOCK.DAT", ios::in | ios::out);
    cout << "ENTER DETAILS FOR THREE ITEMS \n";
    for(int i=0;i<3;i++)
    {
        item[i].readdata();

        file.write((char *) & item[i],sizeof(item[i]));
    }
    file.seekg(0);                // reset to start
    cout << "\nOUTPUT\n\n";
    for(i = 0;  i < 3; i++)
    {
        file.read((char *) & item[i], sizeof(item[i]));
        item[i].writedata();
    }
    file.close();

    return 0;
}
```

PROGRAM 11.6

The output of Program 11.6 would be:

```
ENTER DETAILS FOR THREE ITEMS
Enter name: C++
Enter code: 101
Enter cost: 175
Enter name: FORTRAN
Enter code: 102
Enter cost: 150
Enter name: JAVA
Enter code: 115
Enter cost: 225


OUTPUT

C++          101   175
FORTRAN      102   150
JAVA         115   225
```

The program uses 'for' loop for reading and writing objects. This is possible because we know the exact number of objects in the file. In case, the length of the file is not known, we can determine the file-size in terms of objects with the help of the file pointer functions and use it in the 'for' loop or we may use **while(file)** test approach to decide the end of the file. These techniques are discussed in the next section.

11.8 UPDATING A FILE: RANDOM ACCESS

Updating is a routine task in the maintenance of any data file. The updating would include one or more of the following tasks:

- Displaying the contents of a file.
- Modifying an existing item.
- Adding a new item.
- Deleting an existing item.

These actions require the file pointers to move to a particular location that corresponds to the item/object under consideration. This can be easily implemented if the file contains a collection of items/objects of equal lengths. In such cases, the size of each object can be obtained using the statement

```
int object_length = sizeof(object);
```

Then, the location of a desired object, say the mth object, may be obtained as follows:

```
int location = m * object_length;
```

The **location** gives the byte number of the first byte of the mth object. Now, we can set the file pointer to reach this byte with the help of **seekg()** or **seekp()**.

We can also find out the total number of objects in a file using the **object_length** as follows:

```
int n = file_size/object_length;
```

The file_size can be obtained using the function **tellg()** or **tellp()** when the file pointer is located at the end of the file.

Program 11.7 illustrates how some of the tasks described above are carried out. The program uses the "STOCK.DAT" file created using Program 11.6 for five items and performs the following operations on the file:

1.   Adds a new item to the file.
2.   Modifies the details of an item.
3.   Displays the contents of the file.

```
              FILE UPDATING :: RANDOM ACCESS

        #include <iostream.h>
        #include <fstream.h>
        #include <iomanip.h>

        class INVENTORY
        {
            char name[10];
            int  code;
            float cost;
          public:
            void getdata(void)
            {
                cout << "Enter name: "; cin >> name;
                cout << "Enter code: "; cin >> code;
                cout << "Enter cost: "; cin >> cost;
            }
            void putdata(void)
            {
                cout << setw(10) << name
                     << setw(10) << code
                     << setprecision(2) << setw(10) << cost
                     << endl;
            }
        };  // End of class definition

        int main()
        {
            INVENTORY item;
            fstream inoutfile;              // input/output stream
```

(Contd)

```
inoutfile.open("STOCK.DAT", ios:: ate | ios:: in |
              ios::out | ios::binary);
inoutfile.seekg(0,ios::beg);        // go to start

cout << "CURRENT CONTENTS OF STOCK" << "\n";

while(inoutfile.read((char *) & item, sizeof item))
{
      item.putdata();
}
inoutfile.clear();              // turn of EOF flag

/* >>>>>>>>>>>>> Add one more item <<<<<<<<<<<<<<< */

cout << "\nADD AN ITEM\n";
item.getdata();
char ch;
cin.get(ch);
inoutfile.write((char *) & item, sizeof item);

// Display the appended file

inoutfile.seekg(0);      // go to the start

cout << "CONTENTS OF APPENDED FILE \n";

while(inoutfile.read((char *) & item, sizeof item))
{
   item.putdata();
}


// Find number of objects in the file
int last = inoutfile.tellg();
int n = last/sizeof(item);

cout << "Number of objects = " << n << "\n";
cout << "Total bytes in the file = " << last << "\n";

/* >>>>>>>> MODIFY THE DETAILS OF AN ITEM <<<<<<<<< */

cout << "Enter object number to be updated \n";
int object;
cin >> object;
```

(Contd)

```
            cin.get(ch);

            int location = (object-1) * sizeof(item);

            if(inoutfile.eof())
            inoutfile.clear();

            inoutfile.seekp(location);

            cout << "Enter new values of the object \n";
            item.getdata();
            cin.get(ch);

            inoutfile.write((char *) & item, sizeof item) << flush;

            /* >>>>>>>>>>>> SHOW UPDATED FILE <<<<<<<<<<<<<< */

            inoutfile.seekg(0); //go to the start

            cout << "CONTENTS OF UPDATED FILE \n";

            while(inoutfile.read((char *) & item, sizeof item))
            {
                item.putdata();
            }
            inoutfile.close();

            return 0;
        } //   End of main
```

PROGRAM 11.7

The output of Program 11.7 would be:

```
CURRENT CONTENTS OF STOCK
      AA    11    100
      BB    22    200
      CC    33    300
      DD    44    400
      XX    99    900

ADD  AN  ITEM
Enter  name: YY
Enter  code: 10
Enter  cost: 101
```

```
CONTENTS OF APPENDED FILE
    AA    11      100
    BB    22      200
    CC    33      300
    DD    44      400
    XX    99      900
    YY    10      101

Number of objects = 6
Total bytes in the files = 96
Enter object number to be updated
6
Enter new values of the object
Enter name: ZZ
Enter code: 20
Enter cost: 201
CONTENTS OF UPDATED FILE
    AA    11      100
    BB    22      200
    CC    33      300
    DD    44      400
    XX    99      900
    ZZ    20      201
```

We are using the **fstream** class to declare the file streams. The **fstream** class inherits two buffers, one for input and another for output, and synchronizes the movement of the file pointers on these buffers. That is, whenever we read from or write to the file, both the pointers move in tandem. Therefore, at any point of time, both the pointers point to the same byte.

Since we have to add new objects to the file as well as modify some of the existing objects, we open the file using **ios::ate** option for input and output operations. Remember, the option **ios::app** allows us to add data to the end of the file only. The **ios::ate** mode sets the file pointers at the end of the file when opening it. We must therefore move the 'get' pointer to the beginning of the file using the function **seekg()** to read the existing contents of the file.

At the end of reading the current contents of the file, the program sets the EOF flag on. This prevents any further reading from or writing to the file. The EOF flag is turned off by using the function **clear()**, which allows access to the file once again.

After appending a new item, the program displays the contents of the appended file and also the total number of objects in the file and the memory space occupied by them.

To modify an object, we should reach to the first byte of that object. This is achieved using the statements

```
int location = (object-1) * sizeof(item);
inoutfile.seekp(location);
```

The program accepts the number and the new values of the object to be modified and updates it. Finally, the contents of the appended and modified file are displayed.

Remember, we are opening an existing file for reading and updating the values. It is, therefore, essential that the data members are of the same type and declared in the same order as in the existing file. Since, the member functions are not stored, they can be different.

11.9 ERROR HANDLING DURING FILE OPERATIONS

So far we have been opening and using the files for reading and writing on the assumption that everything is fine with the files. This may not be true always. For instance, one of the following things may happen when dealing with the files:

1. A file which we are attempting to open for reading does not exist.
2. The file name used for a new file may already exist.
3. We may attempt an invalid operation such as reading past the end-of-file.
4. There may not be any space in the disk for storing more data.
5. We may use an invalid file name.
6. We may attempt to perform an operation when the file is not opened for that purpose.

The C++ file stream inherits a 'stream-state' member from the class ios. This member records information on the status of a file that is being currently used. The stream state member uses bit fields to store the status of the error conditions stated above.

The class **ios** supports several member functions that can be used to read the status recorded in a file stream. These functions along with their meanings are listed in Table 11.4.

Table 11.4   Error handling functions

Function	Return value and meaning
eof()	Returns *true* (non-zero value) if end-of-file is encountered while reading; Otherwise returns *false*(zero)
fail()	Returns *true* when an input or output operation has failed
bad()	Returns *true* if an invalid operation is attempted or any unrecoverable error has occurred. However, if it is *false*, it may be possible to recover from any other error reported, and continue operation.
good()	Returns *true* if no error has occurred. This means, all the above functions are false. For instance, if **file.good()** is *true*, all is well with the stream **file** and we can proceed to perform I/O operations. When it returns *false*, no further operations can be carried out.

These functions may be used in the appropriate places in a program to locate the status of a file stream and thereby to take the necessary corrective measures. Example:

```
.....
.....
ifstream infile;
infile.open("ABC");
while(!infile.fail())
{
.....
.....    (process the file)
.....
}
if(infile.eof())
{
         .....              (terminate program normally)
}
else
      if(infile.bad())
{
   ..... (report fatal error)
}
else
{
infile.clear();          // clear error state
.....
.....
}
.....
.....
```

The function **clear()** (which we used in the previous section as well) resets the error state so that further operations can be attempted.

Remember that we have already used statements such as

```
while(infile)
{
     .....
     .....
}
```

and

```
while(infile.read(....))
{
     .....
     .....
}
```

Here, **infile** becomes *false* (zero) when end of the file is reached (and **eof()** becomes *true*).

11.10 COMMAND-LINE ARGUMENTS

Like C, C++ too supports a feature that facilitates the supply of arguments to the **main()** function. These arguments are supplied at the time of invoking the program. They are typically used to pass the names of data files. Example:

```
C > exam data results
```

Here, *exam* is the name of the file containing the program to be executed, and data and results are the filenames passed to the program as *command-line* arguments.

The command-line arguments are typed by the user and are delimited by a space. The first argument is always the filename (command name) and contains the program to be executed. How do these arguments get into the program?

The **main()** functions which we have been using up to now without any arguments can take two arguments as shown below:

```
main(int argc, char * argv[])
```

The first argument **argc** (known as *argument counter*) represents the number of arguments in the command line. The second argument **argv** (known as *argument vector*) is an array of **char** type pointers that points to the command line arguments. The size of this array will be equal to the value of **argc**. For instance, for the command line

```
C > exam data results
```

the value of **argc** would be 3 and the **argv** would be an array of three pointers to strings as shown below:

```
argu[0] ---> exam
argu[1] ---> data
argu[2] ---> results
```

Note that **argv[0]** always represents the command name that invokes the program. The character pointers **argv[1]** and **argv[2]** can be used as file names in the file opening statements as shown below:

```
.....
.....
infile.open(argv[1]);   // open data file for reading
.....
.....
outfile.open(argv[2]); // open results file for writing
.....
.....
```

Program 11.8 illustrates the use of the command-line arguments for supplying the file names. The command line is

```
test ODD EVEN
```

The program creates two files called **ODD** and **EVEN** using the command-line arguments, and a set of numbers stored in an array are written to these files. Note that the odd numbers are written to the file **ODD** and the even numbers are written to the file **EVEN**. The program then displays the contents of the files.

```
                        COMMAND-LINE ARGUMENTS

        #include  <iostream.h>
        #include  <fstream.h>
        #include  <stdlib.h>

        int main(int argc, char * argv[])
        {
            int  number[9]  =  {11,22,33,44,55,66,77,88,99};

            if(argc != 3)
            {
                cout << "argc = " << argc << "\n";
                cout << "Error in arguments \n";
                exit(1);
            }
            ofstream  fout1,  fout2;

            fout1.open(argv[1]);

            if(fout1.fail())
            {
                cout << "could not open the file"
                    << argv[1] << "\n";
                exit(1);
            }

            fout2.open(argv[2]);

            if(fout2.fail())
            {
                cout << "could not open the file "
                    << argv[2]  << "\n";
                exit(1);
            }
```

(Contd)

```
        for(int i=0; i<9; i++)
        {
            if(number[i] % 2 == 0)
            fout2 << number[i] << " ";        // write to EVEN file
            else
            fout1 << number[i] << " ";        // write to ODD file
        }

        fout1.close();
        fout2.close();

        ifstream   fin;
        char   ch;
        for(i=1; i<argc; i++)
        {
            fin.open(argv[i]);
            cout << "Contents of " << argv[i] << "\n";
            do
            {
                fin.get(ch);     // read a value
                cout << ch;      // display it
            }
            while(fin);
            cout << "\n\n";
            fin.close();
        }
        return 0;
}
```

PROGRAM 11.8

The output of Program 11.8 would be:

```
Contents of ODD
11 33 55 77 99

Contents of EVEN
22 44 66 88
```

Summary

- The C++ **I/O** system contains classes such as **ifstream, ofstream** and **fstream** to deal with file handling. These classes are derived from **fstreambase** class and are declared in a   header file *iostream*.
- A file can be opened in two ways by using the constructor function of the class and using the member function **open()** of the class.

- While opening the file using constructor, we need to pass the desired filename as a parameter to the constructor.
- The **open()** function can be used to open multiple files that use the same stream object. The second argument of the **open()** function called file mode, specifies the purpose for which the file is opened.
- If we do not specify the second argument of the **open()** function, the default values specified in the prototype of these class member functions are used while opening the file. The default values are as follows:

```
ios :: in - for ifstream functions, meaning-open for reading only.
ios :: out - for ofstream functions, meaning-open for writing only.
```

- When a file is opened for writing only, a new file is created only if there is no file of that name. If a file by that name already exists, then its contents are deleted and the file is presented as a clean file.
- To open an existing file for updating without losing its original contents, we need to open it in an append mode.
- The **fstream** class does not provide a mode by default and therefore we must provide the mode explicitly when using an object of **fstream** class. We can specify more than one file modes using bitwise OR operator while opening a file.
- Each file has associated two file pointers, one is called input or get pointer, while the other is called output or put pointer. These pointers can be moved along the files by member functions.
- Functions supported by file stream classes for performing I/O operations on files are as follows:

```
put() and get() functions handle single character at a time.
write() and read() functions write and read blocks of binary data.
```

- The class **ios** supports many member functions for managing errors that may occur during file operations.
- File names may be supplied as arguments to the **main()** function at the time of invoking the program. These arguments are known as command-line arguments.

Key Terms

> append mode
> argc
> argument counter
> argument vector
> argv
> **bad()**
> binary data
> binary format
> character format
> **clear()**

> **ios**
> **ios::app**
> **ios::ate**
> **ios::beg**
> **ios::binary**
> **ios::cur**
> **ios::end**
> **ios::in**
> **ios::nocreate**
> ios::out

> command-line
> end-of-file
> eof()
> **fail()**
> file mode
> file mode parameters
> file pointer
> file stream classes
> file streams
> **filebuf**
> files
> **fstream**
> **fstreambase**
> get pointer
> **get()**
> **good()**
> **ifstream**
> input pointer
> input stream

> **ios::noreplace**
> **ios::trunc**
> **iostream**
> **ofstream**
> **open()**
> output pointer
> output stream
> put pointer
> **put()**
> random access
> **read()**
> **seekg()**
> **seekp()**
> **sizeof()**
> streams
> **tellg()**
> **tellp()**
> updating
> **write()**

Review Questions and Exercises

11.1 *What are input and output streams?*

11.2 *What are the steps involved in using a file in a C++ program?*

11.3 *Describe the various classes available for file operations?*

11.4 *What is the difference between opening a file with a constructor function and opening a file with* **open()** *function? When is one method preferred over the other?*

11.5 *Explain how* **while(fin)** *statement detects the end of a file that is connected to fin stream?*

11.6 *What is a file mode? Describe the various file mode options available.*

11.7 *Write a statement that will create an object called* **fob** *for writing, and associate it with a file name DATA.*

11.8 *How many file objects would you need to create to manage the following situations?*
   (a) *To process four files sequentially.*
   (b) *To merge two sorted files into a third file.*
   Explain.

11.9 *Both* **ios::ate** *and* **ios::app** *place the file pointer at the end of the file (when it is opened). What then, is the difference between them?*

11.10 *What does the "current position" mean when applied to files?*

11.11 *Write statements using* **seekg()** *to achieve the following:*
   (a) *To move the pointer by 15 positions backward from current position.*
   (b) *To go to the beginning after an operation is over.*
   (c) *To go backward by 20 bytes from the end.*
   (d) *To go to byte number 50 in the file.*

11.12 *What are the advantages of saving data in binary form?*

11.13 *Describe how would you determine number of objects in a file. When do you need such information?*

11.14 *Describe the various approaches by which we can detect the end-of-file condition successfully.*

11.15 *State whether the following statements are **TRUE** or **FALSE**.*
   (a) *A stream may be connected to more than one file at a time.*
   (b) *A file pointer always contains the address of the file.*
   (c) *The statement*
   `outfile.write((char *) & obj,sizeof(obj));` writes only data in **obj** to **outfile**.
   (d) *The **ios::ate** mode allows us to write data anywhere in the file.*
   (e) *We can add data to an existing file by opening in write mode.*
   (f) *The parameter **ios::app** can be used only with the files capable of output.*
   (g) *The data written to a file with **write()** function can be read with the get() function.*
   (h) *We can use the functions **tellp()** and **tellg()** interchangeably for any file.*
   (i) *Binary files store floating point values more accurately and compactly than the text files.*
   (j) *The **fin.fail()** call returns non-zero when an operation on the file has failed.*

11.16 *Find errors in the following statements:*
   (a)   `ifstream.infile("DATA");`
   (b)   `fin1.getline(); //fin1 is input stream`
   (c)   `if(fin1.eof() == 0) exit(1);`
   (d)   `close(f1);`
   (e)   `infile.open(argc);`
   (f)   `sfinout.open(file,ios::in |ios::out| ios::ate);`

11.17 *Write a program that reads a text file and creates another file that is identical except that every sequence of consecutive blank spaces is replaced by a single space.*

11.18 *A file contains a list of telephone numbers in the following form::*
   John   23456
   Ahmed   9876
     ....

   The names contain only one word and the names and telephone numbers are separated by white spaces. Write a program to read the file and output the list in two columns. The names should be left-justified and the numbers right-justified.

11.19 *Write a program that will create a data file containing the list of telephone numbers given in Exercise 11.18. Use a class object to store each set of data.*

11.20 *Write an interactive, menu-driven program that will access the file created in Exercise 11.19 and implement the following tasks.*
   (a)   *Determine the telephone number of the specified person.*
   (b)   *Determine the name if a telephone number is known.*
   (c)   *Update the telephone number, whenever there is a change.*

12

Templates

12.1 INTRODUCTION

Templates is one of the features added to C++ recently. It is a new concept which enable us to define generic classes and functions and thus provides support for *generic programming*. Generic programming is an approach where generic types are used as parameters in algorithms so that they work for a variety of suitable data types and data structures.

A template can be used to create a family of classes or functions. For example, a class template for an **array** class would enable us to create arrays of various data types such as **int** array and **float** array. Similarly, we can define a template for a function, say **mul()**, that would help us create various versions of **mul()** for multiplying **int**, **float** and **double** type values.

A template can be considered as a kind of macro. When an object of a specific type is defined for actual use, the template definition for that class is substituted with the required data type. Since a template is defined with a *parameter* that would be replaced by a specified data type at the time of actual use of the class or function, the templates are sometimes called *parameterized classes* or *functions*.

12.2   CLASS TEMPLATES

Consider a vector class defined as follows:

```
class vector
{
        int *v;
        int size;
    public:
        vector(int m)              // create a null vector
        {
            v = new int[size = m];
            for(int i=0; i<size; i++)
                v[i] = 0;
        }
        vector(int *a)             // create a vector from an array
        {
            for(int i=0; i<size; i++)
                v[i] = a[i];
        }
        int operator*(vector &y)     // scalar product
        {
            int sum = 0;
            for(int i=0; i<size; i++)
                sum += this -> v[i] * y - v[i];
            return sum;
        }
};
```

The vector class can store an array of **int** numbers and perform the scalar product of two **int** vectors as shown below:

```
int main()
{
        int x[3] = {1,2,3};
        int y[3] = {4,5,6};
        vector v1(3);          // Creates a null vector of 3 integers
        vector v2(3);
        v1 = x;                // Creates v1 from the array x
        v2 = y;
        int R = v1 * v2;
        cout << "R = " R;

        return 0;
}
```

Now suppose we want to define a vector that can store an array of **float** values. We can do this by simply replacing the appropriate **int** declarations with **float** in the **vector** class. This means that we have to redefine the entire class all over again.

Assume that we want to define a **vector** class with the data type as a *parameter* and then use this class to create a vector of any data type instead of defining a new class every time. The template mechanism enables us to achieve this goal.

As mentioned earlier, templates allow us to define generic classes. It is a simple process to create a generic class using a template with an anonymous type. The general format of a class template is:

```
template<class T>
class classname
{
    // .........
    // class member specification
    // with anonymous type T
    // wherever appropriate
    // .........
};
```

The template definition of **vector** class shown below illustrates the syntax of a template:

```
template<class T>
class vector
{
    T* v;        // Type T vector
    int size;
public:
    vector(int m)
    {
        v = new T [size = m];
        for(int i=0; i<size; i++)
            v[i] = 0;
    }
    vector(T* a)
    {
        for(int i=0; i<size, i++)
            v[i] = a[i];
    }
    T operator*(vector &y)
    {
        T sum = 0;
        for(int i=0; i<size; i++)
            sum += this -> v[i] * y - v[i];
        return sum;
    }
};
```

The class template definition is very similar to an ordinary class definition except the prefix **template<class T>** and the use of type **T**. This prefix tells the compiler that we are going to declare a template and use **T** as a type name in the declaration. Thus, vector has become a parameterized class with the type **T** as its parameter. **T** may be substituted by any data type including the user-defined types. Now, we can create vectors for holding different data types.

Example:

```
vector <int>    v1(10);    // 10 element int vector
vector <float>  v2(25);    // 25 element float vector
```

The type **T** may represent a class name as well. Example:

```
vector <complex> v3(5); // vector of 5 complex numbers
```

A class created from a class template is called a *template class*. The syntax for defining an object of a template class is:

```
classname<type> objectname(arglist);
```

This process of creating a specific class from a class template is called *instantiation*. The compiler will perform the error analysis only when an instantiation takes place. It is, therefore, advisable to create and debug an ordinary class before converting it into a template.

Programs 12.1 and 12.2 illustrate the use of a **vector** class template for performing the scalar product of **int** type vectors as well as **float** type vectors.

```
                    EXAMPLE OF CLASS TEMPLATE
    #include <iostream>

    using namespace std;

    const size = 3;

    template <class T>
    class vector
    {
        T* v;       // type T vector
```

(Contd)

```
    public:
        vector()
        {
            v = new T[size];
            for(int i=0;i<size;i++)
                v[i] = 0;
        }
        vector(T* a)
        {
            for(int i=0;i<size;i++)
                v[i] = a[i];

        }
        T operator*(vector &y)
        {
            T sum = 0;
            for(int i=0;i<size;i++)
                sum += this -> v[i] * y.v[i];
            return sum;

        }
};
int main()
{
        int x[3] = {1,2,3};
        int y[3] = {4,5,6};
        vector <int> v1;
        vector <int> v2;
        v1 = x;
        v2 = y;
        int R = v1 * v2;
        cout << "R = " << R << "\n";
        return 0;
}
```

PROGRAM 12.1

The output of the Program 12.1 would be:

```
R = 32
```

ANOTHER EXAMPLE OF CLASS TEMPLATE

```
#include <iostream>

using namespace std;
```

(*Contd*)

```
        const size = 3;
        template <class T>
        class vector
        {
                T* v;            // type T vector
           public:
                vector()
                {
                        v = new T[size];
                        for(int i=0;i<size;i++)
                                v[i] = 0;
                }
                vector(T* a)
                {
                        for(int i=0;i<size;i++)
                                v[i] = a[i];
                }
                T operator*(vector &y)
                {
                        T sum = 0;
                        for(int i=0;i<size;i++)
                                sum += this -> v[i] * y.v[i];

                        return sum;
                }
        };

        int main()
        {
                float x[3] = {1.1,2.2,3.3};
                float y[3] = {4.4,5.5,6.6};
                vector <float> v1;
                vector <float> v2;
                v1 = x;
                v2 = y;
                float R = v1 * v2;
                cout << "R = " << R << "\n";

                return 0;
        }
```

PROGRAM 12.2

The output of the Program 12.2 would be:

```
R = 38.720001
```

12.3 CLASS TEMPLATES WITH MULTIPLE PARAMETERS

We can use more than one generic data type in a class template. They are declared as a comma-separated list within the **template** specification as shown below:

```
template<class T1, class T2, ...>
class classname
{
    .....
    .....        (Body of the class)
    .....
};
```

Program 12.3 demonstrates the use of a template class with two generic data types.

```
                TWO GENERIC DATA TYPES IN A CLASS DEFINITION

    #include <iostream>

    using namespace std;

    template<class T1, class T2>
    class Test
    {
            T1 a;
            T2 b;
       public:
            Test(T1 x, T2 y)
            {
                    a = x;
                    b = y;
            }
            void show()
            {
                    cout << a << " and " << b << "\n";
            }
    };

    int main()
    {
            Test <float,int> test1 (1.23,123);
            Test <int,char> test2 (100,'W');

            test1.show();
            test2.show();

            return 0;
    };
                            PROGRAM 12.3
```

The output of Program 12.3 will be:

```
1.23  and  123
100  and  W
```

12.4   FUNCTION TEMPLATES

Like class templates, we can also define function templates that could be used to create a family of functions with different argument types. The general format of a function template is:

```
template<class T>
returntype functioname (arguments of type T)
{
       // .....
       // Body of function
       // with type T
       // wherever appropriate
       // .....
}
```

The function template syntax is similar to that of the class template except that we are defining functions instead of classes. We must use the template parameter **T** as and when necessary in the function body and in its argument list.

The following example declares a **swap()** function template that will swap two values of a given type of data.

```
template<class  T>
void swap(T&x,  T&y)
{
    T temp = x;
    x = y;
    y = temp;
}
```

This essentially declares a set of overloaded functions, one for each type of data. We can invoke the **swap()** function like any ordinary function. For example, we can apply the **swap()** function as follows:

```
void  f(int m,int n,float a,float b)
{
       swap(m,n);          // swap two integer values
       swap(a,b);          // swap two float values
       // .....
```

This will generate a **swap()** function from the function template for each set of argument types. Program 12.4 shows how a template function is defined and implemented.

```
                    FUNCTION TEMPLATE - AN EXAMPLE

    #include <iostream>

    using namespace std;

    template <class T>
    void swap(T &x, T &y)
    {
         T temp = x;
         x = y;
         y = temp;
    }

    void fun(int m,int n,float a,float b)
    {
         cout << "m and n before swap: " << m << " " << n << "\n";
         swap(m,n);
         cout << "m and n after swap:  " << m << " " << n << "\n";

         cout << "a and b before swap: " << a << " " << b << "\n";
         swap(a,b);
         cout << "a and b after swap:  " << a << " " << b << "\n";
    }

    int main()
    {
         fun(100,200,11.22,33.44);

         return 0;
    }
                         PROGRAM  12.4
```

The output of Program 12.4:

```
m and n before swap:   100 200
m and n after swap:    200 100
a and b before swap:   11.22  33.439999
a and b after swap:    33.439999  11.22
```

Another function often used is **sort()** for sorting arrays of various types such as **int** and **double**. The following example shows a function template for bubble sort:

```
template<class T>
bubble(T a[], int n)
{
        for(int i=0; i<n-1; i++)
        for(int j=n-1; i<j; j--)
             if(a[j] < a[j-1])
             {
                    T temp = v[j];
                    v[j] = v[j-1];
                    v[j-1] = temp;
             }
}
```

Note that the swapping statements

```
T temp = v[j];
v[j] = v[j-1];
v[j-1] = temp;
```

may be replaced by the statement

```
swap(v[j],v[j-1]);
```

where **swap()** has been defined as a function template.

Here is another example where a function returns a value.

```
template<class T>
T max(T x, T y)
{
        return x>y ? x:y;
}
```

A function generated from a function template is called a *template function*. Program 12.5 demonstrates the use of two template functions in nested form for implementing the bubble sort algorithm. Program 12.6 shows another example of application of template functions.

```
                 BUBBLE SORT USING TEMPLATE FUNCTIONS

       #include <iostream>

       using namespace std;

       template<class T>
       void bubble(T a[], int n)
       {
```

(Contd)

```
            for(int i=0;  i<n-1;  i++)
                  for(int j=n-1;  i<j;  j--)
                        if(a[j]  <  a[j-1])
                        {
                                swap(a[j],a[j-1]);  // calls template function
                        }
}

template<class X>
void swap(X &a, X &b)
{
        X temp = a;
        a = b;
        b = temp;
}

int main()
{
        int x[5]  = {10,50,30,40,20};
        float y[5]  = {1.1,5.5,3.3,4.4,2.2};

        bubble(x,5); // calls template function for int values
        bubble(y,5); // calls template function for float values

        cout << "Sorted x-array: ";
        for(int i=0;  i<5;  i++)
        cout << x[i] << " ";
        cout << endl;

        cout << "Sorted y-array: ";
        for(int j=0;  j<5;  j++)
        cout << y[j] << " ";
        cout << endl;

        return 0;
}
```

PROGRAM 12.5

The output of Program 12.5:

```
Sorted x-array: 10 20 30 40 50
Sorted y-array: 1.1 2.2 3.3 4.4 5.5
```

AN APPLICATION OF TEMPLATE FUNCTION

```cpp
#include <iostream>
#include <iomanip>
#include <cmath>

using namespace std;

template <class T>
void roots(T a,T b,T c)
{
    T d = b*b - 4*a*c;
    if(d == 0)              // Roots are equal
    {
        cout << "R1 = R2 = " << -b/(2*a) << endl;
    }
    else if(d > 0)              // Two real roots
    {
        cout << "Roots are real \n";
        float R = sqrt(d);
        float R1 = (-b+R)/(2*a);
        float R2 = (-b-R)/(2*a);
        cout << "R1 = " << R1 << " and ";
        cout << "R2 = " << R2 << endl;
    }
    else                    // Roots are complex
    {
        cout << "Roots are complex \n";
        float R1 = -b/(2*a);
        float R2 = sqrt(-d)/(2*a);
        cout << "Real part = " << R1 << endl;
        cout << "Imaginary part = " << R2;
        cout << endl;
    }
}

int main()
{
    cout << "Integer coefficients \n";
    roots(1,-5,6);
    cout << "\nFloat coefficients \n";
    roots(1.5,3.6,5.0);

    return 0;
}
```

PROGRAM 12.6

The output of Program 12.6 would be:

```
Integer coefficients
Roots are real

R1 = 3 and R2 = 2

Float coefficients
Roots are complex
Real part = -1.2
Imaginary part = 1.375985
```

12.5 FUNCTION TEMPLATES WITH MULTIPLE PARAMETERS

Like template classes, we can use more than one generic data type in the template statement, using a comma-separated list as shown below:

```
template<class T1, class T2, ...>
returntype functionname(arguments of types T1, T2,...)
{
    .....
    .....     (Body of function)
    .....
}
```

Program 12.7 illustrates the concept of using two generic types in template functions.

```
                    FUNCTION WITH TWO GENERIC TYPES

    #include <iostream>
    #include <string>

    using namespace std;

    template<class T1, class T2>
    void display(T1 x, T2 y)
    {
        cout << x << " " << y << "\n";
    }

    int main()
    {
        display(1999, "EBG");
        display(12.34, 1234);
        return 0;
    }
                         PROGRAM 12.7
```

The output of Program 12.7 would be:

```
1999 EBG
12.34 1234
```

12.6 OVERLOADING OF TEMPLATE FUNCTIONS

A template function may be overloaded either by template functions or ordinary functions of its name. In such cases, the overloading resolution is accomplished as follows:

1. Call an ordinary function that has an exact match.
2. Call a template function that could be created with an exact match.
3. Try normal overloading resolution to ordinary functions and call the one that matches.

An error is generated if no match is found. Note that no automatic conversions are applied to arguments on the template functions. Program 12.8 shows how a template function is overloaded with an explicit function.

```
              TEMPLATE FUNCTION WITH EXPLICIT FUNCTION

    #include <iostream>
    #include <string>

    using namespace std;

    template <class T>
    void display(T x)
    {
         cout << "Template display: " << x << "\n";
    }

    void display(int x)          // overloads the generic display()
    {
         cout << "Explicit display: " << x << "\n";
    }

    int main()
    {
         display(100);
         display(12.34);
         display('C');

         return 0;
    }

                            PROGRAM 12.8
```

The output of Program 12.8 would be:

```
Explicit display:100
Template display:12.34
Template display:C
```

 The call **display(100)** invokes the ordinary version of **display()** and not the template version.

12.7   MEMBER FUNCTION TEMPLATES

When we created a class template for vector, all the member functions were defined as inline which was not necessary. We could have defined them outside the class as well. But remember that the member functions of the template classes themselves are parameterized by the type argument (to their template classes) and therefore these functions must be defined by the function templates. It takes the following general form:

```
Template<class T>
returntype classname <T> :: functionname(arglist)
{
      // .....
      // Function body
      // .....
}
```

The **vector** class template and its member functions are redefined as follows:

```
// Class template ..........

template<class T>
class vector
{
        T* v;
        int size;
    public:
        vector(int m);
        vector(T* a);
        T operator*(vector & y);
};

// Member function templates ........
template<class T>
vector<T> :: vector(int m);
```

```
{
    v = new T[size = m];
    for(int i=0; i<size; i++)
        v[i] = 0;
}

template< class T>
vector<T> :: vector(T* a)
{
    for(int i=0; i<size; i++)
        v[i] = a[i];
}

template< class T>
T vector<T> :: operator*(vector & y)
{
    T sum = 0;
    for(int i = 0; i < size; i++)
        sum += this -> v[i] * y.v[i];
    return sum;
}
```

12.8 NON-TYPE TEMPLATE ARGUMENTS

We have seen that a template can have multiple arguments. It is also possible to use non-type arguments. That is, in addition to the type argument **T**, we can also use other arguments such as strings, function names, constant expressions and built-in types. Consider the following example:

```
template<class T, int size>
class array
{
    T a[size];          // automatic array initialization
    // .....
    // .....
};
```

This template supplies the size of the **array** as an argument. This implies that the size of the **array** is known to the compiler at the compile time itself. The arguments must be specified whenever a template class is created. Example:

```
array<int,10>    a1;    // Array of 10 integers
array<float,5>   a2;    // Array of 5 floats
array<char,20>   a3;    // String of size 20
```

The size is given as an argument to the template class.

Summary

- C++ supports a mechanism known as template to implement the concept of generic programming.
- Templates allows us to generate a family of classes or a family of functions to handle different data types.
- Template classes and functions eliminate code duplication for different types and thus make the program development easier and more manageable.
- We can use multiple parameters in both the class templates and function templates.
- A specific class created from a class template is called a template class and the process of creating a template class is known as instantiation. Similarly, a specific function created from a function template is called a template function.
- Like other functions, template functions can be overloaded.
- Member functions of a class template must be defined as function templates using the parameters of the class template.
- We may also use non-type parameters such basic or derived data types as arguments templates.

Key Terms

- bubble sort
- class template
- **display()**
- **explicit** function
- function template
- generic programming
- instantiation
- member function template
- multiple parameters
- overloading
- **parameter**

- parameterized classes
- parameterized functions
- swapping
- **swap()**
- **template**
- template class
- template definition
- template function
- template parameter
- template specification
- templates

Review Questions and Exercises

12.1 *What is generic programming? How is it implemented in C++?*

12.2 *A template can be considered as a kind of macro. Then, what is the difference between them?*

12.3 *Distinguish between overloaded functions and function templates.*

12.4 *Distinguish between the terms class template and template class.*

12.5 *A class (or function) template is known as a parameterized class (or function). Comment.*

12.6 *State which of the following definitions are illegal.*

(a) template<class T>
```
class city
{ ...... };
```
(b) template<class P, R, class S>
```
class city
{ ...... }
```
(c) template<class T, typename S>
```
class city
{ ...... };
```
(d) template<class T, typename S>
```
class city
{ ...... };
```
(e) class<class T, int size=10>
```
class list
{ ...... };
```
(f) class<class T = int, int size>
```
class list
{ ...... };
```

12.7 *Identify which of the following function template definitions are illegal.*

(a) template<class A, B>
```
void fun(A, B)
{ ...... };
```
(b) template<class A, class A>
```
void fun(A, A)
{ ...... };
```
(c) template<class A>
```
void fun(A, A)
{ ...... };
```
(d) template<class T, typename R>
```
T fun(T, R)
{ ...... };
```
(e) template<class A>
```
A fun(int *A)
{ ...... };
```

12.8 *Write a function template for finding the minimum value contained in an array.*

12.9 *Find errors, if any, in the following code segment:*

```
template<class T>
T max(T, T)
{ ...... };
unsigned int m;
int main()
{
     max(m, 100);
}
```

12.10 *Write a class template to represent a generic vector. Include member functions to perform the following tasks:*
   (a)   *To create the vector*
   (b)   *To modify the value of a given element*
   (c)   *To multiply by a scalar value*
   (d)   *To display the vector in the form (10,20,30,......)*

13

Exception Handling

Key Concepts _____

➤ Errors and exceptions
➤ Throwing mechanism
➤ Multiple catching
➤ Rethrowing exceptions

➤ Exception handling mechanism
➤ Catching mechanism
➤ Catching all exceptions
➤ Restricting exceptions thrown

13.1 INTRODUCTION

We know that it is very rare that a program works correctly first time. It might have bugs. The two most common types of bugs are *logic errors* and *syntactic errors*. The logic errors occur due to poor understanding of the problem and solution procedure. The syntactic errors arise due to poor understanding of the language itself. We can detect these errors by using exhaustive debugging and testing procedures.

We often come across some peculiar problems other than logic or syntax errors. They are known as *exceptions*. Exceptions are run time anomalies or unusual conditions that a program may encounter while executing. Anomalies might include conditions such as division by zero, access to an array outside of its bounds, or running out of memory or disk space. When a program encounters an exceptional condition, it is important that it is identified and dealt with effectively. ANSI C++ provides built-in language features to detect and handle exceptions which are basically run time errors.

Exception handling was not part of the original C++. It is a new feature added to ANSI C++. Today, almost all compilers support this feature. C++ exception handling provides a type-safe, integrated approach, for coping with the unusual predictable problems that arise while executing a program.

13.2   BASICS OF EXCEPTION HANDLING

Exceptions are of two kinds, namely, *synchronous exceptions* and *asynchronous exceptions*. Errors such as "out-of-range index" and "over-flow" belong to the synchronous type exceptions. The errors that are caused by events beyond the control of the program (such as keyboard interrupts) are called asynchronous exceptions. The proposed exception handling mechanism in C++ is designed to handle only synchronous exceptions.

The purpose of the exception handling mechanism is to provide means to detect and report an "exceptional circumstance" so that appropriate action can be taken. The mechanism suggests a separate error handling code that performs the following tasks:

1. Find the problem (*Hit the exception*).
2. Inform that an error has occurred (*Throw the exception*).
3. Receive the error information (*Catch the exception*).
4. Take corrective actions (*Handle the exception*).

The error handling code basically consists of two segments, one to detect errors and to throw exceptions, and the other to catch the exceptions and to take appropriate actions.

13.3   EXCEPTION HANDLING MECHANISM

C++ exception handling mechanism is basically built upon three keywords, namely, **try, throw,** and **catch**. The keyword **try** is used to preface a block of statements (surrounded by braces) which may generate exceptions. This block of statements is known as *try block*. When an exception is detected, it is thrown using a **throw** statement in the try block. A *catch block* defined by the keyword **catch** 'catches' the exception 'thrown' by the throw statement in the try block, and handles it appropriately. The relationship is shown in Fig. 13.1.

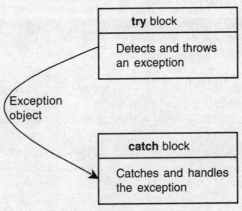

Fig. 13.1   *Try block throwing exception*

The **catch** block that catches an exception must immediately follow the **try** block that throws the exception. The general form of these two blocks are as follows:

```
    . . . . .
    . . . . .
    try
    {
        . . . . .
        throw exception;            // Block of statements which
        . . . . .                   // detects and throws an exception
        . . . . .
    }
    catch(type arg)                 // Catches exception
    {
        . . . . .
        . . . . .                   // Block of statements that
        . . . . .                   // handles the exception
        . . . . .
    }
    . . . . .
    . . . . .
```

When the **try** block throws an exception, the program control leaves the **try** block and enters the **catch** statement of the catch block. Note that exceptions are objects used to transmit information about a problem. If the type of object thrown matches the *arg* type in the **catch** statement, then catch block is executed for handling the exception. If they do not match, the program is aborted with the help of the **abort()** function which is invoked by default. When no exception is detected and thrown, the control goes to the statement immediately after the catch block. That is, the catch block is skipped. This simple try-catch mechanism is illustrated in Program 13.1.

```
                    TRY BLOCK THROWING AN EXCEPTION
    #include <iostream>

    using namespace std;

    int main()
    {
        int a,b;
        cout << "Enter Values of a and b \n";
        cin >> a;
        cin >> b;
        int x = a-b;
        try
        {
```

(Contd)

```
            if(x != 0)
            {
                    cout << "Result(a/x) = " << a/x << "\n";
            }
            else                // There is an exception
            {
                    throw(x);   // Throws int object
            }
        }
        catch(int i)            // Catches the exception
        {
                cout << "Exception caught: x = " << x << "\n";
        }

        cout << "END";

        return 0;
    }
```

PROGRAM 13.1

The output of Program 13.1:

First Run
```
    Enter Values of a and b
    20 15
    Result(a/x) = 4
    END
```

Second Run
```
    Enter Values of a and b
    10 10
    Exception caught: x = 0
    END
```

Program detects and catches a division-by-zero problem. The output of first run shows a successful execution. When no exception is thrown, the **catch** block is skipped and execution resumes with the first line after the **catch**. In the second run, the denominator x becomes zero and therefore a division-by-zero situation occurs. This exception is thrown using the object **x**. Since the exception object is an **int** type, the **catch** statement containing **int** type argument catches the exception and displays necessary message.

Most often, exceptions are thrown by functions that are invoked from within the **try** blocks. The point at which the **throw** is executed is called the *throw point*. Once an exception is thrown to the catch block, control cannot return to the throw point. This kind of relationship is shown in Fig. 13.2.

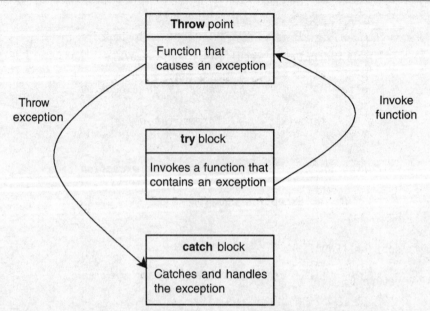

Fig. 13.2 *Function invoked by try block throwing exception*

The general format of code for this kind of relationship is shown below:

```
type function(arg list)  // Function with exception
{
     ......
     ......
     throw(object);         // Throws exception
     ......
     ......
}
......
......
try
{
     ......
     ...... Invoke function here
     ......
}
catch(type arg)              // Catches exception
{
     ......
     ...... Handles exception here
     ......
}
......
```

The **try** block is immediately followed by the **catch** block, irrespective of the location of the throw point.

Program 13.2 demonstrates how a **try** block invokes a function that generates an exception.

```
INVOKING  FUNCTION  THAT  GENERATES  EXCEPTION

// Throw point outside the try block

#include <iostream>

using namespace std;

void divide(int x, int y, int z)
{
        cout << "\nWe are inside the function \n";
        if((x-y) != 0)          // It is OK
        {
            int R = z/(x-y);
            cout << "Result = " << R << "\n";
        }
        else                    // There is a problem
        {
            throw(x-y);         // Throw point
        }
}

int main()
{
        try
        {
            cout << "We are inside the try block \n";
            divide(10,20,30);   // Invoke divide()
            divide(10,10,20);   // Invoke divide()
        }
        catch(int i)      // Catches the exception
        {
            cout << "Caught the exception \n";
        }
        return 0;
}
```

PROGRAM 13.2

The output of the Program 13.2:

```
We are inside the try block

We are inside the function
Result = -3

We are inside the function
Caught the exception
```

13.4 THROWING MECHANISM

When an exception that is desired to be handled is detected, it is thrown using the **throw** statement in one of the following forms:

```
throw(exception);
throw exception;
throw;                    // used for rethrowing an exception
```

The operand object *exception* may be of any type, including constants. It is also possible to throw objects not intended for error handling.

When an exception is thrown, it will be caught by the **catch** statement associated with the **try** block. That is, the control exits the current **try** block, and is transferred to the **catch** block after that **try** block.

Throw point can be in a deeply nested scope within a **try** block or in a deeply nested function call. In any case, control is transferred to the **catch** statement.

13.5 CATCHING MECHANISM

As stated earlier, code for handling exceptions is included in **catch** blocks. A **catch** block looks like a function definition and is of the form

```
catch(type arg)
{
    // Statements for
    // managing exceptions
}
```

The *type* indicates the type of exception that catch block handles. The parameter *arg* is an optional parameter name. Note that the exception-handling code is placed between two braces. The **catch** statement catches an exception whose type matches with the type of **catch** argument. When it is caught, the code in the **catch** block is executed.

If the parameter in the **catch** statement is named, then the parameter can be used in the exception-handling code. After executing the handler, the control goes to the statement immediately following the catch block.

Due to mismatch, if an exception is not caught, abnormal program termination will occur. It is important to note that the **catch** block is simply skipped if the **catch** statement does not catch an exception.

Multiple Catch Statements

It is possible that a program segment has more than one condition to throw an exception. In such cases, we can associate more than one **catch** statement with a **try** (much like the conditions in a **switch** statement) as shown below:

```
try
{
    // try block
}
catch(type1 arg)
{
    // catch block1
}
catch(type2 arg)
{
    // catch block2
}
......
......
catch(typeN arg)
{
    // catch blockN
}
```

When an exception is thrown, the exception handlers are searched *in order* for an appropriate match. The first handler that yields a match is executed. After executing the handler, the control goes to the first statement after the last **catch** block for that **try**. (In other words, all other handlers are bypassed). When no match is found, the program is terminated.

It is possible that arguments of several **catch** statements match the type of an exception. In such cases, the first handler that matches the exception type is executed.

Program 13.3 shows a simple example where multiple catch statements are used to handle various types of exceptions.

MULTIPLE CATCH STATEMENTS

```cpp
#include <iostream>

using namespace std;

void test(int x)
{
    try
    {
        if(x == 1) throw x;                 // int
        else
            if(x == 0) throw 'x';           // char
        else
            if(x == -1) throw 1.0;          // double
        cout << "End of try-block \n";
    }
    catch(char c) // Catch 1
    {
        cout << "Caught a character \n";
    }
    catch(int m)  // Catch 2
    {
        cout << "Caught an integer \n";
    }
    catch(double d)     // Catch 3
    {
        cout << "Caught a double \n";
    }
    cout << "End of try-catch system \n\n";
}

int main()
{
    cout << "Testing Multiple Catches \n";
    cout << "x ==  1 \n";
    test(1);
    cout << "x ==  0 \n";
    test(0);
    cout << "x == -1 \n";
    test(-1);
    cout << "x ==  2 \n";
    test(2);

    return 0;
}
```

PROGRAM 13.3

The output of the Program 13.3:

```
Testing Multiple Catches
x == 1
Caught an integer
End of try-catch system

x == 0
Caught a character
End of try-catch system

x == -1
Caught a double
End of try-catch system0

x == 2
End of try-block
End of try-catch system
```

The program when executed first, invokes the function **test()** with x = 1 and therefore throws x an **int** exception. This matches the type of the parameter **m** in catch2 and therefore catch2 handler is executed. Immediately after the execution, the function **test()** is again invoked with x = 0. This time, the function throws 'x', a character type exception and therefore the first handler is executed. Finally, the handler catch3 is executed when a double type exception is thrown. Note that every time only the handler which catches the exception is executed and all other handlers are bypassed.

When the **try** block does not throw any exceptions and it completes normal execution, control passes to the first statement after the last **catch** handler associated with that try block.

 try block does not throw any exception, when the **test()** is invoked with x = 2.

Catch All Exceptions

In some situations, we may not be able to anticipate all possible types of exceptions and therefore may not be able to design independent **catch** handlers to catch them. In such circumstances, we can force a **catch** statement to catch all exceptions instead of a certain type alone. This could be achieved by defining the **catch** statement using ellipses as follows:

```
catch(...)
{
        // Statements for processing
        // all exceptions
}
```

Program 13.4 illustrates the functioning of catch(...).

```
                        CATCHING ALL EXCEPTIONS

    #include <iostream>

    using namespace std;

    void test(int x)
    {
        try
        {
            if(x == 0) throw x;              // int
            if(x == -1) throw 'x';           // char
            if(x == 1) throw 1.0;            // float
        }
        catch(...)       // catch all
        {
            cout << "Caught an exception \n";
        }
    }

    int main()
    {
        cout << "Testing Generic Catch \n";
        test(-1);
        test(0);
        test(1);

        return 0;
    }

                            PROGRAM 13.4
```

The output of the Program 13.4:

```
Testing Generic Catch
Caught an exception
Caught an exception
Caught an exception
```

Note that all the throws were caught by the **catch(...)** statement.

It may be a good idea to use the **catch(...)** as a default statement alongwith other catch handlers so that it can catch all those exceptions which are not handled explicitly.

Remember, **catch(...)** should always be placed last in the list of handlers. Placing it before other **catch** blocks would prevent those blocks from catching exceptions.

13.6   RETHROWING AN EXCEPTION

A handler may decide to rethrow the exception caught without processing it.   In such situations, we may simply invoke **throw** without any arguments as shown below:

```
throw;
```

This causes the current exception to be thrown to the next enclosing **try/catch** sequence and is caught by a **catch** statement listed after that enclosing **try** block. Program 13.5 demonstrates how an exception is rethrown and caught.

```
                        RETHROWING AN EXCEPTION

    #include <iostream>

    using namespace std;

    void divide(double x, double y)
    {
        cout << "Inside function \n";
        try
        {
            if(y == 0.0)
                throw y;            // Throwing double
            else
                cout << "Division = " << x/y << "\n";
        }
        catch(double)               // Catch a double
        {
            cout << "Caught double inside function \n";
            throw;                  // Rethrowing double
        }
        cout << "End of function \n\n";
    }

    int main()
    {
        cout << "Inside main \n";
        try
        {
```

(Contd)

```
            divide(10.5,2.0);
            divide(20.0,0.0);
    }
    catch(double)
    {
            cout << "Caught double inside main \n";
    }
    cout << "End of main \n";

    return 0;
}
```

PROGRAM 13.5

The output of the Program 13.5:

```
Inside main
Inside function
Division = 5.25
End of function

Inside function
Caught double inside function
Caught double inside main
End of main
```

When an exception is rethrown, it will not be caught by the same **catch** statement or any other **catch** in that group. Rather, it will be caught by an appropriate **catch** in the outer **try/catch** sequence only.

A **catch** handler itself may detect and throw an exception. Here again, the exception thrown will not be caught by any **catch** statements in that group. It will be passed on to the next outer **try/catch** sequence for processing.

13.7   SPECIFYING EXCEPTIONS

It is possible to restrict a function to throw only certain specified exceptions. This is achieved by adding a **throw** *list* clause to the function definition. The general form of using an *exception specification* is:

```
type function(arg-list) throw (type-list)
{
    ......
    ...... Function body
    ......
}
```

The *type-list* specifies the type of exceptions that may be thrown. Throwing any other type of exception will cause abnormal program termination. If we wish to prevent a function from throwing any exception, we may do so by making the *type-list* empty. That is, we must use

```
throw(); // Empty list
```

in the function header line.

A function can only be restricted in what types of exceptions it throws back to the *try* block that called it. The restriction applies only when throwing an exception out of the function (and not within a function).

Program 13.6 demonstrates how we can restrict a function to throw only certain types and not all.

```
                    TESTING THROW RESTRICTIONS

    #include <iostream>

    using namespace std;

    void test(int x) throw(int,double)
    {
        if(x == 0) throw 'x';              // char
        else
            if(x == 1) throw x;            // int
        else
            if(x == -1) throw 1.0;         // double
        cout << "End of function block \n";
    }

    int main()
    {
        try
        {
            cout << "Testing Throw Restrictions \n";
            cout << "x ==  0 \n";
            test(0);
            cout << "x ==  1 \n";
            test(1);
            cout << "x == -1 \n";
            test(-1);
            cout << "x ==  2 \n";
            test(2);
        }
```

(Contd)

```
        catch(char c)
        {
                cout << "Caught a character \n";
        }
        catch(int m)
        {
                cout << "Caught an integer \n";
        }
        catch(double d)
        {
                cout << "Caught a double \n";
        }
        cout << "End of try-catch system \n\n";

        return 0;
    }
```

PROGRAM 13.6

The output of the Program 13.6:

```
Testing Throw Restrictions
x == 0
Caught a character
End of try-catch system
```

Summary

- Exceptions are peculiar problems that a program may encounter at run time.
- Exceptions are of two types: *synchronous* and *asynchronous*. C++ provides mechanism for handling synchronous exceptions.
- An exception is typically caused by a faulty statement in a **try** block. The statement discovers the error and throws it, which is caught by a **catch** statement.
- The catch statement defines a block of statements to handle the exception appropriately.
- When an exception is not caught, the program is aborted.
- A **try** block may throw an exception directly or invoke a function that throws an exception. Irrespective of location of the throw point, the catch block is placed immediately after the try block.
- We can place two or more catch blocks together to catch and handle multiple types of exceptions thrown by a try block.
- It is also possible to make a catch statement to catch all types of exceptions using ellipses as its argument.
- We may also restrict a function to throw only a set of specified exceptions by adding a throw specification clause to the function definition.

Key Terms

- ➤ **abort**() function
- ➤ asynchronous exceptions
- ➤ bugs
- ➤ **catch** block
- ➤ **catch(...)** statement
- ➤ catching mechanism
- ➤ errors
- ➤ exception handler
- ➤ exception handling mechanism
- ➤ exception specifying
- ➤ exceptions
- ➤ logic errors

- ➤ multiple catch
- ➤ out-of-range index
- ➤ overflow
- ➤ rethrowing exceptions
- ➤ synchronous exceptions
- ➤ syntactic errors
- ➤ **throw**
- ➤ throw point
- ➤ **throw** statement
- ➤ **throw()**
- ➤ throwing mechanism
- ➤ **try** block

Review Questions and Exercises

13.1 *What is an exception?*

13.2 *How is an exception handled in C++?*

13.3 *What are the advantages of using exception handling mechanism in a program?*

13.4 *When should a program throw an exception?*

13.5 *When is a **catch(...)** handler is used?*

13.6 *What is an exception specification? When is it used?*

13.7 *What should be placed inside a **try** block?*

13.8 *What should be placed inside a **catch** block?*

13.9 *When do we used multiple **catch** handlers?*

13.10 *State what will happen in the following situations:*

  (a) *An exception is thrown outside a **try** block*

  (b) *No **catch** handler matches the type of exception thrown*

  (c) *Several handlers match the type of exception thrown*

  (d) *A **catch** handler throws an exception*

  (e) *A function throws an exception of type not specified in the specification list*

  (f) ***catch(...)** is the first of cluster of **catch** handlers*

  (g) *Placing **throw()** in a function header line*

  (h) *An exception rethrown within a **catch** block*

13.11 *Identify errors, if any, in the following statements*

```
(a) catch(int a, float b)
    {...}
(b) try
    {throw 100;};
(c) try
    {fun1()}
(d) throw a, b;
```

```
(e) void divide(int a, int b) throw(x, y)
    {......}
(f) catch(int x, ..., float y)
    {......}
(g) try
    {throw x/y;}
(h) try
    {if(!x) throw x;}
    catch(x)
    {cout << "x is zero \n";}
```

13.12 *Explain under what circumstances the following statements would be used:*

```
(a) throw;
(b) void fun1(float x) throw()
(c) catch(...)
```

13.13 *Write a program containing a possible exception. Use a try block to throw it and a catch block to handle it properly.*

13.14 *Write a program that illustrates the application of multiple catch statements.*

13.15 *Write a program which uses **catch(...)** handler.*

13.16 *Write a program that demonstrates how certain exception types are not allowed to be thrown.*

13.17 *Write a program to demonstrate the concept of rethrowing an exception.*

13.18 *Write a program with the following:*
  (a)   *A function to read two double type numbers from keyboard*
  (b)   *A function to calculate the division of these two numbers*
  (c)   *A try block to throw an exception when a wrong type of data is keyed in*
  (d)   *A try block to detect and throw an exception if the condition "divide-by-zero" occurs*
  (e)   *Appropriate catch block to handle the exceptions thrown*

13.19 *Write a main program that calls a deeply nested function containing an exception. Incorporate necessary exception handling mechanism.*

Introduction to the Standard Template Library

14.1 INTRODUCTION

We have seen how templates can be used to create generic classes and functions that could extend support for generic programming. In order to help the C++ users in generic programming, Alexander Stepanov and Meng Lee of Hewlett-Packard developed a set of general-purpose templatized classes (data structures) and functions (algorithms) that could be used as a standard approach for storing and processing of data. The collection of these generic classes and functions is called the *Standard Template Library (STL)*. The STL has now become a part of the ANSI standard C++ class library.

STL is large and complex and it is difficult to discuss all of its features in this chapter. We therefore present here only the most important features that would enable the readers to begin using the STL effectively. Using STL can save considerable time and effort, and lead to high quality programs. All these benefits are possible because we are basically "reusing" the well-written and well-tested components defined in the STL.

STL components which are now part of the Standard C++ Library are defined in the **namespace std**. We must therefore use the **using namespace** directive

```
using namespace std;
```

to inform the compiler that we intend to use the Standard C++ Library. All programs in this chapter use this directive.

14.2 COMPONENTS OF STL

The STL contains several components. But at its core are three key components. They are:

- containers,
- algorithms, and
- iterators.

These three components work in conjunction with one another to provide support to a variety of programming solutions. The relationship between the three components is shown in Fig.14.1. *Algorithms* employ *iterators* to perform operations stored in *containers*.

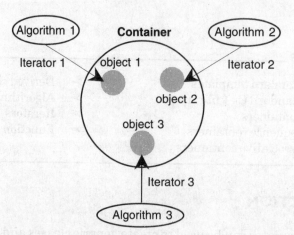

Fig. 14.1 *Relationship between the three STL components*

A *container* is an object that actually stores data. It is a way data is organized in memory. The STL containers are implemented by template classes and therefore can be easily customized to hold different types of data.

An *algorithm* is a procedure that is used to process the data contained in the containers. The STL includes many different kinds of algorithms to provide support to tasks such as initializing, searching, copying, sorting, and merging. Algorithms are implemented by template functions.

An *iterator* is an object(like a pointer) that points to an element in a container. We can use iterators to move through the contents of containers. Iterators are handled just like pointers. We can increment or decrement them. Iterators connect algorithms with containers and play a key role in the manipulation of data stored in the containers.

14.3 CONTAINERS

As stated earlier, containers are objects that hold data (of same type). The STL defines ten containers which are grouped into three categories as illustrated in Fig. 14.2. Table 14.1 gives the details of all these containers as well as header to be included to use each one of them and the type of iterator supported by each container class.

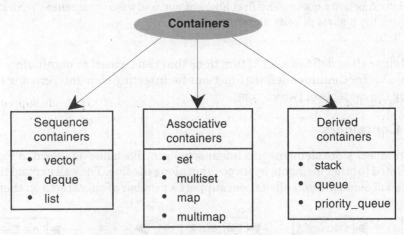

Fig. 14.2   *Three major categories of containers*

Table 14.1   Containers supported by the STL

Container	Description	Header file	Iterator
vector	A dynamic array. Allows insertions and deletions at back. Permits direct access to any element	\<vector\>	Random access
list	A bidirectional, linear list. Allows insertions and deletions anywhere.	\<list\>	Bidirectional
deque	A double-ended queue. Allows insertions and deletions at both the ends. Permits direct access to any element.	\<deque\>	Random access
set	An associate container for storing unique sets. Allows rapid lookup. (No duplicates allowed)	\<set\>	Bidirectional
multiset	An associate container for storing non-unique sets. (Duplicates allowed)	\<set\>	Bidirectional
map	An associate container for storing unique key/value pairs. Each key is associated with only one value (One-to-one mapping). Allows key-based lookup.	\<map\>	Bidirectional

(Contd)

multimap	An associate container for storing key/value pairs in which one key may be associated with more than one value (one-to-many mapping). Allows key-based lookup.	\<map>	Bidirectional
stack	A standard stack. Last-in-first-out(LIFO).	\<stack>	No iterator
queue	A standard queue. First-in-first-out(FIFO).	\<queue>	No iterator
priority-queue	A priority queue. The first element out is always the highest priority element.	\<queue>	No iterator

Each container class defines a set of functions that can be used to manipulate its contents. For example, a vector container defines functions for inserting elements, erasing the contents, and swapping the contents of two vectors.

Sequence Containers

Sequence containers store elements in a linear sequence, like a line as shown in Fig. 14.3. Each element is related to other elements by its position along the line. They all expand themselves to allow insertion of elements and all of them support a number of operations on them.

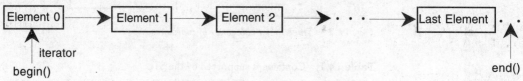

Fig. 14.3   *Elements in a sequence container*

The STL provides three types of sequence containers:

* vector
* list
* deque

Elements in all these containers can be accessed using an iterator. The difference between the three of them is related to only their performance. Table 14.2 compares their performance in terms of speed of random access and insertion or deletion of elements.

Table 14.2   Comparison of sequence containers

Container	Random access	Insertion or deletion in the middle	Insertion or deletion at the ends
vector	Fast	Slow	Fast at back
list	Slow	Fast	Fast at front
deque	Fast	Slow	Fast at both the ends

Associative Containers

Associative containers are designed to support direct access to elements using keys. They are not sequential. There are four types of associative containers:

* set
* multiset
* map
* multimap

All these containers store data in a structure called *tree* which facilitates fast searching, deletion, and insertion. However, these are very slow for random access and inefficient for sorting.

Containers **set** and **multiset** can store a number of items and provide operations for manipulating them using the values as the *keys*. For example, a **set** might store objects of the **student** class which are ordered alphabetically using names as keys. We can search for a desired student using his name as the key. The main difference between a **set** and a **multiset** is that a **multiset** allows duplicate items while a **set** does not.

Containers **map** and **multimap** are used to store pairs of items, one called the *key* and the other called the *value*. We can manipulate the values using the keys associated with them. The values are sometimes called *mapped values*. The main difference between a **map** and a **multimap** is that a **map** allows only one key for a given value to be stored while **multimap** permits multiple keys.

Derived Containers

The STL provides three derived containers namely, **stack**, **queue**, and **priority_queue**. These are also known as *container adaptors*.

Stacks, queues and priority queues can be created from different sequence containers. The derived containers do not support iterators and therefore we cannot use them for data manipulation. However, they support two member functions **pop( )** and **push( )** for implementing deleting and inserting operations.

14.4 ALGORITHMS

Algorithms are functions that can be used generally across a variety of containers for processing their contents. Although each container provides functions for its basic operations, STL provides more than sixty standard algorithms to support more extended or complex operations. Standard algorithms also permit us to work with two different types of containers at the same time. Remember, STL algorithms are not member functions or friends of containers. They are standalone template functions.

STL algorithms reinforce the philosophy of reusability. By using these algorithms, programmers can save a lot of time and effort. To have access to the STL algorithms, we must include **<algorithm>** in our program.

STL algorithms, based on the nature of operations they perform, may be categorized as under:

* Retrieve or non-mutating algorithms
* Mutating algorithms
* Sorting algorithms
* Set algorithms
* Relational algorithms

These algorithms are summarized in Tables 14.3 to 14.7. STL also contains a few numeric algorithms under the header file **<numeric>**. They are listed in Table 14.8.

Table 14.3   Non-mutating algorithms

Operations	Description
adjacent_find( )	Finds adjacent pair of objects that are equal
count( )	Counts occurrence of a value in a sequence
count_if( )	Counts number of elements that matches a predicate
equal( )	True if two ranges are the same
find( )	Finds first occurrence of a value in a sequence
find_end( )	Finds last occurrence of a value in a sequence
find_first_of( )	Finds a value from one sequence in another
find_if( )	Finds first match of a predicate in a sequence
for_each( )	Apply an operation to each element
mismatch( )	Finds first elements for which two sequences differ
search( )	Finds a subsequence within a sequence
search_n( )	Finds a sequence of a specified number of similar elements

Table 14.4   Mutating algorithms

Operations	Description
Copy( )	Copies a sequence
copy_backward( )	Copies a sequence from the end
fill( )	Fills a sequence with a specified value
fill_n( )	Fills first n elements with a specified value
generate( )	Replaces all elements with the result of an operation
generate_n( )	Replaces first n elements with the result of an operation
iter_swap( )	Swaps elements pointed to by iterators
random_shuffle( )	Places elements in random order
remove( )	Deletes elements of a specified value
remove_copy( )	Copies a sequence after removing a specified value
remove_copy_if( )	Copies a sequence after removing elements matching a predicate
remove_if( )	Deletes elements matching a predicate
replace( )	Replaces elements with a specified value

(Contd)

replace_copy( )	Copies a sequence replacing elements with a given value
replace_copy_if( )	Copies a sequence replacing elements matching a predicate
replace_if( )	Replaces elements matching a predicate
reverse( )	Reverses the order of elements
reverse_copy( )	Copies a sequence into reverse order
rotate( )	Rotates elements
rotate_copy( )	Copies a sequence into a rotated
swap( )	Swaps two elements
swap_ranges( )	Swaps two sequences
transform( )	Applies an operation to all elements
unique( )	Deletes equal adjacent elements
unique_copy( )	Copies after removing equal adjacent elements

Table 14.5   Sorting algorithms

Operations	Description
binary_search( )	Conducts a binary search on an ordered sequence
equal_range( )	Finds a subrange of elements with a given value
inplace_merge( )	Merges two consecutive sorted sequences
lower_bound( )	Finds the first occurrence of a specified value
make_heap( )	Makes a heap from a sequence
merge( )	Merges two sorted sequences
nth_element( )	Puts a specified element in its proper place
partial_sort( )	Sorts a part of a sequence
partial_sort_copy()	Sorts a part of a sequence and then copies
Partition( )	Places elements matching a predicate first
pop_heap( )	Deletes the top element
push_heap( )	Adds an element to heap
sort( )	Sorts a sequence
sort_heap( )	Sorts a heap
stable_partition( )	Places elements matching a predicate first matching relative order
stable_sort( )	Sorts maintaining order of equal elements
upper_bound( )	Finds the last occurrence of a specified value

Table 14.6   Set algorithms

Operations	Description
includes( )	Finds whether a sequence is a subsequence of another
set_difference( )	Constructs a sequence that is the difference of two ordered sets
set_intersection( )	Constructs a sequence that contains the intersection of ordered sets
set_symmetric_difference()	Produces a set which is the symmetric difference between two ordered sets
set_union( )	Produces sorted union of two ordered sets

Table 14.7   Relational algorithms

Operations	Description
equal( )	Finds whether two sequences are the same
lexicographical_compare()	Compares alphabetically one sequence with other
max( )	Gives maximum of two values
max_element( )	Finds the maximum element within a sequence
min( )	Gives minimum of two values
min_element( )	Finds the minimum element within a sequence
mismatch( )	Finds the first mismatch between the elements in two sequences

Table 14.8   Numeric algorithms

Operations	Description
accumulate( )	Accumulates the results of operation on a sequence
adjacent_difference( )	Produces a sequence from another sequence
inner_product( )	Accumulates the results of operation on a pair of sequences
partial_sum( )	Produces a sequence by operation on a pair of sequences

14.5   ITERATORS

Iterators behave like pointers and are used to access container elements. They are often used to traverse from one element to another, a process known as *iterating* through the container.

There are five types of iterators as described in Table 14.9.

Table 14.9   Iterators and their characteristics

Iterator	Access method	Direction of movement	I/O capability	Remark
Input	Linear	Forward only	Read only	Cannot be saved
Output	Linear	Forward only	Write only	Cannot be saved
Forward	Linear	Forward only	Read/Write	Can be saved
Bidirectional	Linear	Forward and backward	Read/Write	Can be saved
Random	Random	Forward and backward	Read/Write	Can be saved

Different types of iterators must be used with the different types of containers (See Table 14.1). Note that only sequence and associative containers are traversable with iterators.

Each type of iterator is used for performing certain functions. Figure 14.4 gives the functionality Venn diagram of the iterators. It illustrates the level of functionality provided by different categories of iterators.

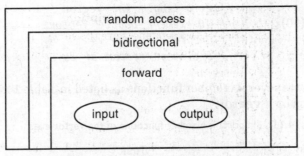

Fig. 14.4 *Functionality Venn diagram of iterators*

The *input* and *output* iterators support the least functions. They can be used only to traverse in a container. The *forward* iterator supports all operations of input and output iterators and also retains its position in the container. A *bidirectional* iterator, while supporting all forward iterator operations, provides the ability to move in the backward direction in the container. A *random access* iterator combines the functionality of a bidirectional iterator with an ability to jump to an arbitrary location. Table 14.10 sum marizes the operations that can be performed on each iterator type.

Table 14.10   Operations supported by iterators

Iterator	Element access	Read	Write	Increment operation	Comparison
Input	->	v = *p		++	==, !=
Output			*p = v	++	
Forward	->	v = *p	*p = v	++	==, !=
Bidirectional	->	v = *p	*p = v	++, - -	==, !=
Random access	->, [ ]	v = *p	*p = v	++, - -, +, -, +=, -=	==, !=, <, >, <=, >=

14.6 APPLICATION OF CONTAINER CLASSES

It is beyond the scope of this book to examine all the containers supported in the STL and provide illustrations. Therefore, we illustrate here the use of the three most popular containers, namely, **vector**, **list**, and **map**.

Vectors

The **vector** is the most widely used container. It stores elements in contiguous memory locations and enables direct access to any element using the subscript operator [ ]. A **vector** can change its size dynamically and therefore allocates memory as needed at run time.

The **vector** container supports random access iterators, and a wide range of iterator operations (See Table 14.10) may be applied to a **vector** iterator. Class **vector** supports a number of constructors for creating **vector** objects.

```
vector<int> v1;              // Zero-length int vector
vector<double> v2(10);       // 10-element double vector
vector<int> v3(v4);          // Creates v3 from v4
vector<int> v(5, 2);         // 5-element vector of 2s
```

The **vector** class supports several member functions as listed in Table 14.11. We can also use all the STL algorithms on a **vector**.

Table 14.11   Important member functions of the vector class

Function	Task
at( )	Gives a reference to an element
back( )	Gives a reference to the last element
begin( )	Gives a reference to the first element
capacity( )	Gives the current capacity of the vector
clear( )	Deletes all the elements from the vector
empty( )	Determines if the vector is empty or not
end( )	Gives a reference to the end of the vector
erase( )	Deletes specified elements
insert( )	Inserts elements in the vector
pop_back( )	Deletes the last element
push_back( )	Adds an element to the end
resize( )	Modifies the size of the vector to the specified value
size( )	Gives the number of elements
swap( )	Exchanges elements in the specified two vectors

Program 14.1 illustrates the use of several functions of the **vector** class template. Note that an iterator is used as a pointer to elements of the vector. We must include header file **<vector>** to use **vector** class in our programs.

USING VECTORS

```
#include <iostream>
#include <vector>        // Vector header file

using namespace std;

void display(vector<int> &v)
{
     for(int i=0;i<v.size();i++)
     {
         cout << v[i] << "  ";
     }
     cout << "\n";
}

int main()
{
```

(Contd)

```
vector<int> v;          // Create a vector of type int
cout << "Initial size = " << v.size() << "\n";

// Putting values into the vector
int x;
cout << "Enter five integer values: ";
for(int i=0; i<5; i++)
{
    cin >> x;
     v.push_back(x);
}
cout << "Size after adding 5 values: ";
cout << v.size() << "\n";

// Display the contents
cout << "Current contents: \n";
display(v);

// Add one more value
v.push_back(6.6);       // float value truncated to int

// Display size and contents
cout << "\nSize = " << v.size() << "\n";
cout << "Contents now: \n";
display(v);

// Inserting elements
vector<int> :: iterator itr = v.begin();    // iterator
itr = itr + 3;          // itr points to 4th element
v.insert(itr,1,9);

// Display the contents
cout << "\nContents after inserting: \n";
display(v);

// Removing 4th and 5th elements
v.erase(v.begin()+3,v.begin()+5);   // Removes 4th and 5th element

// Display the contents
cout << "\nContents after deletion: \n";
display(v);
cout << "END\n";
return(0);
}
```

PROGRAM 14.1

Given below is the output of Program 14.1:

```
Initial size = 0

Enter five integer values:  1 2 3 4 5
Size after adding 5 values:  5
Current contents:
1  2  3  4  5

Size = 6
Contents now:
1  2  3  4  5  6

Contents after inserting:
1  2  3  9  4  5  6

Contents after deletion:
1  2  3  5  6
END
```

The program uses a number of functions to create and manipulate a vector. The member function **size()** gives the current size of the vector. After creating an **int** type empty vector **v** of zero size, the program puts five values into the vector using the member function **push_back()**. Note that **push_back()** takes a value as its argument and adds it to the back end of the vector. Since the vector **v** is of type **int**, it can accept only integer values and therefore the statement

```
v.push_back(6.6);
```

truncates the values 6.6 to 6 and then puts it into the vector at its back end.

The program uses an iterator to access the vector elements. The statement

```
vector<int> :: iterator itr = v.begin();
```

declares an iterator **itr** and makes it to point to the first position of the vector. The statements

```
itr = itr + 3;
v.insert(itr,9);
```

inserts the value 9 as the fourth element. Similarly, the statement

```
v.erase(v.begin()+3,  v.begin()+5);
```

deletes 4th and 5th elements from the vector. Note that **erase(m,n)** deletes only n-m elements starting from mth element and the nth element is not deleted.

The elements of a vector may also be accessed using subscripts (as we do in arrays). Notice the use of **v[i]** in the function **display()** for displaying the contents of **v**. The call **v.size()** in the **for** loop of **display()** gives the current size of **v**.

Lists

The **list** is another container that is popularly used. It supports a bidirectional, linear list and provides an efficient implementation for deletion and insertion operations. Unlike a vector, which supports random access, a list can be accessed sequentially only.

Bidirectional iterators are used for accessing list elements. Any algorithm that requires input, output, forward, or bidirectional iterators can operate on a **list**. Class **list** provides many member functions for manipulating the elements of a list. Important member functions of the **list** class are given in Table 14.12. Use of some of these functions is illustrated in Program 14.2. Header file **<list>** must be included to use the container class **list**.

```
                         USING LISTS

        #include <iostream>
        #include <list>
        #include <cstdlib>    // For using rand() function

        using namespace std;

        void display(list<int> &lst)
        {
              list<int> :: iterator p;
              for(p = lst.begin(); p != lst.end(); ++p)
                     cout << *p << ", ";
              cout << "\n\n";
        }

        int main()
        {
              list<int> list1;      // Empty list of zero length
              list<int> list2(5);   // Empty list of size 5

              for(int i=0;i<3;i++)
                     list1.push_back(rand()/100);

              list<int> :: iterator p;
              for(p=list2.begin(); p!=list2.end();++p)
                     *p = rand()/100;
```

(Contd)

```
                cout << "List1 \n";
                display(list1);
                cout << "List2 \n";
                display(list2);

                // Add two elements at the ends of list1
                list1.push_front(100);
                list1.push_back(200);

                // Remove an element at the front of list2
                list2.pop_front();

                cout << "Now List1 \n";
                display(list1);
                cout << "Now List2 \n";
                display(list2);

                list<int> listA, listB;
                listA = list1;
                listB = list2;

                // Merging two lists(unsorted)
                list1.merge(list2);
                cout << "Merged unsorted lists \n";
                display(list1);

                // Sorting and merging
                listA.sort();
                listB.sort();
                listA.merge(listB);
                cout << "Merged sorted lists \n";
                display(listA);

                // Reversing a list
                listA.reverse();
                cout << "Reversed merged list \n";
                display(listA);

                return(0);
        }
```

PROGRAM 14.2

Output of the Program 14.2 would be:

```
List1
0, 184, 63,

List2
265, 191, 157, 114, 293,

Now List1
100, 0, 184, 63, 200,

Now List2
191, 157, 114, 293,

Merged unsorted lists
100, 0, 184, 63, 191, 157, 114, 200, 293,

Merged sorted lists
0, 63, 100, 114, 157, 184, 191, 200, 293,

Reversed merged list
293, 200, 191, 184, 157, 114, 100, 63, 0,
```

The program declares two empty lists, **list1** with zero length and **list2** of size 5. The **list1** is filled with three values using the member function **push_back()** and math function rand(). The **list2** is filled using a **list** type iterator **p** and a **for** loop. Remember that **list2.begin()** gives the position of the first element while **list2.end()** gives the position immediately after the last element. Values are inserted at both the ends using **push_front()** and **push_back()** functions. The function **pop_front()** removes the first element in the list. Similarly, we may use **pop_back()** to remove the last element.

The objects of list can be initialized with other list objects like

```
listA = list1;
listB = list2;
```

The statement

```
list1.merge(list2);
```

simply adds the **list2** elements to the end of **list1**. The elements in a list may be sorted in increasing order using **sort()** member function. Note that when two sorted lists are merged, the elements are inserted in appropriate locations and therefore the merged list is also a sorted one.

We use a **display()** function to display the contents of various lists. Note the difference between the implementations of **display()** in Program 14.1 and Program 14.2.

Table 14.12   Important member functions of the list class

Function	Task
back( )	Gives reference to the last element
begin( )	Gives reference to the first element
clear( )	Deletes all the elements
empty( )	Decides if the list is empty or not
end( )	Gives reference to the end of the list
erase( )	Deletes elements as specified
insert( )	Inserts elements as specified
merge( )	Merges two ordered lists
pop_back( )	Deletes the last element
pop_front( )	Deletes the first element
push_back( )	Adds an element to the end
push_front( )	Adds an element to the front
remove( )	Removes elements as specified
resize( )	Modifies the size of the list
reverse( )	Reverses the list
size( )	Gives the size of the list
sort( )	Sorts the list
splice( )	Inserts a list into the invoking list
swap( )	Exchanges the elements of a list with those in the invoking list
unique( )	Deletes the duplicating elements in the list

Maps

A map is a sequence of (key, value) pairs where a single value is associated with each unique key as shown in Fig. 14.5. Retrieval of values is based on the key and is very fast. We should specify the key to obtain the associated value.

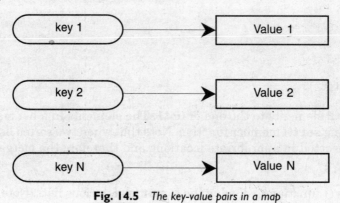

Fig. 14.5   *The key-value pairs in a map*

A **map** is commonly called an *associative array*. The key is specified using the subscript operator [ ] as shown below:

```
phone[ "John" ] = 1111;
```

This creates an entry for "John" and associates(i.e. assigns) the value 1111 to it. **phone** is a **map** object. We can change the value, if necessary, as follows:

```
phone[ "John" ] = 9999;
```

This changes the value 1111 to 9999. We can also insert and delete pairs anywhere in the **map** using **insert( )** and **erase( )** functions. Important member functions of the **map** class are listed in Table 14.13.

Table 14.13   Important member functions of the map class

Function	Task
begin( )	Gives reference to the first element
clear( )	Deletes all elements from the map
empty( )	Decides whether the map is empty or not
end( )	Gives a reference to the end of the map
erase( )	Deletes the specified elements
find( )	Gives the location of the specified element
insert( )	Inserts elements as specified
size( )	Gives the size of the map
swap( )	Exchanges the elements of the given map with those of the invoking map

Program 14.13 shows a simple example of a **map** used as an associative array. Note that **<map>** header must be included.

```
                        USING MAPS

#include <iostream>
#include <map>
#include <string>

using namespace std;
typedef map<string,int> phoneMap;

int main()
{
        string name;
        int number;
```

(Contd)

```
        phoneMap phone;

        cout << "Enter three sets of name and number \n";

        for(int i=0;i<3;i++)
        {
            cin >> name;          // Get key
            cin >> number;        // Get value
            phone[name] = number; // Put them in map
        }

        phone["Jacob"] = 4444;              // Insert Jacob

        phone.insert(pair<string,int> ("Bose", 5555));
        int n = phone.size();
        cout << "\nSize of Map: " << n << "\n\n";

        cout << "List of telephone numbers \n";
        phoneMap::iterator p;
        for(p=phone.begin(); p!=phone.end(); p++)
        {
            cout << (*p).first << "   " << (*p).second << "\n";
        }

        cout << "\n";
        cout << "Enter name: ";            // Get name
        cin >> name;
        number = phone[name];              // Find number
        cout << "Number: " << number << "\n";

        return 0;
    }
```

PROGRAM 14.3

Output of the Program 14.3 would be:

```
Enter three sets of name and number:
Prasanna 1111
Singh 2222
Raja 3333

Size of Map: 5

List of telephone numbers
Bose 5555
Jacob 4444
```

```
Prasanna 1111
Raja 3333
Singh 2222

Enter name: Raja
Number: 3333
```

The program first creates **phone** map interactively with three names and then inserts two more names into the map. Then, it displays all the names and their telephone numbers available in the map. Now the program requests the user to enter the name of a person. The program looks into the map, using the person name as a key, for the associated number and then prints the number.

That the names are printed in alphabetical order, although the original data was not. The list is automatically sorted using the key. In our example, the key is the name of person.

We can access the two parts of an entry using the members **first** and **second** with an iterator of the **map** as illustrated in the program. That is,

```
(*p).first
```

gives the key, and

```
(*p).second
```

14.7   FUNCTION OBJECTS

A function object is a function that has been wrapped in a class so that it looks like an object. The class has only one member function, the overloaded ( ) operator and no data. The class is templatized so that it can be used with different data types.

Function objects are often used as arguments to certain containers and algorithms. For example, the statement

```
sort(array, array+5, greater<int>());
```

uses the function object **greater<int>( )** to sort the elements contained in **array** in descending order.

Besides comparisons, STL provides many other predefined function objects for performing arithmetical and logical operations as shown in Table 14.14. Note that there are function objects corresponding to all the major C++ operators. For using function objects, we must include **<functional>** header file.

Table 14.14   STL function objects in <functional>

Function object	Type	Description
divides<T>	arithmetic	x/y
equal_to<T>	relational	x == y
greater<T>	relational	x > y
greater_equal<T>	relational	x >= y
less<T>	relational	x < y
less_equal<T>	relational	x <= y
logical_and<T>	logical	x && y
logical_not<T>	logical	!x
logical_or<T>	logical	x || y
minus<T>	arithmetic	x - y
modulus<T>	arithmetic	x % y
negate<T>	arithmetic	- x
not_equal_to<T>	relational	x != y
plus<T>	arithmetic	x + y
multiplies<T>	arithmetic	x * y

Note: The variables x and y represent objects of class T passed to the function object as arguments.

Program 14.4 illustrates the use of the function object **greater<>( )** in **sort( )** algorithm.

```
                USE OF FUNCTION OBJECTS IN ALGORITHMS
#include <iostream>
#include <algorithm>
#include <functional>

using namespace std;

int main()
{
    int x[] = {10,50,30,40,20};
    int y[] = {70,90,60,80};

    sort(x,x+5,greater<int>());
    sort(y,y+4);

    for(int i=0; i<5; i++)
        cout << x[i] << " ";
    cout << "\n";

    for(int j=0; j<4; j++)
        cout << y[j] << " ";
    cout << "\n";

    int z[9];
    merge(x,x+5,y,y+4,z);
    for(i=0; i<9; i++)
        cout << z[i] << " ";
    cout << "\n";
    return(0);
}
```

                            PROGRAM 14.4

Output of Program 14.4:

```
50 40 30 20 10
60 70 80 90
50 40 30 20 10 60 70 80 90
```

The program creates two arrays **x** and **y** and initializes them with specified values. The program then sorts both of them using the algorithm **sort( )**. Note that **x** is sorted using the function object **greater<int>( )** and **y** is sorted without it and therefore the elements in **x** are in descending order.

The program finally merges both the arrays and displays the content of the merged array. Note the form of **merge()** function and the results it produces.

Summary

- A collection of generic classes and functions is called the Standard Template Library (STL). STL components are part of C++ standard library.
- The STL consists of three main components: containers, algorithms, and iterators.
- Containers are objects that hold data of same type. Containers are divided into three major categories: sequential, associative, and derived.
- Container classes define a large number of functions that can be used to manipulate their contents.
- Algorithms are standalone functions that are used to carry out operations on the contents of containers, such as sorting, searching, copying, and merging.
- Iterators are like pointers. They are used to access the elements of containers thus providing a link between algorithms and containers. Iterators are defined for specific containers and used as arguments to algorithms.
- Certain algorithms use what are known as function objects for some operations. A function object is created by a class that contains only one overloaded operator () function.

Key Terms

- <algorithm>
- <cstdlib>
- <deque>
- <functional>
- <list>
- <map>

- <numeric>
- <queue>
- <set>
- <string>
- <stack>
- <vector>

> algorithms
> associative containers
> bidirectional iterator
> container adaptors
> containers
> **deque**
> derived containers
> forward iterator
> function object
> generic programming
> input iterator
> iterators
> keys
> linear sequence
> **list**
> **map**
> mapped values
> **multimap**
> multiple keys
> **multiset**
> mutating algorithms

> namespace
> non-mutating algorithms
> numeric algorithms
> output iterator
> **priority_queue**
> **queue**
> random access iterator
> relational algorithms
> sequence containers
> **set**
> set algorithms
> sorting algorithms
> **stack**
> standard C++ library
> standard template library
> templates
> templatized classes
> tree
> using namespace
> values
> **vector**

Review Questions and Exercises

14.1 *What is STL? How is it different from the C++ Standard Library? Why is it gaining importance among the programmers?*

14.2 *List the three types of containers.*

14.3 *What is the major difference between a sequence container and an associative container?*

14.4 *What are the best situations for the use of the sequence containers?*

14.5 *What are the best situations for the use of the associative containers?*

14.6 *What is an iterator? What are its characteristics?*

14.7 *What is an algorithm? How STL algorithms are different from the conventional algorithms?*

14.8 *How are the STL algorithms implemented?*

14.9 *Distinguish between the following:*
   (a) lists and vectors
   (b) sets and maps
   (c) maps and multimaps
   (d) queue and deque
   (e) arrays and vectors

14.10 *Compare the performance characteristics of the three sequence containers.*

14.11 *Suggest appropriate containers for the following applications:*
   (a) Insertion at the back of a container.

(b) *Frequent insertions and deletion at both the ends of a container.*

(c) *Frequent insertions and deletions in the middle of a container.*

(d) *Frequent random access of elements.*

14.12 *State whether the following statements are true or false.*

(a) *An iterator is a generalized form of pointer.*

(b) *One purpose of an iterator is to connect algorithms to containers.*

(c) *STL algorithms are member functions of containers.*

(d) *The size of a vector does not change when its elements are removed.*

(e) *STL algorithms can be used with c-like arrays.*

(f) *An iterator can always move forward or backward through a container.*

(g) *The member function* **end()** *returns a reference to the last element in the container.*

(h) *The member function* **back()** *removes the element at the back of the container.*

(i) *The* **sort()** *algorithm requires a random-access iterator.*

(j) *A map can have two or more elements with the same key value.*

14.13 *Write a code segment that does the following:*

(a) *Defines a vector* **v** *with a maximum size of 10*

(b) *Sets the first element of* **v** *to 0*

(c) *Sets the last element of* **v** *to 9*

(d) *Sets the other elements to 1*

(e) *Displays the contents of* **v**

14.14 *Write a program using the* **find()** *algorithm to locate the position of a specified value in a sequence container.*

14.15 *Write a program using the algorithm* **count()** *to count how many elements in a container have a specified value.*

14.16 *Create an array with even numbers and a list with odd numbers. Merge two sequences of numbers into a vector using the algorithm* **merge()**. *Display the vector.*

14.17 *Create a* **student** *class that includes a student's first name and his roll_number. Create five objects of this class and store them in a list thus creating a phone_lit. Write a program using this list to display the student name if the roll_number is given and vice-versa.*

14.18 *Redo the Exercise 14.17 using a set.*

14.19 *A table gives a list of car models and the number of units sold in each type in a specified period. Write a program to store this table in a suitable container, and to display interactively the total value of a particular model sold, given the unit-cost of that model.*

14.20 *Write a program that accepts a shopping list of five items from the keyboard and stores them in a vector. Extend the program to accomplish the following:*

(a) *To delete a specified item in the list*

(b) *To add an item at a specified location*

(c) *To add an item at the end*

(d) *To print the contents of the vector*

15

Manipulating Strings

15.1 INTRODUCTION

A string is a sequence of characters. We know that C++ does not support a built-in string type. We have used earlier null-terminated character arrays to store and manipulate strings. These strings are called *C-strings* or *C-style strings*. Operations on C-strings often become complex and inefficient. We can also define our own string classes with appropriate member functions to manipulate strings. This was illustrated in Program 7.4 (Mathematical Operation of Strings).

ANSI standard C++ now provides a new class called **string**. This class improves on the conventional C-strings in several ways. In many situations, the string objects may be used like any other built-in type data. Further, although it is not considered as a part of the STL, **string** is treated as another container class by C++ and therefore all the algorithms that are applicable for containers can be used with the **string** objects. For using the **string** class, we must include **<string>** in our program.

The **string** class is very large and includes many constructors, member functions and operators. We may use the constructors, member functions and operators to achieve the following:

- Creating string objects
- Reading string objects from keyboard
- Displaying string objects to the screen
- Finding a substring from a string
- Modifying string objects
- Comparing string objects
- Adding string objects
- Accessing characters in a string
- Obtaining the size of strings
- And many other operations

Table 15.1 gives prototypes of three most commonly used constructors and Table 15.2 gives a list of important member functions. Table 15.3 lists a number of operators that can be used on **string** objects.

Table 15.1 Commonly used string constructors

Constructor	Usage
String();	For creating an empty string
String(const chat *str);	For creating a string object from a null-terminated string
String(const string & str);	For creating a string object from other string object

Table 15.2 Important functions supported by the string class

Function	Task
append()	Appends a part of string to another string
Assign()	Assigns a partial string
at()	Obtains the character stored at a specified location
Begin()	Returns a reference to the start of a string
capacity()	Gives the total elements that can be stored.
compare()	Compares string against the invoking string
empty()	Returns true if the string is empty; Otherwise returns false
end()	Returns a reference to the end of a string
erase()	Removes characters as specified
find()	Searches for the occurrence of a specified substring
insert()	Inserts characters at a specified location
length()	Gives the number of elements in a string
max_size()	Gives the maximum possible size of a string object in a give system
replace()	Replace specified characters with a given string
resize()	Changes the size of the string as specified
size()	Gives the number of characters in the string
swap()	Swaps the given string with the invoking string

Table 15.3   Operators for string objects

Operator	Meaning
=	Assignment
+	Concatenation
+=	Concatenation assignment
= =	Equality
!=	Inequality
<	Less than
<=	Less than or equal
>	Greater than
>=	Greater than or equal
[ ]	Subscription
<<	Output
>>	Input

15.2 CREATING string OBJECTS

We can create **string** objects in a number of ways as illustrated below:

```
string s1;          // Using constructor with no argument
string s2("xyz");   // Using one-argument constructor
s1 = s2;            // Assigning string objects
s3 = "abc" + s2     // Concatenating strings
cin >> s1;          // Reading through keyboard (one word)
getline(cin, s1);   // Reading through keyboard a line of text
```

The overloaded + operator concatenates two string objects. We can also use the operator +=
to append a string to the end of a string. Examples:

```
s3 += s1;           // s3 = s3 + s1
s3 += "abc";        // s3 = s3 + "abc"
```

The operators << and >> are overloaded to handle input and output of string objects. Examples:

```
cin >> s2;          // Input to string object (one word)
cout << s2;         // Displays the contents of s2
getline(cin, s2);   // Reads embedded blanks
```

Using **cin** and >> operator we can read only one word of a string while the **getline()**
function permits us to read a line of text containing embedded blanks.

Program 15.1 demonstrates the several ways of creating string objects in a program.

```
                        CREATING STRING OBJECTS

    #include <iostream>
    #include <string>

    using namespace std;

    int main()
    {
        // Creating string objects
        string s1;                    // Empty string object
        string s2(" New");            // Using string constant
        string s3(" Delhi");

        // Assigning value to string objects
        s1 = s2;                            // Using string object
        cout << "S1 = " << s1 << "\n";

        // Using a string constant
        s1 = "Standard C++";
        cout << "Now S1 = " << s1 << "\n";

        // Using another object
        string s4(s1);
        cout << "S4 = " << s4 << "\n\n";

        // Reading through keyboard
        cout << "ENTER A STRING \n";
        cin >> s4;                          // Delimited by blank space
        cout << "Now S4 = " << s4 << "\n\n";

        // Concatenating strings
        s1 = s2 + s3;
        cout << "S1 finally contains: " << s1 << "\n";

        return 0;
    }
                            PROGRAM 15.1
```

The output of Program 15.1 would be:

```
S1 =  New
Now S1 = Standard C++
S4 = Standard C++

ENTER A STRING
```

```
COMPUTER CENTRE
Now S4 = COMPUTER

S1 finally contains:   New Delhi
```

15.3 MANIPULATING STRING OBJECTS

We can modify contents of **string** objects in several ways, using the member functions such as **insert(), replace(), erase(),** and **append().** Program 15.2 demonstrates the use of some of these functions.

MODIFYING STRING OBJECTS

```cpp
#include <iostream
#include <string>

using namespace std;

int main()
{
    string s1("12345");
    string s2("abcde");

    cout << "Original Strings are: \n";
    cout << "S1: " << s1 << "\n";
    cout << "S2: " << s2 << "\n\n";

    // Inserting a string into another
    cout << "Place S2 inside S1 \n";
    s1.insert(4,s2);
    cout << "Modified S1: " << s1 << "\n\n";

    // Removing characters in a string
    cout << "Remove 5 Characters from S1 \n";
    s1.erase(4,5);
    cout << "Now S1: " << s1 << "\n\n";

    // Replacing characters in a string
    cout << "Replace Middle 3 Characters in S2 with S1 \n";
    s2.replace(1,3,s1);
    cout << "Now S2: " << s2 << "\n";

    return 0;
}
```

PROGRAM 15.2

The output of Program 15.2 given below illustrates how strings are manipulated using string functions.

```
Original Strings are:
S1: 12345
S2: abcde

Place S2 inside S1
Modified S1: 1234abcde5

Remove 5 Characters from S1
Now S1: 12345

Replace Middle 3 Characters in S2 with S1
Now S2: a12345e
```

 Analyse how arguments of each function used in this program are implemented.

15.4 RELATIONAL OPERATIONS

A number of operators that can be used on strings are defined for **string** objects (Table 15.3). We have used in the earlier examples the operators = and + for creating objects. We can also apply the relational operators listed in Table 15.3. These operators are overloaded and can be used to compare **string** objects. The **compare()** function can also be used for this purpose.

```
             RELATIONAL OPERATIONS ON STRING OBJECTS

#include <iostream>
#include <string>

using namespace std;

int main()
{
    string s1("ABC");
    string s2("XYZ");
    string s3 = s1 + s2;

    if(s1 != s2)
        cout << "s1 is not equal to s2 \n";
    if(s1 > s2)
        cout << "s1 greater than s2 \n";
    else
        cout << "s2 greater than s1 \n";
    if(s3 == s1 + s2)
```

(Contd)

```
            cout << "s3 is equal to s1+s2 \n\n";

        int x = s1.compare(s2);
        if(x == 0)
            cout << "s1 == s2 \n";
        else if(x > 0)
            cout << "s1 > s2 \n";
        else                            // x < 0
            cout << "s1 < s2 \n";

        return 0;
    }
```

PROGRAM 15.3

Program 15.3 shows how these operators are used.

This program produces the following output:

```
s1 is not equal to s2
s2 greater than s1
s3 is equal to s1+s2

s1 < s2
```

15.5 STRING CHARACTERISTICS

Class **string** supports many functions that could be used to obtain the characteristics of strings such as size, length, capacity, etc. The size or length denotes the number of elements currently stored in a given string. The capacity indicates the total elements that can be stored in the given string. Another characteristic is the *maximum size* which is the largest possible size of a string object that the given system can support. Program 15.4 illustrates how these characteristics are obtained and used in an application.

OBTAINING STRING CHARACTERISTICS

```
#include <iostream>
#include <string>

using namespace std;

void display(string &str)
{
    cout << "Size = " << str.size() << "\n";
    cout << "Length = " << str.length() << "\n";
    cout << "Capacity = " << str.capacity() << "\n";
    cout << "Maximum Size = " << str.max_size() << "\n";
    cout << "Empty: " << (str.empty() ? "yes" : "no");
```

(Contd)

```
        cout << "\n\n";
}

int main()
{
    string str1;

    cout << "Initial status: \n";
    display(str1);

    cout << "Enter a string (one word) \n";
    cin >> str1;
    cout << "Status now: \n";
    display(str1);

    str1.resize(15);
    cout << "Status after resizing: \n";
    display(str1);
    cout << "\n";

    return 0;
}
```

PROGRAM 15.4

Shown below is the output of Program 15.4:

```
Initial status:
Size = 0
Length = 0
Capacity = 0
Maximum Size = 4294967293
Empty: yes

Enter a string (one word)
INDIA
Status now:
Size = 5
Length = 5
Capacity = 31
Maximum Size = 4294967293
Empty: no

Status after resizing:
Size = 15
Length = 15
Capacity = 31
Maximum Size = 4294967293
Empty: no
```

The size and length of 0 indicate that the string **str1** contains no characters. The size and length are always the same. The **str1** has a capacity of zero initially but its capacity has increased to 31 when a string is assigned to it. The maximum size of a string in this system is 4294967293. The function **empty()** returns **true** if **str1** is empty; otherwise **false**.

15.6 ACCESSING CHARACTERS IN STRINGS

We can access substrings and individual characters of a string in several ways. The **string** class supports the following functions for this purpose:

at()	for accessing individual characters
substr()	for retrieving a substring
find()	for finding a specified substring
find_first_of()	for finding the location of first occurrence of the specified character(s)
find_last_of()	for finding the location of last occurrence of the specified character(s)

We can also use the overloaded [ ] operator (which makes a **string** object look like an array) to access individual elements in a string. Program 15.5 demonstrates the use of some of these functions.

```
                    ACCESSING AND MANIPULATING CHARACTERS

    #include <iostream>
    #include <string>

    using namespace std;

    int main()
    {
        string s("ONE TWO THREE FOUR");

        cout << "The string contains: \n";
        for(int i=0;i<s.length();i++)
                cout << s.at(i);       // Display one character
        cout << "\nString is shown again: \n";
        for(int j=0;j<s.length();j++)
                cout << s[j];

        int x1 = s.find("TWO");
        cout << "\n\nTWO is found at: " << x1 << "\n";

        int x2 = s.find_first_of('T');
        cout << "\nT is found first at: " << x2 << "\n";
```

(Contd)

```
            int x3 = s.find_last_of('R');
            cout << "\nR is last found at: " << x3 << "\n";

            cout << "\nRetrieve and print substring TWO \n";

            cout << s.substr(x1,3);
            cout << "\n";

            return 0;
    }
```

PROGRAM 15.5

Shown below is the output of Program 15.5:

```
The string contains:
ONE TWO THREE FOUR
String is shown again:
ONE TWO THREE FOUR

TWO is found at: 4

T is found first at: 4

R is last fount at: 17

Retrieve and print substring TWO
TWO
```

We can access individual characters in a string using either the member function **at()** or the subscript operator [ ]. This is illustrated by the following statements:

```
cout << s.at(i);
cout << s[i];
```

The statement

```
int x1 = s.find("TWO");
```

locates the position of the first character of the substring "TWO". The statement

```
cout << s.substr(x1,3);
```

finds the substring "TWO". The first argument **x1** specifies the location of the first character of the required substring and the second argument gives the length of the substring.

15.7   COMPARING AND SWAPPING

The **string** supports functions for comparing and swapping strings. The **compare()** function can be used to compare either two strings or portions of two strings. The **swap()** function can be used for swapping the contents of two **string** objects. The capabilities of these functions are demonstrated in Program 15.6.

```
                    COMPARING AND SWAPPING STRINGS

    #include <iostream>
    #include <string>

    using namespace std;

    int main()
    {
      string s1("Road");
      string s2("Read");
      string s3("Red");
      cout << "s1 = " << s1 << "\n";
      cout << "s2 = " << s2 << "\n";
      cout << "s3 = " << s3 << "\n";

      int x = s1.compare(s2);
      if(x == 0)
            cout << "s1 == s2" << "\n";
      else if(x > 0)
            cout << "s1 > s2" << "\n";
      else
          cout << "s1 < s2" << "\n";

      int a = s1.compare(0,2,s2,0,2);
      int b = s2.compare(0,2,s1,0,2);
      int c = s2.compare(0,2,s3,0,2);
      int d = s2.compare(s2.size()-1,1,s3,s3.size()-1,1);

      cout << "a = " << a << "\n" << "b = " << b << "\n";
      cout << "c = " << c << "\n" << "d = " << d << "\n";

      cout << "\nBefore swap: \n";
      cout << "s1 = " << s1 << "\n";
      cout << "s2 = " << s2 << "\n";
      s1.swap(s2);
```

(Contd)

```
        cout << "\nAfter swap: \n";
        cout << "s1 = " << s1 << "\n";
        cout << "s2 = " << s2 << "\n";

        return 0;
    }
```

The output of Program 15.6:

```
    s1 = Road
    s2 = Read
    s3 = Red
    s1 > s2
    a = 1
    b = -1
    c = 0
    d = 0

    Before swap:
    s1 = Road
    s2 = Read

    After swap:
    s1 = Read
    s2 = Road
```

The statement

```
    int x = s1.compare(s2);
```

compares the string **s1** against **s2** and **x** is assigned 0 if the strings are equal, a positive number if **s1** is *lexicographically* greater than **s2** or a negative number otherwise.

The statement

```
    int a = s1.compare(0,2,s2,0,2);
```

compares portions of **s1** and **s2**. The first two arguments give the starting subscript and length of the portion of **s1** to compare to **s2**, that is supplied as the third argument. The fourth and fifth arguments specify the starting subscript and length of the portion of **s2** to be compared. The value assigned to **a** is 0, if they are equal, 1 if substring of **s1** is greater than the substring of **s2**, –1 otherwise.

The statement

```
    s2.swap(s2);
```

exchanges the contents of the strings **s1** and **s2**.

Summary

- Manipulation and use of C-style strings become complex and inefficient. ANSI C++ provides a new class called **string** to overcome the deficiencies of C-strings.
- The string class supports many constructors, member functions and operators for creating and manipulating string objects. We can perform the following operations on the strings:

  - Reading strings from keyboard
  - Assigning strings to one another
  - Finding substrings
  - Modifying strings
  - Comparing strings and substrings
  - Accessing characters in strings
  - Obtaining size and capacity of strings
  - Swapping strings
  - Sorting strings

Key Terms

➤ **<string>**	➤ **insert()**
➤ **append()**	➤ length
➤ **assign()**	➤ **length()**
➤ **at()**	➤ lexicographical
➤ **begin()**	➤ **max_size()**
➤ capacity	➤ maximum size
➤ **capacity()**	➤ relational operators
➤ **compare()**	➤ **replace()**
➤ comparing strings	➤ size
➤ C-strings	➤ **size()**
➤ C-style strings	➤ string
➤ **empty()**	➤ string class
➤ **end()**	➤ string constructors
➤ **erase()**	➤ string objects
➤ **find()**	➤ **substr()**
➤ **find_first_of()**	➤ substring
➤ **find_last_of()**	➤ **swap()**
➤ **getline()**	➤ swapping strings

Review Questions and Exercises

15.1 *State whether the following statements are TRUE or FALSE:*
   (a) *For using* **string** *class, we must include the header <string>.*

(b)   *string objects are null terminated.*
(c)   *The elements of a string object are numbered from 0.*
(d)   *Objects of string class can be copied using the assignment operator.*
(e)   *Function end() returns an iterator to the invoking string object.*

15.2   *How does a string type string differ from a C-type string?*

15.3   *The following statements are available to read strings from the keyboard.*
(a)   `cin >> s1;`
(b)   `getline(cin, s1);`
where s1 is a string object. Distinguish their behaviour.

15.4   *Consider the following segment of a program:*
```
string s1("man"), s2, s3;
s2.assign(s1);
s3 = s1;
string s4("wo" + s1);
s2 += "age";
s3.append("ager");
s1[0] = 'v';
```
State the contents of the objects s1, s2, s3 and s4 when executed.

15.5   *We can access string elements using*
(a)   *at() function*
(b)   *subscript operator [ ]*
Compare their behaviour.

15.6   *Find errors, if any, in the following segment of code.*
```
int len = s1.length();
for(int i=0;i<=len;++i)
    cout << s1.at[ ];
```

15.7   *What does each of the following statements do?*
(a)   `s.replace(n,1,"/");`
(b)   `s.erase(10);`
(c)   `s1.insert(10,s2);`
(d)   `int x = s1.compare(0, s2.size(), s2);`
(e)   `s2 = s1.substr(10, 5);`

15.8   *Distinguish between the following pair of functions.*
(a)   *max_size() and capacity()*
(b)   *find() and rfind()*
(c)   *begin() and rbegin()*

15.9   *Write a program that reads the name*
```
Martin Luther King
```
from the keyboard into three separate string objects and then concatenates them into a new string object using
(a)   *+ operator and*
(b)   *append() function.*

15.10 *Write a program using an iterator and while() construct to display the contents of a string object.*

15.11 *Write a program that reads several city names from the keyboard and displays only those names beginning with characters "B" or "C".*

15.12 *Write a program that will read a line of text containing more than three words and then replace all the blank spaces with an underscore(_).*

15.13 *Write a program that counts the number of occurrences of a particular character, say 'e', in a line of text.*

15.14 *Write a program that reads the following text and counts the number of times the word "It" appears in it.*

> *It is new. It is singular.*
> *It is simple. It must succeed!*

15.15 *Modify the program in Exercise 15.14 to count the number of words which start with the character 's'.*

15.16 *Write a program that reads a list of countries in random order and displays them in alphabetical order. Use comparison operators and functions.*

15.17 *Given a string*

> *string s("123456789");*

Write a program that displays the following:

> *1*
> *232*
> *34543*
> *4567654*
> *567898765*

New Features of ANSI C++ Standard

Key Concepts

- •◦ Boolean type data
- •◦ Wide-character literals
- •◦ Constant casting
- •◦ Static casting
- •◦ Dynamic casting
- •◦ Reinterpret casting
- •◦ Runtime type information

- •◦ Explicit constructors
- •◦ Mutable member data
- •◦ Namespaces
- •◦ Nesting of namespaces
- •◦ Operator keywords
- •◦ Using new keywords
- •◦ New style for headers

16.1 INTRODUCTION

The ISO / ANSI C++ Standard adds several new features to the original C++ specifications. Some are added to provide better control in certain situations and others are added for providing conveniences to C++ programmers. It is therefore important to note that it is technically possible to write full-fledged programs without using any of the new features. Important features added are:

1. New data types
   - ▪ bool
   - ▪ wchar_t
2. New operators
   - ▪ const_cast
   - ▪ static_cast
   - ▪ dynamic_cast

- reinterpret_cast
- typeid
3. Class implementation
   - Explicit constructors
   - Mutable members
4. Namespace scope
5. Operator keywords
6. New keywords
7. New headers

We present here a brief overview of these features.

16.2 NEW DATA TYPES

The ANSI C++ has added two new data types to enhance the range of data types available in C++. They are **bool** and **wchar_t**.

The bool Data Type

The data type **bool** has been added to hold a Boolean value, **true** or **false**. The values **true** and **false** have been added as keywords to the C++ language. The **bool** type variables can be declared as follows.

```
bool b1;                    // declare b1 as bool type
b1 = true;                  // assign true value to it
bool b2 = false;            // declare and initialize
```

The default numeric value of **true** is 1 and **false** is 0. Therefore, the statements

```
cout << "b1 = " << b1;      // b1 is true
cout << "b2 = " << b2;      // b2 is false
```

will display the following output:

```
b1 = 1
b2 = 0
```

We can use the **bool** type variables or the values **true** and **false** in mathematical expressions. For instance,

```
int x = false + 5*m - b1;
```

is valid and the expression on the right evaluates to 9 assuming **b1** is true and **m** is 2. Values of type **bool** are automatically elevated to integers when used in non-Boolean expressions.

It is possible to convert implicitly the data types pointers, integers or floating point values to **bool** type. For example, the statements

```
bool  x  = 0;
bool  y  = 100;
bool  z  = 15.75;
```

assign **false** to **x** and **true** to **y** and **z**.

Program 16.1 demonstrates the features of **bool** type data.

```
                          USE OF bool TYPE DATA
    #include  <iostream>

    using namespace std;

    int main()
    {
            int x1 = 10,x2 = 20,m = 2;
            bool b1, b2;

            b1 = x1 == x2;     // False
            b2 = x1 < x2;              // True

            cout << "b1 is " << b1 << "\n";
            cout << "b2 is " << b2 << "\n";

            bool b3  =   true;
            cout << "b3 is " << b3 << "\n";

            if(b3)
                    cout << "Very Good" << "\n";
            else
                    cout << "Very Bad" << "\n";

            int x3 = false + 5*m-b3;
            b1 = x3;
            b2 = 0;
            cout << "x3 = " << x3 << "\n";
            cout << "Now b1 = " << b1 << " and b2 = " << b2 << "\n";

            return 0;
    }

                          PROGRAM  16.1
```

The output of Program 16.1 would be:

```
b1 is 0
b2 is 1
b3 is 1
Very Good
x3 = 9
Now b1 = 1 and b2 = 0
```

The wchar_t Data Type

The character type **wchar_t** has been defined in ANSI C++ to hold 16-bit wide characters. The 16-bit characters are used to represent the character sets of languages that have more than 255 characters, such as Japanese. This is important if we are writing programs for international distribution.

ANSI C++ also introduces a new character literal known as *wide_character* literal which uses two bytes of memory. Wide_character literals begin with the letter L, as follows:

```
L'xy'  // wide_character literal
```

16.3 NEW OPERATORS

We have used cast operators (also known as *casts* or *type casts*) earlier in a number of programs. As we know, casts are used to convert a value from one type to another. This is necessary in situations where automatic conversions are not possible. We have used the following forms of casting:

```
double x = double(m);    // C++ type casting
double y = (double)n;    // C-type casting
```

Although these casts still work, ANSI C++ has added several new cast operators known as *static casts, dynamic casts, reinterpret casts* and *constant casts*. It also adds another operator known as **typeid** to verify the types of unknown objects.

The static_cast Operator

Like the conventional cast operators, the **static_cast** operator is used for any standard conversion of data types. It can also be used to cast a base class pointer into a derived class pointer. Its general form is:

```
static_cast<type>(object)
```

Here, *type* specifies the target type of the cast, and *object* is the object being cast into the new type. Examples:

```
int m = 10;
double x = static_cast<double> (m);
char ch = static_cast<char> (m);
```

The first statement casts the variable **m** to type **double** and the second casts it to type **char**.

Why use this new type when the old style still works? The syntax of the old one blends into the rest of the lines and therefore it is difficult to locate them. The new format is easy to spot and to search for using automated tools.

The const_cast Operator

The **const_cast** operator is used to explicitly override **const** or **volatile** in a cast. It takes the form

```
const_cast<type>(object)
```

Since the purpose of this operator is to change its **const** or **volatile** attributes, the *target type* must be the same as the *source type*. It is mostly used for removing the const_ness of an object.

The reinterpret_cast Operator

The **reinterpret_cast** is used to change one type into a fundamentally different type. For example, it can be used to change a pointer type object to integer type object or vice versa. It takes the following form:

```
reinterpret_cast<type>(object)
```

This operator should be used for casting inherently incompatible types. Examples:

```
int m;
float x;
int* intptr;
float* floatptr;
intptr = reinterpret_cast<int*> (m);
floatptr = reinterpret_cast<float*> (x);
```

The dynamic_cast Operator

The dynamic cast is used to cast the type of an object at runtime. Its main application is to perform casts on polymorphic objects. Recall that polymorphic objects are created by base classes that contain virtual functions. It takes the form:

```
dynamic_cast<type>(object)
```

The *object* is a base class object whose type is to be checked and casted. It casts the type of object to *type*. It never performs an invalid conversion. It checks that the conversion is legal at runtime. If the conversion is not valid, it returns NULL.

The *type* must be a pointer or a reference to a defined class type. The *argument* object must be expression that resolves to a pointer or reference. The use of the operator **dynamic_cast()** is also called a *type-safe downcast*.

The typeid Operator

We can use the **typeid** operator to obtain the types of unknown objects, such as their class name at runtime. For example, the statement

```
char *objectType = typeid(object).name();
```

will assign the type of "object" to the character array **objectType** which can be printed out, if necessary. To do this, it uses the **name()** member function of the **type_info** class. The object may be of type **int**, **float**, etc. or of any class.

We must include <**typeinfo**> header file to use the operators **dynamic_cast** and **typeid** which provide run-time type information (RTTI).

16.4   CLASS IMPLEMENTATION

ANSI C++ Standard adds two unusual keywords, **explicit** and **mutable**, for use with class members.

The explicit Keyword

The **explicit** keyword is used to declare class constructors to be "explicit" constructors. We have seen earlier, while discussing constructors, that any constructor called with one argument performs *implicit conversion* in which the type received by the constructor is converted to an object of the class in which the constructor is defined. Since the conversion is automatic, we need not apply any casting. In case, we do not want such automatic conversion to take place, we may do so by declaring the one-argument constructor as explicit as shown below:

```
class ABC
{
    int m;
public:
    explicit ABC (int i)    // constructor
    {
        m = i;
    }
    // .............
    // .............
};
```

Here, objects of ABC class can be created using only the following form:

```
ABC  abc1(100);
```

The automatic conversion form

```
ABC  abc1 = 100;
```

is not allowed and illegal. Remember, this form is permitted when the keyword **explicit** is not applied to the conversion.

The mutable Keyword

We know that a class object or a member function may be declared as **const** thus making their member data not modifiable. However, a situation may arise where we want to create a **const** object (or function) but we would like to modify a particular data item only. In such situations we can make that particular data item modifiable by declaring the item as **mutable**. Example:

```
mutable int m;
```

Although a function(or class) that contains **m** is declared **const**, the value of **m** may be modified. Program 16.2 demonstrates the use of a **mutable** member.

```
                       USE  OF  KEYWORD mutable

#include  <iostream>
using  namespace  std;

class ABC
{
        private:
                mutable int m;  // mutable member
        public:
                explicit ABC(int  x  =  0)
                {
                        m = x;
                }
                void change() const    // const function
                {
                        m = m+10;
                }
                int display() const    // const function
                {
                        return m;
                }
};
```

(Contd)

```
int main()
{
        const ABC abc(100);              // const object
        cout << "abc contains: " << abc.display();

        abc.change();                    // changes mutable data
        cout << "\nabc now contains: " << abc.display();
        cout << "\n";

        return 0;
}
```
PROGRAM 16.2

The output of Program 16.2 would be:

```
abc contains: 100
abc now contains: 110
```

Although the function **change()** has been declared constant, the value of **m** has been modified. Try to execute the program after deleting the keyword **mutable** in the program.

16.5   NAMESPACE SCOPE

We have been defining variables in different scopes in C++ programs, such as classes, functions, blocks, etc. ANSI C++ Standard has added a new keyword **namespace** to define a scope that could hold global identifiers. The best example of namespace scope is the C++ Standard Library. All classes, functions and templates are declared within the namespace named **std**. That is why we have been using the directive

```
using namespace std;
```

in our programs that uses the standard library. The **using namespace** statement specifies that the members defined in **std** namespace will be used frequently throughout the program.

Defining a Namespace

We can define our own namespaces in our programs. The syntax for defining a namespace is similar to the syntax for defining a class. The general form of namespace is:

```
namespace namespace_name
{
        // Declaration of
        // variables, functions, classes, etc.
}
```

There is one difference between a class definition and a namespace definition. The namespace is concluded with a closing brace but no terminating semicolon.

Example:

```
namespace TestSpace
{
    int m;
    void display(int n)
    {
        cout << n;
    }
}           // No semicolon here
```

Here, the variable **m** and the function **display** are inside the scope defined by the **TestSpace** namespace. If we want to assign a value to m, we must use the scope resolution operator as shown below.

```
TestSpace::m = 100;
```

Note that **m** is qualified using the namespace name.

This approach becomes cumbersome if the members of a namespace are frequently used. In such cases, we can use a **using** directive to simplify their access. This can be done in two ways:

```
using namespace namespace_name;   // using directive
using namespace_name::member_name;   // using declaration
```

In the first form, all the members declared within the specified namespace may be accessed without using qualification. In the second form, we can access only the specified member in the program. Example:

```
using namespace TestSpace;
m = 100;         // OK
display(200);    // OK

using TestSpace::m;
m = 100;         // OK
display(200);    // Not ok, display not visible
```

Nesting of Namespaces

A namespace can be nested within another namespace. Example:

```
namespace NS1
{
```

```
......
......
namespace NS2
{
    int m = 100;
}
......
......
}
```

To access the variable **m**, we must qualify the variable with both the enclosing namespace names. The statement

```
cout << NS1::NS2::m;
```

will display the value of **m**. Alternatively, we can write

```
using namespace NS1;
cout << NS2::m;
```

Unnamed Namespaces

An unnamed namespace is one that does not have a name. Unnamed namespace members occupy global scope and are accessible in all scopes following the declaration in the file. We can access them without using any qualification.

A common use of unnamed namespaces is to shield global data from potential name classes between files. Every file has its own, unique unnamed namespace.

Program 16.3 demonstrates how namespaces are defined, how they are nested and how an unnamed namespace is created. It also illustrates how the members in various namespaces are accessed.

```
                    USING Namespace SCOPE WITH NESTING

#include <iostream>

using namespace std;

// Defining a namespace
namespace Name1
{
        double x = 4.56;
        int m = 100;

        namespace Name2        // Nesting namespaces
        {
```

(Contd)

```
            double y = 1.23;
        }
}

namespace                       // Unnamed namespace
{
    int m = 200;
}

int main()
{
    cout << "x = " << Name1::x << "\n";          // x is qualified
    cout << "m = " << Name1::m << "\n";
    cout << "y = " << Name1::Name2::y << "\n";   // y is fully qualified
    cout << "m = " << m << "\n";                 // m is global

    return 0;
}
```

                           PROGRAM 16.3

The output of Program:

```
x = 4.56
m = 100
y = 1.23
m = 200
```

 We have used the variable **m** in two different scopes.

Program 16.4 shows the application of both the **using** directive and **using** declaration.

                    ILLUSTRATING THE using KEYWORD

```
#include <iostream>

using namespace std;

// Defining a namespace
namespace Name1
{
    double x = 4.56;
    int m = 100;

    namespace Name2        // Nesting namespaces
```

(Contd)

```
        {
              double y = 1.23;
        }
}

namespace Name3
{
        int m = 200;
        int n = 300;
}

int main()
{
        using namespace Name1;                    // bring members of Name1
                                                  // to current scope
        cout << "x = " << x << "\n";              // x is not qualified
        cout << "m = " << m << "\n";
        cout << "y = " << Name2::y << "\n";       // y is qualified
        using Name3::n;                           // bring n to current scope
        cout << "m = " << Name3::m << "\n";       // m is qualified
        cout << "n = " << n << "\n";              // n is not qualified

        return 0;
}
```

PROGRAM 16.4

The output of Program 16.4 would be:

```
x = 4.56
m = 100
y = 1.23
m = 200
n = 300
```

 How the data members are qualified when they are accessed.

Program 16.5 uses functions in a namespace scope.

USING Functions IN Namespace SCOPE

```
#include <iostream>

using namespace std;

namespace Functions
{
```

(Contd)

```
                int divide(int x,int y)      // definition
                {
                     return(x/y);
                }

                int prod(int x,int y);   // declaration only
      }

      int Functions::prod(int x,int y)  // qualified
      {
                return(x*y);
      }

      int main()
      {
                using namespace Functions;

                cout << "Division: " << divide(20,10) << "\n";
                cout << "Multiplication: " << prod(20,10) << "\n";

                return 0;
      }
```

PROGRAM 16.5

The output of Program 16.5 would be:

```
Division: 2
Multiplication: 200
```

When a function that is declared inside a namespace is defined outside, it should be qualified.

Program 16.6 demonstrates the use of classes inside a namespace.

USING Classes IN Namespace SCOPE

```
#include <iostream>

using namespace std;

namespace Classes
{
      class Test
```

(*Contd*)

```
                    {
                                private:
                                    int m;

                                public:

                                    Test(int a)
                                    {
                                            m = a;
                                    }

                                    void display()
                                    {
                                            cout << "m = " << m << "\n";
                                    }
                    };
        }

        int main()
        {
                // using scope resolution
                Classes::Test T1(200);
                T1.display();

                // using directive
                using namespace Classes;
                Test T2(400);
                T2.display();

                return 0;
        }
```

PROGRAM 16.6

The output of Program 16.6 would be:

```
m = 200
m = 400
```

16.6 OPERATOR KEYWORDS

The ANSI C++ Standard proposes keywords for several C++ operators. These keywords, listed in Table 16.1, can be used in place of operator symbols in expressions. For example, the expression

```
x > y && m != 100
```

may be written as

x > y **and** m **not_eq** 100

Operator keywords not only enhance the readability of logical expressions but are also useful in situations where keyboards do not support certain special characters such as &, ^ and ~.

Table 16.1   Operator keywords

Operator	Operator keyword	Description
&&	and	logical AND
||	or	logical OR
!	not	logical NOT
!=	not_eq	inequality
&	bitand	bitwise AND
|	bitor	bitwise inclusive OR
^	xor	bitwise exclusive OR
~	compl	bitwise complement
&=	and_eq	bitwise AND assignment
|=	or_eq	bitwise inclusive OR assignment
^=	xor_eq	bitwise exclusive OR assignment

16.7 NEW KEYWORDS

ANSI C++ has added several new keywords to support the new features. Now, C++ contains 64 keywords, including **main**. They are listed in Table 16.2. The new keywords are boldfaced.

Table 16.2   ANSI C++ keywords

asm	else	**namespace**	template
auto	enum	new	this
bool	**explicit**	operator	throw
break	**export**	private	**true**
case	extern	protected	try
catch	**false**	public	typedef
char	float	register	**typeid**
class	for	**reinterpret_cast**	**typename**
const	friend	return	union
const_cast	goto	short	unsigned
continue	if	signed	**using**
default	inline	sizeof	virtual
delete	int	static	void
do	long	**static-cast**	volatile
double	main	struct	**wchar_t**
dynamic_cast	**mutable**	switch	while

16.8 NEW HEADERS

The ANSI C++ Standard has defined a new way to specify header files. They do not use **.h** extension to filenames. Example:

```
#include <iostream>
#include <fstream>
```

However, the traditional style **<iostream.h>**, **<fstream.h>**, etc. is still fully supported. Some old header files are renamed as shown below:

Old style	New style
<assert.h>	<cassert>
<ctype.h>	<cctype>
<float.h>	<cfloat>
<limits.h>	<climits>
<math.h>	<cmath>
<stdio.h>	<cstdio>
<stdlib.h>	<cstdlib>
<string.h>	<cstring>
<time.h>	<ctime>

Summary

- ANSI C++ Standard committee has added many new features to the original C++ language specifications.
- Two new data types **bool** and **wchar_t** have been added to enhance the range of data types available in C++.
- The **bool** type can hold Boolean values, **true** and **false**.
- The **wchar_t** type is meant to hold 16-bit character literals.
- Four new cast operators have been added: static_cast, const_cast, reinterpret_cast and dynamic_cast.
- The **static_cast** operator is used for any standard conversion of data types.
- The **const_cast** operator may be used to explicitly change the **const** or **volatile** attributes of objects.
- We can change the data type of an object into a fundamentally different type using the **reinterpret_cast** operator.
- Casting of an object at run time can be achieved by the **dynamic_cast** operator.
- Another new operator known as **typeid** can provide us run time type information about objects.
- A constructor may be declared **explicit** to make the conversion explicit.
- We can make a data item of a **const** object or function modifiable by declaring it **mutable**.

- ANSI C++ permits us to define our own **namespace** scope in our program to overcome certain name conflict situations.
- Namespaces may be nested.
- Members of **namespace** scope may be accessed using either **using** declaration or **using** directive.
- ANSI C++ proposes keywords that may be used in place of symbols for certain operators.
- In new standard, the header files should be specified without **.h** extension and the **using** directive

```
using namespace std;
```

should be added in every program.
- Some old style header files are renamed in the new standard. For example **math.h** file is known as **cmath**.

Key Terms

➤ **and**	➤ **not**
➤ **and_eq**	➤ **not_eq**
➤ ANSI C++	➤ operator keywords
➤ **bitand**	➤ **or**
➤ **bitor**	➤ **or_eq**
➤ **bool**	➤ polymorphic objects
➤ Boolean	➤ reinterpret casts
➤ C_type casting	➤ **reinterpret_cast**
➤ C++ standard	➤ RTTI
➤ C++ type casting	➤ source type
➤ casts	➤ standard library
➤ **compl**	➤ static casts
➤ **const**	➤ **static_cast**
➤ **const** function	➤ **std** namespace
➤ **const** object	➤ target type
➤ **const_cast**	➤ **true** value
➤ constant casts	➤ type casts
➤ current scope	➤ **type_info** class
➤ downcast	➤ type_safe casting
➤ **dynamic_cast**	➤ **typeid**
➤ dynamic casts	➤ **typeinfo** header
➤ **explicit** constructor	➤ unnamed namespaces
➤ **false** value	➤ **using** declaration
➤ global identifiers	➤ **using** directive
➤ **header file**	➤ **using namespace**
➤ implicit conversion	➤ **volatile**
➤ **mutable** member	➤ **wchar_t**
➤ **name()** function	➤ wide_character literal
➤ **namespace** scope	➤ **xor**
➤ nesting namespaces	➤ **xor_eq**

Review Questions and Exercises

16.1 *List the two data types added by the ANSI C++ standard committee?*

16.2 *What is the application of **bool** type variables?*

16.3 *What is the need for **wchar_t** character type?*

16.4 *List the new operators added by the ANSI C++ standard committee?*

16.5 *What is the application of **const_cast** operator.*

16.6 *Why do we need the operator **static_cast** while the old style cast does the same job?*

16.7 *How does the **reinterpret_cast** differ from the **static_cast**?*

16.8 *What is dynamic casting?. How is it achieved in C++?*

16.9 *What is **typeid** operator?. When is it used?*

16.10 *What is explicit conversion?. How is it achieved?*

16.11 *When do we use the keyword **mutable**?*

16.12 *What is a namespace conflict? How is it handled in C++?*

16.13 *What is wrong with the following code segment?*

```
const int m = 100;
int *ptr = &m;
```

16.14 *What is the problem with following statements?*

```
const int m = 100;
double *ptr = const_cast<double*>(&m);
```

16.15 *What will be the output of the following program?*

```
#include<iostream.h>
class Person
{
        // ......
}
int main()
{
        Person John;
        cout << " John is a ";
        cout << typeid(John).name() << "\n";
}
```

16.16 *What is wrong with the following namespace definition?*

```
namespace Main
{
        int main()
        {
                // ......
        }
}
```

16.17 *How do we access the variables declared in a named namespace?*

16.18 *What is the difference between using the **using namespace** directive and using the **using** declaration for accessing **namespace** members.*

16.19 *Write a program to demonstrate the use of **reinterpret_cast** operator.*

16.20 *Define a namespace named **Constants** that contains declarations of some constants. Write a program that uses the constants defined in the namespace **Constants**.*

17

Object-Oriented Systems Development

17.1 INTRODUCTION

Software engineers have been trying various *tools, methods,* and *procedures* to control the process of software development in order to build high-quality software with improved productivity. The methods provide "how to 's" for building the software while the tools provide automated or semi-automated support for the methods. They are used in all the stages of software development process, namely, planning, analysis, design, development and maintenance. The software development procedures integrate the methods and tools together and enable rational and timely development of software systems (Fig.17.1). They provide guideines as to how to apply the methods and tools, how to produce the deliverables at each stage, what controls to apply, and what milestones to use to assess the progress.

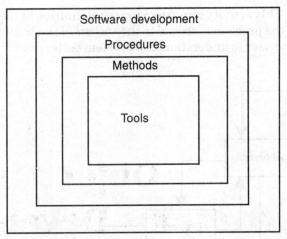

Fig. 17.1   *Software development components*

There exist a number of software development paradigms, each using a different set of methods and tools. The selection of a particular paradigm depends on the nature of the application, the programming language used, and the controls and deliverables required. The development of a successful system depends not only on the use of the appropriate methods and techniques but also on the developer's commitment to the objectives of the system. A successful system must:

1.   satisfy the user requirements,
2.   be easy to understand by the users and operators,
3.   be easy to operate,
4.   have a good user interface,
5.   be easy to modify,
6.   be expandable,
7.   have adequate security controls against misuse of data,
8.   handle the errors and exceptions satisfactorily, and
9.   be delivered on schedule within the budget.

In this chapter, we shall review some of the conventional approaches that are being widely used in software development and then discuss some of the current ideas that are applicable to the object-oriented software development.

17.2   PROCEDURE-ORIENTED PARADIGMS

Software development is usually characterized by a series of stages depicting the various asks involved in the development process. Figure 17.2 illustrates the classic software life cycle that is most widely used for the procedure-oriented development. The classic life cycle is based on an underlying model, commonly referred to as the "water-fall" model. This model attempts to break up the identifiable activities into series of actions, each of which must be completed before the next begins. The activities include problem definition, requirement analysis, design, coding, testing, and maintenance. Further refinements to this model include iteration back to the previous stages in order to incorporate any changes or missing links.

Problem Definition: This activity requires a precise definition of the problem in user terms. A clear statement of the problem is crucial to the success of the software. It helps not only the developer but also the user to understand the problem better.

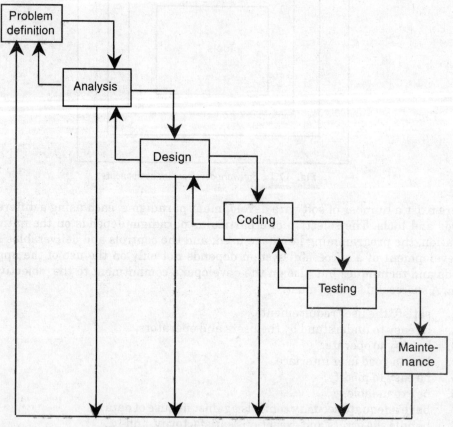

Fig. 17.2 *Classic software development life cycle*
(Embedded 'water-fall' model)

Analysis: This covers a detailed study of the requirements of both the user and the software. This activity is basically concerned with what of the system such as

* what are the inputs to the system?
* what are the processes required?
* what are the outputs expected?
* what are the constraints?

Design: The design phase deals with various concepts of system design such as data strucure, software architecture, and algorithms. This phase translates the requirements into a representation of the software. This stage answers the questions of *how*.

Coding: Coding refers to the translation of the design into machine-readable form. The more detailed the design, the easier is the coding, and better its reliability.

Testing: Once the code is written, it should be tested rigorously for correctness of the code and results. Testing may involve the individual units and the whole system. It requires a detailed plan as to what, when and how to test.

Maintenance: After the software has been installed, it may undergo some changes. This may occur due to a change in the user's requirement, a change in the operating environment, or an error in the software that has not been fixed during the testing. Maintenance ensures that these changes are incorporated wherever necessary.

Each phase of the life cycle has its own goals and outputs. The output of one phase acts as an input to the next phase. Table 17.1 shows typical outputs that could be generated for each phase of the life cycle.

Table 17.1 Outputs of classic software life cycle

Phase	Output
Problem definition (why)	• Problem statement sheet • Project request
Analysis (what)	• Requirements document • Feasibility report • Specifications document • Acceptance test criteria
Design (how)	• Design document • Test class design
Coding (how)	• Code document (program) • Test plan • User manual
Testing (what and how)	• Tested code • Test results • System manual
Maintenance	• Maintenance log sheets • Version documents

The software life cycle, as described above, is often implemented using the *functional decomposition technique*, popularly known as *top-down, modular* approach. The functional decomposition technique is based on the interpretation of the problem space and its translaion into the solution space as an inter-dependent set of functions. The functions are decomposed into a sequence of progressively simpler functions that are eventually implemented. The final system is seen as a set of functions that are organized in a top-down hierarchical structure.

There are several flaws in the top-down, functional decomposition approach. They include:

1. It does not allow evolutionary changes in the software.
2. The system is characterized by a single function at the top which is not always true. In fact many systems have no top.

3. Data is not given the importance that it deserves.

4. It does not encourage reusability of the code.

17.3 PROCEDURE-ORIENTED DEVELOPMENT TOOLS

A large number of tools are used in the analysis and design of the systems. It is important to note that the process of systems development has been undergoing changes over the years due to continuous changes in the computer technology. Consequently, there has been an evolution of new system development tools and techniques. These tools and techniques provide answers to the *how* questions of the system development.

The development tools available today may be classified as the *first generation, second generation,* and *third generation* tools. The first generation tools developed in the 1960's and 1970's are called the traditional tools. The second generation tools introduced in the late 1970's and early 1980's are meant for the structured systems analysis and design and therefore they are known as the structured tools. The recent tools are the third generation ones evolved since late 1980's to suit the *object-oriented* analysis and design.

Table 17.2 shows some of the popular tools used for various development processes under the three categories. Although this categorization is questionable, it gives a fair idea of the growth of the tools during the last three decades.

Table 17.2   System development tools

Process	First generation	Second generation	Third generation
Physical processes	System flowcharts	Context diagrams	Inheritance graphs Object-relationship charts
Data representation	Layout forms Grid charts	Data dictionary	Objects object dictionary
Logical processes	Playscript English narrative	Decision tables &trees Data flow diagrams	Inheritance graphs Data flow diagrams
Program representation	Program flowcharts I/O layouts	Structure charts Warnier /Orr diagrams	State change diagrams Ptech diagrams Coad/Yourdon charts

This section gives an overview of some of the most frequently used first and second generation tools. Object-oriented development tools will be discussed later in this chapter (as and when they are required).

System flowcharts: A graphical representation of the important inputs, outputs, and data flow among the key points in the system.

Program flowcharts: A graphical representation of the program logic.

Playscripts: A narrative description of executing a procedure.

Layout forms: A format designed for putting the input data or displaying results.

Grid charts: A chart showing the relationship between different modules of a system.
Context diagrams: A diagram showing the inputs and their sources and the outputs and their destinations. A context diagram basically outlines the system boundary.
Data flow diagrams: They describe the flow of data between the various components of a system. It is a network representation of the system which includes processes and data files.
Data dictionary: A structured repository of data about data. It contains a list of terms and their definitions for all the data items and data stores.
Structure chart: A graphical representation of the control logic of functions (modules) representing a system.
Decision table: A table of contingencies for defining a problem and the actions to be taken. It presents the logic that tells us what action to take when a given condition is true or otherwise.
Decision tree: A graphic representation of the conditions and outcomes that resemble the branches of a tree.
Warnier/Orr diagrams: A horizontal hierarchy chart using nested sets of braces, psuedo-codes, and logic symbols to indicate the program structure.

17.4 OBJECT-ORIENTED PARADIGM

The object-oriented paradigm draws heavily on the general systems theory as a conceptual background. A system can be viewed as a collection of *entities* that interact together to accomplish certain objectives (Fig. 17.3). Entities may represent physical objects such as equipment and people, and abstract concepts such as data files and functions. In object-oriented analysis, the entities are called *objects*.

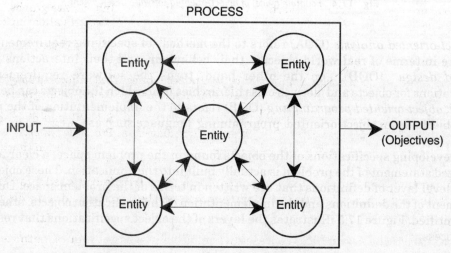

Fig. 17.3 *A system showing inter-relationship of entities*

As the name indicates, the object-oriented paradigm places greater emphasis on the objects that encapsulate data and procedures. They play the central role in all the stages of the software development and, therefore, there exists a high degree of overlap and iteration between the stages. The entire development process becomes evolutionary in nature. Any graphical representation of the object-oriented version of the software development life cycle must, therefore, take into account these two aspects of overlap and iteration. The result is a "fountain model" in place of the classic "water-fall" model as shown in Fig. 17.4. This model depicts that the development reaches a higher level only to fall back to a previous level and then again climbing up.

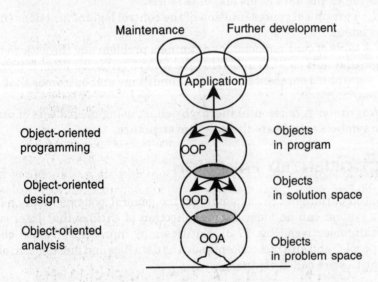

Fig. 17.4 *Fountain model of object-oriented software development*

Object-oriented analysis (OOA) refers to the methods of specifying requirements of the software in terms of real-world objects, their behaviour, and their interactions. *Object-oriented design* (OOD), on the other hand, turns the software requirements into specifications for objects and derives class hierarchies from which the objects can be created. Finally, *object-oriented programming* (OOP) refers to the implementation of the program using objects, in an object-oriented programming language such as C++.

By developing specifications of the objects found in the problem space, a clear and well-organized statement of the problem is actually built into the application. These objects form a high-level layer of definitions that are written in terms of the problem space. During the refinement of the definitions and the implementation of the application objects, other objects are identified. Figure 17.5 illustrates the layers of the object specifications that result from this process.

All the phases in the object-oriented approach work more closely together because of the commonality of the object model. In one phase, the problem domain objects are identified, while in the next phase additional objects required for a particular solution are specified. The design process is repeated for these implementation-level objects.

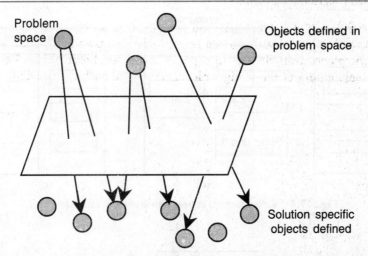

Fig. 17.5   *Layers of object specifications*

In contrast to the traditional top-down functional decomposition approach, the object-oriented approach has many attributes of both the top-down and bottom-up designs. The top funcional decomposition techniques can be applied to the design of individual classes, while the final system can be constructed with the help of class modules using the bottom-up approach.

17.5   OBJECT-ORIENTED NOTATIONS AND GRAPHS

Graphical notations are an essential part of any design and development process, and object-oriented design is no exception. We need notations to represent classes, objects, subclasses, and their inter-relationships. Unfortunately, there are no standard notations for representing the objects and their interactions. Authors and researchers have used their own notations. Some of them are used more frequently while others are not. Figures 17.6 through 17.14 show some of the commonly used notations to represent the following:

1.   Classes and objects.
2.   Instances of objects.
3.   Message communication between objects.
4.   Inheritance relationship.
5.   Classification relationship.
6.   Composition relationship.
7.   Hierarchical chart.
8.   Client-server relationship.
9.   Process layering.

We must use these notations and graphs wherever possible. They improve not only the clarity of the processes but also the productivity of the software developers.

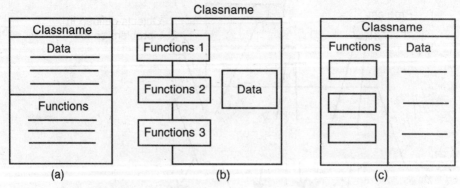

Fig. 17.6   *Various forms of representation of classes/objects*

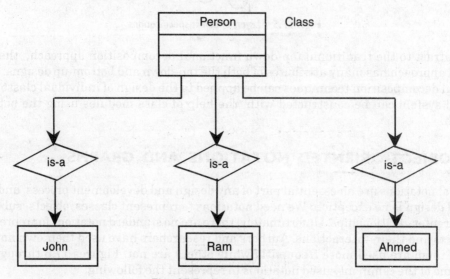

Fig. 17.7   *Instances of objects*

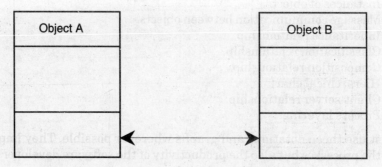

Fig. 17.8   *Message communication between objects*

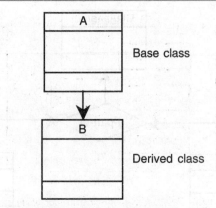

Fig. 17.9 *Inheritance relationship*

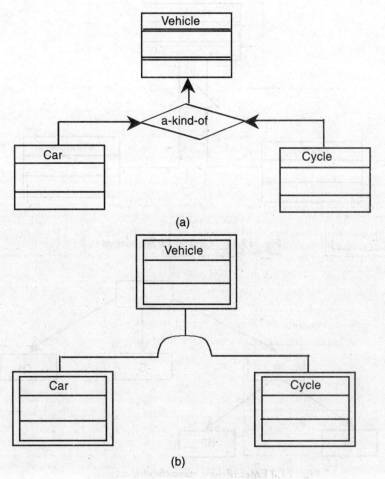

(a)

(b)

Fig. 17.10 *Classification relationship*

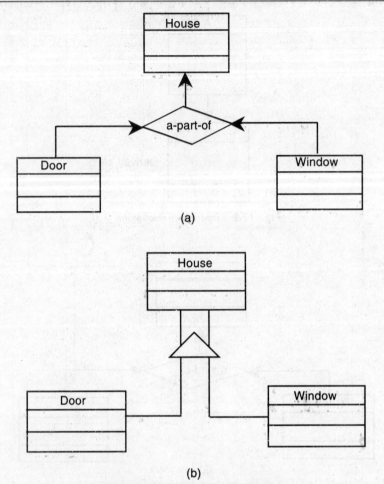

(a)

(b)

Fig. 17.11   *Composition relationship*

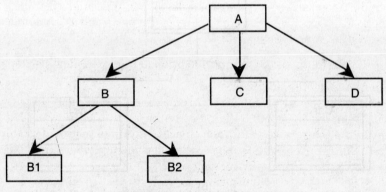

Fig. 17.12   *Hierarchical chart*

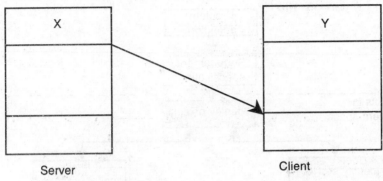

Fig. 17.13 *Client-server relationship*

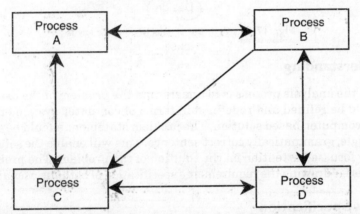

Fig. 17.14 *Process layering (A process may have typically five to seven objects)*

17.6 STEPS IN OBJECT-ORIENTED ANALYSIS

Object-oriented analysis provides us with a simple, yet powerful, mechanism for identifying objects, the building block of the software to be developed. The analysis is basically concerned with the decomposition of a problem into its component parts and establishing a logical model to describe the system functions.

The object-oriented analysis (OOA) approach consists of the following steps:

1. Understanding the problem.
2. Drawing the specifications of requirements of the user and the software.
3. Identifying the objects and their attributes.
4. Identifying the services that each object is expected to provide (interface).
5. Establishing inter-connections (collaborations) between the objects in terms of services required and services rendered.

Although we have shown the above tasks as a series of discrete steps, the last three activities are carried out inter-dependently as shown in Fig. 17.15.

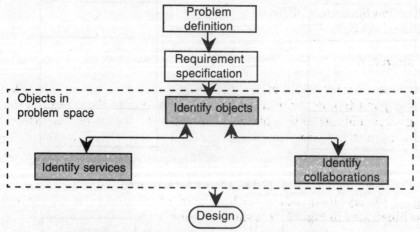

Fig. 17.15 *Activities of object-oriented analysis*

Problem Understanding

The first step in the analysis process is to understand the problem of the user. The problem statement should be refined and redefined in terms of computer system engineering that could suggest a computer-based solution. The problem statement should be stated, as far as possible, in a single, grammatically correct sentence. This will enable the software engineers to have a highly focussed attention on the solution of the problem. The problem statement provides the basis for drawing the requirements specification of both the user and the software.

Requirements Specification

Once the problem is clearly defined, the next step is to understand what the proposed system is required to do. It is important at this stage to generate a list of user requirements. A clear understanding should exist between the user and the developer of what is required. Based on the user requirements, the specifications for the software should be drawn. The developer should state clearly:

- What outputs are required.
- What processes are involved to produce these outputs.
- What inputs are necessary.
- What resources are required.

These specifications often serve as a reference to test the final product for its performance of the intended tasks.

Identification of Objects

Objects can often be identified in terms of the real-world objects as well as the abstract objects. Therefore, the best place to look for objects is the application itself. The application may be analyzed by using one of the following two approaches:

1. Data flow diagrams (DFD)
2. Textual analysis (TA)

Data flow diagram

The application can be represented in the form of a data flow diagram indicating how the data moves from one point to another in the system. The boxes and *data stores* in the data flow diagram are good candidates for the objects. The process *bubbles* correspond to the procedures. Figure 17.16 illustrates a typical data flow diagram. It is also known as a *data flow graph or a bubble chart*.

A DFD can be used to represent a system at any level of abstraction. For example, the DFD shown in Fig. 17.16 may be expanded to include more information (such as payment details) or condensed as illustrated in Fig. 17.17 to show only one bubble.

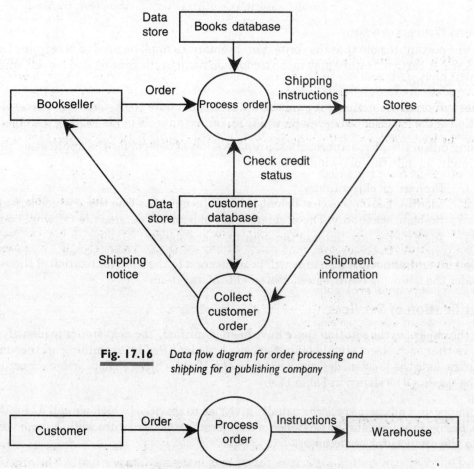

Fig. 17.16   *Data flow diagram for order processing and shipping for a publishing company*

Fig. 17.17   *Fundamental data flow diagram*

Textual analysis

This approach is based on the textual description of the problem or proposed solution. The description may be of one or two sentences or one or two paragraphs depending on the type and complexity of the problem. The nouns are good indicators of the objects. The names can further be classified as *proper nouns, common nouns*, and *mass or abstract nouns*. Table 17.3 shows the various types of nouns and their meaning.

Table 17.3 Types of nouns

Type of noun	Meaning	Example
Common noun	Describe classes of things (entites)	Vehicle, customer income, deduction
Proper noun	Names of specific things	Maruti car, John, ABC company
Mass or abstract noun	Describe a quality, Quantity or an activity associated with a noun	Salary-income house-loan, feet, traffic

It is important to note that the context and semantics must be used to determine the noun categories. A particular word may mean a common noun in one context and a mass or abstract noun in another.

These approaches are only a guide and not the ultimate tools. Creative perception and intuition of the experienced developers play an important role in identifying the objects.

Using one of the above approaches, prepare a list of objects for the application problem. This might include the following tasks:

1. Prepare an object table.
2. Identify the objects that belong to the solution space and those which belong to the problem space only. The problem space objects are outside the software boundary.
3. Identify the attributes of the solution space objects.

Remember that not all the nouns will be of interest to the final realization of the solution. Consider the following requirement statements of a system:

Identification of Services

Once the objects in the solution space have been identified, the next step is to identify a set of services that each object should offer. Services are identified by examining all the verbs and verb phrases in the problem description statement. Verbs which can note actions or occurrences may be classified as shown in Table 17.4.

Doing verbs and *compare verbs* usually give rise to services (which we call as functions in C++). *Being verbs* indicate the existence of the classification structure while *having* verbs give rise to the composition structures.

Table 17.4 Classification of verbs

Types of verb	Meaning	Examples
Doing verbs	operations	read , get, display, buy
Being verbs	classifications	is an, belongs to
Having verbs	composition	has an, is part of
Compare verbs	operations	is less than, is equal to
Stative verbs	invariance-condition	to be present, are owned

Establishing Interconnections

This step identifies the services that objects provide and receive. We may use an information flow diagram (IFD) or an entity-relationship (ER) diagram to enlist this information. Here, we must establish a correspondence between the services and the actual information (messages) that are being communicated.

17.7 STEPS IN OBJECT-ORIENTED DESIGN

Design is concerned with the mapping of objects in the problem space into objects in the solution space, and creating an overall structure (architectural model) and computational models of the system. This stage normally uses the bottom-up approach to build the structure of the system and the top-down functional decomposition approach to design the class member functions that provide services. It is particularly important to construct structured hierarchies, to identify abstract classes, and to simplify the inter-object communications. Reusability of classes from the previous designs, classification of the objects into subsystems and determination of appropriate protocols are some of the considerations of the design stage. The object oriented design (OOD) approach may involve the following steps:

1. Review of objects created in the analysis phase.
2. Specification of class dependencies.
3. Organization of class hierarchies.
4. Design of classes.
5. Design of member functions.
6. Design of driver program.

Review of Problem Space Objects

An exercise to review the objects identified in the problem space is undertaken as a first step in the design stage. The main objective of this review exercise is to refine the objects in terms of their attributes and operations and to identify other objects that are solution specific. Some guidelines that might help the review process are:

1. If only one object is necessary for a service (or operation), then it operates only on that object.
2. If two or more objects are required for an operation to occur, then it is necessary to identify which object's private part should be known to the operation.
3. If an operation requires knowledge of more than one type of objects, then the operation is not functionally cohesive and should be rejected.

Applying these guidelines will help us refine the services of the objects. Further, the redundant or extraneous objects are removed, synonymous services are combined and the names of the operations (functions) are improved to denote clearly the kind of processing involved.

Class Dependencies

Analysis of relationships between the classes is central to the structure of a system. Therefore, it is important to identify appropriate classes to represent the objects in the solution space and establish their relationships. The major relationships that are important in the context of design are:

1. Inheritance relationships.
2. Containment relationships.
3. Use relationships.

Inheritance relationship is the highest relationship that can be represented in C++. It is a powerful way of representing a hierarchical relationship directly. The real appeal and power of the inheritance mechanism is that it allows us to reuse a class that is almost, but not exactly, what we want and to tailor the class in a way that it does not introduce any unwanted side effects into the rest of the class. We must review the attributes and operations of the classes and prepare a *inheritance relationship* table as shown in Table 17.5

Table 17.5   Inheritance relationship table

Class	Depends on
A	......
B	A
C	A
D	B
B1	B
B2	B

Containment relationship means the use of an object of a class as a member of another class. This is an alternative and complimentary technique to use the class inheritance. But, it is often a tricky issue to choose between the two techniques. Normally, if there is a need to override attributes or functions, then the inheritance is the best choice. On the other hand, if we want to represent a property by a variety of types, then the containment relationship is the right method to follow. Another place where we need to use an object as a member is when we need to pass an attribute of a class as an argument to the constructor of another class. The "another" class must have a member object that represents the argument. The inheritance represents *is_a* relationship and the containment represents *has_a* relationship.

Use relationship gives information such as the various classes a class uses and the way it uses them. For example, a class **A** can use classes **B** and **C** in several ways:

* **A** reads a member of **B**.
* **A** calls a member of **C**.
* **A** creates **B** using new operator.

The knowledge of such relationships is important to the design of a program.

Organization of Class Hierarchies

In the previous step, we examined the inheritance relationships. We must re-examine them and create a class hierarchy so that we can reuse as much data and/or functions that have been designed already. Organization of the class hierarchies involves identification of common attributes and functions among a group of related classes and then combining them to form a new class. The new class will serve as the super class and the others as subordinate classes (which derive attributes from the super class). The new class may or may not have the meaning of an object by itself. If the object is created purely to combine the common attributes, it is called an *abstract class*.

This process may be repeated at different levels of abstraction with the sole objective of extending the classes. As hierarchy structure becomes progressively higher, the amount of specification and implementation inherited by the lower level classes increases. We may repeat the process until we are sure that no new class can be formed. Figure 17.18 illustrates a two-level iteration process.

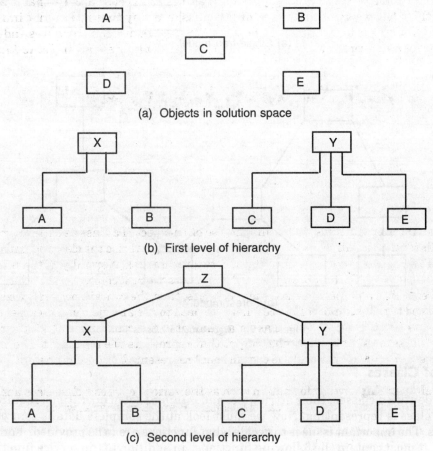

(a) Objects in solution space

(b) First level of hierarchy

(c) Second level of hierarchy

Fig. 17.18 *Level of class hierarchies*

The process of a class organization may finally result in a *single-tree model* as shown in Fig. 17.19(a) or *forest model* as shown in Fig. 17.19(b).

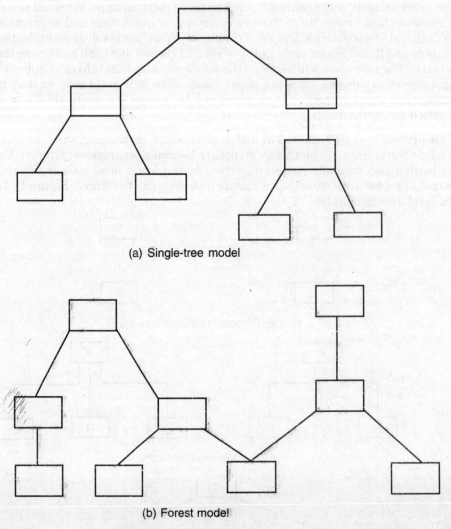

(a) Single-tree model

(b) Forest model

Fig. 17.19   *Organisation of classes*

Design of Classes

We have identified classes, their attributes, and *minimal* set of operations required by the concept a class is representing. Now we must look at the complete details that each class represents. The important issue is to decide what functions are to be provided. For a class to be useful, it must contain the following functions, in addition to the service functions:

1. Class management functions.

    * How an object is created?
    * How an object is destroyed?
2. Class implementation functions.
    What operations are performed on the data type of the class?
3. Class access functions.
    How do we get information about the internal variables of the class?
4. Class utility functions.
    How do we handle errors?

Other issues that are to be considered are:

* What kind of access controls are required for the base classes?
* Which functions can be made virtual?
* What library classes are expected to be used in a class?
* The design of the individual classes has a major impact on the overall quality of the software.

Given below are some guidelines which should be considered while designing a class:

1. The public interface of a class should have only functions of the class.
2. An object of one class should not send a message directly to a member of another class.
3. A function should be declared public only when it is required to be used by the objects of the class.
4. Each function either accesses or modifies some data of the class it represents.
5. A class should be dependent on as few (other) classes as possible.
6. Interactions between two classes must be explicit.
7. Each subordinate class should be designed as a specialization of the base class with the sole purpose of adding additional features.
8. The top class of a structure should represent the abstract model of the target concept.

Design of Member Functions

We have so far identified

1. classes and objects,
2. data members,
3. interfaces,
4. dependencies, and
5. class hierarchy (structure).

It is time now to consider the design of the member functions. The member functions define the operations that are performed on the object's data. These functions behave like any other C function and therefore we can use the top-down functional decomposition technique to design them as shown in Fig. 17.20.

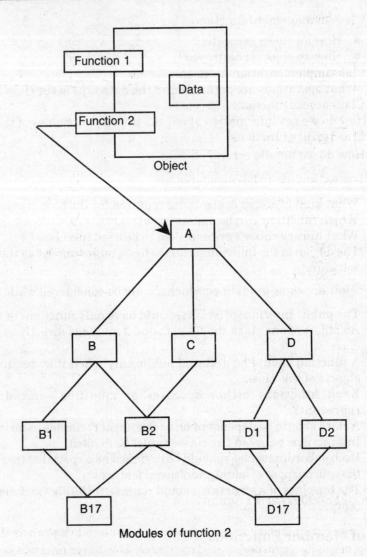

Fig. 17.20   *Top-down design of functions*

We may also apply the *structured design* techniques to each module. The basic structured techniques supported by C++ are shown in Fig. 17.21. We may implement them in any combination and in any order using one-entry, one-exit concept.

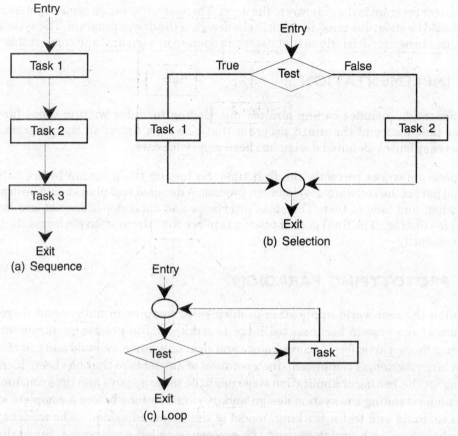

Fig. 17.21 *Structured design techniques*

Design of the Driver Program

Every C++ program must contain a **main()** function code known as the driver program. The execution of the program begins and ends here. The driver program is mainly responsible for:

1. receiving data values from the user,
2. creating objects from the class definitions,
3. arranging communication between the objects as a sequence of messages for invoking the member functions, and
4. displaying output results in the form required by the user.

All activities, including processing during the execution of the program, result from the mutual interactions of the objects. One major design decision to be made is the logical order of the message passing.

The driver program is the gateway to the users. Therefore, the design of user-system interface (USI) should be given due consideration in the design of the driver program. The system should be designed to be user-friendly so that users can operate in a natural and comfortable way.

17.8   IMPLEMENTATION

Implementation includes coding and testing. Coding includes writing codes for classes, member functions and the **main** program that acts as a driver in the program. Coding becomes easy once a detailed design has been done with care.

No program works correctly the first time. So testing the program before using is an essential part of the software development process. A detailed test plan should be drawn as to what, when and how to test. The class interfaces and class dependencies are important aspects for testing. The final goal of testing is to see that the system performs its intended job satisfactorily.

17.9   PROTOTYPING PARADIGM

Most often the real-world application problems are complex in nature and therefore the structure of the system becomes too large to work out the precise requirements at the beginning. Some particulars become known and clear only when we build and test the system. After a large system is completed, incorporation of any feature that has been identified as "missing" at the testing or application stage might be too expensive and time consuming. One way of understanding the system design and its ramifications before a complete system is built is to build and test a working model of the proposed system. The model system is popularly known as a *prototype,* and the process is called *prototyping*. Since the object-oriented analysis and design approach is evolutionary, it is best suited for *prototyping paradigm* which is illustrated in Fig. 17.22.

A prototype is a scaled down version of the system and may not have stringent performance criteria and resource requirements. Developer and customer agree upon certain "outline specifications" of the system and a prototype design is proposed with the outline requirements and available resources. The prototype is built and evaluated. The major interest is not in the prototype itself but in its performance which is used to refine the requirement specifications. Prototypes provide an opportunity to experiment and analyze various aspects of the system such as system structure, internal design, hardware requirements and the final system requirements. The benefits of using the prototype approach are:

* We can produce understandable specifications which are correct and complete as far as possible.
* The user can understand what is being offered.
* Maintenance changes that are required when a system is installed, are minimized.
* Development engineers can work from a set of specifications which have been tested and approved.

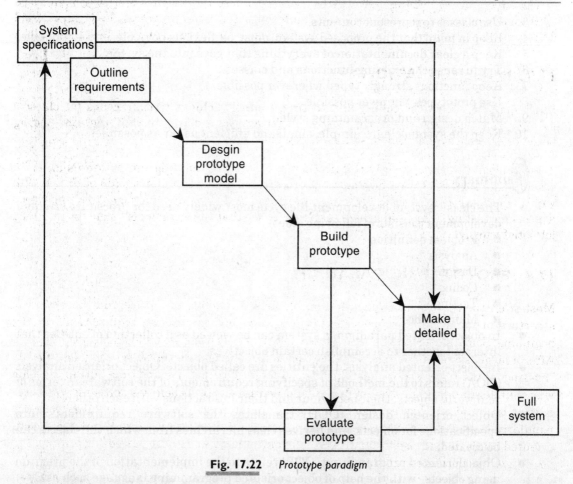

Fig. 17.22   *Prototype paradigm*

Prototype is meant for experimenting. Most often it cannot be tuned into a product. However, occasionally, it may be possible to tune a prototype into a final product if proper care is taken in redesigning the prototype. The best approach is to throw away the prototype after use.

7.10 WRAPPING UP

We have discussed various aspects of the object-oriented analysis and design. Remember, there is no one approach that is always right. You must consider the ideas presented here as only guidelines and use your experience, innovation and creativity wherever possible.

Following are some points for your thought and innovation:

1. Set clear goals and tangible objectives.
2. Try to use existing systems as examples or models to analyze your system.

3. Use classes to represent concepts.
4. Keep in mind that the proposed system must be flexible, portable, and extendable.
5. Keep a clear documentation of everything that goes into the system.
6. Try to reuse the existing functions and classes.
7. Keep functions strongly typed wherever possible.
8. Use prototypes wherever possible.
9. Match design and programming style.
10. Keep the system clean, simple, small and efficient as far as possible.

Summary

* The classic system development life cycle most widely used for procedure oriented development consists of following steps.
    * Problem definition
    * Analysis
    * Design
    * Coding
    * Testing
    * Maintenance
* In object oriented paradigm, a system can be viewed as a collection of entities that interact together to accomplish certain objectives.
* In object oriented analysis, the entities are called objects. Object oriented analysis (OOA) refers to the methods of specifying requirements of the software in terms of real world objects, their behaviour and their interactions with each other.
* Object oriented design (OOD) translates the software requirements into specifications for objects, and derives class hierarchies from which the objects can be created.
* Object oriented programming (OOP) refers to the implementation of the program using objects, with the help of object oriented programming language such as C++.
* The object oriented analysis (OOA) approach consists of the following steps:
    * Defining the problem.
    * Estimating requirements of the user and the software.
    * Identifying the objects and their attributes.
    * Identifying the interface services that each object is supposed to provide.
    * Establishing interconnections between the objects in terms of services required and services rendered.
* The object oriented design (OOD) approach involves the following steps:
    * Review of objects created in the analysis phase.
    * Specification of class dependencies.
    * Organization of class hierarchies.
    * Design of classes.
    * Design of member functions.
    * Design of driver program.
* One way of understanding the system design and its ramifications before a complete system is built is to build and test a working model of the proposed system. This model system is called the prototype, and the process is called prototyping.

* The benefits of using the prototype approach are:
   ■ You can produce understandable specifications which are correct and complete as far as possible.
   ■ The user can understand what is being offered.
   ■ Maintenance changes that are required when a system is installed are minimized.
   ■ Development engineers can work from a set of specifications, which have been tested and approved.

Key Terms

➤ abstract class
➤ abstract nouns
➤ a-kind-of
➤ analysis
➤ a-part-of
➤ being verbs
➤ bubble chart
➤ class hierarchies
➤ classes
➤ classic life cycle
➤ classification relationship
➤ client-server relationship
➤ coding
➤ collaborations
➤ common nouns
➤ compare verbs
➤ composition relationship
➤ containment relationship
➤ context diagrams
➤ data dictionary
➤ data flow diagrams
➤ decision table
➤ decision tree
➤ design
➤ development tools
➤ doing verbs
➤ driver program
➤ entities
➤ entity relationship diagram
➤ entity-relationship
➤ fist generation
➤ flowcharts
➤ forest model
➤ fountain model
➤ functional decomposition
➤ grid charts

➤ loop
➤ maintenance
➤ mass nouns
➤ member functions
➤ message communications
➤ methods
➤ modular approach
➤ object-oriented analysis
➤ object-oriented design
➤ object-oriented paradigm
➤ object-oriented programming
➤ objects
➤ playscripts
➤ problem definition
➤ problem space
➤ procedure-oriented paradigm
➤ procedures
➤ process layering
➤ program flowcharts
➤ proper nouns
➤ prototype
➤ prototyping
➤ prototyping paradigm
➤ second generation
➤ selection
➤ sequence
➤ single-tree model
➤ software life cycle
➤ solution space
➤ stative verbs
➤ structure chart
➤ structured design
➤ structured tools
➤ system flowcharts
➤ testing
➤ textual analysis

➤ has-a relationship	➤ third generation
➤ having verbs	➤ tools
➤ hierarchical chart	➤ top-down approach
➤ information flow diagram	➤ traditional tools
➤ inheritance relationship	➤ use relationship
➤ instances of objects	➤ Warnier diagrams
➤ is-a relationship	➤ water-fall model
➤ layout forms	

Review Questions and Exercises

17.1 *List five most important features, in your opinion, that a software developer should keep in mind while designing a system.*

17.2 *Describe why the testing of software is important.*

17.3 *What do you mean by maintenance of software? How and when is it done?*

17.4 *Who are the major players in each stage of the systems development life cycle?*

17.5 *Is it necessary to study the existing system during the analysis stage? If yes, why? If no, why not?*

17.6 *What are the limitations of the classic software development life cycle?*

17.7 *"Software development process is an iterative process". Discuss.*

17.8 *Distinguish between the "water-fall" model and the "fountain" model.*

17.9 *Distinguish between object-oriented systems analysis and systems design. Which of the two requires more creative talents of the system developer?*

17.10 *Distinguish between the following.*
   (a) *Classification relationship and composition relationship.*
   (b) *Inheritance relationship and client-server relationship.*
   (c) *Objects in problem space and objects in solution space.*
   (d) *Data flow diagrams and hierarchical charts.*

17.11 *Discuss the application of structured design techniques in object-oriented programming.*

17.12 *What are the critical issues that are to be considered while designing the driver program? Why?*

17.13 *"No program works correctly first time." Comment.*

17.14 *What is prototyping? How does it help improve the system design?*

17.15 *State whether the following statements are TRUE or FALSE.*
   (a) *An important consideration when designing a new system is the end-user.*
   (b) *The user has no role in the analysis and design of a system.*
   (c) *A decision table is a pictorial representation of data flow.*
   (d) *The only useful purpose of data flow diagrams is documentation.*
   (e) *Data flow diagrams stress logical flow of data versus physical flow of data.*
   (f) *Computer outputs can be designed in such a way that it is a humanizing force.*
   (g) *Structured programming techniques have no place in the object-oriented program design.*
   (h) *A prototype cannot be improved into a final product.*

Appendix A

Differences Between ANSI C, C++ and ANSI C++

A.1 INTRODUCTION

C++ is a superset of ANSI C. It has many additional features, which can be grouped into two categories, namely,

1. features that are improvements over ANSI C to enhance programming style in a non-object-oriented environment, and
2. features that are added to aid object-oriented programming.

Although a majority of the programs written in ANSI C will run under C++ compiler, a few may not. They may require minor modifications before they are compatible to the C++ environment. This appendix summarizes instances where an ANSI C program is not a C++ program, and highlights the features added to ANSI C to make it an object-oriented programming language.

A.2 WHERE ANSI C IS NOT C++

Keywords

In order to add features to C, a number of new keywords have been added to ANSI C. These are:

C++ additions

asm	**catch**	**class**	**delete**
friend	**inline**	**new**	**operator**

private	protected	public	template
this	throw	try	virtual

ANSI C++ additions

bool	export	reinterpret_cast	typename
const_cast	false	static_cast	using
dynamic_cast	mutable	true	wchar_t
explicit	namespace	typeid	

ANSI C programs using any of these keywords as identifiers are not C++ programs.

Length of Identifiers

C++ does not put any limit on the length of identifiers. Some C implementations may impose restrictions on the length.

Declarations

In ANSI C, a global variable can be declared several times without using the **extern** specifier. C++ does not permit this. It must be declared only once without **extern** and all the remaining must use the **extern** specifier.

Global const

In ANSI C, a global **const** has an external linkage. But it is not true in C++ where all **const** values are **static** by default and thus become local.

Character Constants

In ANSI C, the character constants are of type **int**. C++ treats the character constants as type **char**. This is necessary because the compiler needs to distinguish between the two overloaded functions based on their arguments. For example, the declarations such as

```
void display(int);
void display(char);
```

are valid in C++. When we call the function

```
display('A');
```

the compiler will call **display(char)** and not **display(int)**.

Enumerated Data Type

The **enum** data type differs slightly in C++. The **enum** tag name is considered a type name in C++. ANSI C defines the type **enum** to be **int**, whereas in C++, each enumerator is the type of its enumeration. This means that C++ does not allow for an **int** value to be automatically converted to an **enum** value. Example:

```
enum colour {yellow, green, blue};
colour paint;          // declare paint of type colour
paint = green;         // valid, green is of type colour
paint = 5;             // invalid, 5 is of type int
paint = colour(5);     // valid
```

Another difference is that ANSI C allows an **enum** to be defined within a structure, but the **enum** is globally visible. In C++, an **enum** defined within a structure is only visible inside the structure.

The C++ also supports the creation of anonymous enum's (i.e. enum's without tags) as shown below:

```
enum{yellow, green, blue};
```

Main Function

C++ forces the **main()** function to return a value of type **int**. Therefore, all **main()** functions should have an explicit **return(0)** statement.

Function Prototype

The supply of function prototypes is a must in C++. The function declaration must define not only the return type but also the types of parameters the function is going to use. This is not essential in ANSI C. Therefore, all the old C type functions will work under ANSI C but will not in C++.

Functions with No Arguments

Functions declared with an empty argument list are treated differently in C++ and ANSI C. For example, a function declaration such as

```
int test();
```

means 'unspecified number of arguments' in ANSI C and 'exactly zero arguments' in C++. Therefore, the function **test()** can be called with arguments in ANSI C. But it will be an error in C++. Function declarations with no arguments for use in both ANSI C and C++ programs should be declared explicitly as follows:

```
int test(void);
```

Function Header

K&R C defines a function header as follows:

```
double mul(m,a)
int m;
float a;
```

```
{
.....
.....
}
```

While this is acceptable in ANSI C as well as C++, this style is likely to be dropped in the future versions of C++. It is better to define the function header using a prototype-like format as shown below:

```
double mul (int m, float a)
{
.....
.....
}
```

void Data Type

The void specifier can be used to define a pointer to a generic item. There is a significant difference in how C++ and ANSI C handle the assignment of **void** pointers to other pointer types. In ANSI C, we can assign void pointer to other pointer types without using a cast.

Example:

```
void *a;
char *c;
c = a;        // assign void pointer to char pointer
```

This will not work in C++. A void pointer cannot be assigned directly to other type pointers in C++. This can be done using the cast operator as follows:

```
c = (char *) a;
```

Remember, in both the cases, a pointer of type void can be assigned any type. That is

```
a = c;
```

will work both in ANSI C and C++.

const Variables

const means different things in C++ and ANSI C. In ANSI C, it means that 'it cannot be changed' to any ordinary variable. In C++, it is intended to replace the use of **#define** to create the symbolic constants. The symbolic constants have no type information whereas **const** values in C++ can have types specified explicitly. For example, the statement

```
const int N = 100;
```

creates a constant **N** of type **int**.

This information can help the compiler detect errors such as calling a function with arguments of the wrong type.

The other main difference is that in C++, we can use a **const** in a constant expression. For example, we can use **const** value to declare the size of an array.

```
const size = 30;
char buffer[size];
```

This is illegal in C. Note that when we omit the type, C++ uses **int**. One another difference is that C++ requires the **const** variables to be initialized at the time of declaration. ANSI C does not. That is,

```
const max;
```

is legal in ANSI C, but not in C++. This must be written as

```
const max = 100;
```

Character Array Initialization

When initializing character arrays in ANSI C, we can declare the array size as equivalent to the number of characters in the string. Example:

```
char name[4] = "GOOD";
```

That is, we need not provide any extra space for the terminating character \0. The above initialization is not legal in C++. The size of the array must include an extra space for holding the null character \0.

goto Jump

ANSI C allows a **goto** to jump into a block of code, past a variable declaration and initialization. Example:

```
.....
goto label1;
.....
{
    int x = 1;
    .....
    .....
    label1;
}
.....
.....
```

C++ does not permit a **goto** to skip an initialization as shown above.

A.3 C++ EXTENSIONS TO ANSI C

C++ is an attempt to improve upon C by expanding its features to support new software development concepts such as object-oriented programming. This section summarizes the new features that are added to the ANSI C.

Comments

C++ supports one more type of comment in addition to the existing comment style /*.......*/. This is useful for one-line comments as shown below:

```
// This is a C++ one-line comment
```

In general, the /*.....*/ style is used for a group of lines and the //.... style is used for the single line comments.

Casts

C++ introduces a new type of cast syntax as shown below:

```
m = long(n);    // new C++ cast
```

C++ also supports C-type cast:

```
m = (long) n;    // C-type cast
```

Declarations

Unlike ANSI C which requires all the declarations to be made at the beginning of the scope, C++ permits us to make declarations at any point in the program. This enables us to place the declarations closer to the point of their use.

Scope Resolution

A new operator :: known as the scope resolution operator has been introduced to access an item that is outside the current scope. This operator is also used for distinguishing class members and defining class methods.

New Keywords

In order to add new features, it was necessary to create a number of new keywords. They are listed in Section A.2 in this Appendix.

Struct and Union Tags

In C++, both structs and unions are treated as types of classes and their tag names as type names. For example,

```
struct item{int cost; float weight};
item a;
```

are valid statements in C++. However, the older syntax is also acceptable. The structs and unions can contain functions as members in addition to data members.

Anonymous Unions

In C++, we can declare unions without tag names. For example,

```
union
{
        int height;
        float weight;
}
```

is a legal declaration in C++. The members can be directly accessed by the name.

```
height = 175;
weight = 70;
```

Free Store Operators

C++ defines two new operators **new** and **delete** to manage the dynamic memory allocation function. They can be used in places of **malloc()** and **free()** used in ANSI C. Example:

```
void fun(void)
{
        float *p;
        p = new float;
        *p = 25.79;
        delete p;
}
```

References

C++ allows the use of a reference, which is simply another name of the variable that is being initialized.

```
int m = 100;
int &x = m;
```

x is an alternative name for **m**. If we add, say 10, to **x**:

```
x = x + 10;
```

we have, in effect, added 10 to **m**.

Inline Functions

To eliminate the cost of calls to small functions, C++ supports a concept known as inline functions. These functions are specified with keyword **inline** as shown below:

```
inline int mul(int a, int b)
{
       return (a * b);
}
```

An *inline* function is inserted wherever a call to that function appears. This is called *inline expansion*. All inline functions must be defined before they are called.

Default Function Arguments

In C++, we can force the arguments to default to predefined values. These values are specified in the function prototype as shown below:

```
void func1(int a, int b=2, int c=3);
```

Typical function calls could be:

```
func1(5,10);
func1(10);
func1(5,10,15);
```

Function Overloading

Function names can be overloaded in C++. That is, we can assign the same name to two or more distinct functions. Example:

```
int mul(int a, int b);          // prototype
float mul(float x, float y);    // prototype
```

The function name **mul()** is overloaded, meaning that it has more than one implementation. The execution of the correct implementation is decided by the compiler by matching the type of the arguments in the function call with the types in the function prototypes.

Operator Overloading

C++ allows overloading of most operators. This feature allows us to change the meaning of the operators. For example, we can add two user-defined data types using the operator +. The concept of operator overloading is extensively used in manipulating the class type objects. Example:

```
Object1 = Object1 + Object2;
```

C++ works by creating functions that define the actions performed on non-intrinsic types by an operator. *An operator function* is declared using the **operator** keyword and the operator symbol.

Classes

C++ extends the syntax of struct to allow the inclusion of functions in structures. The new syntax is termed as *class* in C++. Classes offer a method of grouping together data and functions that can operate on this data. They also provide a mechanism for restricted access to specific data.

It is also possible to derive a class from one or more base classes. A derived class inherits all the members of its base class. Access privileges of the inherited members can be changed by the derived class through access specifiers. Derived classes provide the capability of building a hierarchical structure of objects.

The classes provide the programmer with a tool for creating new data types that can be used as conveniently as the built-in types.

Pointers

Pointers are declared and referenced similar to C. However, C++ adds the concepts of constant pointer and pointer to constant:

```
char * const ptr1;     // constant pointer
```

We cannot modify the address that **ptr1** is initialized to:

```
char const * ptr2;     // pointer to a constant
```

The contents of what **ptr2** is pointing to cannot be changed through indirection.

Templates

Templates, a feature added to C++, enable us to define generic classes and functions that can be used to create a family of classes and functions with different data types.

Exception Handling

C++ adds a mechanism to locate and manage certain disastrous error conditions known as exceptions during the execution of a program.

Input/Output in C++

All I/O functions available in C are supported by C++ as well. However, in addition to what C provides, C++ adds a few unique features of its own. It supports several functions that allow reading and writing of data in both formatted and unformatted forms.

A.4   ANSI C++ ADDITIONS TO C++

ANSI C++ has added several new features to the original C++ specifications. Important features added are:

Data types
* bool
* wchar_t

Operators
* const_cast
* static_cast
* reinterpret_cast
* typeid

Class member qualifiers
* Explicit constructor
* Mutable members
* Namespace scope
* Operator keywords
* New style headers
* New keywords

These features are discussed in detail in Chapter 16.

A.5 STANDARD TEMPLATE LIBRARY

A large number of generic classes and functions have been developed that could be used as a standard approach for storing and processing of data. These classes and functions, collectively known as the Standard Template Library, have now become a part of ANSI C++ class library. The important features of the Standard Template Library are presented in Chapter 14.

Appendix B
Executing Turbo C++

B.1 INTRODUCTION

All programs in this book were developed and run under Turbo C++ compiler Version 3.0, in an MS-DOS environment on an IBM PC compatible computer. We shall discuss briefly, in this Appendix, the creation and execution of C++ programs under Turbo C++ system.

B.2 CREATION AND EXECUTION OF PROGRAMS

Executing a computer program written in any high-level language involves several steps, as listed below:

1. Develop the program (source code).
2. Select a suitable file name under which you would like to store the program.
3. Create the program in the computer and save it under the filename you have decided. This file is known as *source code file*.
4. Compile the source code. The file containing the translated code is called *object code file*. If there are any errors, debug them and compile the program again.
5. Link the object code with other library code that are required for execution. The resulting code is called the *executable code*. If there are errors in linking, correct them compile the program again.
6. Run the executable code and obtain the results, if there are no errors.
7. Debug the program, if errors are found in the output.
8. Go to Step 4 and repeat the process again.

These steps are illustrated in Fig. B.1. The exact steps depend upon the program environment and the compiler used. But, they will resemble the steps described above.

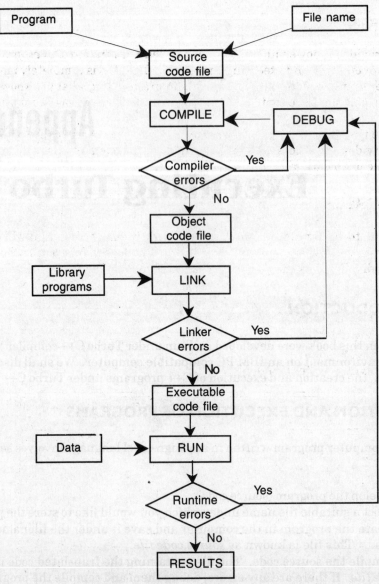

Fig. B.1   *Program development and execution*

Turbo C++ and Borland C++ are the two most popular C++ compilers. They provide ideal platforms for learning and developing C++ programs. In general, both Turbo C++ and Borland C++ work the same way, except some additional features supported by Borland C++ which are outside the scope our discussions. Therefore, whatever we discuss here about Turbo C++ applies to Borland C++ as well.

B.3   TURBO C++

Turbo C++ provides a powerful environment called *Integrated Development Environment* (**IDE**) for creating and executing a program. The IDE is completely menu-driven and allows the user to create, edit, compile and run programs using what are known as *dialogue boxes*. These operations are controlled by single keystrokes and easy-to-use menus.

We first use the editor to create the source code file, then compile, link and finally run it. Turbo C++ provides error messages, in case errors are detected. We have to correct the errors and compile the program again.

B.4   IDE SCREEN

It is important to be familiar with the details of the IDE screen that will be extensively used in the program development and execution. When we invoke the Turbo C++, the IDE screen will be displayed as shown in Fig. B.2. As seen from the figure, this screen contains four parts:

* Main menu (top line)
* Editor window
* Message window
* Status line (bottom line)

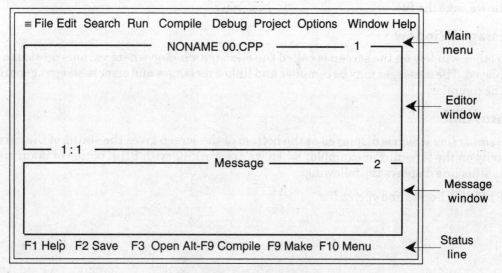

Fig. B.2   *IDE opening screen*

Main Menu

The *main menu* lists a number of items that are required for the program development and execution. They are summarized in Table B.1.

Table B.I Main menu items

Item	Options
–	Displays the version number, clears or restores the screen, and execut various utility programmes supplied with Turbo C++
File	Loads and saves files, handless directories invokes DOS, and exists Turbo C+
Edit	Performs various editing functions
Search	Performs various text searches and replacements
Run	Complies, links and runs the program currently loaded in the environment
Compile	Compiles the program currently in the environment
Debug	Sets various debugger options, including setting break points
Projects	Manages multifile projects
Options	Sets various compiler, linker, and environmental options
Window	Controls the way various windows are displayed
Help	Activates the context–sensitive Help system

The *main menu* can be activated by pressing the F10 key. When we select an item on the main menu, a *pull-down menu*, containing various options, is displayed. This allows us to select an action that relates to the main menu item.

Editor Window

The *editor window* is the place for creating the source code of C++ programs. This window is named NONAME00.CPP. This is the temporary name given to a file which can be changed while we save the file.

Message Window

The other window on the screen is called the *message window* where various messages are displayed. The messages may be compiler and linker messages and error messages generated by the compiler.

Status Line

The *status line* which is displayed at the bottom of the screen gives the status of the current activity on the screen. For example, when we are working with FILE option of main menu, the status line displays the following:

F1 Help | Locate and open a file

B.5   INVOKING TURBO C++

Assuming that you have installed the Turbo C++ compiler correctly, go to the directory in which you want to work. Then enter TC at the DOS system prompt:

`C:>TC`

and press RETURN. This will place you into the IDE screen as shown in Fig. B.2. Now, you are ready to create your program.

B.6   CREATING SOURCE CODE FILE

Once you are in the IDE screen, it is simple to create and save a program. The F10 key will take you to main menu and then move the cursor to *File*. This will display the file dialogue window containing various options for file operations as shown in Fig. B.3. The options include, among others, opening an existing file, creating a new file and saving the new file.

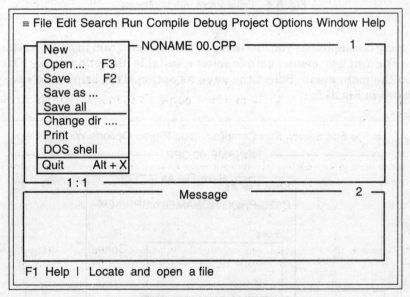

Fig. B.3   *File dialogue window*

Since you want to create a new file, move the cursor to **New** option. This opens up a blank window called *editing window* and places the cursor inside this window. Now the system is ready to receive the program statements as shown in Fig. B.4.

```
≡ File Edit Search Run Compile Debug Project Options Window Help
┌─────────────────── NONAME 00.CPP ──────────────── 1 ──┐
# include  <iostream. h>
main()
{
    cout  <<  "C++ is better than  C";
    return 0;
}

└── 1 : 1 ──────────────────────────────────────────────┘
┌───────────────────── Message ──────────────── 2 ──┐



└──────────────────────────────────────────────────┘
F1 Help F2 Save  F3 Open Alt-F9  Compile F9 Make  F10 Menu
```

Fig. B.4   *Editor screen with statements*

Once the typing is completed, you are ready to save the program in a file. At this time, you must go to *the File dialogue* menu again to select a suitable file option. Press **F10** and select **File** option on the main menu. Select the **save as** option. This brings the save editor file window as shown in Fig. B.5.

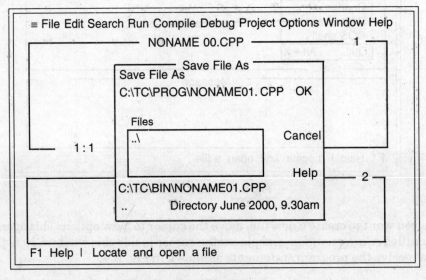

Fig. B.5   *Save editor file window*

Now, you may change the file name NONAMEOO.CPP (shown in the editor file window) to the name you have selected. Make sure that your name has the extension **.CPP** to indicate to the compiler that your program is a C++ one and not C. Let's Assume that you have selected **test.cpp** as name. Press RETURN key and the program is saved in the file **test.cpp**.

B.7   COMPILING THE PROGRAM

When you select the **compile** option on the main menu, the *compile dialogue* window is displayed as shown in Fig. B.6. The *compile* to OBJ option allows you to compile the current file in the editor to an object file. In the present case, **test.obj** file is created, if there are no errors in your program. If there are any errors, appropriate error messages are displayed in the message window.

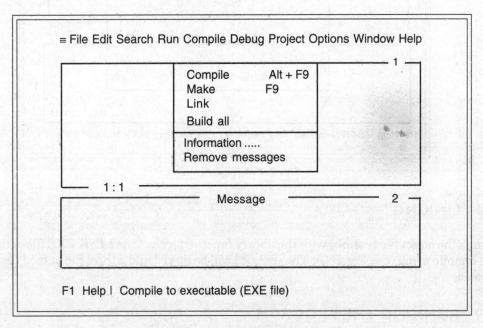

Fig. B.6   *Compile dialogue menu*

During compilation, a window called *compilation window* will appear on the screen as shown in Fig. B.7. If there are no errors during compilation, this window will display **"Success: Press any key"** message. The entries for warning and errors will be 0.

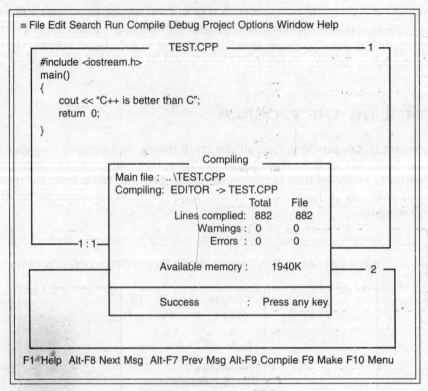

Fig. B.7   *Compilation window*

B.8   LINKING

To link the object file **test.obj** with the library functions, select the **LINK EXE** file option from the compile menu (See Fig. B.6). The **test.obj** will be linked and a third file named **test.exe** is created.

B.9   RUNNING THE PROGRAM

You have reached successfully the final stage of your excitement. Now, select the **Run** from the main menu and again **Run** from the run *dialogue window* (See Fig. B.8). You will see the screen flicker briefly. Surprisingly, no output is displayed. Where has the output gone? It has gone to a place known as *user screen*.

In order to see the user screen, select **window** from the main menu and then select *user screen* from the window dialogue menu (See Fig.B.9). The IDE screen will disappear and the user screen is displayed containing output of the program **test.cpp** as follows:

```
C > TC
```

Note that, at this point, you are outside the IDE. To return to IDE, press RETURN key.

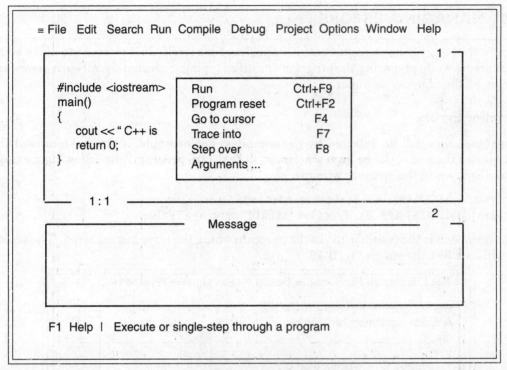

Fig. B.8   *Run dialogue menu*

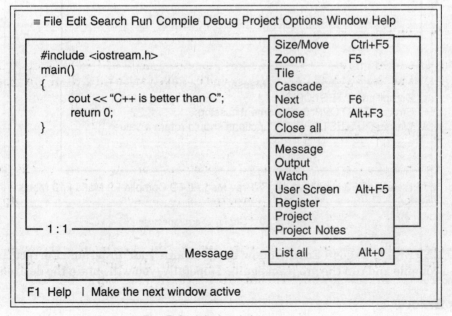

Fig. B.9   *Window dialogue menu*

B.10   MANAGING ERRORS

It is rare that a program runs successfully the first time itself. It is common to make some syntax errors while preparing the program or during typing. Fortunately, all such errors are detected by the compiler or linker.

Compiler Errors

All syntax errors will be detected by the compiler. For example, if you have missed the semicolon at the end of the **return** statement in **test.cpp** program, the following message will be displayed in the message window.

```
Error...\TEST.CPP 6: Statement missing;
Warning...\TEST.CPP 7: Function should return a value
```

The number 6 is the possible line in the program where the error has occurred. The screen now will look like the one in Fig. B.10.

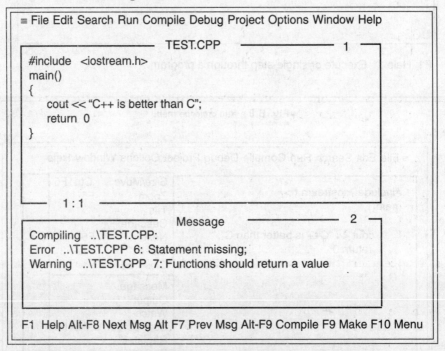

```
≡ File Edit Search Run Compile Debug Project Options Window Help
┌──────────────────── TEST.CPP ──────────────── 1 ─┐
│ #include   <iostream.h>                            │
│ main()                                             │
│ {                                                  │
│     cout << "C++ is better than C";                │
│     return  0                                      │
│ }                                                  │
│                                                    │
└─ 1 : 1 ───────────────────────────────────────────┘
┌──────────────────── Message ──────────────── 2 ─┐
│ Compiling   ..\TEST.CPP:                           │
│ Error  ..\TEST.CPP  6: Statement missing;          │
│ Warning   ..\TEST.CPP  7: Functions should return a value │
│                                                    │
└────────────────────────────────────────────────┘
F1  Help Alt-F8 Next Msg Alt F7 Prev Msg Alt-F9 Compile F9 Make F10 Menu
```

Fig. B.10   *Display of error message*

Press ENTER key to go to **Edit** window that contains your program. Correct the errors and then compile and run the program again. Hopefully, you will obtain the desired results.

Linker Errors

It is also possible to have errors during the linking process. For instance, you may not have included the file *iostream.h*. The program will compile correctly, but will fail to link. It will display an error message in the *linking window*. Press any key to see the message in the message window.

Run-time Errors

Remember compiling and linking successfully do not always guaranty the correct results. Sometimes, the results may be wrong due logical errors or due to errors such as stack overflow. System might display the errors such as *null pointer assignment*. You must consult the manual for the meaning of such errors and modify the program accordingly.

B.11   HANDLING AN EXISTING FILE

After saving your file to disk, your file has become a part of the list of files stored in the disk. How do we retrieve such files and execute the programs written to them? You can do this in two ways:

1.   Under DOS prompt
2   Under IDE

Under DOS prompt, you can invoke as follows:

```
C > TC   TEST.CPP
```

Remember to type the complete and correct name of the file with **.cpp** extension. This command first brings Turbo C++ IDE and then loads **edit window** containing the file **test.cpp**.

If you are working under IDE, then select **open** option from the *file menu*. This will prompt you for a file name and then loads the file as you respond with the correct file name. Now you can edit the program, compile it and execute it as before.

B.12   SOME SHORTCUTS

It is possible to combine the two steps of compiling and linking into one. This can be achieved by selecting **Make EXE file** from the compile dialogue window.

We can shorten the process by combining the execution step as well with the above step. In this case, we must select **Run** option from the run dialogue window. This causes the program to be compiled, linked and executed.

Many common operations can be activated directly without going through the main menu, again and again. Turbo C++ supports what are known as *hot keys* to provide these shortcuts. A list of hot keys and their functions are given Table B.2. We can use them whenever necessary.

Hot key	Meaning
F1	Activates the online Help system
F2	Saves the file currently being edited
F3	Loads a file
F4	Executives the program unit the cursor is reached
F5	Zooms the active window
F6	Switches between windows
F7	Traces program; skips function calls
F8	Traces program; skips function calls
F9	Compiles and links programs
F10	Activates the main menu
ALT-O	Lists open windows
ALT-n	Activates window n (n must be 1 through 9)
ALT-F1	Shows the previous help screen
ALT-F3	Deletes the active window
ALT-F4	Opens an Inspector window
ALT-F5	Opens an Inspector window
ALT-F7	Previous error
ALT-F8	Next error
ALT-F9	Compiles file to .OBJ
ALT-SPACEBAR	Activates the main menu
ALT-C	Activates the Compile menu
ALT-D	Activates the Debug menu
ALT-E	Activates the Edit menu
ALT-F	Activates the File menu
ALT-H	Activates the Help menu
ALT-O	Activates the Options menu
ALT-P	Activates the Project menu
ALT-R	Activates the Run menu
ALT-S	Activates the Run menu
ALT-W	Activates the Window menu
ALT-X	Quits Turbo C++
CTRL-F1	Requests help about the item the cursor is on
CTRL-F2	Resets the program
CTRL-F3	Shows the function call stack
CTRL-F4	Evaluates an expression
CTRL-F5	Changes the size or location of the active window
CTRL-F7	Sets a watch expression (debugging)
CTRL-F8	Sets or clears a break point
CTRL-F9	Executes the current program

Appendix C
Executing C++ Under Windows

C.I INTRODUCTION

C++ is one of the most popular languages due to its power and portability. It is available for different operating systems such as DOS, OS/2, UNIX, Windows and many others. C++ programs when implemented under Windows are called Visual C++ programs. Therefore, there is no difference between C++ and Visual C++ programs in terms of programming but the difference lies in terms of implementation.

A C++ compiler designed for implementation under Windows is known as Visual C++. A C++ program running under MS-DOS will also run successfully under Windows. This is because, the rules of programming are the same; only the environment of implementation is different and is shown in Fig. C.1.

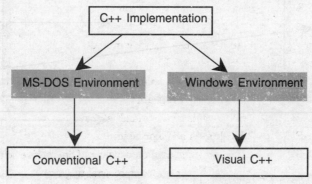

Fig. C.I *C++ implementation environments*

A C++ programmer can easily become a Visual C++ programmer if he knows how to use the implementation tools of his Visual C++ system. In this Appendix, we introduce the features of Microsoft Visual C++ and discuss how to create, compile and execute C++ programs under Windows.

The Microsoft Corporation has introduced a Windows based C++ development environment named as **Microsoft Visual C++** (MSVC). This development environment integrates a set of tools that enable a programmer to create and run C++ programs with ease and style. Microsoft calls this integrated development environment (IDE) as **Visual Workbench. Microsoft Visual Studio**, a product sold by Microsoft Corporation, also includes Visual C++, in addition to other tools like Visual Basic, Visual J++, Visual Foxpro, etc.

C.2   THE VISUAL WORKBENCH

It is important to be familiar with the Visual Workbench that will be extensively used in the program development. The Visual Workbench is a visual user interface designed to help implement C++ programs. This contains various tools that are required for creating, editing, compiling, linking and running of C++ programs under Windows. These tools include File, Edit, Search, Project, Resource, Debug, Tools, Window and Help.

When we invoke the Microsoft Visual C++ (Version 6.0), the initial screen of the Visual Workbench will be displayed as shown in Fig. C.2. As seen from the figure, this screen contains five parts: (1) Title bar (2) Main menu (3) Tool bar (4) Developer window (5) Status line.

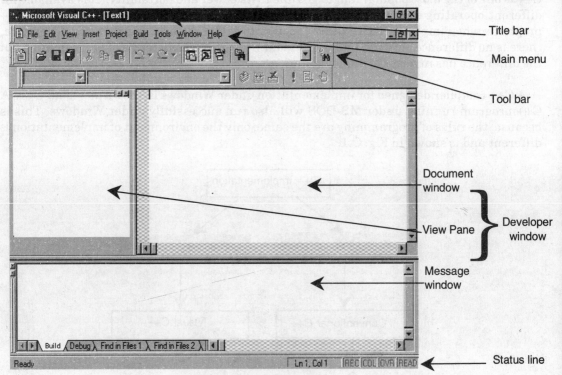

Fig. C.2   *Visual workbench opening screen*

Main Menu

The main menu lists a number of items that are required for program development and execution. They are summarized in Table C.1.

Table C.1   Main menu of visual workbench

Item	Functions / Options
File	Creates a new file or opens an existing file for editing. Closes and saves files. Exits the Visual Workbench.
Edit	Performs various editing functions, such as searching, deleting, copying, cutting and pasting.
View	Enable different views of screen, output, workspace.
Insert	Insertion of Graphics resources like pictures, icons, HTML, etc. can be done.
Project	Sets up and edits a project (a list of files).
Build	Compiles the source code in the active window. Builds an executable file. Detects errors.
Tools	Customizes the environment, the editors and the debugger.
Window	Controls the visibility of various Windows involved in an application development.
Help	Provides help about using Visual C++ through Microsoft Developer Network Library (MSDN Library). Online help also can be received provided an Internet connection.

Once a main menu item is selected, a pull-down menu, containing various options, is displayed. This allows us to select an action/command that relates to the main menu item.

It is likely that an option in the pull-down menu is grayed. This means that the particular option is currently not available or not valid. For example, the Save option in the File menu will be grayed if the workspace is empty.

Some options are followed by three periods (...). Such an option, when selected, will display a submenu known as dialog box suggesting that some more input is required for that option to get implemented. Options followed by the symbol ▶ means we have to select a choice from the list.

Tool Bar

The tool bar resides just below the main menu. This provides a shortcut access to many of the main menu's options with a single mouse click. Figure. C.3 shows some important tool bar commands that can be used from anywhere within the Workbench. Several tool bars like Standard, Build, Edit, Wizard Bar, etc. are available which can be enabled/disabled from the screen using Tools/Customize option.

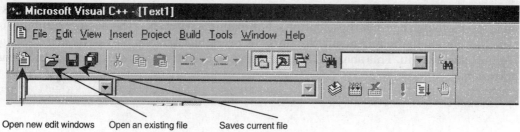

Fig. C.3   *Tool bar actions*

Developer Window

Just below the tool bar is the developer window. It is initially divided into three parts as shown in Fig. C.2.

* View Pane (on the left)
* Document window (on the right)
* Message window (at the bottom)

The view pane has three tabs for ClassView, FileView and InfoView. Once we have a project going, the ClassView will show us the class hierarchy and the FileView will show us the files used. InfoView will allow us to navigate through the documentation.

The document window, also known as workspace, is the place where we enter or display our programs. The message window displays messages such as warnings and errors when we compile the programs.

Accessing Menu Items

Before we proceed further, it is important to know how to access the menu items. There are two ways of accomplishing this:

1. Using the mouse
2. Using the keyboard

Mouse Actions

Using the mouse for accessing an item is the most common approach in Windows programming. We can perform the following actions with the mouse:

* Move the mouse pointer to a desired location by moving the mouse without pressing any button.
* Click the left mouse button when the pointer is over the preferred option.

Keyboard Actions

Though the use of mouse is a must for Windows-based applications, the accessing can also be done through keyboard. Simultaneously pressing the ALT key and the underscored letter of the menu item required will activate the corresponding pull-down menu. The underscored letter is known as hot key. Once a pull-down menu is displayed, using the down/up arrow keys an option can be highlighted and then pressing the ENTER key will activate that option.

Some of the options in a pull-down menu can be directly activated by using their hot key combinations shown against these options. For example, Ctrl+N is the hot key combination for the New option in the File menu. Similarly by pressing Ctrl+S, a file can be saved without using pull-down menu. This shortcut approach can be used from anywhere within the Visual Workbench.

C.3   IMPLEMENTING VISUAL C++ PROGRAMS

Developing and implementing a computer program written in any high-level language involves several steps already described in Appendix B.

C.4   CREATING A SOURCE CODE FILE

When you have installed the Microsoft Visual C++ compiler correctly, you can start the Visual Workbench from Microsoft Windows. To start the Visual Workbench, simply select the Visual C++ icon from the Programs group and click on it. This will bring up the Visual Workbench screen as shown in Fig. C.2. Once you are in the Visual Workbench screen, it is simple to create and save a program.

Entering the Program

The first thing you need to do before entering a program is to open a new file. Select the File menu from the main menu. This will display a pull-down file menu as shown in Fig. C.4. The options include, among others, opening an existing file, creating a new file and saving the new file.

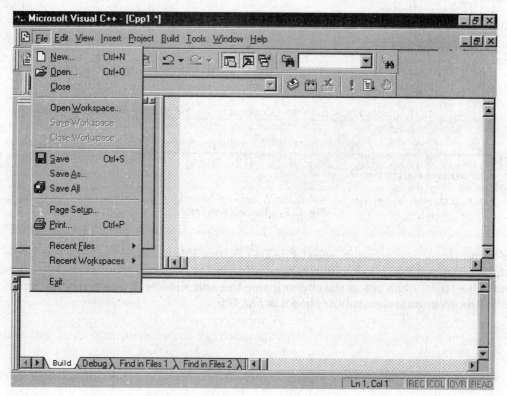

Fig. C.4   *Visual C++ Workbench file menu*

Since, you want to create a new file, choose New ... option which will bring up the New dialog box as shown in Fig. C.5 displaying a list of different types of programming files.

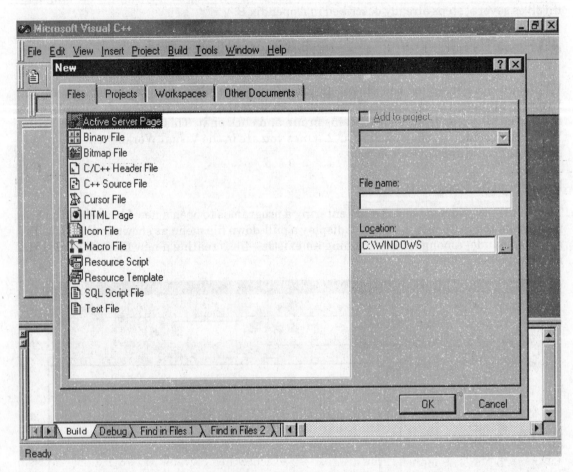

Fig. C.5   *The new dialog box*

For entering a new program, select File/C++ Source File option and then click on the OK button. This opens up a blank window (similar to Fig. C.2) with the window title as 'Microsoft Visual C++ - [CPP]' and places the cursor inside this edit window. Now the system is ready to receive the program statements as shown in Fig. C.6.

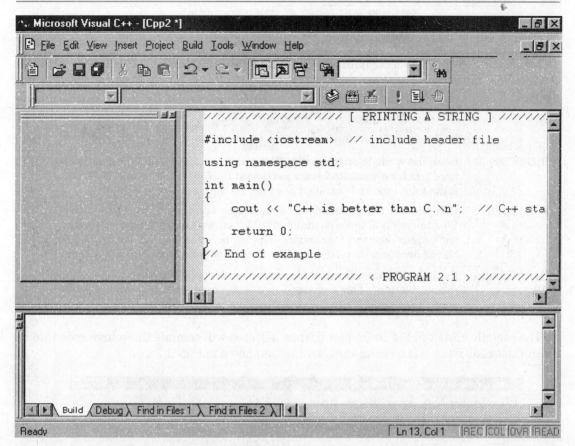

Fig. C.6   *Edit window with the sample program*

Saving the Program

Once the typing is completed, you are ready to execute the program. Although a program can be compiled and run before it is saved, it is always advisable to save the program in a file before compilation. You can do so by doing one of the following:

1. Using File/Save command
2. Pressing the Ctrl+S hot key combination
3. Clicking on the third button from left on the toolbar.

When a file is saved for the first time, the system will present you with a save dialog box. Save this under the file name TEST.CPP.

After the file is saved, the title in the title bar will show the saved file's name.

C.5 COMPILING AND LINKING

In Visual C++, the process of compiling and linking all the source files to create an executable file is called "building". There are three ways of compiling a type source code and is shown in Table C.2.

Table C.2 Three ways of compiling

Command	Action
Build/Compile	Compiles a single program file. The result is an object file. This option is used when we want to check a particular file for syntax errors. Note that it does not link and therefore does not produce any executable file.
Build/Build	Compiles all the modified/new source files and then links all the object files to create a new executable file. When we are working on a project, we usually use this command. That is because we may change a few things here and there and want to compile only those modified programs.
Build/Rebuild All	Compiles all the files in a project and links them together to create an executable file. This command is usually used when we want to make sure that everything in the project has been built again.

The compile option in the Build menu when selected will compile the source code into an executable code if there is no errors or warnings as shown in Fig. C.7.

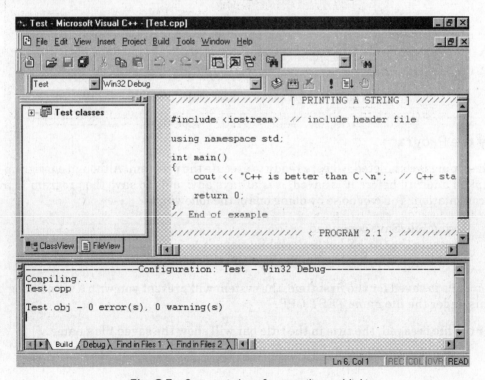

Fig. C.7 *Output window after compiling and linking*

While compiling a C++ source file the Visual C++ application will prompt a message to build a new workspace. Workspace is nothing but an area where we can have a number of source files, their compilation files and linking files saved altogether known as Project. This will be used when we have to create a application with multiple source files.

Executable File

The executable file TEST.EXE will be added to the Build menu as shown in the Fig. C.8 after a zero error(s) and zero warning(s) compilation.

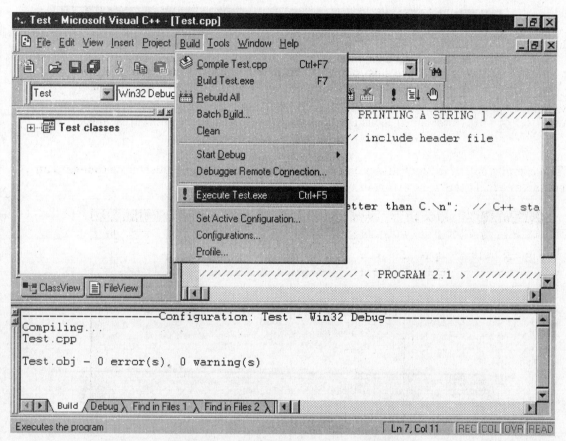

Fig. C.8 *Build menu after successful compilation*

The output window indicates that there are no warnings and no errors. The Compile command has successfully generated the executable file TEST.EXE.

C.6 RUNNING THE PROGRAM

You have reached successfully the final stage of your excitement. Now, to run the program, click the Execute TEST.EXE option in Build menu. The output will be generated in a new windows as shown in Fig. C.9.

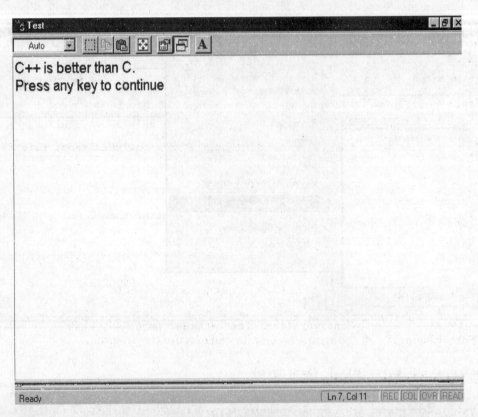

Fig. C.9   *Output generated*

C.7 MANAGING ERRORS

It is rare that a program runs successfully the first time itself. When the program contains errors, they are displayed in the message window as shown in Fig. C.10.

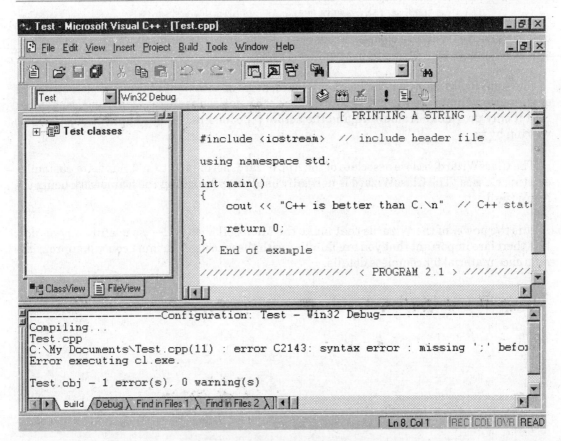

Fig. C.10 *Output window error messages*

You can double-click on a syntax error in the message window to go to the line containing that problem. Fix all the errors, recompile and execute the program.

C.8 OTHER FEATURES

Windows programmers now have a wider range of tools that can be used for the development of object-oriented systems. Microsoft has provided, among others, the following three tools that would benefit the programmers:

* Foundation Class Library
* Application Wizard
* Class Wizard

The Microsoft Foundation Class (MFC) library contains a set of powerful tools and provides the users with easy-to-use objects. Proper use of MFC library would reduce the length of code and development time of an application.

The AppWizard, short for Application Wizard, helps us to define the fundamental structure of a program and to create initial applications with desired features. However, remember that it only provides a framework and the actual code for a particular application should be written by us.

The ClassWizard, a close associate of the AppWizard, permits us to add classes or customize existing classes. The ClassWizard is normally used after designing the framework using the AppWizard.

It is the power of the Wizards that make the Microsoft Visual C++ so useful and popular. It is therefore important that you are familiar with these tools. You must consult appropriate reference material for complete details.

Appendix D

Glossary of ANSI C++ Keywords

asm   It is to embed the assembly language statements in C++ programs. Its use is implementation dependent.

auto   It is a storage class specifier for the local variables. An auto variable is visible only in the block or function where it is declared. All the local variables are of type auto by default.

bool   It is a data type and is used to hold a Boolean value, **true** or **false.**

break   A **break** statement is used to cause an exit from the loop and switch statements. It is used to provide labels in a switch statement.

catch   **catch** is used to describe the *exception handler* code that catches the exceptions (unusual conditions in the program).

char   It is a fundamental data type and is used to declare character variables and arrays.

class   **class** is used to create user-defined data types. It binds together data and functions that operate on them. Class variables known as *objects* are the building blocks of OOP in C++.

const   It is a data type qualifier. A data type qualified as **const** may not be modified by the program.

const_cast It is a casting operator used to explicitly override **const** or **volatile** objects.

continue It causes skipping of statements till the end of a loop in which it appears. It is similar to saying "go to end of loop".

default   It is a **default** label in a switch statement. The control is transferred to this statement when none of the case labels match the expressions in switch.

delete   It is an operator used to remove the objects from memory that were created using new operator.

do   **do** is a control statement that creates a loop of operations. It is use with another keyword *while* in the form:

```
do
{
      statements
}
while(expression);
```

The loop is terminated when the expression becomes zero.

double   It is a floating-point data types specifier. We use this specification double the number of digits after decimal point of a floating-point valu

dynamic_cast It is a casting operator used to cast the type of an object at runtime. main application is to perform casts on polymorphic objects.

else   **else** is used to specify an alternative path in a two-way branch contro execution. It is used with if statement in the form:

```
if(expression)
      statement-1;
else
      statement-2;
```

The statement-1 is executed if expression is nonzero; otherw statement-2 is executed.

enum   It is used to create a user-defined integer data type. Example:

```
enum E{e1,e2,...};
```

where e1, e2, ... are enumerators which take integer values. E is a d type and can be used to declare variables of its type.

explicit   It is a specifier to a constructor. A constructor declared as expl cannot perform implicit conversion.

export   It is used to instantiate non-inline template classes and functions fr separate files.

extern   **extern** is a storage class specifier which informs the compiler that variable so declared is defined in another source file.

false   It is a Boolean type constant. It can be assigned to only a **bool** t variable. The default numeric value of **false** is 0.

loat   It is a fundamental data type and is used to declare a variable to stor single-point precision value.

for   **for** is a control statement and is used to create a loop of iterat operations. It takes the form:

```
for(e1; e2; e3) statement;
```

The *statement* is executed until the expression e2 becomes zero. 1 expression e1 is evaluated once in the beginning and e3 is evaluated the end of every iteration.

friend   **friend** declares a function as a **friend** of the class where it is declar A function can be declared as a friend to more than one class. A **frie** function, although defined like a normal function, can have access to the members of a class to which it is declared as **friend**.

goto   **goto** is a transfer statement that enables us to skip a group statements unconditionally. This statement is very rarely used.

if	if is a control statement that is used to test an expression and transfer the control to a particular statement depending upon the value of expression. if statement may take one of the following forms:

        (i) `if (expression)`
                `statement-1;`
            `statement-2;`
        (ii) `if (expression)`
                `statement-1;`
       `else`
                `statement-2;`

In form (i), if the expression is nonzero (true), statement-1 is executed and then statement-2 is executed. If the expression is zero (false), statement-1 is skipped. In form (ii), if the expression is nonzero, statement-1 is executed and statement-2 will be skipped; if it is zero, statement-2 is executed and statement-1 is skipped.

inline	**inline** is a function specifier which specifies to the compiler that the function definition should be substituted in all places where the function is called.
int	It is one of the basic data types and is used to declare a variable that would be assigned integer values.
long	**long** is a data type modifier that can be applied to some of the basic data types to increase their size. When used alone as shown below, the variable becomes signed

        `long int.`
        `long m;`

mutable	It is a data type modifier. A data item declared **mutable** may be modified even if it is a member of a **const** object or **const** function.
namespace	It is used to define a scope that could hold global identifiers. Example:

```
namespace name
{
    Declaration of identifiers
}
```

new	It is an operator used for allocating memory dynamically from free store. We can use new in place of **malloc()** function.
operator	**operator** is used to define an operator function for overloading an operator for use with class objects. Example:

        `int operator*(vector &v1, vector &v2);`

private	It is a visibility specifier for class members. A member listed under private is not accessible to any function other than the member functions of the class in which it is used.
protected	Like private, protected is also a visibility specifier for class members. It makes a member accessible not only to the members of the class but also to the members of the classes derived from it.
public	This is the third visibility specifier for the class members. A member declared as public in a class is accessible publicly. That is, any function can access a public member.
register	**register** is a storage class specifier for integer data types. It tells the compiler that the object (variable) should be accessible as quickly as possible. Normally, a CPU register is used to store such variables.

reinterpret_cast	It is a casting operator and is used to change one type into a fundamentally different type.
return	It is used to mark the end of a function execution and to transfer the control back to the calling function. It can also return a value of an expression to the calling function. Example:

```
return(expression);
```

short	Similar to long, it is also a data type modifier applied to integer base types. When used alone with a variable, it means the variable is signed short int.
signed	It is a qualifier used with character and integer base type variables to indicate that the variables are stored with the sign. The high-order bit is used to store the sign bit, 0 meaning positive, 1 meaning negative. A signed char can take values between -127 to +127 whereas an unsigned char can hold values from 0 to 255. The default integer declaration assumes a signed number.
sizeof	**sizeof** is an operator used to obtain the size of a type or an object, in bytes. Example:

```
int m = sizeof(char);
int m = sizeof(x);
```

where x is an object or variable.

static	**static** is a storage class specifier. This can be used on both the local and global variables, but with a different meaning. When it is applied to a local variable, permanent storage is created and it retains its value between function calls in the program. When it is applied to a global variable, the variable becomes internal to the file in which it is declared.
static_cast	It is a casting operator and may be used for any standard conversion of data types.
struct	**struct** is similar to a class and is used to create user-defined data types. It can group together the data items and functions that operate on them. The only difference between a class and struct is that, by default, the struct members are public while the class members become private.
switch	It is a control statement that provides a facility for multiway branching from a particular point. Example:

```
switch (expression)
{
        case labels
}
```

Depending on the value of expression, the control is transferred to a particular label.

Template	**template** is used to declare generic classes and functions.
this	It is a pointer that points to the current object. This can be used to access the members of the current object with the help of the arrow operator.
Throw	**throw** is used in the exception handling mechanism to "throw" an exception for further action.

true   It is a Boolean type constant. It can be assigned to only a **bool** type variable. The default numeric value of **true** is 1.

try   It is also a keyword used in the exception handling mechanism. It is used to instruct the compiler to try a particular function.

typedef   **typedef** is used to give a new name to an existing data type. It is usually used to write complex declarations easily.

typeid   It is an operator that can be used to obtain the types of unknown objects.

typename   It is used to specify the type of template parameters.

union   It is similar to **struct** in declaration but is used to allocate storage for several data items at the same location.

using   It is a **namespace** scope directive and is used to declare the accessibility of identifiers declared within a **namespace** scope.

unsigned   It is a type modifier used with integer data types to tell the compiler that the variables store non-negative values only. This means that the high-bit is also used to store the value and therefore the size of the number may be twice that of a signed number.

virtual   **virtual** is a qualifier used to declare a member function of a base class as "virtual" in order to perform dynamic binding of the function. It is also used to declare a base class as virtual when it is inherited by a class through multiple paths. This ensures that only one copy of the base class members are inherited.

void   ╷   **void** is a data type and is used to indicate the objects of unknown type. Example:

```
void *ptr;
```

is a generic pointer that can be assigned a pointer of any type. It is also used to declare a function that returns nothing. Another use is to indicate that a function does not take any arguments. Example:

```
void print(void);
```

volatile   It is a qualifier used in variable declarations. It indicates that the variable may be modified by factors outside the control of the program.

wchar_t   It is a character data type and is used to declare variables to hold 16-bit wide characters.

while   **while** is a control statement used to execute a set of statements repeatedly depending on the outcome of a test. Example:

```
while (expression)
{
        statements
}
```

The statements are executed until the expression becomes zero.

Appendix E

C++ Operator Precedence

The Table E.1 below lists all the operators supported by ANSI C++ according to their precedence (i.e. order of evaluation). Operators listed first have higher precedence than those listed next. Operators at the same level of precedence (between horizontal lines) evaluate either left to right or right to left according to their associativity.

Table E.I C++ Operators

Operator	Meaning	Associativity	Use
: :	global scope	right to left	::name
: :	class, namespace scope	left to right	name : : member
.	direct member	left to right	object.member
->	indirect member		pointer->member
[ ]	subscript		pointer[expr]
( )	function call		expr(arg)
( )	type construction		type(expr)
++	postfix increment		m++
--	postfix decrement		m--
Sizeof	size of object	right to left	sizeof expr
sizeof	size of type		sizeof (type)
++	prefix increment		++m
--	prefix decrement		--m
typeid	type identification		typeid(expr)
const_cast	specialized cast		const_cast<expr>
dynamic_cast	specialized cast		dynamic_cast<expr>
reinterpret_cast	specialized cast		reinterpret_cast<expr>
static_cast	specialized cast		static_cast<expr>
( )	traditional cast		(type)expr
~	one's complement		~expr
!	logical NOT		! expr
-	unary minus		- expr
+	unary plus		+ expr
&	address of		& value
*	dereference		* expr
new	create object		new type
new [ ]	create array		new type [ ]
delete	destroy object	right to left	delete ptr
delete [ ]	destroy arrary		delete [ ] ptr

.*	member dereference	left to right	object.*ptr_to_member
->*	indirect member dereference		ptr->*ptr_to_member
*	Multiply	left to right	expr1 * expr2
/	Divide		expr1 / expr2
%	Modulus		expr1 % expr2
+	add	left to right	expr1 + expr2
-	subtract		expr1 - expr2
<<	left shift	left to right	expr1 << expr2
>>	right shift		expr1 >> expr2
<	less than	left to right	expr1 < expr2
<=	less than or equal to		expr1 <= expr2
>	greater than		expr1 > expr2
>=	greater than or equal to		expr1 >= expr2
==	equal	left to right	expr1 == expr2
!=	not equal		expr1 != expr2
&	bitwise AND	left to right	expr1 & expr2
^	bitwise XOR	left to right	expr1 ^ expr2
|	bitwise OR	left to right	expr1 ^| expr2
&&	logical AND	left to right	expr1 && expr2
||	logical OR	left to right	expr1 || expr2
?:	conditional expression	left to right	expr1 ? expr2: expr3
=	assignment	right to left	x = expr
*=	multiply update		x *= expr
/=	divide update		x /= expr
%=	modulus update		x %= expr
+=	add update		x += expr
-=	substract update		x - = expr
<<=	left shift update		x <<= expr
>>=	right shift update		x >>= expr
&=	bitwise AND update		x &= expr
|=	bitwise OR update		x |= expr
^=	bitwise XOR update		x ^= expr
throw	throw exception	right to left	throw expr
,	comma	left to right	expr1, expr2

Appendix F
Points to Remember

1. Computers use the binary number system which uses binary digits called as bits.
2. The basic unit of storage in a computer is a byte represented by eight bits.
3. A computer language is a language used to give instructions to a computer.
4. A compiler translates instructions in programming language to instructions in machine language.
5. Application software is a software that is designed to solve a particular problem or to provide a particular service.
6. Systems software is a software that is designed to support the development and execution of application programs.
7. An operating system is a system software that controls and manages the computing resources such as the memory, the input and output devices, and the CPU.
8. An algorithm is a detailed, step-by-step procedure for solving a problem.
9. The goal of a software design is to produce software that is reliable, understandable, cost effective, adaptable, and reusable.
10. Abstraction is the process of highlighting the essential, inherent aspects of an entity while ignoring irrelevant details.
11. Encapsulation (or information hiding) is the process of separating the external aspects of an object from the internal implementation details which should be hidden from other objects.
12. Modularity is the process of dividing a problem into smaller pieces so that each smaller module can be dealt with individually.
13. Organizing a set of abstractions from most general to least general is known as *inheritance hierarchy*.
14. Object-oriented programming is a paradigm in which a system is modeled as a set of objects that interact with each other.
15. In C++ an abstraction is formed by creating a class. A class encapsulates the attributes and behaviors of an object.
16. The data members of a class represent the attributes of a class.
17. The member functions of a class represent the behaviors of a class.

18. A base class is one from which other, more specialized classes are derived.

19. A derived class is one that inherits properties from a base class.

20. Polymorphism is the capability of something to assume different forms. In an object-oriented language, polymorphism is provided by allowing a message or member function to mean different things depending on the type of object that receives the message.

21. Instantiation is the process of creating an object from a class.

22. We must use the statement #include <iostream> a preprocessor directive that includes the necessary definitions for performing input and output operations.

23. The C++ operator << , called the insertion operator, is used to insert text into an output stream.

24. The C++ operator >>, called the extraction operator, is used to insert text into an input stream.

25. All C++ programs begin executing from the **main**. Function **main** returns an integer value that indicates whether the program executed successfully or not. A value of 0 indicates successful execution, while the value 1 indicates that a problem or error occurred during the execution of the program.

26. A value is returned from a function using the **return** statement. The statement

    ```
    return 0;
    ```
    returns the value 0.

27. A C++ style comment begins with // and continues to the end of the line.

28. A C++ identifiers consists of a sequence of letters (upper and lowercase), digits, and underscores. A valid name cannot begin with a digit character.

29. C++ identifiers are case sensitive. For example, **Name** and **name** refer to two different identifiers.

30. A variable must be defined before it can be used. Smart programmers give a variable an initial value when it is defined.

31. The automatic conversion specifies that operands of type **char** or **short** are converted to type **int** before proceeding with operation.

32. For an arithmetic operation involving two integral operands, the automatic conversion specifies that when the operands have different types, the one that is type **int** is converted to **long** and a **long** operation is performed to produce a **long** result.

33. For an arithmetic operation involving two floating-point operands, the automatic conversion specifies that when the operands are of different types, the operand with lesser precision is converted to the type of the operand with greater precision.

34. A mixed-mode arithmetic expression involves integral and floating-point operands. The integral operand is converted to the type of the floating-point operand, and the appropriate floating-point operation is performed.

35. The precedence rules of C++ define the order in which operators are applied to operands. For the arithmetic operators, the precedence from highest to lowest is unary plus and minus; multiplication, division, and modules; and addition and subtraction.

36. It is a good programming practice to initialize a variable or an object when it is declared.

37. When a floating-point value is stored in an integer variable, the floating-point value is converted to an integer value by truncating its decimal value.

38. The keyword **const** is used to define variables or objects that should not be modified.

39. When writing a program that accepts input interactively it is important that the program issues prompts that clearly indicate the type and the form of the input.

40. The compound assignment operators + =, - =, * =, / =, % = perform an arithmetic operation on a variable and store the resulting value back into the variable.

41. C++ supports special operators, ++ and −, for incrementing and decrementing integral and floating-point objects.

42. A logical expression evaluates to **true** if the value of the expression is either a nonzero integer value or the **bool** value **true**.

43. A logical expression evaluates to **false** if the value of the expression is integer zero or the **bool** value **false.**

44. The relational operators also produce logical values. The relational operators fall into two categories; *equality* and *ordering*.

45. The equality operators = = and ! = and the ordering operators <, < =, >, and >= are defined for all fundamental and pointer types.

46. The **if** statement has two forms. In both forms, a logical expression is evaluated and if that expression is **true**, an action is executed. In one of the forms, an action is also specified for, when the evaluated expression is **false**.

47. The expression used to determine the course of action for a conditional or iterative construct is sometimes known as a *test expression*.

48. The **switch** statement takes actions based upon the value of an integral expression. The programmer specifies the case values of interest for that expression, and for each case value the desired action is specified.

49. Types defined by a programmer are known as user-defined or derived types.

50. The **enum** statement is a method for organizing a collection of integral constants into a type.

51. A loop is a group of statements whose actions are repeated using an iterative construct.

52. The **while** statement permits actions to be repeated while a given logical expression evaluates to **true**. If the logical expression is initially false, then the action of the construct is never executed; otherwise, the action is repeatedly executed until the test expression evaluates to **false**.

53. The **do** statement is similar in nature to the **while** statement; however, its action is always executed at least once. This is because its test expression is evaluated only after its body is executed.

54. The **for** statement is a generalization of the **while** construct that has a test expression, a one-time loop initialization section and an increment section. All sections of a **for** statement are optional. In particular, if the test expression is omitted, then the value **true** is used instead.

55. A **typedef** statement creates a new name for an existing type. Both the new and old names can be used in subsequent definitions.

56. In C++, we can declare a variable as close as possible to its first use.

57. The **class** describes all the properties of a data type, and an object is an entity created according to that description.

58. Information to a function is passed via parameters. The function's result is normally brought back as the return value. The type of value brought back by a function is the return type. A function that does not return a value has the type **void**.

59. The parameters in the invocation are called the *actual parameters*. The actual parameters are represented in the invoked function by its *formal parameters*.

60. When a function is called, flow of control is transferred from the calling function to the called function. When the called function completes, control is transferred back to the calling function.

61. Before a function is called, it must be prototyped or defined. A prototype is a description of the function's interface. The prototype specifies the return type, function name, and the form of the parameters list.

62. One method of passing actual parameters is the pass-by-value method. When an actual parameter is passed in this method, the formal parameter is initialized to the value of the actual parameter. Subsequent changes to the formal parameter do not affect the actual parameter.

63. A function is a mechanism that enables us to use modular programming and facilitates software reuse.

64. A statement block in a program is a set of statements within curly braces.

65. A nested block is a statement block occurring within another statement block.

66. A **return** statement supplies a value from the called function to the calling function.

67. A local variable is a variable defined within a statement block.

68. A global variable is a variable defined above all the functions in a program.

69. Functions can use local and global variables and even other functions, in their implementations.

70. While calling a function, a programmer supplies actual parameters of the correct form. If the actual parameters are not of the correct form, the compiler will attempt to perform conversions to put the actual parameters in the correct form.

71. Variable names can be reused as long as the declarations associated with the names occur in different blocks.

72. The scope resolution operator :: can be used to reference a global variable whose name has been reused in the local scope.

73. Global fundamental types are initialized to zero by default.

74. Typical programs use multiple files. The files are individually compiled and linked together to produce an executable version of the program.

75. A reference to a global variable in an implementation file requires that the global variable be either defined or declared using an **extern** statement within the translation unit of that implementation file.

76. A global variable can be defined only once in the global scope of the program.

77. A C++ program should provide a prototype for each function used in the program.

78. While ANSI C allows function prototype, in C++ it is mandatory.

79. Function arguments can be assigned the default values only in the function prototype. This should be done form *right* to *left*.

80. If you are moving from C to C++, start using the qualifier **const** to define constants instead of using **#define** statement.

81. When determining the minimum array size needed to hold a string, remember to add a place for the terminating null character.

82. Remember that when you use a declaration statement to initialize a pointer, the pointer, not the variable pointed to, is initialized.

83. Always set a pointer to an appropriate address before applying the dereferencing operator * to it.

84. Note that adding 1 to a pointer variable increases its value by the number of bytes of the type to which it points.

85. Arrays are used for defining a variable that represents a list of variables of same type.

86. In defining an array, we must specify the size of the array, that is, the number of elements in the array. The size must be a bracketed expression whose terms represent literal constants.

87. The typical array is a one-dimensional list. However, multidimensional arrays can also be defined.

88. By using the subscript operator [ ], we can reference an individual element of the array.

89. Each element has its own subscript value; The first element in the array has a subscript of 0, the second element has a subscript of 1, and so on. The last element has a subscript that is one less than the size of the list.

90. Once subscripted, an individual array element can be used like any other variable. That is, it can be accessed, assigned, displayed, extracted to, passed as a value or reference parameter, and so on.

91. An array is not a first-class variable. As such, we cannot use an array as the target of an assignment or as the return value for a function. In addition, when an array is passed as a parameter, it must be passed by reference.

92. When defining a function with an array parameter, the formal parameter definition does not need to include the size of the first dimension.

93. The elements of an array are always stored in contiguous memory. For a one-dimensional array, at the beginning of its memory will be the first element, next will be the second element, and so on. For multidimensional arrays the array elements are stored in row-major order.

94. The traditional way to represent a string value is a character string. When an array is used to represent a character string, a null value '\0' is stored in the element that immediately follows the last character in the string.

95. Elements of a global array whose base type is a fundamental type are initialized to 0 by default.

96. Elements of a local array whose base type is a class type are not initialized by default.

97. Elements of an array whose base type is a class type are initialized using the default constructor of the base type.

98. Elements of an array (of fundamental type) can be set to specific values in their definition using initialization lists. If the initialization list does not specify sufficient values, the unspecified elements are set to 0 .

99. A pointer is a variable whose value is the address of another variable.

100. Pointers should be different type for each type of variable. There are even pointer types whose variable are pointers to other pointers.

101. The location of a variable can be obtained using the address operator &.

102. The literal 0 can be assigned to any pointer type object. In this context, the literal 0 is known as the null address.

103. The value of the object at a given location can be obtained using the indirection operator * on the location.

104. The indirection operator produces an lvalue.

105. The null address is not a location which can be dereferenced.

106. The member selector operator -> allows a particular member of object to be dereferenced.

107. Pointer operators may be compared using the equality and relational operators.

108. The increment and decrement operators may be applied to pointer objects.

109. Pointers can be passed as reference parameters by using the indirection operator.

110. An array name is viewed by C++ as constant pointer. This fact gives us flexibility in which notation to use when accessing and modifying the values in a list.

111. Command-line parameters are communicated to programs using pointers.

112. We can define variables that are pointers to functions. Such variables are typically used as function parameters. This type of parameter enables the function that uses it to have greater flexibility in accomplishing its task.

113. Increment and decrement of pointers follow the pointer arithmetic rules. If **ptr** points to the first element of an array, then **ptr+1** points to the second element.

114. The name of an array of type **char** contains the address of the first character of the string.

115. When reading a string into a program, always use the address of the previously allocated memory. This address can be in the form of an array name or a pointer that has been initialized using **new**.

116. Structure members are **public** by default while the class members are **private** by default.

117. When accessing the class members, use the dot operator if the class identifier is the name of the class and use the arrow operator if the identifier is the pointer to the class.

118. Use **delete** only to delete the memory allocated by **new**.

119. It is a good practice to declare the size of an array as a constant using the qualifier **const**.

120. C++ supports two types of parameters, namely, value parameters and reference parameters.

121. When a parameter is passed by value, a copy of the variable is passed to the called function. Any modifications made to the parameter by the called function change the copy, not the original variable.

122. When a reference parameter is used, instead of passing a copy of the variable, a reference to the original variable is passed. Any modifications made to the parameter by the called function change the original variable.

123. When an **iostream** object is passed to a function, either an extraction or an insertion operation implicitly modifies the stream. Thus, stream objects should be passed a reference.

124. A reason to use a reference parameter is for efficiency. When a class object is passed by value, a copy of the object is passed. If the object is large, making a copy of it can be expensive in terms of execution time and memory space. Thus objects that are large, or objects whose size is not known are often passed by reference. We can ensure that the objects are not modified by using the **const** modifier.

125. A const modifier applied to a parameter declaration indicates that the function may not change the object. If the function attempts to modify the object, the compiler will report a compilation error.

126. A reference variable must be initialized when it is declared.

127. When you are returning an address from a function, never return the address of local variable though, syntactically, this is acceptable.

128. If a function call argument does not match the type of a corresponding reference parameter, C++ creates an anonymous variable of the correct type, assigns the value of the argument to it and causes the reference parameter to refer the variable.

129. A function that returns a reference is actually an alias for the "referred-to" variable.

130. We can assign a value to a C++ function if the function returns a reference to a variable. The value is assigned to the referred-to variable.

131. C++'s default parameter mechanism provides the ability to define a function so that a parameter gets a default value if a call to the function does not give a value for that parameter.

132. Function overloading occurs when two or more function have the same name.

133. The compiler resolves overloaded function calls by calling the function whose parameters list best matches that of the call.

134. Casting expressions provide a facility to explicitly convert one type to another.

135. A cast expression is useful when the programmer wants to force the compiler to perform a particular type of operation such as floating-point division rather than integer division.

136. A cast expression is useful for converting the values that library function return to the appropriate type. This makes it clear to other programmers that the conversion was intended.

137. An *inline function* must be defined before it is called.

138. An *inline function* reduces the function call overhead. Small functions are best declared inline within a class.

139. In a multiple-file program, you can define an external variable in one and only one file. All the other files using that variable have to declare it with the keyword **extern**.

140. An abstract data type (ADT) is well-defined and complete data abstraction that uses the principle of information-hiding.

141. An ADT allows the creation and manipulation of objects in a natural manner.

142. If a function or operator can be defined such that it is not a member of the class, then do not make it a member. This practice makes a nonmember function or operator generally independent of changes to the class's implementation.

143. In C++, an abstract data type is implemented using classes, functions, and operators.

144. Constructors initialize objects of the class type. It is standard practice to endure that every object has all of its data members appropriately initialized.

145. A default constructor is a constructor that requires no parameters.

146. A copy constructor initializes a new object to be a duplicate of a previously defined source object. If a class does not define a copy constructor, the compiler automatically supplies a version.

147. A member assignment operator copies a source object to the invoking target object in an assignment statement. If a class does not define a member assignment operator, the compiler automatically supplies a version.

148. When we call a member function, it uses the data members of the object used to invoke the member function.

149. A class constructor, if defined, is called whenever a program creates an object of that class.

150. When we create constructors for a class, we must provide a default constructor to create uninitialized objects.

151. When we assign one object to another of the same class, C++ copies the contents of each data member of the source object to the corresponding member of the target object.

152. A member function operates upon the object used to invoke it, while a friend function operates upon the objects passed to it as arguments.

153. The qualifier **const** appended to function prototype indicates that the function does not modify any of the data members. A **const** member function can be used by **const** objects of the class.

154. The client interface to a class object occurs in the **public** section of the class definition.

155. Any member defined in any section — whether **public, protected,** or **private** — is accessible to all of the other members of its class.

156. Members of a **protected** section are intended to be used by a class derived from the class.

157. Data members are normally declared in a **private**. By restricting outside access to the data members in a class, it is easier to ensure the integrity and consistency of their values.

158. Members of **private** section of a class are intended to be used only by the members of that class.

159. An & in the return type for a function or operator indicates that a reference return is being performed. In a reference return, a reference to the actual object in the return expression rather than a copy is returned. The scope of the returned object should not be local to the invoked function or operator.

160. When creating a **friend** function, use the keyword friend in the prototype in the class definition, but do not use this keyword in the actual function definition. Friend functions are defined outside the class definition.

161. Friend functions have access to the private and protected members of a class.

162. An operator can be overloaded many times using distinct signatures.

163. If we want to overload a binary operator with two different types of operands with non class as the first operand, we must use a friend function to define the operator overloading.

164. Do not use implicit type conversions unless it is necessary. If they are used arbitrarily, it can cause problems for future users of the class.

165. Whenever we use **new** in a constructor to allocate memory, we should use **delete** in the corresponding destructor to free that memory.

166. The relationship "is_ a" indicates inheritance. For example, a car is a kind of vehicle.

167. The relationship "has_a" indicates containment. For example, a car has an engine. Aggregate objects are constructed using containment.

168. Both inheritance and containment facilitate software reuse.

169. A new class that is created from an existing class using the principle of inheritance is called a *derived class or subclass*. The parent class is called the *base class or superclass*.

170. When an object that is a instance of derived class is instantiated, the constructor for the base class is invoked before the body of the constructor for the derived class is invoked.

171. A class intended to be a base class usually should use **protected** instead of **private** members.
172. When a derived class object is being created, first its base classes constructors are called before its own constructor. The destructors are called in the reverse order.
173. A constructor of a derived class must pass the arguments required by its base class constructor.
174. A derived class uses the member functions of the base class unless the derived class provides a replacement function with the same name.
175. A derived class object is converted to a base class object when used as an argument to a base class member function.
176. Derived class constructors are responsible for initializing any data members added to those inherited from the base class. The base class constructors are responsible for initializing the inherited data members.
177. When passing an object as an argument to the function, we usually use a reference or a pointer argument to enable function calls within the function to use virtual member function.
178. Declare the destructor of a base class as a virtual function.
179. Destructors are called in reverse order from the constructor calls. Thus, the destructor for a derived class is called before the destructor of the base or superclass.
180. With **public** inheritance, the **public** members of the base class are public members of the derived class. The **private** members of the base class are not inherited and, therefore, not accessible in the derived class.
181. With **protected** inheritance, **public** and **protected** members of the base class become **protected** members of the derived class. The **private** members of the base class are not inherited.
182. With multiple inheritance, a derived class inherits the attributes and behaviors of all parent classes.
183. With **private** inheritance, **public** and **protected** members of the base class become **private** members of the derived class. Private members are not inherited.
184. If a derived class has a base class as a multiple ancestor (through multiple inheritance), then declare the base class as **virtual** in the derived class definition. This would ensure the inheritance of just one object of the base class.
185. A pointer to a base class can be used to access a member of the derived class, as long as that class member is inherited from the base.
186. Polymorphism is a mechanism that permits the same interface to invoke different functions or operators depending upon the type of objects using the interface.
187. Another method of achieving syntactic polymorphism is the use of function and class templates.
188. C++ achieves polymorphism through virtual functions.
189. A virtual function is required to be a member function.
190. If a function of a derived class has the same name and type as a virtual function of its base class, then the member function of the derived class overrides the base class function.
191. With a virtual function, the decision on which actual function is being invoked in an interface is delayed until run time. The decision will be based upon the type of object

being accessed by a pointer or reference object, rather than by the type of the pointer or reference object.

192. By declaring an array of pointers for a common base type, the array can be used to represent a heterogeneous list — the individual elements can point to objects of the different derived types from that base class.

193. When a virtual function is invoked by dereferencing one of the elements in a heterogeneous list, the action to be taken can be specific to the derived type of the object to which the pointer refers. Such code will continue to work properly even if a new derived type is defined and one of its objects is added to the list.

194. Destructors for a base class are typically virtual. That way, regardless of the context of the destruction, the appropriate destructor is invoked.

195. A pure virtual function is a virtual function to which the null address, has been assigned.

196. A pure virtual function has no implementation.

197. It is not possible to construct an object from a class with a pure virtual function because the construction cannot be completed.

198. A class with a pure virtual function is an abstract base class.

199. An abstract base class is used to describe the common interface of its derived classes.

200. A function template is a mechanism for generating a new function.

201. A class template is mechanism for generating a new class.

202. A template parameter can be either a type or a value.

203. All of the template parameters in a function template definition must be used in the function interface. The template parameters can also be used in the function body.

204. The proposed C++ standard describes a standard template library that in part includes template versions of common computing tasks such as searching and sorting.

205. All of the template parameters in a class template must be used in the definition of the class interface.

206. Through the use of class templates, we can develop a container class that represents lists in an array like manner. A major reason that such a container class is preferred to standard arrays is that the container class does not suffer array use limitations (e.g. a container class can be the return type of a function or be a value parameter).

207. The standard template library defines a collection of common container classes for list representation. The representations differ in how the elements of the list can be accessed. Various container classes support random access of the elements, sequential access of the elements, and associative access of the elements.

208. Often a container class will have an iterator class associated with it. The iterator class provides the means for iteratively accessing the various elements of the list.

209. Exception handling is designed for dealing with synchronous errors.

210. Exceptions are thrown in **try** block in a function or in a function called directly or indirectly form the **try** block.

211. Once an exception is thrown, control cannot return directly to the **throw** point.

212. Exception are caught by the closest **catch** statement that matches the type of exception thrown.

213. By default, if no matching **catch** handler is found, the program terminates.

214. An exception thrown outside a **try** block will cause the program to terminate.
215. The **catch (...)** can catch all types of exceptions.
216. When a **catch** handler finishes executing, control goes to the first statement after the last **catch** block.
217. When **try** blocks are nested, if a matching handler is not found in the inner **try** block, the search continues in the enclosing **try** block.
218. The **catch(...)** should always be placed last in the list of handlers following a **try** block.
219. C++ views each file a sequential stream of bytes.
220. We must include the header files <iostream> and <fstream> to perform **C++ file I/O** operations.
221. Files are opened simply by instantiating objects of stream classes **ifstream**, **ofstream** and **fstream**.
222. Opening an existing file for output erases the data in the file, unless we specify append mode.
223. Even though we may think of the streams **cin** and **cout** as text files, we should neither declare them nor use them to invoke **open()** and **close()** functions.
224. We must use **get(char *)** when we need to examine every character including white space.
225. The flags set by **setf()** remain effective until they are reset or unset.
226. A format flag can be reset any number of times in a program.
227. The **setf()** function sets the specified flags and leaves others unchanged.
228. The file mode parameters **ios :: app** and **ios :: ate** when used to open a file, take us to the end of the file. However, with **ios :: app**, we can only append data to the file while with **ios :: ate** we may add or modify data anywhere in the file.
229. The parameter **ios: :app** can be used only with the file capable of output.
230. Creating a stream using **ifstream** implies input and creating a stream using **ofstream** implies output. Therefore, in these cases, it is not necessary to provide the mode parameters.
231. The **fstream** class does not provide a mode by default and therefore, use must provide the mode explicitly when using an object of **fstream** class.
232. It is a good programming practice to close all **fstream** objects when we have finished using them.
233. Functions **put()** and **get()** are designed for handling single character at a time, while **write()** and **read()** are designed to handle blocks of binary data.
234. The member function **eof** of **ios** determines if the end of the file indicator has been set. End-of-file is set after an attempted read fails.
235. To use C++ **strings**, we must include the header file <**string**> of **C++** standard library.
236. C++ strings are not null terminated.
237. Using **STL** containers can save considerable time and effort, and result in higher quality programs.
238. To use containers, we must include appropriate header files.
239. **STL** includes a large number of algorithms to perform certain standard operations on containers.
240. **STL** algorithms use iterators to perform manipulation operations on containers.
241. We may use **const**-cast operator to remove the constantness of objects.

242. We may use **mutable** specifier to the members of **const** member functions or **const** objects to make them modifiable.

243. We must restrict the use of runtime type information functions only with polymorphic types.

244. When we suspect any side-effects in the constructors, we must use **explicit** constructors.

245. We must provide parentheses to all arguments in macro functions.

Appendix G
Glossary of Important C++
and OOP Terms

#define	A C++ preprocessor directive that defines a substitute text for a name.
#include	A preprocessor directive that causes the named file to be inserted in place of the #include.
Abstract Class	A class that serves only as a base class from which classes are derived. No objects of an abstract base class are created. A base class that contains pure virtual functions is an abstract base class.
Abstract Data Type (ADT)	An abstraction that describes a set of objects in terms of an encapsulated or hidden data and operations on that data.
Abstraction	The act of representing the essential features of something without including much detail.
Access Operations	Operations which access the state of a variable or object but do not modify it.
Address	A value that identifies a storage location in memory.
Alias	Two or more variables that refer to the same data are said to be aliases of one another.
Anonymous Union	An unnamed union in C++. The members can be used like ordinary variables.
ANSI C	Any version of C that conforms to the specifications of the American National Standards Institute Committee X3J.
ANSI C++	Any version of C++ that conforms to the specifications of the American National Standards Institute. At the time of writing this, the standards exist only in draft form and a lot of details are still to be worked out.
Array	A collection of data elements arranged to be indexed in one or more dimensions. In C++, arrays are stored in contiguous memory.
ASCII	American Standard Code for Information Interchange. A code to represent characters.

Assignment Statement	An operation that stores a value in a variable.
Attribute	A property of an object. It cannot exist independently of the object. Attributes may take other objects as values.
Automatic Variable	*See* temporary variable.
Base Class	A class from which other classes are derived. A derived class can inherit members from a base class.
Bit	Binary digit; either of the digits 0 or 1.
Bit Field	A group of contiguous bits taken together as a unit. This C++ language feature allows the access of individual bits.
Bit Flip	The inversion of all bits in an operand. See also complement.
Bitmapped Graphics	Computer graphics where each pixel in the graphic output device is controlled by a single bit or a group of bits.
Bitwise Operator	An operator that performs Boolean operations on two operands, treating each bit in an operand as individual bits and performing the operation bit by bit on corresponding bits.
Block	A section of code enclosed in curly braces.
Borland C++	A version of the C++ language for personal computers developed by Borland. This is the high-end version of Borland's Turbo-C++ product.
Breakpoint	A location in a program where normal execution is suspended and control is turned over to the debugger.
Byte	A group of eight bits.
C	A general-purpose computer programming language developed in 1974 at Bell Laboratories by Dennis Ritchie. C is considered to be medium-to high level language.
C++	An object-oriented language developed by Bjarne Stroutstrup as a successor of C.
Call by Reference	A function call mechanism that passes arguments to a function by passing the addresses of the arguments.
Call by Value	A function call mechanism that passes arguments to a function by passing a copy of the value of the arguments.
Cast	To convert a variable from one type to another type by explicitly.
Class	A group of objects that share common properties and relationships. In C++, a class is a new data type that contains member variables and member 0 functions that operate on the variables. A Class is defined with the keyword **class**.

Class Hierarchy	Class hierarchy consists of a base class and derived classes. When a derived class has a single base class, it is known as single inheritance. When a derived class has more than one base class (multiple inheritance), it is known as **class network**.
Class Network	A collection of classes, some of which are derived from others. A class network is a class hierarchy generalized to allow for multiple inheritance. It is sometimes known as forest model of classes.
Class Object	A variable whose type is a class. An instance of a class.
Classification structure	A tree or network structure based on the semantic primitives of inclusion and membership which indicates that inheritance may implement specialization or generalization. Objects may participate in more than one such structure, giving rise to multiple inheritance.
Class-oriented	Object-based systems in which every instance belongs to a class, but classes may not have super classes.
Client	An object that uses the services of another object called server. That is, clients can send messages to servers.
Coding	The act of writing a program in a computer language.
Comment	Text included in a computer program for the sole purpose of providing information about the program. Comments are a programmer's notes to himself and future programmers. The text is ignored by the compiler.
Comment Block	A group of related comments that convey general information about a program or a section of program.
Compilation	The translation of source code into machine code.
Compiler	A system program that does compilation.
Complement Composition	An arithmetic or logical operation. A logical complement is the same as an invert or NOT operation.
Structure	A tree structure based on the semantic primitive part of which indicates that certain objects may be assembled from the collection of other objects. Objects may participate in more than one such structure.
Conditional Compilation	The ability to selectively compile parts of a program based on the truth of conditions tested in conditional directives that surround the code.
Constructor	A special member function for automatically creating an instance of a class. This function has the same name as the class.
Container Class	A class that contains objects of other classes.
Control Statement	A statement that determines which statement is to be executed next based on a conditional test.

Control Variables	A variable that is systematically changed during the execution of the loop. When the variable reaches a predetermined value, the loop is terminated.
Copy Constructuor	The constructor that creates a new class object from an existing object of the same class.
Curly Braces	One of the characters { or }. They are used in C++ to delimit groups of elements to treat them as a unit.
Data Flow Diagram (DFD)	A diagram that depicts the flow of data through a system and the processes that manipulate the data.
Data Hiding	A property whereby the internal data structure of an object is hidden from the rest of the program. The data can be accessed only by the functions declared within the class (of that object).
Data Member	A variable that is declared in a class declaration.
Debugging	The process of finding and removing errors from a program.
Decision Statement	A statement that tests a condition created by a program and changes the flow of the program based on that decision.
Declaration	A specification of the type and name of a variable to be used in a program.
Default Argument	An argument value that is specified in a function declaration and is used if the corresponding actual argument is omitted when the function is called.
De-referencing Operator	The operator that indicates access to the value pointed to by a pointer variable or an addressing expression. *See* also indirection operator.
Derived Class	A class that inherits some or all of its members from another class, called **base class**.
Destructor	A function that is called to deallocate memory of the objects of a class.
Directive	A command to the preprocessor (as opposed to a statement to produce machine code).
Dynamic Binding	The addresses of the functions are determined at run time rather than compile time. This is also known as late binding.
Dynamic Memory Allocation	The means by which data objects can be created as they are needed during the program execution. Such data objects remain in existence until they are explicitly destroyed. In C++, dynamic memory allocation is accomplished with the operators **new** (for creating data objects) and **delete** (for destroying them).
Early Binding	*See* static binding.

Encapsulation	The mechanism by which the data and functions (manipulating this data) are bound together within an object definition.
Enumerated Data Type	A data type consisting of a named set of values. The C++ compiler assigns an integer to each member of the set.
Error State	For a stream, flags that determine whether an error has occurred and, if so, give some indication of its severity.
Escape Character	A special character used to change the meaning of the character(s) that follow. This is represented in C++ by the backslash character '\'.
Executive File	A file containing machine code that has been linked and is ready to be run on a computer.
Extensibility	A feature that allows the extension of existing code. This allows the creation of new objects from the existing ones.
Extraction Operator	The operator >>, which is used to read input data from keyboard.
Fast Prototyping	A top-down programming technique that consists of writing the smallest portion of a specification that can be implemented that will still do something.
File	A group of related records treated as a unit.
Format State	For a stream, flags and parameters that determine how output values will be printed and (to a lesser extent) how input values will be read.
Free Store	A pool of memory from which storage for objects is allocated. It is also known as heap.
Friend	A function that has access to the private members of a class but is not itself a member of the class. An entire class can be a friend of another class.
Friend	A function that although not a member of a class is able to access the private members of that class.
Function	A procedure that returns a value.
Function Declaration	This provides the information needed to call a function. The declaration gives the name of the function, its return type, and the type of each argument.
Function Prototype	A function declaration.
Generic Class	*See* parameterized class.
Generic Pointer	A pointer that can point to any variable without restriction as to the type of variable. A pointer to storage without regard to content.
Global Variables	Variables that are known throughout an entire program.
Header File	A file containing the declarations that are to be used in one or more source files. A header file is normally included in a source file with an #include directive.
Header File	*See* include file.

Heap	*See* free storage.
Heap	A portion of money used by new to get space for the structures and classes returned by new. Space is returned to this pool by using the delete operator.
Heterogeneous List	A list of class objects, which can belong to more than one class. Processing heterogeneous lists is an important application of polymorphism.
Homogeneous List	A list of class objects all of which belong to the same class.
I/O Manipulators	Functions that when "output" or "input" cause no I/O, but set various conversion flags or parameters.
Implementation	The source code that embodies the realization of the design.
Include File	A file that is merged with source code by invocation of the preprocessor directive #include. Also called a header file.
Index	A value, variable or expression that selects a particular element of an array.
Indirect Operator	*See* de-referencing operator.
Indirection Operator	The operator *, which is used to access a value referred to by a pointer.
Information Hiding	The principle which states that the state and implementation of an object or module should be private to that object or module and only accessible via its public interface. *See* encapsulation.
Inheritance	A relationship between classes such that the state and implementation of an object or module should be private to that object or module and only accessible via its public interface. *See* encapsulation.
Inheritance Path	A series of classes that provide a path along which inheritance can take. For example, if class B is derived from A, class C is derived from class B, and class D is derived from class C, then class D inherits from class A via the inheritance path ABCD.
Initialization List	In the definition of a constructor, the function heading can be followed by a colon and a list of calls to other constructors. This initialization list can contain calls to (1) constructors for base classes and (2) constructors for class members that are themselves class objects.
Inline Function	A function definition such that each call to the function is, in effect, replaced by the statements that define the function.

Insertion Operator	The operator <<, which is used to send output data to the screen.
Instance	An instance of a class is an object whose type is the class in question.
Instance Variable	A data member that is not designated as static. Each instance of a class contains a corresponding data object for each nonstatic data member of the class. Because the data objects are associated with each instance of the class, rather than with the class itself, we refer to them as **instance** variables.
Instantiation	The creation of a data item representing a variable or a class (giving a value to something).
Interface	The visible methods of an object.
Intermediate Base Class	A class that lies on an inheritance path connecting a base class and a derived class. For example, if class C is derived from class B and class B is derived from class A, then B is an intermediate base class lying on the inheritance path between the base class A and the derived class C.
Late Binding	*See* dynamic binding.
Left Shift	The operation of moving the bits field left by a specified amount and filling the vacated positions with zeros.
Library	A collection of files.
Lifetime	The lifetime of an object is the time period from when the object is created till the time it is destroyed.
Linkage	The property of an identifier that governs its accessibility in different source files. An identifier with internal linkage is accessible only in the source file in which it is declared. An identifier with an external linkage is accessible in all the source files of a program.
Local Variable	A variable whose scope is limited to the block in which it is declared.
Logical Operator	A C++ operator that performs a logical operation on its two operands and returns a true or a false value.
Macro	A short piece of text, or text template, that can be expanded ino a longer text.
Macro Processor	A program that generates code by replacing values into positions in a defined template.
Manipulator	A data object that is used with the insertion and extraction operators as if it were a value to be inserted into a stream or a data object whose value is to be extracted from a stream. A manipulator causes a specified operation to be performed on the stream.

Mask   A pattern of bits for controlling the retention or elimination of another group of bits.

Member   A data object (variable), function, or operator declared in a class declaration and (for a function or operator) not designated as a friend. See data member, member function.

Member Function   A function declared within a class and not declared as a friend. These functions can have access to the data members and define operations that can be performed on the data.

Member Pointer   A pointer that designates a member of a class. Member pointers are distinct from, and must not be confused with pointers that designate data objects.

Member Variable   See data member.

Message   Information sent to an object. A message generally produces an internal change in the object that receives it, and object may respond to the message by returning a reply. In C++ , we send messages by applying member functions to the class objects.

Message Passing   The philosophy that objects only interact by sending messages to each other. The messages request for some operations to be performed.

Method   The means by which an object receives and responds to a particular kind of message. In C++, a method is a member function.

Multiple Inheritance A language feature that allows a derived class to have more than one base class.

New-line Character   A character that causes an output device to go to the beginning of a new line.

Non Significant Digits Leading digits that do not affect the value of a number (0s for a positive number, 1s for a negative number in complement form).

Normalization   The shifting of a floating-point fraction (and adjustment of the exponent) so there are no leading non significant digits in the fraction.

Null   A constant of value 0 that points to nothing.

Null Pointer   A pointer that does not point to any data object. In C++, the null pointer can be represented by the constant 0.

Null Character   The character whose integer code is 0. The null character is used for terminating strings.

Object   An entity that can store data and, send and receive messages. An instance of a class.

Object-based   Systems are object-based when they allow objects to encapsulate both the data and methods and when they enforce the object identity.

Object-Oriented   Object-oriented systems are object-based, and also support inheritance between classes and superclasses and allow objects to send messages to themselves.

Object-Oriented Design   A method of realizing the system requirements it terms of classes, class hierarchies and their interrelationships.

Object-Oriented Analysis   A method of analysis in which the system requirements are identified in terms of objects and their interactions.

Object-Oriented Programming   Implementation of programs using the objects in an object-oriented language like C++.

Octal Number   A base-eight number.

One's Complement   An operation that flips all the bits in a integer. Ones become zeros and zeros become ones.

Operator   A symbol that represents an action to be performed.

Overflow Error   An arithmetic error caused by the result of an arithmetic operation being greater than the space the computer provides to store the result.

Overloading   A language feature that allows a function or operator to be given more than one definition. The types of the arguments with which the function or operator is called, determines which definition will be used.

Overriding   The ability to change the definition of an inherited method or attribute in a subclass.

Parameter   A data item to which a value may be assigned.

Parameterized Class A class definition that depends on a parameter. A family of classes can be defined by setting the parameter to different data types. It is also known as *generic class*.

Parameterized Macro A macro consisting of a template with insertion points for the introduction of parameters.

Persistence   The property of objects to persist in terms of identity, state and description through time, regardless of the computer session which creates or uses them. The objects are stored and ready for use, on secondary storage.

Pointer   A data type that holds the address of a location in memory.

Polymorphism   A property by which we can send the same message to objects of several different classes, and each object can respond in a different way depending on its class. We can send such a message without knowing to which of the classes the objects belongs. In C++, polymorphism is implemented by means of virtual functions and dynamic binding.

Preprocessor   A part of the compiler that manipulates the program text before any further compiling is done. Three important tasks of the preprocessor are (1) to replace each **#include** directive with the contents of the designated file, (2) to replace each escape sequence with the designated character, and (3) to process macro definitions and expand macro calls.

Preprocessor   A program that performs preliminary processing with the purpose of expanding macro code templates to produce C++ code.

Preprocessor Directive   A command to the preprocessor.

Private Base Class   A base class which allows its public and protected members to be inherited as "private" members of the derived class. Thus, the inherited members are accessible to the members and friends of the derived class, but they are not accessible to the users of the derived class.

Private Member   A class member that is accessible only to the member and friend functions of the class. A private member of a base class is not inherited by a derived class.

Program Header   The comment block at the beginning of a program.

Programming   The process of expressing the solution to a problem in a language that represents instructions for a computer.

Protected Member   A protected member is the same as a private member except that a protected member of a base class is inherited by a derived class, whereas a private member is not. For details of inheritance, *see* public base class and private base class.

Pseudocode   A coding technique where precise descriptions of procedures are written in easy-to-read language constructs without the bother of precise attention to the syntax rules of a computer language.

Public Member   A class member that is accessible to all users of the class. The access is not restricted to the member and friend functions of the class alone. A public member of a base class is inherited by a derived class. For more details on inheritance, *see* private base class and public base class.

Public Base Class	A base class which allows its public and protected members to be inherited as, respectively, public and protected members of the derived class. Thus, the public members that are accessible to users of the base class are also accessible to users of the derived class. Also, protected members retain their protected status so that they can be inherited in turn by classes derived from a class that itself inherited them.
Pure Virtual Function	A virtual function that is declared in a base class but not defined there. The responsibility for defining the function falls on the derived classes, each of which generally provides a different definition. It is illegal to create instances of a class that declares a pure virtual function. So, such a class is necessarily an abstract base class.
Qualifier	A word used to modify the meaning of a data declaration.
Recursion	Recursion occurs when a function calls itself directly or indirectly. (For a recursive definition, *see* recursion).
Relational Operator	An identifier that serves as an alternate name for a variable. A reference is defined in terms of an existing name for the variable and becomes an alias of that name. It provides a means, whereby the names of the data objects can, in effect, be passed to and returned by the functions and operators.
Relational Operator	An operator that compares two operands and reports either true or false based on whether the relationship is true of false.
Return Statement	A statement that signals the completion of a function and causes control to return to the caller.
Reusability	A feature which is supported in object-oriented programming. This allows the reuse of existing classes without redefinition.
Right Shift	The operation of moving the bits in a bit field right by a specified amount.
Rounding Error	An error due to truncation in rounding.
Scope	The scope of an identifier is the portion of the program text in which that identifier is accessible.
Scope	The scope of a variable is the portion of a program where the name of the variable is known.
Scope Resolution Operator	The operator which is usually used to indicate the class in which an identifier is declared.
Segmentation violation	An error caused by a program trying to access memory outside its address space. Caused by de-referencing a bad pointer.

Server	An object which performs operations according to the client's requests but may not act upon other objects. It may only send messages to other objects as a result of a request from them, unless it is also a client of other servers. *See Client.*
Significant Digit	A digit that must be kept to preserve a given accuracy.
Single Inheritance	The situation in which a derived class has only one base class.
Source Code	Symbolic coding in its original form before it is translated by a computer.
Source File	A file containing source code.
Stack	An area of memory used to hold a list of data and instructions on a temporary basis.
Stack Overflow	An error caused by a program using too much temporary space (stack space) for its variables. Caused by a big program or by infinite recursion.
Stack Variable	*See* temporary variable.
Static Binding	The opposite of dynamic binding. The functions are bound to the code to be executed at compile time. It is also known as *early binding*.
Static Member	A class member designated as static. A static data member declares a class variable — a variable associated with the class itself rather than with any instance of the class.
Storage Class	An attribute of a variable definition that controls how the variable will be stored in memory.
Stream	A source from which input data can be obtained or a destination to which output data can be sent.
Structure	In object-oriented analysis, this is a linked set of objects. Structures are of three main kinds — Classification, Composition and Use.
Structure	A hierarchical set of names that refers to an aggregate of data items that may have different attributes.
Subclass	A class which has link to a more general class.
Superclass	A class which has one or more members which are (more specialized) classes themselves.
Syntax	Rules that govern the construction of statements.
Syntax Error	An error in the proper construction of a C++ expression.
Temporary Variable	A variable whose storage is allocated from the stack. The variable is initialized each time the block in which it is defined is entered. It exists only during the execution of that block.

This	This is a pointer to the current object. It is passed implicitly to an overloaded operator function.
Translation	Creation of a new program in an alternate language logically equivalent to an existing program in a source language.
Truncation	An operation on a real number whereby any fractional part is discarded.
Turbo C++	A version of the C++ language for personal computers developed by Borland.
Type Conversion	A conversion of a value from one type to another.
Typecast	*See* cast.
Typedef Name	A name given to a type via a type-name definition introduced by the keyword **typedef**.
Union	A data type that allows different data types to be assigned to the same storage location.
Value	A quantity assigned to a constant.
Variable	A name that refers to a value. The data represented by the variable name can, at different times during the execution of a program, assume different values.
Variable Name	The symbolic name given to a section of memory used to store a variable.
Virtual Base Class	A base class that has been qualified as virtual in the inheritance definition. In multiple inheritance, a derived class can inherit the members of a base class via two or more inheritance paths. If the base class is not virtual, the derived class will inherit more than one copy of the members of the base class. For a virtual base class, however, only one copy of its members will be inherited regardless of the number of inheritance paths between the base class and the derived class.
Virtual Function	A function qualified by the **virtual** keyword. When a virtual function is called via a pointer, the class of the object pointed to determines which function definition will be used. Virtual functions implement polymorphism, whereby objects belonging to different classes can respond to the same message in different ways.
Visibility	The ability of one object to be a server to others.
Void	A data type in C++. When used as a parameter in a function call, it indicates there is no return value. void+ indicates that a generic pointer value is returned. When used in casts, it indicates that a given value is to be discarded.
Windows	A graphical partition of screen for user interface.

Appendix H

C++ Proficiency Test

State whether the following statements are true or false

1. A C++ program is identical to a C program with minor changes in coding
2. Bundling functions and data together is known as data hiding.
3. In C++, a function contained within a class is called a member function.
4. Object modeling depicts the real-world entities more closely than do functions.
5. In using object-oriented languages like C++, we can define our own data types.
6. When a C++ program is executed, the function that appears first in the program is executed first.
7. In a 32-bit system, the data types **float** and **long** occupy the same number of bytes.
8. In an assignment statement such as

   ```
   int x = expression;
   ```

   the value of x is always equal to the value of the expression on the right.
9. In C++, declarations can appear almost anywhere in the body of a function.
10. C++ does not permit mixing of variables of different data types in an arithmetic expression.
11. The value of the expression 13%4 is 3.
12. Assuming the value of variable x as 10, the output of the statement

    ```
    cout << x--;
    ```

    will be 10.
13. The expression **for(; ;)** is the same as a **while** loop with a test expression of **true**.
14. In C++, arithmetic operators have a lower precedence than relational operators.
15. In C++, only **int** type variables can be used as loop control variables in a **for** loop.
16. A **do** loop is executed at least once.

17. The **&&** and | | operators compare two boolean values.
18. The control variable of a **for** loop can be decremented inside the **for** statement.
19. The **break** statement is used to exit from all the nested loops.
20. The **default** case is required in the **switch** selection structure.
21. The **continue** statement inside a **for** loop transfers the control to the top of the loop.
22. The **goto** statement cannot be used to transfer the control out of a nested loop.
23. A conditional expression such as

    ```
    (x < y) ? x : y
    ```

    can be used anywhere a value can be.
24. A structure and a class use similar syntax.
25. Memory space for a structure member is created when the structure is declared.
26. If **item1** and **item2** are variables of type structure **Item**, then the assignment operation

    ```
    item1 = item2;
    ```
    is legal.
27. When calling a function, if the arguments are passed by reference, the function works with the actual variables in the calling program.
28. A structure variable cannot be passed as an argument to a function.
29. A C++ function can return multiple values to the calling function.
30. A function call of a function that returns a value can be used in an expression like any other variable.
31. We need not specify any return type for a function that does not return anything.
32. A set of functions with the same return type are called overloaded functions.
33. Only when an argument has been initialized to zero value, it is called the default argument.
34. A variable declared above all the functions in a program can be accessed only by the **main( )** function.
35. A static automatic variable retains its value even after exiting the function where it is defined.
36. We can use a function call on the left side of the equal sign when the function returns a value by reference.
37. Returning a reference to an automatic variable in a called function is a logic error.
38. Reference variables should be initialized when they are declared.
39. Using **inline** functions may reduce execution time, but may increase program size.
40. A C++ array can store values of different data types.
41. Referring to an element outside the array bounds is a syntax error.
42. When an array name is passed to a function, the function access a copy of the array passed by the program.
43. The extraction operator >> stops reading a string when a space is encountered.
44. Objects of the **string** class can be copied with the assignment operator.
45. Strings created as objects of the **string** class are zero-terminated.
46. Pointers of different types may not be assigned to one another without a cast operation.
47. Not initializing a pointer when it is declared is a syntax error.
48. Data members in a class must be declared **private**.

49. Data members of a class cannot be initialized in the class definition.
50. Members declared as **private** in a class are accessible to all the member functions of that class.
51. In a class, we cannot have more than one constructor with the same name.
52. A member function declared **const** cannot modify any of its class's member data.
53. In a class, members are private by default.
54. In a structure, members are public by default.
55. A member variable defined as **static** is visible to all classes in the program.
56. An object declared as **const** can be used only with the member functions that are also declared as **const**.
57. A member function can be declared **static**, if it does not access any non-static class members.
58. A non member function may have access to the **private** data of a class if it is declared as a **friend** of that class.
59. The precedence of an operator can be changed by overloading it.
60. Using the keyword **operator**, we can create new operators in C++.
61. We can convert a user-defined class to a basic type by using a one-argument constructor.
62. We can always treat a base-class object as a derived-class object.
63. A derived class cannot directly access the **private** members of its base class.
64. In inheritance, the base-class constructors are called in the order in which inheritance is specified in the derived class definition.
65. Inheritance is used to improve data hiding and encapsulation.
66. We can convert a base-class pointer to a derived class pointer using a cast.
67. When deriving a class from a base class with **protected** inheritance, **public** members of the base class became **protected** members of the derived class.
68. When deriving a class from a base class with **public** inheritance, **protected** members of the base class become **public** members of the derived class.
69. A **protected** member of a base class cannot be accessed from a member function of the derived class.
70. In case constructors are not specified in a derived class, the derived class will use the constructors of the base class for constructing its objects.
71. The scope-resolution operator tells us what base class a class is derived from.
72. A derived class is often called a subclass because it represents a subset of its base class.
73. It is permitted to make an object of one class a member of another class.
74. Virtual functions permit us to use the same function call to execute member functions of different classes.
75. A pointer to a base class can point to an object of a derived class of that base class.
76. An **abstract** class is never used as a base class.
77. A pure virtual function in a class will make the class abstract.
78. A derived class can never be made an **abstract** class.
79. A **static** function can be invoked using its class name and function name.
80. The input and output stream features are provided as a part of C++ language.
81. A file pointer always contains the address of the file.
82. Templates create different versions of a function at runtime.
83. Template classes can work with different data types.
84. A template function can be overloaded by another template function with the same function name.

85. A function template can have more than one template argument.
86. Class templates can have only class-type as parameters.
87. A program cannot continue to execute after an exception has occurred.
88. An exception is always caused by a syntax error.
89. After an exception is processed, control will return to the first statement after the **throw**.
90. An exception should be thrown only within a **try** block.
91. If no exceptions are thrown in a **try** block, the **catch** blocks for that **try** block are skipped and the control goes to the first statement after the last **catch** block.
92. The statement **throw**; rethrows an exception.
93. Two **catch** handlers cannot have the same type.
94. Exceptions are thrown from a **throw** statement to a **catch** block.
95. STL algorithms can work successfully with C-like arrays.
96. Algorithms can be added easily to the STL, without modifying the container classes.
97. A **map** can store more than one element with the same key value.
98. A **vector** can store different types of objects.
99. In an associative container, the keys are stored in sorted order.
100. In a **deque**, data can be quickly inserted or deleted at either end.
101. Two functions cannot have the same name in ANSI C++.
102. The modulus operator(%) can be used only with integer operands.
103. Declarations can appear anywhere in the body of a C++ function.
104. All the bitwise operators have the same level of precedence in Java.
105. If $a = 10$ and $b = 15$, then the statement $x = (a > b)\,?\,a : b$; assigns the value 15 to x.
106. In evaluating a logical expression of type

```
boolean expression - 1  &&  boolean expression - 2
```

both the boolean expressions are not always evaluated.
107. In evaluating the expression $(x == y\ \&\&\ a < b)$ the boolean expression $x == y$ is evaluated first and then $a < b$ is evaluated.
108. The **default** case is required in the **switch** selection structure.
109. The **break** statement is required in the default case of a **switch** selection structure.
110. The expression $(x == y\ \&\&\ a < b)$ is true if either $x == y$ is true or $a < b$ is true.
111. A variable declared inside the **for** loop control cannot be referenced outside the loop.
112. Objects are passed to a function by use of call-by-reference only.
113. We can overload functions with differences only in their return type.
114. It is an error to have a function with the same signature in both the super class and its subclass.
115. Derived classes of an abstract class that do not provide an implementation of a pure virtual function are also abstract.
116. Members of a class specified as **private** are accessible only to the functions of the class.
117. A function declared as **static** cannot access **non-static** class members.
118. A **static** class function can be invoked by simply using the name of the function alone.
119. It is perfectly legal to assign an object of a base class to a derived class reference without a cast.
120. It is perfectly legal to assign a derived class object to a base class reference.
121. All functions in an **abstract** base class must be declared pure virtual.

122. The length of a **string** object **s1** can be obtained using the expression **s1.length**.
123. A **catch** can have comma-separated multiple arguments.
124. It is an error to catch the same type of exception in two different **catch** blocks associated with a particular **try** block.
125. Throwing an **exception** always causes program termination.

Part B
Fill in the Blanks Questions

1.   The wrapping up of data and functions into a single unit is called _____.
2.   The process by which objects of one class acquire the attributes of objects of another class is known as _____.
3.   The insulation of data from direct access by unauthorized functions is called _____.
4.   _____ means the ability that one thing can take several distinct forms.
5.   _____ are used to document a program.
6.   The _____ object extracts values from the keyboard.
7.   The object used to display information on the screen in _____.
8.   Every C++ program begins execution at the function _____.
9.   Every C++ statement ends with a _____.
10.   The _____ operator can be used only with integer operands.
11.   Objects communicate with each other by sending _____.
12.   Relational operators have a _____ precedence than arithmetic operators.
13.   The && operator combines two _____ type values.
14.   The _____ statement causes an exit from the innermost loop or switch.
15.   The **continue** statement inside a loop causes the control to go to _____.
16.   A relational operator combines two operands and yields a _____ type result.
17.   _____ are used to change the order of precedence in evaluation of expressions.
18.   A function prototype tells the compiler the return type, name, and _____.
19.   Global variables exist for the life of the _____.
20.   A function cannot modify its argument that has been declared as _____.
21.   If we want a function to work on the original argument in the calling function, we must pass the argument to the function by _____.
22.   A function that has return type _____ does not return anything.
23.   A C++ statement that invokes a function is known as _____.
24.   A storage class specifies two things for a variable. One is visibility and the other is _____.
25.   The storage class _____ is used to a variable to retain its value when a function is not executing.
26.   The _____ enables access to a global variable with the same name as a variable in the current scope.
27.   The default access mode for class members is _____.

28. In a class, a member declared as _____ is not accessible from outside the class.
29. A constructor's name is the same as _____.
30. When two objects of a class are created, _____ copies of data members and _____ copies of member functions are stored in memory.
31. Class members are accessed using the _____ operator in conjunction with the name of the object of a class.
32. Member functions of a class are normally declared as _____.
33. A _____ data member represents class-wise information.
34. The _____ operator dynamically allocates memory for an object of a specified type.
35. A member function declared static can access only _____ class members.
36. An array element is accessed using _____ number.
37. The elements of an array of size 5 are numbered from _____ to _____.
38. When a multidimensional array is accessed, each array index is surrounded by _____.
39. C-style strings are _____ of type char.
40. The individual items in an array are called _____ while the individual items in a class are called _____.
41. The keyword _____ is used to overload an operator.
42. The _____ and _____ of operators cannot be changed by overloading them.
43. Call by reference is achieved by applying _____ operator to the formal parameters.
44. Conversion from a basic type to a class type may be achieved using _____.
45. Conversion from a class type to another class type or any basic type requires the use of _____ operator in the source class.
46. _____ is a way to add features to existing classes without rewriting them.
47. When the class B is inherited from the class A, class A is called the _____ class and class B is called the _____ class.
48. The process of inheriting features from many basic classes is known as _____.
49. The members declared as _____ or _____ in the base class may be accessed from a member function of the derived class.
50. In protected derivation, public members of the base class become _____ members of the derived class.
51. In a multipath inheritance, the duplication of inherited members from the grandparent class can be avoided by declaring the grandparent class as _____ while declaring the intermediate base classes.
52. A class that is designed only to act as a base class but not used to create objects is known as _____ class.
53. Inheritance represents _____ relationship between classes and composition represents _____ relationship between classes.
54. The _____ operator is used to specify a particular class.

55. A function call resolved at run time is referred to as _____ binding.
56. When we use the same function name in both the base and derived classes dynamic binding is achieved by declaring the base class function as _____.
57. A _____ function causes its class to be abstract.
58. A virtual function can be made pure virtual function by placing _____ at the end of its prototype in the class definition.
59. The only integer that can be assigned to a pointer is _____.
60. A pointer is a variable for storing _____.
61. The content of an int type pointer increases by _____ bytes whenever the increment operator is applied to it.
62. A pointer to _____ can hold pointers to any data type.
63. While passing arguments to a function, passing them by pointers allow the function to _____ the arguments in the calling function.
64. The base class for most of the input and output stream classes is the _____ class.
65. Output operations are supported by the _____ class.
66. The class _____ declares input functions such as get() and read().
67. When using manipulator functions to alter the output format parameters of streams, we must include the header file _____.
68. The default precision for printing floating point numbers is _____ digits.
69. The flag _____ causes the display of trailing zeros.
70. To write data that contains variables of type to an object of type of stream, we should use _____ function.
71. The function _____ writes a single character to the associated stream.
72. To place the input pointer in a specified location in the file, we must use the _____ function.
73. Opening a file in ios::out mode also opens it in the _____ mode by default.
74. The read() and write() functions handle data in _____ form.
75. We must open the file using _____ option for performing both input and output operations.
76. Command-line arguments are accessed through arguments to _____.
77. A _____ provides a convenient way to create a family of classes and functions.
78. A function template definition begin with the keyword _____.
79. A call instantiated from a class template is called a _____.
80. All functions instantiated from a function template have the same name; therefore, the compiler applies the concept of _____ resolution to invoke the required function.
81. A template argument is preceded by the keyword _____.
82. A template function works with _____ data types.
83. An exception is typically caused by _____ error.
84. Exception are thrown from a _____ statement to a _____ block.
85. The code that is likely to produce an exception is enclosed in a _____ block.

86. The catch handler _____ will catch all types of exceptions.
87. By default, if no handler is found for an exception, the program _____.
88. The container deque is a _____ type container.
89. The three STL container adapters are stack, queue, and _____.
90. The STL algorithms operate on container elements indirectly using _____.
91. A _____ is an appropriate container if we are given an element's key value and we want to quickly access the corresponding value.
92. In a _____ container, the data can be quickly inserted or deleted at either end.
93. In _____ containers, keys are stored in sorted order.
94. For using function objects, we must include the header file _____.
95. For using the algorithm accumulate(), we must include the header file _____.
96. The _____ operator is used to change the constantness of objects.
97. The operator _____ returns a reference to a type-info object.
98. Non standard casts between unrelated types may be achieved by using the operator _____.
99. The operator _____ qualifies a member with its namespace.
100. The use of specifier _____ to a data item permits us to modify it even when it is a member of a const object.

Part C
Multiple-choice Questions _____

1. The range of values for the long type data on a 16-bit machine is
   A. -2^{31} to $2^{31} - 1$
   B. -2^{64} to 2^{64}
   C. -2^{63} to $2^{63} - 1$
   D. -2^{32} to $2^{32} - 1$
2. Which of the following represent(s) a hexadecimal number?
   A. 570
   B. (hex) 5
   C. 0X9F
   D. 0X5
3. Which of the following assignments are valid?
   A. float x = 123.4;
   B. long m = 023;
   C. int n = (int)false;
   D. double y = 0X756;
4. What will be the result of the expression 13 & 25?
   A. 38
   B. 25
   C. 9
   D. 12

5. What will be result of the expression 9 | 9?
    A. 1
    B. 18
    C. 9
    D. None of the above

6. Which of the following are correct?
    A. int a = 16, a >> 2 = 4
    B. int b = – 8, b >> 1 = – 4
    C. int a = 16, a >>> 2 = 4
    D. int b = – 8, b >>> 1 = – 4
    E. All the above

7. What will be the values of x, m, and n after execution of the following statements?

```
int x, m, n;
m = 10;
n = 15;
x = ++m + n++;
```

    A. x = 25, m = 10, n = 15
    B. x = 27, m = 10, n = 15
    C. x = 26, m = 11, n = 16
    D. x = 27, m = 11, n = 16

8. If m and n are **int** type variables, what will be the result of the expression

    m % n

    when m = 5 and n = 2?
    A. 0
    B. 1
    C. 2
    D. None of the above

9. If m and n are **int** type variables, what will be the result of the expression

    m % n

    when m = – 14 and n = – 3?
    A. 4
    B. 2
    C. – 2
    D. – 4
    E. None of the above

10. Consider the following statements:

```
int x = 10, y = 15;
x = ((x<y) ? (y+x) : (y-x));
```

What will be the value of x after executing these statements?
A.   10
B.   25
C.   15
D.   5
E.   Error. Cannot be executed.

11. Which of the following operators could be overloaded?
A.   −
B.   +
C.   + =
D.   ::
E.   sizeof

12. What is the result of the expression

(1 & 2) + (3 | 4)

in base ten?
A.   1
B.   2
C.   8
D.   7
E.   3

13. A variable is defined within a block in body of a function. Which of the following are true?
A.   It is visible throughout the function.
B.   It is visible from the point of definition to the end of the program.
C.   It is visible from the point of definition to the end of the block.
D.   It is visible throughout the block.

14. Which of the following are correct?
A.   A relational expression yields an int type result.
B.   A relational expression yields a bool type result.
C.   A logical operator compare two bool type values.
D.   A logical operator combines two bool type values.

15. Which of the following will produce a value of 22 if x = 22.9?
A.   ceil(x)
B.   log(x)
C.   abs(x)
D.   floor(x)

16. Which of the following will produce a value of 10 if x = 9.7?
A.   floor(x)
B.   abs(x)
C.   log(x)
D.   ceil(x)

17. Which of the following expressions are illegal?
A.   (10 | 5)
B.   (false && true)
C.   bool x = (bool)10;
D.   float y = 12.34;

18. When the **break** statement is encountered inside a loop, which one of the following occurs?
    A. Control goes to the end of the program
    B. Control leaves the function that contains the loop
    C. Causes an exit from the innermost loop containing it
    D. Causes an exit from all the nested loop

19. When the **continue** statement is executed within a loop, the control goes to
    A. the next statement in the loop
    B. the top of the loop
    C. the statement immediately after the loop
    D. the beginning of the program
    E. the end of the program

20. Which of the following are illegal loop constructs?

    A.
```
while(int i > 0)
{i--;   other statements;}
```
    B.
```
for(int i = 10, int j = 0; i+j > 5; i = i-2, j++)
{
      Body statements
}
```
    C.
```
int i = 10;
while(i)
{
      Body statements
}
```
    D.
```
int i = 1, sum = 0;
do  {loop statements}
while(sum < 10  || i < 5);
```

21. Consider the following code

```
if(number >= 0)
    if(number > 0)
    cout << "Number is positive\n";
else
    cout << "Number is negative\n";
```

    What will be the output if number is equal to 0?
    A. Number is negative
    B. Number is positive
    C. Both A and B
    D. None of the above

22. Which of the following control expressions are valid for an **if** statement?
    A. an integer expression
    B. a boolean expression
    C. either A or B
    D. Neither A nor B

23. In the following code snippet, which lines of code contain error?

```
int j = 0;
while(j < 10) {
j++;
if(j == 5) continue loop;
cout << "j is" << j;  }
```

    A.   Line 2
    B.   Line 3
    C.   Line 4
    D.   Line 5
    E.   None of the above

24.   Consider the following code:

```
char c = 'a';
switch(c)
{
        case 'a':
        cout << "A";
        case 'b':
        cout << "B";         break;
        default:
        cout "C";
}
```

   For this code, which of the following statements are true?
    A.   output will be A
    B.   output will be A followed by B
    C.   output will be A, followed by B, and then followed by C.
    D.   code is illegal and therefore will not compile

25.   Which of the following cannot be passed to a function?
    A.   Reference variable
    B.   Arrays
    C.   Class objects
    D.   Header files

26.   Which of the following statements are true when a function is called by reference?
    A.   The called function copies the values into a new set of variables.
    B.   The formal arguments in the called function becomes aliases to the actual arguments in the calling function.
    C.   The called function has access to the original data in the calling program.
    D.   The called function cannot access the values of actual arguments.

27.   Which of the following represent correct form of function prototype?
    A.   float volume(int x, float y);
    B.   float volume(int x, y);
    C.   volume(int x, int y);
    D.   float volume(int, float);
    E.   float volume(int, float) { }

28. Which of the following apply to a **static** member variable?
    A.   It is initialized to zero when the first object of its class is created.
    B.   A separate copy of the variable is created for each object.
    C.   It retains the value till the end of the program.
    D.   It is visible to all the classes in the program.
29. Which of the following properties are true for a **static** member function?
    A.   It has access to all the members of its class.
    B.   It has access to only other static members of its class.
    C.   It can be called using the class name, instead of objects.
    D.   It can access only non-static members of its class.
30. The following function prototypes use default arguments. Which of them are illegal?
    A.   void prod(int a, int b, int c=10);
    B.   void prod(int a=10, int b, int c);
    C.   void prod(int a=10, int b=5, int c);
    D.   void prod(int a, int b=5, int c=10);
    E.   void prod(int a=10, int b=5, int c=10);
31. Which of the following are valid methods for accessing the first element of the array **item**?
    A.   item.1
    B.   item[1]
    C.   item[0]
    D.   item(0)
    E.   item.0
    F.   item[i]
32. Which of the following function prototypes are not valid?
    A.   void mean(const int[ ]);
    B.   void mean(const int[ ], int);
    C.   void array(int [ ], [ ]);
    D.   void xyz(int a[ ][5]);
    E.   void xyz(int a[ ][ ]);
    F.   void xyz(int a[5][ ]);
33. Which of the following array initialization statements are valid?
    A.   double a[3] = {1.0, 2.0, 3.0};
    B.   double a[3] = {1.0, 2.0};
    C.   double a[ ] = {1.0, 2.0};
    D.   double a[3] = 0.0;
    E.   double a[2] = {1.0, 2.0, 3.0}
34. Which of the following are legal declaration of a reference?
    A.   int &a = 10;
    B.   int &a = m;
    C.   int &a = m++;
    D.   int &a = sqr(m);
    E.   int *a = &15;
35. Which of the following statements are illegal?
    A.   int *p = new int(15);
    B.   int *p = new int;
    C.   int *p = new int[10];

D.   delete p[ ];

E.   delete p;

F.   delete [ ] p;

36. If p and q are pointers of type int and m is an int type variable, which of the following are legal?

A.   p – q

B.   p + q

C.   n + p

D.   n – q

E.   p – n

37. In **public** derivation accessibility of members of base class undergo the following modifications in the derived class:

A.   public becomes protected

B.   protected becomes private

C.   private becomes private

D.   public becomes public

E.   protected becomes protected

F.   private is not inherited

Which of the above are correct?

38. In **private** derivation, accessibility of base members undergo the following modifications in the derived class:

A.   public becomes protected

B.   public becomes private

C.   protected becomes protected

D.   protected becomes private

E.   private becomes private

F.   private is not inherited

Which of the above are correct?

39. In **protected** derivation, accessibility of base members undergo the following changes in the derived class:

A.   public becomes protected

B.   public becomes private

C.   protected becomes protected

D.   protected becomes private

E.   private becomes protected

F.   private is not inherited

Which of the above are correct?

40. The following examples show that the class C is derived from classes A and B. Which of them are legal?

A.   class C : public A, public B

B.   class C : public A : public B

C.   class C : public A, B

D.   class C : private A, public B

E.   class C :: public A, public B

41. The major goal of inheritance in C++ is
     A. To facilitate the conversion of data types
     B. To help modular programming
     C. To facilitate the reusability of code
     D. To extend the capabilities of a class
     E. To hide the details of base classes

42. Consider the following class definition.

```
class Person
{
};
class Student : protected Person
{
};
```

What happens when we try to compile this class?
     A. Will not compile because class body of person is not defined
     B. Will not compile because the class body of Student is not defined
     C. Will not compile because class Person is not public inherited
     D. Will compile successfully.

43. Consider the following class definitions:

```
class Maths
{
    Student student1;
};
class Student
{
    String name;
};
```

This code represents:
     A. an 'is a' relationship
     B. a 'has a' relationship
     C. both
     D. neither

44. Which of the following are overloading the function

```
int sum(int x, int y)  {  }
```

     A. int sum(int x, int y, int z) { }
     B. float sum(int x, int y) { }
     C. int sum(float x, float y) { }
     D. int sum(int a, int b) { }
     E. float sum(int x, int y, float z) { }

45.   What is the error in the following code?

```
class Test
{
     virtual void display( );
}
```

A.   No error
B.   Function **display( )** should be declared as **static**
C.   Function display() should be defined
D.   **Test** class should contain data members

46.   Which of the following declarations are illegal?
A.   void *ptr;
B.   char *str1 = "xyz";
C.   char str2 = "abc";
D.   const *int p1;
E.   int * const p2;

47.   The function **show()** is a member of the class **A** and **abj** is a object of A and **ptr** is a pointer to A. Which of the following are valid access statements?
A.   abj.show();
B.   abj→show();
C.   ptr→show();
D.   ptr.show();
E.   ptr*show();
F.   (*ptr).show();

48.   We can make a class abstract by
A.   Declaring it abstract using the static keyword
B.   Declaring it abstract using the virtual keyword
C.   Making at least one member function as virtual function
D.   Making at least one member function as pure virtual function
E.   Making all member functions **const**.

49.   Consider the following code:

```
class A
{ public : virtual void show() = 0; };

class B : public A
{ public : void display()
       { cout << "B"; }  };

class C : public A
{  public : void show()
        { cout << "C"; }  };
```

Which of the following statements are illegal?

A. C c1;
B. A a1;
C. B b1;
D. A * arr[2];
E. arr[0] = &c1;
F. arr[1] = &b1;

50. The **friend** functions are used in situations where
   A. We want to exchange data between classes
   B. We want to have access to unrelated classes
   C. Dynamic binding is required
   D. We want to create versatile overloaded operators

51. By default, all C++ compilers provide a copy constructor. This constructor is invoked when
   A. An argument is passed by reference to a function
   B. An argument passed to a function is a pointer
   C. An argument is passed by value
   D. A function returns a value to an object

52. Which of the following ways are legal to access a class data member using the **this** pointer.
   A. this → x
   B. this.x
   C. *this.x
   D. *(this.x)
   E. (*this).x

53. Which of the following statements are true with respect to the use of **friend** keyword inside a class?
   A. A private data member can be declared as a friend.
   B. A function may be declared as a friend.
   C. A class may be declared as a friend.
   D. An object may be declared as a friend.

54. What are the functions that can have access to the protected members of a class?
   A. A function that is a friend of the class.
   B. A member function of any class in the program.
   C. A member function of a class that is a friend of the class.
   D. A function is the program that is declared as static.
   E. A member function of a derived class.

55. Which of the following are not keywords?
   A. NULL
   B. abstract
   C. protected
   D. mutable
   E. string

56. Which of the following are keywords?
   A. switch
   B. integer

C.   default
D.   bool
E.   object

57.   Which of the following keywords are used to control access to a class member?
A.   default
B.   break
C.   protected
D.   goto
E.   public

58.   Which of the following keywords were added by ANSI C++?
A.   asm
B.   explicit
C.   enum
D.   extern
E.   typename
F.   using

59.   Which of the following statements are valid array declaration?
A.   int number(5);
B.   float average[5];
C.   double[5] marks;
D.   counter int[5];
E.   int x[5], y[10];

60.   What will be the content of array variable table after executing the following code

```
for(int i=0; i<3; i++)
    for(int j=0, j<3; j++)
        if(j == i) table[i][j] = 1;
        else table[i][j] = 0;
```

A.			B.			C.			D.		
0	0	0	1	0	0	0	0	1	1	0	0
0	0	0	1	1	0	0	1	0	0	1	0
0	0	0	1	1	1	1	0	0	0	0	1

61.   Which of the following methods belong the **string** class?
A.   length( )
B.   compareTo( )
C.   equals( )
D.   substring( )
E.   All of them
F.   None of them

62.   Given the code

```
string s1 = "yes";
string s2 = "yes";
string s3 = string s3(s1);
```

Which of the following would equate to **true**?

A.   s1 == s2
B.   s1 = s2
C.   s3 == s1
D.   s1.equals(s2)
E.   s3.equals(s1)

63. Suppose that s1 and s2 are two strings. Which of the statements or expressions are correct?
A.   string s3 = s1 + s2;
B.   string s3 = s1 – s2;
C.   s1 <= s2
D.   s1.compareTo(s2);
E.   int m = s1.length( );

64. Given the code

```
string s("abc");
```

Which of the following calls are valid?
A.   s.trim( )
B.   s.replace('a', 'A')
C.   s.substring(3)
D.   s.toUpperCase( )

65. Given the declarations

```
bool b;
int x1 = 100, x2 = 200, x3 = 300;
```

Which of the following statements are evaluated to *true*?
A.   b = x1 * 2 == x2;
B.   b = x1 + x2 != 3 * x1;
C.   b = (x3 - 2*x2 < 0) || ((x3 = 400) < 2*x2);
D.   b = (x3 - 2*x2 > 0) || ((x3 = 400) < 2*x2);

66. In which of the following code fragments, the variable x is evaluated to 8.
A.   int x = 32;
     x = x >> 2;
B.   int x = 33;
     x = x >> 2;
C.   int x = 35;
     x = x >> 2;
D.   int x = 16;
     x = x >> 1;

67. Which of the following represent legal flow control statements?
A.   break;
B.   break( );
C.   continue outer;
D.   continue(inner);

E.   return;

F.   exit( );

68. Templates enables us to create a range of related
  A.   classes
  B.   variables
  C.   arrays
  D.   functions
  E.   main() functions

69. The actual source code for implementing a template function is created when
  A.   the function is actually executed
  B.   the declaration of the function appears
  C.   the definition of the function appears
  D.   the function is invoked

70. An exception is caused by
  A.   a hardware problem
  B.   a problem in the operating system
  C.   a syntax error
  D.   a run-time error

71. An exception may be thrown from
  A.   a throw statement in a catch block
  B.   a try block in a function
  C.   a function called in a try block
  D.   a return statement in a function

72. Which of the following statements are true?
  A.   A program can continue to run after an exception has occurred
  B.   After the exception is handled in a catch block, the control goes to the next catch block
  C.   When a catch block finishes executing, the control goes to the first statement after the last catch block
  D.   When an exception is thrown, the first catch block is executed
  E.   If no handler is found for an exception, the program terminates

73. Which one of the following is an associative container?
  A.   list
  B.   queue
  C.   map
  D.   string

74. Which one of the following is a sequence container?
  A.   stack
  B.   deque
  C.   queue
  D.   set

75. Which of the following containers support the random access iterator?
  A.   priority-queue
  B.   multimap
  C.   list
  D.   vector
  E.   multiset

76. Which of the following are non-mutating algorithms?
    A.   search()
    B.   accumulate()
    C.   for_each()
    D.   rotate()
    E.   count()

77. Which of the following functions give the current size of a **string** object?
    A.   max_size()
    B.   capacity()
    C.   size()
    D.   find()
    E.   length()

78. Consider the following code:

```
class Base
{
    private : int x;
    protected : int y;
};
class Derived : Public Base
{
    int a, b;
    void change()
    {
      a = x;
      b = y;
    }
};
int main()
{
    Base base;
    Derived derived;
    base.y = 0;
    derived.y = 0;
    derived.change();
}
```

Which of the lines in the above program will produce compilation errors?
    A.   a = x;
    B.   b = y;
    C.   base.y;
    D.   derived.y;
    E.   derived.change();

79. Which of the following statements are true in C++?

    A.   Classes cannot have data as public members
    B.   Structures cannot have functions as members

C.   Class members are public by default

D.   None of these

80.   What would be the output of the following program?

```
int main()
{
    int x,y=10,z=10;
    x = (y == z);
    cout << x;
    return 0;
}
```

A.   0

B.   1

C.   10

D.   Error

Part D
Short Answer Questions

1.   What is the **main( )** function? How is it different from other functions?

2.   What are the valid types of data that the **main()** can return?

3.   Given the command line

```
prog_10 input.dat
```

how would you open the file **input.dat**?

4.   How does the function declaration

```
int fun();
```

differ in C and C++?

5.   Compare the behaviour of the operator **sizeof()** in C and C++.

6.   How does the use of keyword **struct** differ in C and C++?

7.   What is the advantage of using named constants instead of literal constants in a program?

8.   What is the difference between the following two declarations?

```
extern int m;
int m = 0;
```

9.   How do the following two compare?

(a)   `#define max(x,y) (((x)>(y) ? (x) : (y))`

(b)   `inline int max(int x, int y)`
      `{ return (x>y) ? x : y; }`

10. When the following code is executed, what will be the values of x and y?

```
int x=1, y=0;
y = x++
```

11. What are the values of m and n after the following two statements are executed?

```
int m=5;
int n=m++ * ++m;
```

12. Use type casts to the following statements to make the conversion explicit and clear.

```
float x = 10 + intNumber;
int m = 10.0 * intNumber/floatNumber;
```

13. What are lvalues and rvalues?
14. What are **new** and **delete**?
15. What is the difference between using **new** and **malloc()** to allocate memory?
16. In the following statements, state whether the functions **fun1** and **fun2** are value-returning functions or void functions.

    (a)   `x = 10 * fun1(m,n) + 5;`
    (b)   `fun2(m,n);`

17. What is the difference between using the following statements?

    (a)   `cin >> ch;`
    (b)   `cin.get(ch);`

18. Write a single input statement that reads the following three lines of input from the screen.

```
100    200
300
400
```

19. What is the problem with the following code?

```
int array[5],i;
for(i=0;i<=5;i++)
     cout << array[i];
```

20. Comment on the following code:

```
int x[3] = { 1,2,3 };
for(int i=1;i<=3;i++)
     cout << " " << x[i];
```

21. Suppose we want to store and process a table of item names and their cost. Can we use a two-dimensional array? Explain.

22. A character array is created as follows:

```
char *cpr = new char[20];
```

How could we delete the memory created using the operator **delete**?

23. In the statement given below, what is the order of evaluation of operators?

```
y = a* ++b + m/2;
```

24. What is the situation where we need the use of **goto** statement?

25. Given the declarations

```
int test(int x);
int mul(void);
```

State whether the following function calls are legal.

```
test(sizeof(int));
test(mul());
```

26. Given the array declaration

```
int x[10];
```

what does

```
*(x+3)
```

mean?

27. Given the statements

```
int y[5];
int *p = y;
```

is the following statement legal?

```
p[3] = 10;
```

28. How does a C-string differs from a C++ type string?

29. Does an array of characters represent a character string?

30. What is the difference between the following two statements?

```
const int M = 100;
#define M 100
```

31. Given the statement

    ```
    const int size = 5;
    ```

    can we declare an array as follows?

    ```
    int x[size];
    ```

32. A character array **name** is defined as follows:

    ```
    char name[30] = "Anil Kumar";
    ```

    what will be the values of **m** and **n** in the following statements?

    ```
    int m = sizeof(name);
    int n = strlen(name);
    ```

33. Write a function **change()** to exchange to double values.

34. Write a function to sort a list of double values using the function **change()**.

35. What will be the value of **test** after the following code is executed?

    ```
    int m = 10, n = -1, test = 1;
    if(m<15)
         if(n>1)
            test = 2;
    else
         test = 3;
    ```

36. Rewrite the following code using a **while** loop structure.

    ```
    int i;
    for(i=0;x<5;++i)
    {
         // C++ statements
    }
    ```

37. When do we need to use the following statement?

    ```
    for( ; ; )
    ```

38. What is wrong with the following function definition? Correct the error.

    ```
    double divide(int m, int n)
    {
         return m/n;
    }
    ```

39.   What will be the output of the following code?

```
for(int m=0;m<5;m++)
      cout << m;
```

40.   Will the following code work? If not, why?

```
int main()
{
      cout << test();
      return 0;
}
float test()
{
      // Function code
}
```

41.   If the total mark is below 300, we want to print "FAIL" and if it is 300 and above but less than 359, we want to print "PASS". If it is 360 or more, we do not want to print anything. Will the following code achieve this? If not, correct the code.

```
if(total >= 300)
      if(total < 360)
            cout << "PASS";
else
      cout << "FAIL";
```

42.   Rewrite the following sequence of **if ... then** statements using a single **if ... then ... else** sequence.

```
if(m%2 == 0)
      cout << "m is even number \n";
if(m%2 != 0)
{
      cout << "m is odd number \n";
      cout << "m = " << m << "\n";
}
```

43.   Simplify the following code segment, if possible.

```
if(value > 100)
      cout << "Tax = 10";
if(value < 25)
      cout << "Tax = 0";
if(value >= 25 && value <= 100)
      cout << "Tax = 5";
```

44.   What does the following loop print out?

```
int m = 1;
while(m < 11)
{
     m++;
     cout << m++;
}
```

45.   Write a code segment, using nested loops, to display the following output:

```
1  2  3  4  5
1  2  3  4
1  2  3
1  2
1
```

46.   A program uses a function named **convert()** in addition to its **main** function. The function main declares a variable x within its body and the function **convert()** declares two variables **y** and **z** within its body, **z** is made static. A fourth variable **m** is declared ahead of both the functions. State the visibility and lifetime of each of these variables.

47.   What is the output of the following program?

```
#include <iostream>
using namespace std;
void stat()
{
     int m = 0;
     static int n = 0;
     m++;
     n++;
     cout << m << "   " << n << "\n";
}
int main()
{
     stat();
     stat();
     return 0;
}
```

48.   Replace **if ... else** ladder by a **switch** statement in the following code segment.

```
if(x == 5)
     a++;
```

```
        else if(x == 6)
              b++;
        else if(x == 9)
              c++;
```

49.   What is the output of the following code segment?

```
      int n = 0;
      int i = 1;
      do
      {
            cout << i;
            i++;
      }
      while(i <= n)
```

50.   What is the output of the following code segment?

```
      int n = 0;
      for(int i=1;i<=n;i++)
            cout << i;
```

51.   Why is it inappropriate to use a **float** type variable as a loop control variable?
52.   What is the output of the following statement?

```
      cout<< "He \n said \n \" Hello \ " \n";
```

53.   What is the primary purpose of C++ union types?
54.   What are the two basic differences between a structure and an array?
55.   Distinguish between a **struct** and a **class** in C++.
56.   Name the three language features that characterize object-oriented programming languages.
57.   What is the difference between static and dynamic binding of an operation to an object?
58.   How would you write a generic version of **max** function that would return the largest of the two given values of any data type?
59.   Compare the relationship between classes in composition and inheritance.
60.   Distinguish between **virtual** functions and pure **virtual** functions.
61.   Distinguish between static typing and dynamic typing.
62.   What is the application of **reinterpret_cast** operator?
63.   What is an abstract base class?
64.   What is a pure **virtual** member function?
65.   What is the application of **public**, **protected**, and **private** keywords?
66.   Why do we declare some data members of a class as **private**?
67.   Where and why do we need to use **virtual** functions?
68.   What is dynamic binding? When do we use it?
69.   What is a down cast? When do we use it?
70.   Why do we need to use constructors?

71. What is a copy constructor? What is its purpose?
72. What is a default constructor?
73. What is '**this**'?
74. How are the overloaded operator functions useful in object-oriented design?
75. What is 'has a' relationship? How is this implemented?
76. What is 'is a' relationship? How is this implemented?
77. Will the following code work correctly?

```
void fun(int m)
{
    // code here
}
void fun(unsigned char m)
{
    // code here
}
int main()
{
    fun('X');
    return 0;
}
```

78. What is wrong with the following code?

```
class ABC
{
    private:
        const int m = 10;
    public:
        // code here
};
```

79. When do we need to declare member functions **const**?
80. Consider the following code:

```
class B{ };
class D1 : public B{ };
class D2 : public B{ };
class DD : public D1, public D2{ };
```

How can we prevent the creation of two copies of base class **B** in a **DD** object?

81. In the code given below what access rights does **DD** have over the members of **B**?

```
class B{ };
class D1 : virtual public B{ };
class D2 : virtual private B{ };
class DD : public D1, public D2{ };
```

82. If a compiler does not support the **bool** type data, how could we simulate the same in our programs?

83. What is the wild pointer? What happens when a program has a wild pointer?

84. What are the C++ operators that cannot be overloaded?

85. Can we use the operator * to operate as ** operator to work as an exponentiation operator?. If not, why?

86. When should we use an **inline** function?

87. Does an inline function increase the code size and improve performance?

88. When do we use default parameters in a function definition?

89. A static member function is similar to a friend function. Comment.

90. How is a static member function invoked?

91. When should a function throw an exception?

92. Why do we need to use exception-handling mechanism?

93. What should be placed in a **catch** block?

94. How could we specify the types of objects a function can throw?

95. What is the STL?

96. What is a container?

97. What is the difference between a function template and template function?

98. How can templates increase the code reuse?

99. Why do we need to use namespaces in our programs.

100. What is the use of the following code?

```
class student
{
    static int m = 0;
    student()
    {
        m++;
    }
    .....
    .....
};
```

101. Which of the following expressions are wrong?

    (a)   11% 2
    (b)   -11 % 2
    (c)   11 % -2
    (d)   -11 % -2
    (e)   11.0 % 2.0

102. What will be the output of the following program segment.

```
{
    int m = 1;
    {
        int n = 2;
```

```
            cout << m << "   " << n << endl;
        }
        cout << m << "   " << n << endl;
    }
```

103. What will be output of the following program?

```
    #include <iostream>
    using namespace std;

    bool test = false;
    int main()
    {
        bool test = true;
        cout << "test = " << test << "\n";
        cout << "test = " << :: test << "\n";
        return 0;
    }
```

104. Consider the following statement:

```
    double average = (double)(total/10);
```

If the **int** variable **total** contains a sum of ten integer values, will the statement evaluate to the correct answer? If not why?

105. Write an expression that evaluates to **true** if the **int** variable **x** is even and evaluates to **false** if it is odd.

106. In the expression

```
    x = (x == x)
```

what should be the type of **x** to make the expression legal?

107. State which of the following statement are illegal, if **m** is a integer and x is a double.

```
    (a)  x = (double)m;
    (b)  m = (int)x;
    (c)  x = true;
    (d)  x = x + 1;
    (e)  x = (double).(true);
    (f)  m = m + false/true;
```

108. If **p** is a pointer of type **int** and **q** is a pointer of type **float**, state which of the following statements are legal.

```
    (a)  p = int *(q);
    (b)  p = (int*) q;
```

```
(c)  p = int (*q);
(d)  p = (int*)(q);
(e)  *p = 25, *q = 7.5, *p = *p + *q;
```

109. Which of the following are legal ANSI C++ statements

```
(a)  char array[3] = "abc";
(b)  int *p = new int(7.5);
(c)  use namespace std;
(d)  #include <iostream.h>
(e)  int *p = new int[5];
```

110. If **b1** and **b2** are bool type expressions, how do the following two statements differ?

```
(a)  if(b1 && b2)
        x = x+1;
(b)  if(b1)
        if(b2)
           x = x+1;
```

111. What is wrong, if any, in the following function implementation?

```
double luxuryTax(double value)
{
     if(value <= 5000)
         return 0.15 * value;
     if(value <= 3000)
         return 0.10 * value;
     if(value <= 10000)
         return 0.20 * value;
     else
         return 0.25 * value;
}
```

112. Write the body of the following function that would return **true** if the value of one of the three variables is equal to the sum of the values of other two variables; otherwise would return **false**.

```
bool test(float a, float b, float c)
{
      // body
}
```

113. Which of the following function headers are correctly written?

```
(a)  void test(void)
(b)  int sum(a, b)
(c)  void tax(float x=0.0)
(d)  double return(double x)
(e)  real max()
```

114. State which of the following loop segments will not compile correctly? Why? Assume that all variables have been declared and initialized properly.

```
(a)  do
         m += m;
     while(x < 0)
(b)  do
     {
         x++;
     }
     while(x < 100)
(c)  for(int m=0;m<5;)
         sum = sum + m;
(d)  while x!= -1
         sum = sum + x;
         x = x - 1;
```

115. What will be the output of the following program segment?

```
int x = 1234;
int d,y = 0;
while(x > 0)
{
        d = x%10;
        x /= 10;
        y = 10 * y + d;
}
cout << n << endl;
```

116. Describe the output of the following program segment.

```
int m = 0;
while(++m <= 5)
{
        if(m == 3) continue;
        cout << m << "\n";
}
```

117. Consider the following code:

```
void swap(int x, int y)
{
        int temp = x;
        x = y;
        y = temp;
}

void interchange()
{
    int m = 10;
    int n = 20;
    swap(m,n);
    cout << "m = " << m << "\n";
    cout << "n = " << n << "\n";
}
```

What is the output?

118. What is wrong with the following code?

```
class A
{
        protected: int x;
};
class B : public A
{
    public:
        void set(A a, int y)
        {
          a.x = y;
        }
};
```

119. What is the difference between a **set** and a **map**.

120. What is the difference between the C header **<string.h>** and C++ header **<string>**?

Answer Key

PART A   True / False Answers

1.	F	2.	F	3.	T	4.	T	5.	T	6.	F	7.	T	8.	F	9.	T	10.	F
11.	F	12.	T	13.	T	14.	F	15.	F	16.	T	17.	F	18.	T	19.	F	20.	F
21.	T	22.	F	23.	T	24.	T	25.	F	26.	T	27.	T	28.	F	29.	F	30.	T
31.	F	32.	F	33.	F	34.	F	35.	T	36.	T	37.	T	38.	F	39.	T	40.	F
41.	F	42.	F	43.	T	44.	T	45.	F	46.	T	47.	F	48.	F	49.	T	50.	T
51.	F	52.	T	53.	T	54.	T	55.	F	56.	T	57.	T	58.	T	59.	F	60.	F
61.	T	62.	F	63.	T	64.	T	65.	F	66.	T	67.	T	68.	F	69.	F	70.	T
71.	F	72.	F	73.	T	74.	T	75.	T	76.	F	77.	T	78.	F	79.	T	80.	F
81.	F	82.	F	83.	T	84.	T	85.	T	86.	F	87.	F	88.	F	89.	F	90.	T
91.	T	92.	T	93.	F	94.	T	95.	T	96.	T	97.	F	98.	F	99.	T	100.	T
101.	F	102.	T	103.	T	104.	F	105.	T	106.	T	107.	F	108.	F	109.	F	110.	F
111.	T	112.	F	113.	F	114.	F	115.	T	116.	T	117.	T	118.	F	119.	F	120.	T
121.	F	122.	F	123.	F	124.	F	125.	F										

PART C   Multiple Choice Questions

1.	A	2.	C & D	3.	A, B & D	4.	C	5.	C
6.	A, B & C	7.	C	8.	B	9.	D	10.	B
11.	A, B & C	12.	D	13.	C	14.	B & D	15.	D
16.	D	17.	C	18.	C	19.	B	20.	A & C
21.	A	22.	B	23.	A	24.	B	25.	D
26.	B & C	27.	A & D	28.	A & C	29.	B & C	30.	B & C
31.	C & F	32.	C, E & F	33.	A, B & C	34.	B	35.	D
36.	A, C & E	37.	D, E & F	38.	B, D & F	39.	A, C & F	40.	A & D
41.	C & D	42.	D	43.	B	44.	A, C & E	45.	A
46.	C	47.	A, C & F	48.	D	49.	A, D & E	50.	B & D
51.	C & D	52.	A & E	53.	B & C	54.	A, C & E	55.	A, B & E
56.	A, C & D	57.	C & E	58.	B, E & F	59.	B	60.	D
61.	A	62.	A & C	63.	A, C & E	64.		65.	A & C
66.	A, B, C & D	67.	A, C & E	68.	A, C & D	69.	D	70.	D
71.	A, B & C	72.	A, C & E	73.	C	74.	B	75.	D
76.	A & E	77.	C & E	78.	A, C, D & E	79.	B	80.	B

Bibliography

Balagurusamy, E, *Programming in ANSI C*, Tata McGraw-Hill, 1992.

Barkakati, Nabajyoti, *Object-Oriented Programming in* C++, SAMS, 1991.

Cohoon and Davidson, *C++ Program Design,* McGraw-Hill, 1999.

Cox, B J and Andrew J Novobilski, *Object-Oriented Programming — An Evolutionary Approach*, Addison-Wesley, 1991.

Dehurst, Stephen C and Kathy T. Stark, *Programming in C++*, Prentice-Hall, 1989.

Deitel and Deitel, *C++ How to Program,* Prentice-Hall, 1998.

Eckel, Bruce, *Using C++*, Osborne McGraw-Hill, 1989.

Gorlen K, *Data Abstraction and Object-Oriented Programming in C++*, Wiley, 1990.

Ladd S. Robert, *C++ Techniques and Applications*, M&T Books, 1990.

Lafore, Robert, *Object-Oriented Programming in Tu. bo C++*, Waite Group, 1999.

Lippman, Stanley B and Josee Lajoie, *C++ Primer*, Addison-Wesley, 1998.

Schildt, Herbert, *Using Turbo C++*, Osborne McGraw-Hill, 1990.

Stroustroup, Bjarne, *The C++ Programming Language*, 3rd edition, Addison-Wesley, 1997.

Stroustroup, Bjarne and Margaret A Ellis, *The Annotated C++ Reference Manual*, Addison-Wesley, 1990.

Voss, Grey, *Object-Oriented Programming — An Introduction*, Osborne McGraw-Hill, 1991.

Wiener, Richard S and Lewis J Pinson, *The C++ Workbook*, Addison-Wesley, 1990.

Index